ULYSSES S. GRANT

Warrior and Statesman

A Matthew Brady photograph of General U. S. Grant

ULYSSES S. GRANT

Warrior and Statesman

BY

MAJOR GENERAL ULYSSES S. GRANT 3RD.

WILLIAM MORROW & COMPANY, INC.

New York 1969

Printed in the United States of America.

Library of Congress Catalog Card Number 68-57446

Contents

Illustrations appear between pages 96–97

List of Maps

Preface

To My Children:

In his essay "Bringing Up Children," Plutarch, popular biographer of the ancients, tells us that it is a splendid thing to have noble ancestors, "but the glory belongs to the ancestors." Your mother and I have been fortunate in giving you as ancestors, on both sides of the family, a fairly consistent line of solid citizens—good men and women and at least two really great men, your Grandfather Elihu Root and your Great-Grandfather Grant. The former lived long enough to know you and for you to know him. Surely each of you has definite recollections of him, of his wise consideration for us all, of his great gifts and sense of humor, of his great personality. These recollections you will cherish more and more as you come to appreciate him with the enhanced standards of maturity.

But your Great-Grandfather Grant you never knew. You, his direct descendants (and your children as well), should know him as we in the family knew him and thought of him. You should know more of the truth about him than has been told by the conventional historians, who have apparently never been able to understand him, and the political writers, who for some reason have hated him as the politicians did. Of course, there have been a few biographers who made an honest effort to understand him and, writing without malice or envy, have to some extent succeeded in leaving for posterity a fairly correct picture of him. Kenneth P. Williams, Robert R. McCormick, William C. Church, James Grant Wilson, Horace Porter, Judge Louis A. Coolidge, the British General J. F. C. Fuller, John Russell Young, and several others have written understandingly and sympathetically, generally basing their stories on reliable records; but even they have not fully seized and pictured the gracious, kindly, good man that the family knew him to be, the devoted husband and most affectionate father.

Although I have access to many records and recollections that were not at hand for them, and have knowledge of many family traditions and stories, I am not at all sure that I shall be able to do better, as I am limiting my "family portrait" to one volume. So this historical portrait which I boldly undertake must be restricted to the man. It will repeat the oft-told facts of history only in so far as they are necessary to an understanding of the background of my narrative.

Napoleon said that history was but a fable agreed upon, and Carlyle, himself a serious writer of history, alleged it was but a summary of rumors. Probably no great man has ever suffered as much as President Grant from the readiness of the public to accept false tales at their face value, and the tendency of writers of books and articles to repeat untruths, provided they were sensational enough to ensure sales. Recently a book, edited by a professional historian of good repute, has appeared. It contains some outrageous and manifestly false but detailed accounts of your great-grandfather's behavior during the Vicksburg campaign, which Dr. Kenneth P. Williams after due research has proved to be entirely untrue. And yet the story has been swallowed whole by two other professional historians and incorporated in their books, which some people doubtless will read and a few believe! Apparently both the professional historian and the publisher succumb to the temptation to profit from scandal. They know that many plain people like to read it. Alleged foibles of the great bring them down to an everyday level and make them feel nearer the heights that others achieved.

It may well be futile, therefore, to attempt to refute fables that have gained some sort of recognition by mere repetition. It may be futile to try to restore the picture of at least one great man to its true outlines, seeking to write history, which Cicero called "the evidence of ages, the light of truth, the life of memory, and the school of life." However, the great, whose reputation rests on a true record of their accomplishments, have a right to expect that some of their descendants will attempt to set the record straight, when it seems to be slipping too far from the facts.

Ulysses S. Grant, 3rd

ULYSSES S. GRANT

Warrior and Statesman

I

The Boy and the Cadet

ON APRIL 27, 1822, along toward 5 A.M., Ulysses S. Grant was born in a modest two-room, frame cabin on a bluff overlooking the Ohio River. Here the river and its tributary, Great Indian Creek, form a peninsula called Point Pleasant. This little boy was destined to do great things in the world after he had grown to man's estate, graduated from the United States Military Academy, and rendered distinguished service in the war with Mexico. In the Civil War he was to prove himself one of the great military commanders of history and vanquish the powerful and determined armed strength of the Confederacy of eleven states that had seceded from the Union. He was to play a most important part in persuading the vanquished states to rejoin the Union. Descendants of those Confederate soldiers, once in rebellion, have since fought shoulder to shoulder, in five foreign wars, with descendants of the Union soldiers —a rare phenomenon in the history of civilization.

The child born in April 1822 was the son of Jesse Root Grant and Hannah Simpson Grant and the oldest son in the eighth generation of descent from Matthew and Priscilla Grant, who had emigrated from England in 1630 to help settle the American continent. In this long line of conscientious New England ancestors there were many who achieved local distinction and office; at least one member of each generation took a fighting part in some war. Jesse's grandfather, Captain Noah Grant, served in the French and Indian War at Lake George and in 1756 received a gratuity from the Connecticut Assembly for "extraordinary services and good conduct in ranging and scouting." He was lost on one such expedition from Fort William Henry. Another Noah Grant, born

1705, "was 2nd Lieutenant and Captain of 4 Company; 8th Regiment of Trained Bands," and Justice of the Peace. Still another Noah Grant, born 1747, had been a sea captain and surveyor. Jesse Grant's father was also named Noah Grant. As a lieutenant and captain he served throughout the American Revolution. He married three times, once to Mrs. Rachel Kelly, Ulysses' grandmother, daughter of Colonel Miller of Jamestown, Virginia.

Ulysses' mother, from whom he inherited many admirable characteristics, came from a family that had settled in Pennsylvania in 1705 and was living in Montgomery County when she married Jesse Grant in June 1821. The ladies of her family had turned out during the Battle of Germantown and fed the wounded and weary soldiers of the Revolutionary Army who had taken refuge nearby.

Jesse realized that the best thing he ever did was to marry Hannah Simpson. To her worth he paid this tribute: "Her steadiness, firmness, and strength of character have been the stay of the family through life. She was always careful, and most watchful over her children; but never austere, and not opposed to their free participation in innocent amusements." Neighbors who knew her called her a "noble woman." Her oldest grandson, Frederick Dent Grant, said of her in later years: "She was one of the most modest and unselfish of women. Her intimate friends greatly appreciated her rare worth and excellent qualities, many of which the general inherited. Devoted as she was to him, his honors and success never betrayed her into an act or remark which would indicate that her head was turned by them. She was glad and thoughtful, and, with the loving faithfulness of a Christian mother, she had long made his welfare the subject of earnest prayer. She had faith in his future, though not great worldly expectations, and during the last years of his life, her interest in his future had special reference to that part on which they have both now entered."

The affection and esteem the future Commander in Chief and President felt for his mother and his sense of intimate companionship with her is best evidenced by the following letter he wrote to her from West Point when he was a cadet:

I have occasionally been called upon to be separated from you, but never did I feel the full force and effect of this separation as I do now. I seem alone in the world without my mother. There have been so many ways in which you have advised me, when in the quiet of home I have been pursuing my studies, that I cannot tell you how much I miss you. I was so often alone with you, and you so frequently spoke to me in private, that the solitude of my situation here at the Academy among my silent books, and in my lonely room, is all the more striking. It reminds me the more forcibly of home, and most of all, dear mother, of you. But in the midst of all this, your kindly instructions and admonitions are ever present with me. I trust they may never be absent from me, as long as I live. How often do I think of them, and how well they strengthen me in every good word and work! My dear mother, should I progress well with my studies at West Point, and become a soldier of my country, I am looking forward with hope to have you spared to share with me in any advancement I may make. *I see now in looking over the records here how much American soldiers of the right stamp are indebted to good American mothers.* When they go to the fields, what prayers go with them; what tender testimonials of affection and counsel are in their knapsacks! I am struck, in looking over the history of the noble struggle of our fathers for national independence, at the evidence of the good influence exerted upon them by the women of the Revolution.

I have always suspected that when Captain Noah Grant returned from his service in the army of the Revolution, he found the family homestead in Windsor, Connecticut, so full of brothers and sisters and their children that he felt constrained to join the tide of immigrants moving west. After the death of his wife he accompanied his son, Peter, and two younger children to Westmoreland County, Pennsylvania. There he married Rachel Miller Kelly, of Virginia, and continued on to Deerfield, Ohio. Peter settled in Maysville, Kentucky, in 1807. He married, fathered nine children, and prospered, becoming one of the wealthy men on the western frontier. In 1829 he drowned in the Kanawha River. After the death of his second wife in 1805, Captain Noah's other children settled near Deerfield, Ohio.

Jesse Grant found a home with Judge Tod and his wife, who treated him almost as if he were their own son. He spoke of Mrs. Tod in later years as the most admirable woman he had ever known. Of an independent nature, Jesse, when old enough to learn a trade, joined his older half-brother, Peter, who owned a tannery. After leaving Peter's employ, he lived with the Brown family in Deerfield and came to know their son, John Brown of Harpers Ferry fame. Jesse in after years always spoke of him as "a man of great purity of character, of high moral and physical courage, but a fanatic and extremist in whatever he advocated."

In June 1821, Jesse Grant settled at Point Pleasant, Ohio, where he brought his bride. A year after the birth of Ulysses they moved to Georgetown, Ohio, where they resided until the boy went to the United States Military Acadamy at West Point, New York. After accumulating a capital of $100,000 and retiring from the tannery business, Jesse became mayor of Bethel, Ohio, and later postmaster in Covington, Kentucky.

When Albert D. Richardson, Frank A. Burr, and Hamlin Garland were writing their biographies of General Grant, they interviewed surviving neighbors and friends of his boyhood. Thus they discovered and recorded a great many incidents and anecdotes of his boyhood in Georgetown, Ohio. While the stories are interesting and probably illustrative of the impression the boy made on people, their historic accuracy may be doubtful in some cases. I never heard him reminisce about his boyhood, and all the "firsthand" information we have is based on his *Memoirs* and some records left by his father. It may be safely said, however, that there was general agreement among his associates and teachers that he was always dependable, a boy whose common sense and resourcefulness in an emergency could be relied upon; he was gentle and considerate of others, "a refined boy," "the soul of honor," with some facility in drawing and a special gift for handling horses. One witness who can certainly be relied upon was Daniel Ammen, a schoolmate and playmate, who afterward became an admiral in the U.S. Navy and left the following statement:

Grant was one of the most remarkable lads I ever knew. We grew up side by side until I went to sea in 1836. We went riding, fishing, swimming and playing together. His mother was one of the most interesting and charming women I ever knew. She was exceedingly kind, ladylike and mild-mannered. I suspect that Grant inherited his kindly disposition from her, for I think his father was rather aggressive.

As a boy, Grant was kindness itself. I never saw him have a show of resentment, and I do not believe that he ever felt a tinge of it. He was never rude, oppressive or disagreeable to other children. He had perfect respect for everybody's feelings and a forbearance that was almost beyond Christianity.

His family say that I once saved his life. He was then about nine years old, and I some two years his senior. We went fishing, one day, in a swollen stream near our homes. While indulging in the sport he stepped on a poplar log, which was very slippery, and fell in. He was rather a sturdy lad, and made a vigorous attempt to get out, but the rushing tide bore him downstream. I ran along after him until I reached a foothold among some willows. As he came by I reached out, caught him by the clothing and pulled him ashore. I don't suppose I should ever have remembered the incident but that he had on a red-striped Marseilles waist, which was my envy and which I thought would be totally ruined by the ducking he had received.

The friendship which sprang up between us then has never dimmed. While he was growing up there was never any evidence of the great ability that has been drawn upon for the good of the country during the crisis through which we have safely passed. But in those characteristics of kindness, self-confidence and perfect self-possession, which I remember so well, Grant the man is but the higher development of Grant as I remember him in childhood.

It was a healthy though rugged life, but it offered good conditions under which to grow up. Devising recreation, outdoor exercise, and sport was left largely to individuals, so that resourcefulness and ingenuity were certainly developed to an extent not possible for children today with their organized play. At the age of seven or eight years Ulysses began hauling all the wood used in the family house and shops. He could not load the timbers on wagons or unload it at its destination; this heavy work was done by grownups. At the age of eleven Ulysses was strong enough to hold a plow, and from then until age seventeen he did all kinds of farm work that was done with horses: clearing land, furrowing, bringing in the crops when harvested. In those days on the frontier work around the house and farm was part of every young boy's training and education. Young Grant acquired a fondness for farming and a certain confidence in his ability to produce harvests which stood him in good stead in later life.

Garland, in his biography of Grant, quotes Judge Marshall (a neighbor in Georgetown) as relating that Ulysses at the age of eleven was much interested in a trick pony at a little circus. The clown in charge of the pony offered $5.00 to any boy who could ride the pony.

He was a fat bay pony, with no mane, and nothing at all to hang to. Ulysses looked on for a while, saw several of the other boys try and fail, and at last said, "I believe I can ride that pony." . . . The pony reared, kicked, and tried all the tricks he knew, but was unable to throw the boy, who had observed the pony's ability to shift his rather loose skin suddenly from the center of his back to the right or left, dropping the rider.—This ability to estimate a situation factually and calmly, and then act to meet it, was to prove very useful to the commanding general of the Union Army.—The clown finally acknowledged defeat and paid.

Ulysses was a favorite with the girls because of his gentleness and consideration of them, and probably also because he had command of a team of horses and could do errands for them and take them for sleigh rides in winter.

At that time, he tells us, "there were no free schools, and none in which the scholars were classified. They were all supported by subscription, and a single teacher—who was often a man or a woman incapable of teaching much, even if they imparted all they knew—would have thirty or forty scholars, male and female, from the infant learning the A B C's up to the young lady of eighteen and the boy of twenty, studying the highest branches taught—the three R's, Reading, 'Riting, and 'Rithmetic. I never saw an algebra, or other mathematical work higher than the arithmetic in Georgetown until after I was appointed to West Point. I then bought a work on algebra in Cincinnati; but having no teacher, it was Greek to me."

Ulysses attended the subscription school in the village, except during the winters of 1836–37 and 1838–39. The first he spent in Maysville, Kentucky, attending the school of Richeson and Rand, and the second he spent in Ripley, Ohio, at a private school. Professor Richeson of the Maysville Seminary later said he "ranked high in all his classes, and his deportment was exceptionally good. He was a member of the Philomathean [Debating] Society." The society's records indicate that his side practically always won the debates, and a friend named Markland has stated that "he was a good debater" although he would "rather pay six-and-a-quarter-cents fine than declaim"—an early recognition of his aversion to public speaking.

As to the two terms spent at the school in Ripley, Ohio, Hamlin Garland quotes the following impressions of one of Ulysses Grant's classmates:

> Lys, or Lyssus, as we called him, boarded with R. M. Johnson, a tanner, whom Jesse Grant knew by way of business dealings. He was then about sixteen years old, and in appearance was short, stout, stubby, and hearty, but rather sluggish in mind and body. I was in the same class with him. We studied algebra together. He was excellent in mathematics. We studied Latin also, as beginners. He was not much of a talker—was rather quiet and serious. We all spent a good deal of time on the river in little boats. He played ball,

and was good at it. When roused, was strong and active. He used to wrestle some, but I never knew him to fight, and he was never quarrelsome.

His habits were good. I don't remember of his using tobacco or liquor. He never talked about military life. He never went on trips or excursions with us, except in our boating or skating; he was occupied with his studies. Everybody liked him, for he was so amiable and friendly and helpful. He was a good student, though we did not consider him a brilliant boy in studies.

Our text-books were the English Reader and its Sequel, Lindley Murray's Grammar, Haven's Speller and Definer, Comstock's Philosophy. Then, we had a geography with pictures of Indians and Chinese in it. I don't remember the name of it. It was a queer little book. Grant stood well in all his classes, but he was specially good in mathematics.

Another classmate had been impressed by his asking many questions and seeming to want to get information and opinions from everybody on nearly everything.

Of these boyhood days Ulysses himself reminisced happily that he remembered no scolding or punishment by his parents, no objection "to rational enjoyments, such as fishing, going to the creek a mile away to swim in summer, taking a horse and visiting my grandparents in the adjoining county, fifteen miles off, skating on the ice in winter, or taking a horse and sleigh when there was snow on the ground."

Of course the young boy had some adventures on these drives. For instance he tells of going to Flat Rock, Kentucky, about seventy miles away, to visit a Mr. Payne, brother of a Georgetown neighbor whom Ulysses took with him. His host had a fine saddle horse which attracted the attention of young Grant. Mr. Payne was somewhat surprised when his visitor offered to exchange one of the horses he had driven from Georgetown for the saddle horse. After being assured that the Grant boy had authority to trade a family horse, he agreed to the exchange—but with the statement that, as far as he knew, the saddle horse had never been in harness. Hitched to a farm wagon, the horse showed no signs of viciousness and the trade was consummated, ten dollars' difference being paid to the Grant boy.

The next day on the drive home (with the Payne boy as a companion) a ferocious dog frightened the horses and caused them to run away. Grant's new animal kicked at every jump he made but the young driver managed to stop them before any damage was done or the horses had run into anything. "After giving them a little rest to quiet their fears, we started again," as General Grant remembered it in future years. "That instant the new horse kicked and started to run once more. The road we were on struck the turnpike within half a mile of the point where the second runaway commenced, and there was an embankment twenty or more feet deep on the opposite side of the pike. I got the horses stopped on the very brink of the precipice. My new horse was terribly frightened and trembled like an aspen; but he was not half so frightened as my companion, Mr. Payne, who deserted me after this last experience, and took passage on a freight-wagon for Maysville. Every time I attempted to start my new horse would commence to kick. I was in quite a dilemma for a time. Once in Maysville, I could borrow a horse from an uncle who lived there; but I was more than a day's travel from that point. Finally I took out my bandanna . . . and with this blindfolded my horse. In this way I reached Maysville safely the next day, no doubt much to the surprise of my friend."

Another horse story was told by Mr. John D. White, a North Carolinian who ran the school in Georgetown. Grant later termed the story "nearly true." According to Mr. White, young Grant very much wanted to acquire a colt owned by a Mr. Ralston, who lived a few miles from the village. Ulysses' father had told him to offer twenty dollars for the colt—all it was worth in his opinion—but to go to twenty-five dollars if necessary. According to the story, the boy made the offer to Mr. Ralston, telling him that he was authorized to offer twenty dollars but if he could not get it for that, he might pay twenty-five. Of course he had to pay the twenty-five. This story of his boyish ingenuousness and frankness caused him much embarrassment when it got to be known in the village.

The question of what to name the boy seems to have caused serious discussions in the family. According to a Grant biographer, Lloyd Lewis, the problem was settled at a family conference in which each one present wrote the name he or she favored on a slip of paper and put it in a hat. The two names finally drawn were "Hiram," proposed by his Grandfather Simpson, and "Ulysses," proposed by Grandmother Simpson, who had been much impressed with Fenelon's description of Ulysses' character in his *Adventures of Telemaque.* Fenelon describes the Greek hero thus: "Your father Ulysses is the wisest of mankind; his heart is of unfathomable depth; his secret lies beyond the line of subtlety and fraud. He is the friend of truth, and says nothing that is false; but when it is necessary, he conceals what is true; his wisdom is, as it were, a seal upon his lips, which is never broken, but for an important purpose." The boy was christened Hiram Ulysses.

Subsequently, before he went to West Point, the future general, seeing the initials H.U.G. on a trunk or satchel, felt that that would invite teasing. So he began signing himself "Ulysses H. Grant" or "U. H. Grant." Many of his signatures early in his West Point career were so signed. However, Congressman Thomas L. Hamer, who appointed him to West Point, thought his middle name was "Simpson" and put "Ulysses S." in the appointment correspondence with West Point. Ulysses made an effort to have the name corrected at the academy but was confronted with either legal action or facing the interpretation that Ulysses S. Grant had been appointed, and if he was not Ulysses S. Grant he had not been appointed! Of a practical turn of mind, he acceded to the change and from then on was known and signed himself as U. S. Grant or Ulysses S. Grant, the "S." standing for nothing except the mistake of Mr. Hamer.

During the Christmas holidays of 1838, Ulysses' father had received a letter from the Honorable Thomas Morris, then U.S. Senator from Ohio. After reading it he turned to his son and said: "Ulysses, I believe you are going to receive the appointment."

"What appointment?" the boy asked.

"To West Point; I have applied for it."

"But I won't go," said Ulysses.

The father then said he thought the boy would go, and Ulysses thought so, too, if his father did. He really had no objections to going to West Point. Rather he had an exaggerated idea of the requirements necessary to enter and pass the course. He modestly doubted that he could do it, and he dreaded the prospect of failing. His appointment ultimately came to fill a vacancy left by a boy named Bailey, appointed in 1837, who had resigned when he found he would not be able to pass the January examination.

Jesse Grant had asked Senator Morris to obtain the appointment because Grant and Congressman Hamer had differed in politics; Hamer was a Democrat, Jesse a Whig, and they had had a warm discussion over President Jackson. Grant had hesitated, therefore, to make the request of Mr. Hamer directly.

* * *

Although the idea of four years at West Point and the consequent military career did not at all appeal to the youngster from Georgetown, Ohio, there was the prospect of travel: visiting large cities like Philadelphia and New York on his way to West Point and the interest of getting there by steamboat trip up the Ohio, the canal-boat voyage from Pittsburgh to Harrisburg, the railroad trip from Harrisburg to Philadelphia at the breathless rate of twelve miles an hour (he had never seen a railroad before). And the sight of the varied topography and scenery, especially in going through the mountains of western Pennsylvania, was the sort of experience he had longed for.

In Philadelphia, the first big city he had ever seen, he stayed with his mother's cousins, the Hares, and enjoyed his walks through the streets and visits to the historic shrines and the theaters. He stayed there for five days and was reprimanded by his father for "dallying by the way so long." According to Garland, Elizabeth Hare, who had been like a sister to Hannah Simpson in their girlhood, wrote of Ulysses as "a rather awkward country lad, wearing plain clothes and large coarse shoes as broad at the toes as at the widest part of the soles." The stay in New York was not as long and inevitably ended with the steamer trip up the Hudson River to West Point, and the climb up to the Parade Ground and registration at Roe's Hotel on May 25, 1839. He signed his name "Ulysses H. Grant" and then reported to the adjutant's office.

Somewhat to his surprise he passed the examination and was admitted to the Military Academy. (The examination eliminated over thirty per cent of the candidates.) He could now be measured for his uniform. The $100 he had earned driving people and goods around Georgetown had to be deposited on his entering West Point. To this deposit was added his cadet pay each month. A cadet never had any cash given him while at the academy. Against the deposits, expenses were charged and on graduation he was paid any balance remaining. Lloyd Lewis somewhere found that the swallow-tailed dress coat cost $10.88, the gig-top cap $2.44, the white pantaloons "as tight as my skin" $10.50 a dozen. There were of course other items, like the shako, but these prices must raise our admiration for the value of the American dollar in 1840, compared to its value today and the present cost of uniforms.

Hamlin Garland has an excellent description of the treatment given the new cadets, called "plebes" by the upperclassmen, as their initial training for the army. It was mostly in the nature of developing in them upright posture, precise muscular control, and other faculties needed for military appearance, as well as learning uniform marching and the manual of arms which are such important parts of the school of the soldier. It was a grueling and hard experience and must have been particularly trying for the country boy from Ohio. But however disagreeable at the time, a plebe's training certainly gives excellent and desirable results. Mild-mannered Ulysses, accustomed to meet new experiences without complaint, seems to have passed through the plebe-summer weeks without any special incident.

When the names of the new cadets were posted on the bulletin board, the upperclassmen made a point of examining the list for any peculiarity of name or place that would justify a nickname. Of course, the initials "U.S." stood out and suggested many possibilities. It was probably a first classman named William Tecumseh Sherman who suggested that "Uncle Sam" would be the proper name for this particular new cadet. Consequently, he was generally known as "Sam Grant" during his four years at West Point and afterward in the army.

After plebe camp was over at the end of August 1839, the cadets went into barracks, and apparently Cadet Grant roomed with Cadet Rufus Ingalls. "There always was mirth when Ingalls was present, he was ever cheerful, never selfish, and full of quaint humor. It was from their room in the North Barracks that Sam Grant wrote to his cousin, McKinstry Griffith, in Bethel, about "This prettiest of places . . . the most beautiful place I have ever seen." Underneath the window was the Hudson "with its bosom studded with hundreds of snowy sails." He went on with a reference to the house in which Washington lived, the path Kosisuscko [sic] used to follow while thinking of his country and ours, and the home of Benedict Arnold across the river—"that BASE AND HEARTLESS traitor to his country and his God. I do love the place, it seems as though I could live here forever, if my friends would only come too."

He went on to tell his cousin: "We have tremendous long and hard lessons to get, in both French and algebra." The midyear examination in January is a "hard one, they say; but I am not frightened yet. . . . I would not go away on any account," because "if a man graduates here, he is safe for life, let him go where he will." After wishing that some of the pretty girls of Bethel were there, he goes on: "I came near forgetting to tell you about our demerit system or 'black marks.' They give a man one of these 'black marks' for almost nothing, and if he gets two hundred a year they dismiss him. To show how easy one can get these, a man by the name of Grant, of this State, got eight of these 'marks' for not going to church. He was also put under arrest so he can not leave his room perhaps for a month, all this for not going to church. We are not only obliged to go to church, but must march there by companies."

It must be added that the number of these demerits which young Grant got affected his class standing very harmfully, although the offenses were more numerous than serious. In fact, they were nearly all for minor offenses such as being late for formation, having a button unbuttoned at parade, or slouchiness of one kind or another; but they did pull his class standing down.

Although mild in manner, quiet and anything but a troublemaker, Ulysses gained a reputation for manliness and courage by knocking down a much larger cadet who persisted in trying to shove him out of his place in line even after having been warned not to attempt it again. Although we do not know, it may be presumed that he received some demerits for this insistence on his rights.

The food in the mess hall seems to have been very poor in those days, and the cadets naturally put their ingenuity to work in obtaining and even preparing in their rooms additional, more palatable food. For instance, on one occasion Cadets Grant and Deshon were roasting a turkey over the coals in their fireplace, when a tactical officer, Lieutenant William N. Grier, burst in after an imperative knock. Lieutenant Grier had recently returned from Indian fighting in the West to serve as instructor in cavalry tactics. The two cadets sprang to attention, standing close together in front of the fireplace. As the officer walked around looking at the way clothing was stowed away, bedding was piled, shoes were shined, *et cetera,* they tried to keep between him and the fireplace. After he had looked everywhere but directly in the fireplace, he mentioned that there was a strange odor of something burning, to which Cadet Grant without any change of expression replied, "Yes, sir, I have noticed it myself." After cautioning them to make sure that nothing was on fire, Lieutenant Grier left the room, and I am sure the two cadets mentally classified him as a perfect gentleman.

The life in barracks was very simple and had the virtue that it was democratic and all fared alike. The scion of a slaveholding family in

Virginia had to do his own work, as did the farm boy from the West. General D. M. Frost later wrote:

> Each Saturday it was down on your knees and scrub the floor. The barracks were dismal, barn-like structures with bare floors and very scanty furnishings. We had no servants at all. We had to carry water, make up our beds, etc. There were no such luxuries as bathrooms then. We had to pump our own water, and carry it upstairs whenever we found it necessary to take a bath.
>
> I remember Grant well. He was a small fellow, active and muscular. His hair was reddish-brown, and his eyes gray-blue. We all liked him, and he took rank soon as a good mathematician and engineer, and as a capital horseman. He had no bad habits whatever, and was a great favorite, though not a brilliant fellow.
>
> He couldn't, or wouldn't, dance. He had no facility in conversation with the ladies, a total absence of elegance and naturally showed off badly in contrast with the young southern men, who prided themselves on being finished in the ways of the world.

General Longstreet, in the class ahead of Grant, remembered that "so perfect was his sense of honor that in the numerous cabals which were often formed his name was never mentioned, for he never did anything which could be subject to criticism or reproach. He soon became the most daring horseman in the Academy." And General Rufus Ingalls believed that:

> . . . when our school days were over, if the average opinion of the members of the class had been taken everyone would have said: "There is Sam Grant; he is a splendid fellow, a good, honest man against whom nothing can be said and from whom everything may be expected." He had the most scrupulous regard for truth. He never held his word light. He never said an untruthful word, even in jest. He was of a reflective mind, and at times very reticent and somber. Something seemed working deep down in his thoughts—things he knew as little about as we. There would be days, even weeks, at a time when he would be silent and somber—not morose. He was a cheerful man, and yet he had these moments when he seemed to feel some premonition of a great future, wondering what he was to do and what he was to become. He was moved by a very sincere motive to join the Dialectic Society, which was the only literary society we had. I did not belong, but Grant joined, while we were roommates, with the aim to improve his manner of expressing himself.

He was elected by his fellow members president of the society.

W. B. Franklin, who stood head of the class, later said: "He had a sense of humor. No man can be called 'a good fellow,' as Grant was, and be a dullard."

The following extract from *The Pointer* of November 1, 1946 confirms General Franklin's recollection that the quiet and often silent cadet did have a sense of humor:

> The old expression "curiosity killed the cat" has a little more meaning to A-1 Co.'s Jack Forest now. The other night, while having nothing else to do, he hit upon the idea of taking off the plate that covers the old outlet circuits on the walls in Central Barracks. On his first try he was rewarded by an old dusty note on which appeared, "All right, now that you have satisfied your curiosity put the darn thing back." On the back it read, "SUCKER LIST—Grant, U.S. 1st Cl. 1840."

In later years Grant wrote in his *Memoirs:*

> A military life had no charms for me, and I had not the faintest idea of staying in the army even if I should be graduated, which I did not expect. The encampment which preceded the commencement of academic studies was very wearisome and uninteresting. When the 28th of August came—the date for breaking up camp and going into barracks—I felt as though I had been at West Point always, and that if I stayed to graduation I would have to remain always. I did not take hold of my studies with avidity—in fact, I rarely ever read over a lesson the second time during my entire cadetship. I could not sit in my room doing nothing. There is a fine library connected with the Academy, from which cadets can get books to read in their quarters. I devoted more time to these than to books relating to the course of studies. Much of the time, I am sorry to say, was devoted to novels, but not those of a trashy sort. I read all of Bulwer's then published, Cooper's, Marryat's, Scott's, Washington Irving's works, Lever's, and many others, that I do not now remember. Mathematics was very easy to me, so that when January came I passed the examination, taking a good standing in that branch. In French—the only other study at that time in the first year's course—my standing was very low. In fact, if the class had been turned the other end foremost, I should have been near head. I never succeeded in getting squarely at either end of my class in any one study during the four years. I came near it in French, artillery, infantry, and cavalry tactics, and conduct.
>
> Early in the session of the Congress which met in December, 1839, a bill was discussed abolishing the Military Academy. I saw in this an honorable way to obtain a discharge, and read the debates with much interest, but with impatience at the delay in taking action, for I was selfish enough to favor the bill. It never passed, and a year later, although the time hung drearily with

me, I would have been sorry to have seen it succeed. My idea then was to get through the course, secure a detail for a few years as assistant professor of mathematics at the Academy, and afterward obtain a permanent position as professor in some respectable college, but circumstances always did shape my course different from my plans.

Nevertheless on September 14, 1839, he had signed the usual agreement to serve for eight years—that is, for four years after graduating from the Military Academy.

Although Hamlin Garland could find no record of Ulysses' having gone to Benny Havens, a perfectly respectable tavern a short distance from the military reservation but "off limits" for cadets, he did visit the tavern once. His purpose was to commit a military offense involving no dishonorable act or moral turpitude but which would cause his dismissal. Accordingly, one day he put on his full-dress uniform and walked down to Benny Havens and back. On his walk he met several officers whom he passed boldly and saluted with precision. They must have surmised from the conspicuousness and flagrancy of his action that he had authority to be out. In any case, he was not reported and could only conclude that fate did not intend him to be dismissed. Perhaps he also gained confidence through learning of the protective power of boldness and its effect on others.

The second cadet year passed easily enough. Furlough, as it came nearer, was the great focus of the hopes and thoughts of all the cadets, and indeed Cadet Grant enjoyed his holiday tremendously. Since he had entered West Point his father and mother had moved to Bethel, a small settlement a few miles nearer Cincinnati than Georgetown had been, and there Ulysses was bound. Miss Kate Lowe, later Mrs. Rothery, who made the canal-boat trip from Harrisburg to Hollidayburg, said "that Grant at that time was a fine-looking, smooth-faced young man with clear eyes and good features, but was chiefly attractive on account of his splendid carriage and soldierly bearing. He was fastidious in dress, wearing always white duck trousers and blue sack coat . . . he must have had a fresh pair for every day in the week."

On his reaching home his mother said, "Ulysses, you've grown much straighter!"

"Yes," he answered, "that was the first thing they taught me."

The summer was thoroughly enjoyed by the young cadet, and most of it was spent with his former schoolmates, visiting Georgetown and other nearby places that were a part of his younger days. It was always hard to go back to the drums and fifes of the military life, with its restrictions and constant attention to little details. With unusual fervor for him, he in later life said, "I enjoyed this vacation beyond any other period of my life."

Back at West Point he continued the even tenor of his ways. One academy incident involved Grant and a classmate named Franklin Gardner, who was showing the members of his section a newly acquired and quite large watch that contained an alarm. When the assembly suddenly was sounded, the watch happened to be in the hands of Cadet Grant, who hastily stuffed it in the chest of his dress coat and marched up to the recitation room with the remainder of his section. While he was at the blackboard in the midst of a recitation, the instructor, Lieutenant Zealous B. Tower, and the section were surprised to hear the ringing of a loud bell. Lieutenant Tower at first thought the noise came from outside; he had the door into the hall closed. Cadet Grant continued his recitation apparently unmoved and hardly aware of the bell, and of course the instructor and most of the class did not know the source of the alarm. Finally, the ringing stopped and soon afterward the cadet finished his recitation still unperturbed. Nothing more was said at the time, but after the class was dismissed and the members of the section were all told whence the alarm had come, they enjoyed the incident hugely.

His classmate and one-time roommate, General Rufus Ingalls, later during the Civil War, said in answer to a question:

> Grant was such a quiet, unassuming fellow when a cadet that nobody would have picked him out as one who was destined to occupy a conspicuous place in history; and yet he had certain qualities which attracted attention and commanded the respect of all those in the Corps with him. He was always frank, generous and manly. At cavalry drill he excelled every one in his class. He used to take great delight in mounting and breaking in the most intractable of the new horses that were purchased from time to time and put in the squad. He succeeded in this, not by punishing the animal he had taken in hand, but by patience and tact, and his skill in making the creature know what he wanted to have it do. . . . In his studies he was lazy and careless. Instead of studying a lesson, he would merely read it over once or twice; but he was so quick in his perceptions that he usually made very fair recitations even with so little preparation.

During his last two years at West Point, mounted cavalry drill was re-established. This was an especially delightful addition to the curriculum for Grant. Apparently the plebes were allowed to go to the riding hall to watch the drill, and Egbert Viele, who had arrived in June 1842, said:

> It was as good as any circus to see Grant ride. . . . There was a dark bay horse that was so fractious that it was about to be condemned. . . . Grant selected it for his horse. He bridled, mounted, and rode it every day at parade; and how he did ride! He handled the refractory creature as a giant would a child. The whole class would stand around admiring his wonderful command of the beast and his graceful evolutions.

Finally, as graduation approached in June 1843, Plebe James B. Fry (who later became a general) entered the riding hall and witnessed a somewhat historic event. The graduating class was there and the hall was full of spectators, including Superintendent Delafield, professors, and official visitors. After the usual cavalry drill, Sergeant Herschberger, the riding master, lifted the jumping bar somewhat above his head and then called for Cadet Grant. Fry saw a slender little cadet dash from the ranks on a big sorrel, then wheel and gallop down the hall. At the extreme end of the hall the rider turned and galloped toward the bar, then rose into the air and over the bar. To Fry it seemed "as if man and beast has been welded together." This jump established a high-jump world record that held for many years; and I remember fifty years later seeing the record of it when I visited the Imperial Riding School in Vienna, Austria.

It should be added that Cadet Grant developed considerable skill in drawing and painting while at West Point. I remember seeing four water colors of his, one of them in the U.S. Military Academy Museum. Members of the family noted that he was always much pleased to have anyone compliment his drawings, but he seemed to take no special interest in any compliments on his military achievements.

In spite of his lack of confidence when he was appointed to West Point, Cadet Grant graduated twenty-first in his class of thirty-nine cadets. This does not seem to be a very high standing; demerits for minor offenses and difficulties with foreign languages held him down. However, an officer who later made a study of the class standing of a number of prominent officers said "a popular fallacy is that U. S. Grant graduated low in his class. He stood approximately in the middle and relatively higher than the following: Jefferson Davis, Joseph Hooker, Don Carlos Buell, James Longstreet, Winfield Scott Hancock, George A. Custer, George Pickett, John B. Hood, Philip Sheridan, Hunter Liggett and Robert L. Bullard." It is interesting in this connection that a study made by Lloyd Lewis shows sixty-five per cent of the cadets from the Middle West failed to graduate; sixty per cent from the South met the same fate; but there was only forty-per-cent failure among cadets from the New England states, New York, New Jersey, and Pennsylvania. This was undoubtedly due to the better schools in the East, and indicates the greater difficulty encountered by cadets from the Middle West and the South in achieving a high standing.

On graduation Cadet Grant naturally asked for assignment and commission in one of the mounted regiments, but was commissioned brevet second lieutenant in the Fourth Infantry with station at Jefferson Barracks, Missouri. The Regular Army at that time was not large enough to absorb the full complement of graduates from West Point, and a number of each class had to be satisfied with brevet commissions until a vacancy occurred. No one in his class was recommended for assignment to the corps of engineers or the ordnance.

II

The Years Between

MEANWHILE, in 1841, at Bethel, Ohio, Jesse Grant had established a tannery in accordance with a partnership agreement with E. A. Collins, a tanner of Bethel. By the terms, Jesse gave up his part in the retail trade and concentrated on becoming a wholesaler, while Collins moved to Galena, Illinois, with the combined stock of prepared hides and opened a retail store there. Jesse Grant's business career was as successful as his son's West Point years.

In preparation for welcoming his son home in June 1843, Jesse bought a colt, unbroken to harness, knowing that this would please Ulysses. The home-coming was a very agreeable, happy time for the young lieutenant. At Bethel he got word of his assignment to the Fourth Infantry and, on July 28, orders to proceed to Jefferson Barracks.

The principal official duty of Grant at this time was that of ordering an officer's uniform and sword. Of his first experience when arrayed in his uniform he afterward wrote:

> The conceit was knocked out of me by two little circumstances that happened soon after the arrival of the clothes, which gave me a distaste for military uniform that I never recovered from. Soon after the arrival of the suit I donned it, and put off for Cincinnati on horseback. While I was riding along a street of that city, imagining that every one was looking at me with a feeling akin to mine when I first saw General Scott, a little urchin, bareheaded, barefooted, with dirty and ragged pants held up by a single gallows—that's what suspenders were called then—and a shirt that had not seen a washtub for weeks, turned to me and cried: "Soldier! will you work? No,

sir—ee; I'll sell my shirt first!!" The horse-trade and its dire consequences were recalled to mind.

The other circumstance occurred at home. Opposite our house in Bethel stood the old stage-tavern where "man and beast" found accommodation. The stable-man was rather dissipated, but possessed of some humor. On my return I found him parading the streets and attending in the stable barefooted, but in a pair of sky-blue nankeen pantaloons—just the color of my uniform trousers—with a strip of white-cotton sheeting sewed down the outside seams in imitation of mine. The joke was a huge one in the mind of many of the people, and was much enjoyed by them; but I did not appreciate it so highly.

Grant reported at Jefferson Barracks on September 30, 1843, and found there eight companies of the 4th Infantry and eight companies of the 3rd Infantry. The post commander was Stephen Kearny, and the colonel of the 4th Infantry, Josiah Vose, was a fine old gentleman but too aged for drill and other activities. The regiment, then, was run by Lieutenant Colonel John Garland and his adjutant, Lieutenant Charles Hoskins. The post was in some turmoil over the court-martial of a Lieutenant Don Carlos Buell, class of 1841, for having struck an enlisted man with his saber. He had been set free by the court; however, General Scott in Washington disapproved the finding of the court as inconsistent with the evidence. President Tyler, to whom the question was referred, ordered that the matter be dropped.

Like all the infantry regiments in the Regular Army at that time, the 4th was very much reduced. When special-duty details—such as musicians, blacksmiths, clerks, and noncommissioned officers—were eliminated, there were only about 449 enlisted men and 21 officers left for strictly military duty, with 36 enlisted men to a company. The new lieutenant, Sam Grant, had been assigned to Company I, but was assigned temporarily to command Company F.

At this time he was not joining his brother officers in trips to the diversions of St. Louis, nine miles away, but was concentrating on studies. Correspondence with Professor Church at West Point had given him assurance that he would be called back as an instructor as soon as a vacancy occurred in the department of mathematics; so he mapped out a course of study in mathematics and history by way of preparation for the call that might come within a year or two. However, this hope was never realized. The Mexican War interfered.

A senior captain in the 4th Infantry, who apparently was president of the bachelor officers' mess, was Robert C. Buchanan. He was a martinet with a rather interfering personality, although he had shown himself brave enough in the Indian fighting from which he had recently come. He seems to have considered the shy young officer Grant a ready victim for his criticism.

One of Lieutenant Grant's classmates—and a roommate—at West Point had been Frederick T. Dent, whose father had a considerable estate located on the Gravois Road between Jefferson Barracks and St. Louis. This classmate, who had been assigned to the Sixth Infantry in Indian Territory, had made Grant promise that he would call on the family at White Haven, to which Ulysses rode on horseback one day and where he was greeted by the youngest daughter of the family, Emmy. She seemed very much impressed with the young officer and only after some hesitation admitted that Mr. Dent lived there. Fred Dent's mother and sister Ellen came out and greeted Ulysses and made him welcome. They explained that the oldest daughter, Julia, had completed finishing school and was visiting Colonel John O'Fallon's family in St. Louis. She returned home February 1844. The father, "Colonel" Frederick Dent (the military title was entirely honorary), was of an old Maryland family. He had come to Missouri and purchased an estate of 925 acres. He was an important citizen in his new surroundings, of definitely southern opinions, and a slave owner; however, he was doubtless a considerate and kind master to his slaves. Further, he was generous, impulsive, consequently at times cantankerous. Mrs. Dent seemed to have taken quite a fancy to the young lieutenant, but Colonel Dent did not appear to be so enthusiastic about the young officer, who, in his opinion, needed watching as a "Yankee."

There were other children: John C.; George, 22, and married; Frederick, 23, and absent with his regiment; and Louis, 20. With Julia's return Lieutenant Grant's visits to White Haven increased in frequency and length, and a sense of mutual appreciation and liking seemed to spring up between the couple. This was evidenced by little Emmy's childish jealousy, which led her to reproach the lieutenant for now being more Julia's beau than hers.

Ulysses' social life probably helps explain an incident with Captain Buchanan, who had adopted a rule "that any officer late at mess should be fined a bottle of wine." Even if the tardy person came in just after the soup was served, Buchanan imposed the penalty. Grant was unfortunate. His frequent visits to White Haven were not always over in time for prompt return to mess, and in ten days' time the lieutenant was fined three times. The manner of the president of the mess was irritating: "Grant, you are late, as usual; another bottle of wine, sir." "Mr. President, I have been fined three bottles of wine within the last ten days and if I am fined again I shall be obliged to repudiate." "Mr. Grant, young people should be seen, not heard." From this it will be seen that "old Buch" was consistently annoying, but when confronted with a definite refusal, firmly stated, he gave some ground.

Another run-in with the senior captain illustrates the lieutenant's fearlessness and his resentment of any doubt expressed as to the truth of his statements: "The lieutenant was drilling his company when his commanding officer came by with some other officers and asked: 'Where are the rest of your men, Lieutenant?' 'Absent, by your leave, sir.' 'That is not true.' Grant turned to the sergeant, told him to take command," and dismissed the company; "then putting the point of his sword to the officer's breast said: 'Unless you apologize at once for this insult, I will run you through.' The officer apologized." We may be sure that these two incidents were still remembered and harbored in bitterness by the older captain, when the lieutenant, upon his promotion to captain, reported to Brevet Lieutenant Colonel Buchanan at Fort Humboldt in 1853.

The time at Jefferson Barracks otherwise passed happily enough. There were parties and dances at the post and occasionally in St. Louis. Caroline O'Fallon was a great friend of Julia and of her beau, and Julia remembered her in after years as "the beautiful angel of her childhood." Other friends were the Longs, the Fentons, the Sappingtons. The young people gathered of evenings to dance and sing, and Grant and his fellow officers were frequent participants. But the chief recreation for both Lieutenant Grant and Julia Dent was their horseback rides, on which Julia rode a handsome bay mare called Missouri Belle.

Lloyd Lewis relates:

> One day when they were riding, cries of "Help" brought them to a Negro who had cut his foot with an ax. Grant stopped the flow of blood with his handkerchief, asked Julia to hold it and told the old darkey to press both thumbs against the arteries. With the ax Grant cut bark from an oak tree, bruised it on top of a stump and poulticed the gashed flesh. The Negro's wife

and two little girls came up wailing. The wife objected when Grant tore out the back of her husband's vest to bind up the poultice. Grant calmed her with a promise to get her husband a new one. Lifting the man onto his horse, Grant took the Negroes to their cabin and left, saying he would be back tomorrow at four in the afternoon. At the appointed hour he was there, and a surgeon with him—and a new army vest. The injured man's eyes shone. Julia with her slave and a basket of food happened to arrive at the same time, and the surgeon, dressing the wound, told her, in mock seriousness, that the lieutenant should be a doctor rather than a soldier.

In the meantime the annexation of Texas gave rise to violent discussion all through the country, particularly in Congress and the press. Naturally, as it involved the possibility of war with Mexico, annexation was uppermost in the minds of the troops at Jefferson Barracks and their families. On April 20, 1844, the 3rd Infantry was ordered to the vicinity of Fort Jessup, Louisiana. Evidently the 4th Infantry was likely to follow the 3rd; therefore Lieutenant Grant applied for a leave of absence to visit his family and on May 1 received twenty days' leave. He took the first steamer for Cincinnati, and the ship was hardly out of sight when a messenger rode to the wharf to call him back, as orders had come for the regiment to move on May 7. By the next boat there came a letter from a friend, Charles E. Jarvis, telling him of these orders and recommending that he not open any other letter from headquarters until his leave was up. Jarvis assured him that he would take all of Sam's belongings with him.

The leave at home, which Grant had looked forward to with such anticipation, was now spoiled. In his *Memoirs* he wrote:

I now discovered that I was exceedingly anxious to get back to Jefferson Barracks, and I understood the reason without explanation from anyone. My leave of absence required me to report for duty at Jefferson Barracks at the end of twenty days. I knew my Regiment had gone up the Red River, but I was not disposed to break the letter of my leave; besides, if I had proceeded to Louisiana direct, I could not have reached there until after the expiration of my leave. Accordingly, at the end of the twenty days I reported to Lieutenant Ewell, commanding at Jefferson Barracks (who later was to be one of General Lee's Corps Commanders), handing him at the same time my leave of absence. After noticing the phraseology of the order—leaves of absence were generally worded, "at the end of which time he will report for duty with his proper command"—he said he would give me an order to join my Regiment in Louisiana. I then asked for a few days' leave before starting, which he readily granted.

In regard to Lieutenant Ewell, he added, "He was a man much esteemed, and deservedly so, in the old army, and proved himself a gallant and efficient officer in two wars—both, in my estimation, unholy."

He quickly obtained a horse and started for White Haven, but was caught in crossing Gravois Creek by the high water caused by recent rains. Having always had a superstition that, after starting to go anywhere or do anything, he should not turn back or stop until the thing intended was accomplished, he started across the stream. His horse was soon swimming and carried down stream by the current; but he succeeded in reaching the other bank, his clothes thoroughly soaked. However, he did reach his destination, where he borrowed a dry suit from his future brother-in-law. It did not fit but served the necessity of the moment. He further related:

> Before I returned I mustered up courage to make known, in the most awkward manner imaginable, the discovery I had made on learning that the 4th Infantry had been ordered away from Jefferson Barracks. The young lady afterward admitted that she too—although until then she had never looked upon me other than as a visitor whose company was agreeable to her—had experienced a depression of spirits she could not account for when the Regiment left. Before separating it was definitely understood that at a convenient time we would join our fortunes, and not let the removal of a regiment trouble us. This was May 1844. It was the 22nd of August 1848 before the fulfillment of this agreement. My duties kept me on the frontier of Louisiana with the Army of Observation during the pendency of annexation; and afterward I was absent through the war with Mexico—provoked by the action of the army if not by the annexation itself. During that time there was a constant correspondence between Miss Dent and myself, but we only met once in the period of four years and three months. In May 1845 I procured a leave for twenty days, visited St. Louis and obtained the consent of the parents to the union, which had not been asked before.

Having in mind the assurance of Professor Church that he would be designated as the latter's assistant professor, he had continued his studies in preparation for this detail and reviewed the West Point course in mathematics and read many valuable historical works and an occasional novel. He had made notes on what he'd read with comments he thought appropriate, but he never recovered this journal after the regiment left Jefferson Barracks. It was not found among the effects packed up and mailed him. For years afterward he lived in fear that this diary would fall into the hands of some malicious person who would publish it, and cause him as much embarrassment and heartache as Mr. White's story of his youthful horse trade or the later caricaturing of his uniform.

The ordering of the two regiments to Louisiana was allegedly for the purpose of preventing smuggling between the United States and Mexico, but it was generally suspected that this military action had been taken in anticipation of the annexation of Texas. In discussing the matter, Lieutenant Grant had expressed himself in opposition to the United States' taking advantage of the annexation of Texas to acquire Mexican territory. Evidently he spoke with clarity and decision, because Mrs. Dent, after he had expressed his opinion, said, "That young man explains politics so clearly I can understand the situation perfectly."

Finally, just before leaving Missouri, he and Julia persuaded her brother to ride horseback to the wedding he was going to attend and let them take the carriage. Julia explained in later years:

> We were going to a morning wedding and Lieutenant Grant was also invited. He came for us on horseback and asked my brother's permission to drive me in exchange for his saddle. . . . The day was beautiful, the roads were a little heavy from previous rains, but the sun shone in splendor.
>
> We had to cross a little bridge that spanned a ravine and when we reached it I was surprised and a little concerned to find the gulch swollen . . . the water reaching to the bridge. I noticed, too, that Lieutenant Grant was very quiet, and that and the high water bothered me. I asked several times if he thought the water dangerous to breast, and told him I would go back rather than take any risks. He assured me, in his brief way, that it was perfectly safe, and in my heart I relied upon him.
>
> Just as we reached the old bridge, I said, "Now, if anything happens, remember I shall cling to you, no matter what you say to the contrary."
>
> He simply said, "All right," and we were over the planks in less than a minute. Then his mood changed, he became more social and in asking me to be his wife, used my threat as a theme.
>
> After dinner that afternoon, Lieutenant Grant asked me to set the day. I wanted to be engaged, and told him that it would be much nicer than getting married—a sentiment he did not approve. We were very quiet at the house that evening and neither said a word of the secret. . . . He was too shy to ask Father.

The Dents' old family servant, Mary Robinson, is reported to have said that Lieutenant Grant's shyness was justified, as old Mr. Dent had opposed his courting Miss Julia and did everything he could to prevent the match; but Mrs. Dent had taken a fancy to young Grant. Colonel Dent was well acquainted with the marriage of Jessie Benton, daughter of his great friend Senator Benton, to young Lieutenant Frémont of the Topographical Engineers. The latter's financial situation and frequent absences of considerable duration on exploring expeditions seemed to Mr. Dent rather hard on the wife, and he did not fancy the prospect for his daughter Julia.

The 4th Infantry had gone by boat to New Orleans and then back up the Red River to Natchitoches, the oldest city in Louisiana. Three days after his arrival there, Lieutenant Grant wrote his old friend, Mrs. Bailey, in Georgetown, Ohio, telling so much of the trip and the camp that the entire letter deserves quotation:

Camp Salubrity
Near Natchitoches Louisiana
June 6th, 1844

Mrs. Bailey

My journey fortunately is at an end, and agreeably to your request, and my own pleasure. I hasten to notify you of my safe arrival here. It always affords me pleasure to write to old acquaintances, and much more to hear from them, so I would be pleased if the correspondence would not stop here. As long as my letters are answered, if agreeable to you I will continue to write.

My trip to this place "forty days journey in the wilderness" was marked with no incident, save one, worth relating and that one is laughable, curious, important, surprising etc. etc. but I cant tell it now. It is for the present a secret but I will tell it to you some time. You must not guess what it is for you will go wrong. On my route I called around by the way of St. Louis and Jefferson Barracks where I spent four or five days very pleasantly among my newly made acquaintances. From St. Louis to N. Orleans I had a very pleasant trip on a large and splendid boat, with pleasant passengers and not much crowded. As we approached the South the sun became sensibly warmer, and the Musquitoes decidedly more numerous. By the time we got to N. Orleans my hands and face bore the strongest evidence of the number and size of this insect in a southern climate. I was but one day in Orleans which was spent in runing over the City just fast enough to tire myself out and get but little good of my visit. But from what I saw I think it would be a pleasant place to live and it is now contemplated that my regiment will go in that neighborhood in case Texas should not be annexed to the U. States, but in case of the annexation we will probably have to go much farther West than we are now. Probably to the Rio Colorado. From N. Orleans to Natchitoches I had the bad fortune to travel on a small boat considerably crowded, through a hot country, with gambling going on day and night. Some of the passengers had very cut throat appearances. From Natchitoches I had to walk (or pay an extravagant price for a conveyance) three miles through the hotest sun I think I ever felt. I found my regiment camping out in small linen tents on the top of a high Sandy ridge and in the midst of a pine forest. The great elevation of our situation and the fact that one of the best springs of water in the State puts out here are the only recommendations the place has. We are about three miles from any place, there is no conveyance to take us from one place to another, and every thing is so high that we can't afford to keep a horse or other conveyance of our own. I could walk myself but for the intensity of the heat. As for lodgings I have a small tent that the rain runs through as it would through a sieve. For a bedstead I have four short pine sticks set upright and plank running from the two at one end to the other. For chairs I use my trunk and bed, and as to a floor we have no such a luxury yet. Our meals are cooked in the woods by servants that know no more about culinary matters than I do myself. But with all these disadvantages my appetite is becoming extravigant [sic]. I would like to have our old West Point board again that you may have heard so much about. As for the troublesome insects of creation they abound here. The swamps are full of Aligators, and the woods full of Red bugs and ticks; insects that you are not troubled with in Ohio, but are the plague of this country. They crawl entirely under the skin when they git on a person and it is impossible to keep them off.—So much for Camp Salubrity.—I should be happy to get an answer to this as early as possible, and if nothing more, a Post Script from the young ladies. Ladies are always so much better at giving the news than others, and then there is nothing doing or said about Georgetown that I would not like to hear. They could tell me of all the weddings etc. etc. that are talked of. Give my love to every body in Georgetown.

Lt. U. S. Grant
4th Infantry

P.S. I give my title in signing this not because I wish people to know what it is but because I want to get an answer to this and put it there that a letter may be directed so, as to get to me.

USG

Camp life was not too strenuous or serious for the moment. Various sports and pastimes were organized by the officers. As General Ingalls wrote:

We were having high old times. We had a set of officers, splendid fellows, but wilder than the characters in "Charles O'Malley," while Twiggs, the colonel, was away endeavoring to get his regiment remounted and put upon a footing with the First Dragoons. So the scenes enacted at Fort Jessup during the time Grant was stationed in Louisiana would make a volume of better reading than "Charles O'Malley," if we had as good an author as Lever to put them in shape.

But when the colonel was present things were entirely different. He was a very superior officer. After the Florida war his command had been dismounted and its designation as the Second Dragoons changed to the Rifle Regiment. Not only Twiggs but all the officers were dissatisfied with this, and at the time of which I speak Twiggs was in Washington getting it restored as a mounted regiment, and discipline was a little lax, but when he returned things were very soon put in good shape.

During the absence of which I speak, Grant would occasionally relieve the monotony of the staid life at Camp Salubrity by coming over and enjoying the hilarity at Fort Jessup. I remember his first arrival. He came in one day upon a frisky pony of very small size, and the boys laughed at him, for he was usually in the habit of seeking the largest and most vicious horse he could find. At that visit we had an interesting renewal of our early acquaintance.

The two regiments—the one to which Grant belonged and the one in which I held a commission—remained during 1844 and 1845 in this dismal country, and I saw him frequently. He would come over and take his chance at gander pulling, horse racing and the usual sports of our camp, at which he was a good hand. We had something new going on every day. Our post was situated half way between the Red and Sabine rivers, where there was very little underbrush. Game was plentiful, woodcock and large quantities of water-fowl. We would drive deer and shoot birds as one of the features of our recreation. Grant was not much of a shot. He never seemed to take great interest in the sports of the field, but could ride anything in the shape of a horse, and was a manly, popular young officer.

Congress on March 1, 1845, voted the annexation of Texas, expecting to ratify the step on July 4. The new President, James Knox Polk, when inaugurated, had optimistically hoped that the differences with Mexico would be settled by diplomacy. However, the young officers in their Louisiana camps felt confident that "the army of observation" would soon become an "army of occupation." Accordingly, Lieutenant Grant on April 1 of that hot spring asked for a thirty-five days' leave to visit St. Louis. The application did not state that the principal and urgent reason for the leave was to obtain from his future father-in-law the approval of his engagement, Colonel Dent not having answered Lieutenant Grant's request by letter. Her father had told Julia, "You are too young and the boy is too poor. He hasn't anything to give you." In reply, Julia afterward related, "I rose in my wrath and I said I was poor too and hadn't anything to give him." Indeed, Colonel Dent was not too well fixed financially. He had land and slaves, but the cash return was limited and he was also inclined to become embroiled in lawsuits that were expensive.

It so happened that old Colonel Dent was at a disadvantage when Lieutenant Grant rode up to White Haven to ask for his daughter's hand. According to Julia's account years afterward, the whole family had been on the front porch saying good-by to Colonel Dent, who was going to Washington on business. They were kissing him farewell and filling his pockets with memoranda of things he was to buy in the East, when suddenly a horseman rode up: "Her Lieutenant in a new uniform —her beautiful young man!"

The young officer swung off of his horse, came up to the porch, and, evidently recognizing the strategic moment, asked Colonel Dent for Julia's hand. "Father being in a hurry to get off, consented." With equal perspicacity the young officer realized that his hope to have the wedding take place during his few days' leave must be given up for the present. The leave was over too quickly and the lieutenant after his last ride with his fiancée boarded a steamer and after a brief farewell started downstream to his regiment, once more leaving Julia waiting.

Meanwhile, General Zachary Taylor (he was brevet brigadier general with a fine reputation as an Indian fighter, but in the Regular Army only a colonel) had been designated to take command of the army at New Orleans, to which place the two infantry regiments on the Red River were moved. The city was very quiet because of the number of residents who had left town to escape the ravages of yellow fever, which had attacked the old French city.

General Taylor sailed on July 23 with the 3rd Infantry for Corpus Christi, and the major part of the 4th followed on the side-wheeler *Dayton* in September. Lieutenant Grant, back with his Company I, took the sailing ship *Suviah* a day or two later. From the deck of the ship he saw the wreck of the *Dayton* where it had blown up on September 13, killing eight members of the 4th Infantry, two of whom had been cadets at West Point with him.

Lieutenant Grant later told of his adventure on this trip, his first sea voyage:

After I had gone ashore, and had been on guard several days at Shell Island—quite six miles from the ship—I had occasion, for some reason or other, to return on board. While on the *Suviah*—I think that was the name of our vessel—I heard a tremendous racket at the other end of the ship, and much and excited sailor language, such as "Damn your eyes," etc. In a moment or two the captain—who was an excitable little man, dying with consumption, and not weighing much over a hundred pounds—came running out, carrying a saber nearly as large and as heavy as he was, and crying that his men had mutinied. It was necessary to sustain the captain without question, and in a few minutes all the sailors charged with mutiny were in irons. I rather felt for a time a wish that I had not gone aboard just then. As the men charged with mutiny submitted to being placed in irons without resistance, I always doubted if they knew that they had mutinied until they were told.

By the time I was ready to leave the ship again I thought I had learned enough of the working of the double and single pulley by which passengers were let down from the upper deck of the ship to the steamer below, and determined to let myself down without assistance. Without saying anything of my intentions to any one, I mounted the railing, and taking hold of the center-rope just below the upper block, I put one foot on the hook below the lower block and stepped off. Just as I did so some one called out, "Hold on!" It was too late. I tried to "hold on" with all my might, but my heels went up, and my head went down so rapidly that my hold broke, and I plunged foremost into the water, some twenty-five feet below, with such velocity that it seemed to me I never would stop. When I came to the surface again, being a fair swimmer, and not having lost my presence of mind, I swam around until a bucket was let down for me, and I was drawn up without a scratch or injury. I do not believe there was a man on board who sympathized with me in the least when they found me uninjured. I rather enjoyed the joke myself. The captain of the *Suviah* died of his disease a few months later, and, I believe, before the mutineers were tried. I hope they got clear, because, as before stated, I always thought the mutiny was all in the brain of a very weak and sick man.

After reaching shore, or Shell Island, the labor of getting to Corpus Christi was slow and tedious. There was, if my memory serves me, but one small steamer to transport troops and baggage when the Fourth Infantry arrived. Others were procured later. The distance from Shell Island to Corpus Christi was some sixteen or eighteen miles. The channel to the bay was so shallow that the steamer, small as it was, had to be dragged over the bottom when loaded. Not more than one trip a day could be effected. Later this was remedied by deepening the channel and increasing the number of vessels suitable to its navigation.

The American army was now occupying the territory between the Nueces River and the Rio Grande, which Mexico had always claimed did not belong to Texas. Neither Texas nor Mexico had ever done very much to settle it, so that it was practically still uninhabited. Corpus Christi itself was a small trading post with a population of about a hundred persons and a trade mostly in tobacco carried on with smugglers and some North American tradesmen.

After a camp site had been cleared and the adjoining thickets more or less freed of their rattlesnake population, the place became quite habitable except for the heat. Captain E. Kirby Smith, coming with Fred Dent and the 5th Infantry, wrote home that the river itself delighted the eyes, "winding through the Prairie like a blue ribbon carelessly thrown on a green robe." The violent storms on occasion stranded enough green turtles to fill wagons. Oysters were raked out of the river mouth in basketfuls. From the prairies, officers and men brought in large numbers of deer, duck, wild turkeys, and jacksnipe. Lieutenant Grant tried hunting only once, when his friend, Calvin Benjamin, of the 4th Artillery, persuaded him to go after turkeys. But as Grant afterward told it, he stood admiring the big birds as they flew from a pecan tree over his head, without thinking of taking a shot at them. From this experience he decided he was not especially qualified for the sport and went back to camp leaving Benjamin to get what birds he wanted.

The officers also learned much about the country, escorting supply trains and paymasters' wagons to San Antonio where General Taylor had a small garrison. Lieutenant Grant tells of one of these trips and of an encounter with wolves:

> The prairie-grass was tall and we could not see the beasts, but the sound indicated that they were near. To my ear it appeared that there must have been enough of them to devour our party, horses and all, at a single meal. The part of Ohio that I hailed from was not thickly settled, but wolves had been driven out long before I left. Benjamin was from Indiana, still less populated, where the wolf yet roamed over the prairies. He understood the nature of the animal and the capacity of a few to make believe there was an unlimited number of them. He kept on toward the noise unmoved. I followed in his

trail, lacking the moral courage to turn back. . . . But Benjamin did not propose turning back. When he did speak it was to ask, "Grant, how many wolves do you think there are in that pack?" Knowing where he was from, and suspecting that he thought I would over-estimate the number, I determined to show my acquaintance with the animal by putting the estimate below what possibly could be correct, and answered, "Oh, about twenty," very indifferently. He smiled and rode on. In a minute we were close upon them, and before they saw us. There were just *two* of them. Seated upon their haunches, with their mouths close together, they had made all the noise we had been hearing for the past ten minutes. I have often thought of this incident since when I have heard the noise of a few disappointed politicians who had deserted their associates. There are always more of them before they are counted.

Gradually General Taylor assembled his "army of occupation" at Corpus Christi. Altogether it consisted of seven companies of the 2nd Regiment of Dragoons, four companies of Light Artillery, five regiments of infantry—the 3rd, 4th, 5th, 7th, and 8th—and one regiment of artillery acting as infantry; there were not more than 3,000 men in all. General Taylor commanded the whole. There were troops enough in one body to establish a drill and discipline sufficient to fit men and officers for all they were capable of in case of battle. The rank and file were men who had enlisted in time of peace to serve for $7 a month, and were necessarily inferior as material to the average volunteers enlisted later in the war expressly to fight. The men engaged in the Mexican War were brave, and the officers of the Regular Army, from highest to lowest, were educated in their profession. "A more efficient army for its number and armament I do not believe ever fought a battle than the one commanded by General Taylor in his first two engagements on Mexican or Texas soil," Grant wrote.

General Taylor proved an outstandingly efficient commander in the field, and under his leadership his little army carried out a great campaign into Mexico, going as far as Buena Vista, where the last battle of that campaign was fought. Before meeting the enemy there, considerable numbers of General Taylor's troops were taken from him and transferred to General Scott's army, then on its way to Vera Cruz. There was a great contrast between the two commanding generals in the matter of appearance. General Scott, a large and imposing man who took a great deal of interest in his appearance and uniforms, had come to be known in the army as "Old Fuss and Feathers." This was without any reflection on his leadership. On the other hand, General Taylor paid little attention to presenting a military appearance, or what is usually so considered. He wore civilian clothes more or less while in command in the field, did not carry a sword, often rode his horse with one leg over the pommel, and otherwise may have been the example from which Lieutenant Grant was persuaded that the question of uniform, sword, and other military paraphernalia had little to do with effective military leadership.

In the meantime, on September 30, 1845, Brevet Second Lieutenant Grant received his promotion to second lieutenant. While this brought him assignment to another regiment, 7th Infantry, he found that the officer, Franklin Gardner, who was assigned to fill his vacancy in the 4th Infantry did not want his transfer either; so by mutual agreement they arranged for reassignment to the regiments with which they had been serving.

III

The War with Mexico

THE presence of the army in the disputed territory farthest from the Mexican settlement did not provoke hostilities, as President Polk had hoped. Evidently it was necessary that the Mexicans attack Taylor's army so that Congress could resolve "whereas, war exists by the acts of the Mexican Army," and then prosecute the contest with vigor. General Taylor was loath to bring on this situation, in spite of the hints he received from the government in Washington. The government was compelled, then, to give him explicit orders to invade Mexican territory. The nearest Mexican settlement of any size was Matamoros, about 150 miles from Corpus Christi.

The country thereabout was lacking in fresh water, and the length of each day's march had to be regulated by the distance between water holes. At that time there was not a single habitation, cultivated field, or herd of domestic animals between Corpus Christi and Matamoros. The provision of the necessary transportation was a very real, practical problem for General Taylor and his staff to solve.

Wagons and harnass [sic] could easily be supplied from the North; but mules and horses could not so readily be brought. The American traders and Mexican smugglers came to the army's relief. Contracts were made for mules at from $8 to $11 each. The smugglers furnished the animals, and took their pay in goods of the description before mentioned. I doubt whether the Mexicans received in value from the traders $5 per head for the animals they furnished, and still more, whether they paid anything but their own time in procuring them. Such is trade; such is war. The Government paid in hard cash to the contractor the stipulated price.

Between the Rio Grande and the Nueces there was at the time a large band of wild horses feeding; as numerous, probably, as the band of buffaloes roaming farther north was before its rapid extermination commenced. The Mexicans used to capture these in large numbers and bring them into the American settlements and sell them. A picked animal could be purchased at from $8 to $12, but taken at wholesale they could be bought for $36 a dozen. Some of these were purchased for the Army, and answered a most useful purpose. The horses were generally very strong, formed much like the Norman horse, and with very heavy manes and tales. A number of officers supplied themselves with these, and they generally rendered as useful service as the northern animal; in fact they were much better when grazing was the only means of supplying forage.

During the short period that he served with the 7th Infantry, pending his transfer back to the 4th, Lieutenant Grant served in the company of Captain Holmes, who afterward became a lieutenant general in the Confederate Army. On retransfer to the 4th Infantry, the lieutenant was assigned to the company of Captain McCall, who resigned from the army after the Mexican War but promptly volunteered on the outbreak of the Civil War and soon rose to the rank of major general in the Union Army. He was highly esteemed as a soldier and a gentleman.

Lieutenant Grant remembered that the preparations for the advance from Corpus Christi consisted principally of securing mules and getting them broken to the harness:

The process was slow, but amusing. The animals sold to the Government were all young and unbroken, even to the saddle, and were quite as wild as the wild horses of the prairie. Usually a number would be brought in by a company of Mexicans, partners in the delivery. The mules were first driven into a stockade, called a *corral,* inclosing an acre or more of ground. The Mexicans—who were all experienced in throwing the lasso—would go into the *corral* on horseback, with their lassos attached to the pommels of their saddles. Soldiers detailed as teamsters and blacksmiths would also enter the *corral,* the former with ropes to serve as halters, the latter with branding-irons and a fire to keep the irons heated. A lasso was then thrown over the neck of a mule, when he would immediately go to the length of his tether, first one end, then the other, in the air. While he was thus plunging and gyrating, another lasso would be thrown by another Mexican, catching the animal by a fore foot. This would bring the mule to the ground, when he was seized and held by the teamsters while the blacksmith put upon him, with hot irons, the initials "U.S." Ropes were then put about the neck, with a slip-noose which would tighten around the throat if pulled. With a man on each side holding these ropes, the mule was released from his other bindings and allowed to rise. With more or less difficulty he would be conducted to a picket-rope outside and fastened there. The delivery of that mule was then complete. This process was gone through with every mule and wild horse with the army of occupation.

The method of breaking them was less cruel and much more amusing. It is a well-known fact that where domestic animals are used for specific purposes from generation to generation the descendants are easily, as a rule, subdued to the same uses. At that time in northern Mexico the mule, or his ancestors, the horse and the ass, was seldom used except for the saddle or pack. At all events, the Corpus Christi mule resisted the new use to which he was being put. The treatment he was subjected to in order to overcome his prejudices was summary and effective.

Excepting perhaps some former teamsters, the soldiers, most of whom were enlisted in large cities, had no experience in handling animals. But somehow the job got done. Five mules were allotted to each wagon, and a soldier detailed as teamster would select at the picket rope five animals of the same color and general appearance for his team. With a full corps of assistants—other teamsters—he would proceed to get his mules together. In twos the men would approach each animal selected, avoiding its heels as far as possible. Two ropes would be put about the neck of each animal with a slip noose, so that he could be choked if too unruly. The mules were then led out, harnessed by force, and hitched to the wagon in the position they had to keep ever after. Two men remained on either side of the lead mule with lassos about its neck, and one man retained the same restraining influence over each of the others. All being ready, the hold would be slackened and the team started.

The first motion was generally five mules in the air at one time, backs bowed, hind feet extended to the rear. After repeating this movement a few times the leaders would start to run. This would bring the breeching tight against the mules at the wheels, which they seemed to regard as a most unwarrantable attempt at coercion. They resisted by taking a seat, sometimes going so far as to lie down. In time all were broken in to do their duty submissively if not cheerfully; but there never was a time during the war when it was safe to let a Mexican mule get entirely loose. Their drivers were all teamsters by the time they got through. Grant recalled:

. . . one case of a mule that had worked in a team under the saddle, not only for some time at Corpus Christi, where he was broken, but all the way to the point opposite Matamoros, then to Camargo, where he got loose from his fastenings during the night. He did not run away at first, but stayed in the neighborhood for a day or two coming up sometimes to the feed trough even; but on the approach of the teamster he always got out of the way. At last growing tired of the constant effort to catch him, he disappeared altogether. Nothing short of a Mexican with his lasso could have caught him. Regulations would not have warranted the expenditure of a dollar in hiring a man with a lasso to catch that mule; but they did allow the expenditure "of the mule" on a certificate that he had run away without any fault of the quartermaster on whose returns he was borne, and also the purchase of another to take his place. I am a competent witness, for I was regimental quartermaster at the time.

In connection with the shortage of transportation, the story has been passed on, from ear to ear like Homer's poems, that the brigade commander ordered the loaded wagons of the 4th Infantry to be parked for inspection on a certain day. He proceeded to check on whether orders were being observed as to what could be carried along with the regiment in the coming campaign. As the commander proceeded down the line of company wagons he found in one a little bundle of books—pertinent infantry regulations, army regulations, and one or two on general subjects relating to the art of war. He asked to whom they belonged, and when the owner spoke up he was ordered to take them off the wagon immediately as an unauthorized addition to the load. One of the other officers attending the inspection seemed a little nervous after this incident and finally decided that he had better make a clean breast of what he had put in his company wagons. He saluted and said that he had a little jug of whiskey which he had thought would be useful on the road in case anybody fainted or otherwise became exhausted. To this the brigade commander is said to have replied: "That's all right, anything within reason; but so and so is loading the wagon down with books!"

It is well here to summarize what had been going on in Mexico City. The Herrera government had been overthrown by a bloodless palace revolution on December 30, 1845, and General Paredes was chosen as temporary president. President Polk had sent Slidell as special emissary to Mexico to discuss the settlement of questions arising out of the annexation of Texas; but the Herrera government had refused to see him or discuss the matter. Paredes took the same position, saying in his proclamation, "I did not admit Mr. Slidell because the dignity of the nation would repel this new insult," adding a list of complaints as to what the Americans had done. "Hostilities therefore had been begun by the United States of America, who have undertaken new conquests in the territory lying within the line of the departments of Tamaulipas and Nuevo León. . . ."

The State Department's negotiations and program with Mexico were somewhat delayed in order to permit as far as possible a settlement with England in regard to the Oregon boundary. When that was amicably settled, General Taylor with his army of less than 3,000 men started advancing to the mouth of the Rio Grande on March 8, 1846. One battery, the siege guns, and all the convalescent troops were sent on by water to Brazos Santiago, at the mouth of the Rio Grande, a guard being left at Corpus Christi to look out for the public property there and take care of those too sick to be removed. The remainder of the army, probably about 2,500 men, was divided into three brigades, with the cavalry independent. Colonel Twiggs, with seven companies of dragoons and a battery of light artillery, also moved on March 8. He was followed by the three infantry brigades with a day's interval between the commands. Thus the rear brigade did not move from Corpus Christi until March 11. In his *Memoirs,* General Grant specifically states as a matter to be noted:

> General Taylor was opposed to anything like plundering by the troops, and in this instance, I doubt not, he looked upon the enemy as the aggrieved party and was not willing to injure them further than his instructions from Washington commanded. His orders to the troops enjoined scrupulous regard for the rights of all peaceable persons. and the payment of the highest price for all supplies taken for the use of the army.

The column did not encounter any serious obstacle or opposition until it reached the mouth of the Little Colorado River, which was quite wide there and of sufficient depth for navigation. The opposition seems to have consisted only of a large number of buglers scattered in the woods and concealed. Like the wolves previously spoken of, they gave an impression of a larger number than was actually present. As a few of our cavalry dashed in and forded and swam the stream, all opposition soon dispersed without any noticeable exchange of fire. The troops waded the stream, which was up to their necks in the deepest part. Artillery and wagons were swung across with rope pulleys.

Toward the middle of March the advance of the army reached the Rio Grande and went into camp near the banks of the river, opposite the city of Matamoros and almost under the guns of a small fort at the lower end of town. No habitations had been passed in the march from Corpus Christi. Construction of a small fort was begun immediately. It was laid out by the engineers, to be built by the soldiers under supervision of their officers, with the chief engineer retaining general supervision. Some Mexican troops crossed the river above the Americans' camp, making it unsafe for small groups of men to go far beyond their camp limits. The Mexicans captured two companies of dragoons, commanded by Captains Thornton and Hardee. (The latter became a general in the Confederate Army and wrote the tactics used at first by both armies in the Civil War.) Both Lieutenant Theodore Porter of the 4th Infantry and Colonel Cross, the assistant quartermaster general, were killed when out with inadequate guards.

A supply base was established at Point Isabel, on the coast north of the mouth of the Rio Grande, twenty-five miles away. Mexicans hovered around in such numbers that it was not safe to send a wagon train for supplies with any escort that could be spared. Work on the fort was pushed as much as possible with the forces available, but even so it was not in defendable condition until the latter part of April, when supplies had become very short. The 7th Infantry, Major Jacob Brown commanding, marched in to garrison it with a few pieces of artillery. All the supplies on hand—with the exception of enough to carry the rest of the army to Point Isabel—were left with the garrison, and the rest of the command commenced its march, taking every wagon. Early on the second day of the march the force reached its destination without opposition from the Mexicans, but there was some delay in getting supplies ashore from the vessels at anchor in the open roadstead.

The little garrison up the river was besieged by the Mexicans while General Taylor was away with the bulk of his army. Lying in their tents on the seashore the troops could hear the artillery at the fort on the Rio Grande distinctly. *The war had begun.*

There was no way of communicating with the small besieged garrison, and doubtless General Taylor had some anxious moments. However, on May 7 the wagons were all loaded, and General Taylor started his return with an army—reinforced at Point Isabel but still less than 3,000 strong—to relieve the garrison on the Rio Grande. Grant's *Memoirs* state:

The road from Point Isabel to Matamoros is over an open, rolling, treeless prairie, until the timber that borders the bank of the Rio Grande is reached. This river, like the Mississippi, flows through a rich alluvial valley in the most meandering manner, running toward all points of the compass, at times, within a few miles. Formerly the river ran by Resaca de la Palma, some four or five miles east of the present channel. The old bed of the river at Resaca had become filled at places, leaving a succession of little lakes. The timber that had formerly grown upon both banks, and for a considerable distance out, was still standing. This timber was struck six or eight miles out from the besieged garrison, at a point known as Palo Alto—"tall trees" or "woods."

Early in the forenoon of the 8th of May, as Palo Alto was approached, an army, certainly outnumbering our little force, was seen, drawn up in line of battle just in front of the timber. Their bayonets and spear-heads glistened in the sunlight formidably. The force was composed largely of cavalry armed with lances. Where we were the grass was tall, reaching nearly to the shoulders of the men, very stiff, and each stock was pointed at the top, and hard and almost as sharp as a darning-needle. General Taylor halted his army before the head of the column came in range of the artillery of the Mexicans. He then formed a line of battle, facing the enemy. His artillery, two batteries and two eighteen-pounder iron guns, drawn by oxen, was placed in position at intervals along the line. A battalion was thrown to the rear, commanded by Lieutenant-Colonel Childs, of the artillery, as reserves. These preparations completed, orders were given for a platoon of each company to stack arms and go to a stream off to the right of the command, to fill their canteens and also those of the rest of their respective companies. When the men were all back in their places in line, the command to advance was given. As I looked down that long line of about three thousand armed men, advancing toward a larger force also armed, I thought what a fearful responsibility General Taylor must feel, commanding such a host and so far away from friends. The Mexicans immediately opened fire upon us, first with artillery and then with infantry. At first their shots did not reach us, and the advance was continued. As we got nearer, the cannon balls commenced going through the ranks. They hurt no one, however, during this advance, because they would strike the ground long before they reached our line, and ricochetted through the tall grass so slowly that the men would see them and open ranks and let them pass. When we got to a point where the artillery could be used with effect, a halt was called, and the battle opened on both sides.

This was to be Lieutenant Grant's first battle, the first time that the future commanding general of two million men was to be under fire, starting his military career in earnest. Therefore, the following account which he wrote to his fiancée back in Missouri seems to be of sufficient interest, historically and personally, for quotation in full. It evidences two of his characteristics in any account of events in which he took part —namely, his modesty and failure to take advantage of any opportunity to do a little boasting, as most of us would do in writing to our future wives; and the details he observed in connection with what others were doing.

Head Quarters Mexican Army
May 11th 1846

Miss Julia B. Dent
Sappington Post Office
St. Louis County, Mo.

My dear Julia,

After two hard fought battles against a force far superior to our own in numbers Gen. Taylor has got possession of the enemy's camp and now I am writing on the head of one of the captured drums. I wrote to you from Point Isabel and told you of the march we had and of the suspected attack upon the little force left near Matamoros. About two days after I wrote we left Point Isabel with about 300 waggons loaded with Army supplies. For the first 18 miles our course was uninterrupted but at the end of that distance we found the Mexican Army under the command of General Arista drawn up in line of battle waiting our approach. Our waggons were immediately parked and Gen. Taylor marched us up towards them. When we got in range of their artillery they let us have it right and left. They had I believe 12 pieces. Our guns were then rounded at them and so the battle commenced. Our artillery amounted to 8 guns of 6 pound calibre and 2 eighteen pounders. Every moment we could see the charges from our pieces cut a way through their ranks making a perfect road, but they would close up the interval without showing signs of retreat. Their officers made an attempt to charge upon us but the havoc had been so great that their soldiers could not be made to advance. Some of the prisoners that we have taken say that their officers cut and slashed among them with their sabres at a dreadful rate to make them advance but it was no use, they would not come. This firing commenced at ½ past 2 o'clock and was nearly constant from that until sundown. Although the balls were whizzing thick and fast about me I did not feel a sensation of fear until nearly the close of the firing a ball struck close by me killing one man instantly, it knocked

Capt. Page's under jaw entirely off and broke in the roof of his mouth, and knocked Lt. Wallen and one Sergeant down besides, but they were not much hurt. Capt. Page is still alive. When it became too dark to see the enemy we encamped upon the field of battle and expected to conclude the fight the next morning. Morning came and we found that the enemy had retreated under cover of night. So ended the battle of the 8th of May. The enemy numbered three to our one besides we had a large waggon train to guard. It was a terrible sight to go over the ground the next day and see the amount of life that had been destroyed. The ground was literally strewed with the bodies of dead men and horses. The loss of the enemy is variously estimated from about 300 to 500. Our loss was comparatively small. But two officers were badly wounded, two or three slightly. About 12 or 15 of our men were killed and probably 50 wounded. When I can learn the exact amount of loss I will write and correct the statements I have made if they are not right. On the 9th of May about noon we left the field of battle and started on our way to Matamoros. When we advanced about six miles we found that the enemy had taken up a new position in the midst of a dense wood, and as we have since learned they had received a reinforcement equal to our whole numbers. Grape shot and musket balls were let fly from both sides making dreadful havoc. Our men continued to advance and did advance in spite of the shots, to the very mouths of the cannon and killed and took prisoner the Mexicans with them, and drove off with their own teams, taking cannon ammunition and all, to our side. In this way nine of their big guns were taken and their own ammunition turned against them. The Mexicans fought very hard for an hour and a half but seeing their means of war fall from their hands in spite of all their efforts they finally commenced to retreat helter skelter. A great many retreated to the banks of the Rio Grande and without looking for means of crossing plunged into the water and no doubt many of them were drowned. Among the prisoners we have taken there are 14 officers and I have no idea how many privates. I understand that General Larega, who is a prisoner in our camp, has said that he has fought against several different nations but ours are the first that he ever saw who would charge up to the very mouths of cannon.

In this last affray we had three officers killed and some 8 or ten wounded. How many of our men suffered has not yet been learned. The Mexicans were so certain of success that when we took their camp we found their dinners on the fire cooking. After the battle the woods was strewed with the dead. Waggons have been engaged drawing their bodies to bury. How many waggon loads have already come in and how many are still left would be hard to guess. I saw 3 large waggon loads at one time myself. We captured, besides the prisoners, 9 cannon, with a small amount of ammunition for them, probably 1,000 or 1,500 stand of fire arms, sabres, swords, etc. Two hundred and fifty thousand rounds of ammunition for them, over four hundred mules and pack saddles or harness. Drums, musical instruments, camp equipage, etc., etc., innumerable. The victory for us has been a very great one. No doubt you will see accounts enough of it in the papers. There is no great sport in having bullets flying about one in every direction but I find they have less horror when among them than when in anticipation. Now that the war has commenced with such vengeance I am in hopes my Dear Julia that we will soon be able to end it. In the thickest of it I thought of Julia. How much I should love to see you now to tell you all that happened. Mr. Hazlitt came out alive and whole. When we have another engagement, if we do have another at all, I will write again; that is if I am not one of the victims. Give my love to all at White Haven and do write soon my dear Julia. I think you will find that history will count the victory just achieved one of the greatest on record. But I do not want to say too much about it until I see the account given by others. Don't forget to write soon to your most devoted

Ulysses

P.S. I forgot to tell you that the fortification left in charge of Maj. Brown in command of the 7th Inf. was attacked while we were at Point Isabel and for five days the Mexicans continued to throw in shells. There were but 2 killed, Maj. Brown & one soldier, and 2 wounded.

Another letter appears to be of sufficient interest to quote and complement the narrative from the young officer's point of view.

Ponti Agrudo, Mexico
September 6th, 1846

My Dearest Julia,

We have left Camargo on our way for Monteray [sic], where it is possible we will have a grand fight. We are now within six days march of Monteray but it is probable we will not start from here, or from Sir Albo, quite a fine city twelve miles from Ponti Agrudo, for some ten or twelve days yet. When we do start I will write again if an opportunity occurs to send the letter. I am much in hopes my Dearest Julia after this move our difficulties will be brought to a close, and I be permitted to visit the North again. If ever I get to the States again it will be but a short time till I will be with you Dearest Julia. If these Mexicans were any kind of people they would have given us a chance to whip them enough some time ago and now the difficulty would be over; but I believe they think they will out-do us by keeping us running over the country after them. I have traveled from Matamoros here, by land, a distance of two hundred miles. In this distance there are at least fifteen thousand persons almost every one a farmer and on the whole road there are not, I don't believe, ten thousand acres of land cultivated. On our way we passed through

Reynoso, Old Reynoso Camargo, & Nier, all of them old deserted looking places, that is if you only look at the houses, but if you look at the people you will find that there is scarcely an old wall standing that some family does not live behind. It is a great mystery to me how they live. Fred [Frederick T. Dent] is not with us yet. If he does not make haste he will not have the pleasure of making himself heard of more than heard from, as you told me he said he would. Have you heard from John [John C. Dent] since he started with Col. Kearny? No doubt he is heartily tired of soldiering by this time. I suppose you have heard long ago of the freak Col. Harney took? He is now some place further interior than we are. Whether he and his six hundred men are ever heard of again I think a doubtful matter. So much exposure as the troops have been subjected to has been the cause of a great deal of sickness, especially among the volunteers. I think about one in five is sick all the time. The regulars stand it some better but there is a great deal of sickness with them too. Gen. Taylor is taking but six thousand men with him to Monteray. The most of the volunteers he has left behind.

Julia aren't you getting tired of hearing of war, war, war? I am truly tired of it. Here it is now five months that we have been at war and as yet but two battles. I do wish this would close. If we have to fight I would like to do it all at once and then make friends.

It is now above two years that we have been engaged Julia and in all that time I have seen you but once. I know though you have not changed and when I do go back I will see the same Julia I did more than two years ago. I know I shall never be willing to leave Gravois again until Julia is mine forever! How much I regret that we were not united when I visited you more than a year ago. But your Pa would not have heard to anything of the kind at that time. I hope he will make no objections now! Write to me very often Julia. You know how happy I am to read your letters. Mr. Hazlitt is very well. Give my love to all at White Haven. Have Ellen & Ben Farrer made up yet? The time is now getting pretty well up and I am afraid that I may lose my bet.

Ulysses

The army continued the march until it reached the "Black Fort," a strong fortification enclosed on all sides and well garrisoned by the Mexicans. Its guns commanded the approaches of the city of Monterrey as far as their range extended. There were two detached spurs of hills or mountains to the west and southwest of the city which were also fortified, and on one of the hills stood the Bishop's Palace. For more details we quote from Grant's *Memoirs.*

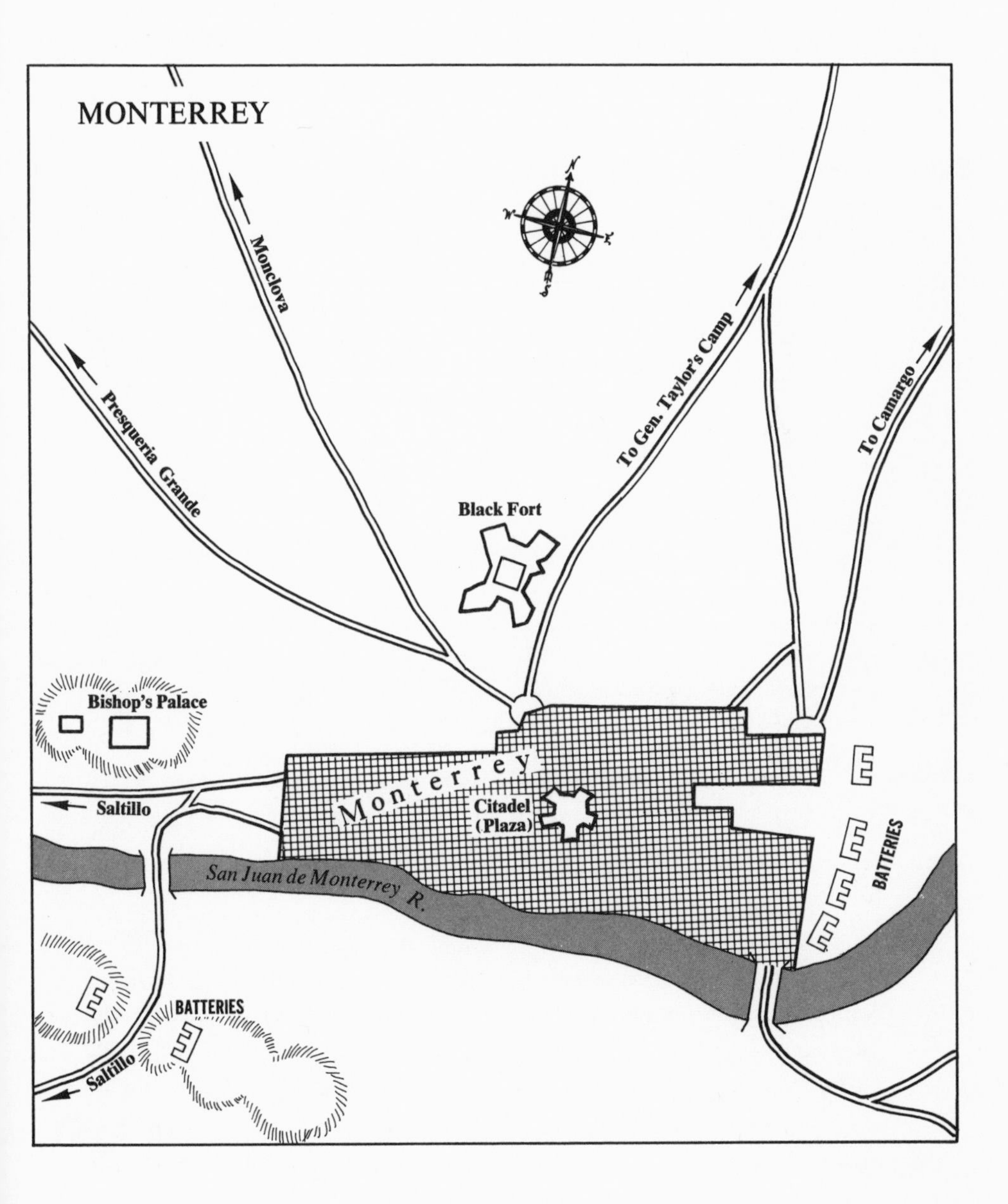
MONTERREY
Monclova
Presqueria Grande
To Gen. Taylor's Camp
To Camargo
Black Fort
Bishop's Palace
Saltillo
Monterrey
Citadel
(Plaza)
BATTERIES
San Juan de Monterrey R.
BATTERIES
Saltillo

The road to Saltillo leaves the upper or western end of the city under the fire of the guns from these heights. . . . The plaza in the center of the city was the citadel, properly speaking. All the streets leading from it were swept by artillery, cannon being entrenched behind temporary parapets. The housetops near the plaza were converted into infantry fortifications by the use of sandbags for parapets. Such were the defenses of Monterey [sic] in September 1846. General Ampudia, with a force of certainly ten thousand men, was in command. General Taylor's force was about sixty-five hundred strong, in three divisions, under Generals Butler, Twiggs, and Worth. The troops went into camp at Walnut Springs, while the engineer officers, under Major Mansfield—a General in the late war—commenced their reconnaissance. . . .

General Worth, with his division somewhat reinforced, was given the task of gaining possession of the Saltillo road, and of carrying the detached works outside the city in that quarter. He started on his march early in the afternoon of the 20th [September]. The divisions under Generals Butler and Twiggs were drawn up to threaten the east and north sides of the city and the works on those fronts, in support of the movement under General Worth. Worth's was regarded as the main attack on Monterey, and all other operations were in support of it. His march this day was uninterrupted; but the enemy was seen to reinforce heavily about the Bishop's Palace and the other outside fortifications. . . .

General Worth that night reached the defensible position outside the range of the enemy's guns on the heights northwest of the city. Captain Sanders and Lieutenant George G. Meade, afterwards the Commander of the victorious national army at Gettysburg, made a reconnaissance to the Saltillo Road during the night. General Taylor posted a battery of two 24-pounder howitzers and a 10-inch mortar where it could play on the Black Fort. A natural depression in the plain was sufficiently deep to protect men standing in it from the fire of the Fort and the battery planted on the crest nearest the enemy. The 4th Infantry, with six reduced companies only, was to support the artillerymen while entrenching themselves and their guns. I was to remain in charge of the camp and public property at Walnut Springs.

At daylight the next morning fire was opened on both sides, and continued with what seemed to me at that day, great fury. My curiosity got the better of my judgment, and I mounted a horse and rode to the front to see what was going on. I had been there but a short time when an order to charge was given; and, lacking the moral courage to return to camp—where I had been ordered to stay—I charged with the regiment. As soon as the troops were out of the depression they came under the fire of the Black Fort. As they advanced they got under fire from batteries guarding the east or lower end of the city, and of musketry. About one third of the men engaged in the charge were killed or wounded in the space of a few minutes. We retreated to get out of the fire—not backward, but eastward, and perpendicular to the direct road running into the city from Walnut Springs. I was, I believe, the only person in the 4th Infantry in the charge who was on horseback. When we got to a place of safety the regiment halted and drew itself together—what was left of it. The adjutant of the regiment, Lieutenant Hoskins, who was not in robust health, found himself very much fatigued from running on foot in the charge and retreat, and, seeing me on horseback, expressed a wish that he could be mounted also. I offered him my horse, and he accepted the offer. A few minutes later I saw a soldier, a quartermaster's man, mounted, not far away. I ran to him, took his horse, and was back with the regiment in a few minutes. In a short time we were off again; and the next place of safety from the shots of the enemy that I recollect of being in was a field of cane or corn to the northeast of the lower batteries. The adjutant to whom I had loaned my horse was killed, and I was designated to act in his place.

This charge was ill conceived or badly executed. We belonged to the brigade commanded by Lieutenant-Colonel Garland, and he had received orders to charge the lower batteries of the city, and carry them if he could without too much loss, for the purpose of creating a diversion in favor of Worth, who was conducting the movement which it was intended should be decisive. By a movement by the left flank Garland could have led his men beyond the range of the fire from Black Fort, and advanced towards the northeast angle of the city, as well covered from fire as could be expected. There was no undue loss of life in reaching the lower end of Monterey, except that sustained by Garland's command. . . . Quitman's brigade . . . reached the eastern end of the city and they came under cover of the houses there without much loss, capturing a little battery of the enemy that was covering the lower end of the city. An entrance into the east end of the city was thus secured. General Worth had reached the Saltillo road and turning from his new position had captured the forts on both heights in that quarter, giving him possession of the western end of Monterey; but the Black Fort to the north and the plaza in the center of the city were still in possession of the enemy.

Nothing much was done by the Americans on the 22nd; but the enemy kept up a relatively harmless fire from the Black Fort and the batteries still in their possession at the east end of the city. The latter were evacuated during the night, so that the Americans held undisputed possession of the east end of Monterey. Twiggs's division was at the lower end of the city and well covered from the fire of the enemy; but the streets leading to the plaza were commanded from all directions by artillery. The flat roofs of the one or two story houses were manned by Mexican troops protected from musketry fire by sand-bags. Advances into the city were thus attended with much danger. "While moving along streets which did not lead to the plaza, our men were protected from the fire and from the view of the enemy, except at crossings; but at these a volley of musketry and a discharge of grape-shot were invariably encountered. The 3rd and 4th regiments of infantry made an advance nearly to the plaza in this way, and with heavy loss. The loss of the 3rd Infantry in commissioned officers was especially severe. There were only five companies of the regiment and not over twelve officers present, and five of these officers were killed. When within a square of the plaza this small command—10 companies in all—was brought to a halt. . . .

We had not occupied this position long when it was discovered that our ammunition was growing low. I volunteered to go back to the point we had started from, report our position to General Twiggs, and ask for ammunition to be forwarded. . . . My ride back was an exposed one. Before starting I adjusted myself on the side of my horse farthest from the enemy; and with only one foot holding to the cantle of the saddle, and an arm over the neck of the horse exposed, I started at full run. It was only at street crossings that my horse was under fire; but these I crossed at such a flying rate that generally I was past and under cover of the next block of houses before the enemy fired. I got out safely without a scratch.

On this ride the lieutenant saw a sentinel in front of one house, stopped and dismounted and went in only to find it occupied by wounded American officers and soldiers, whose painful situation he promised to report. However, the two regiments were withdrawn, before the ammunition could be collected for them, and they succeeded in retiring without any great loss. But the wounded officers and solders left behind fell into the hands of the enemy.

While this was going on at the east, General Worth, with a small division of troops, was advancing toward the plaza from the opposite end of the city. He resorted to a better expedient for getting to the plaza—the citadel—than we did on the east. Instead of moving by the open streets, he advanced through the houses, cutting passageways from one to the other. Without much loss of life he got so near the plaza during the night that before morning Ampudia, the Mexican commander, made overtures for the surrender of the city and garrison. This stopped all further hostilities. The terms of surrender were soon agreed upon. The prisoners were paroled and permitted to take their horses and personal property with them.

My pity was aroused by the sight of the Mexican garrison of Monterey marching out of town as prisoners, and no doubt the same feeling was experienced by most of our army who witnessed it.

After the surrender the Americans remained in Monterrey on excellent terms with the inhabitants.

At this time General Winfield Scott was in command of the Army of the United States; but this war was a political war fought for political objectives, and General Scott was known to have aspirations to the presidency. Therefore, the President had selected Brevet Brigadier General Zachary Taylor to command the first expedition into Mexico. Taylor was not thought to have any such ambitions. However, the success of his campaign and the talk about it in the country at large had caused General Taylor to become, probably without his knowledge, a very promising candidate for the presidency. Like General Scott, he too was a Whig, and therefore in the opposition party to the Administration. Evidently the selection of a commander in chief to carry on the Mexican War, which had developed more importance and success than was anticipated, had become a very important problem for the President. There was no other physically qualified officer of adequate rank to lead an army on this mission of conquest. The President did consult with General Scott and asked him for his plan for the invasion of Mexico. From the start Scott had been opposed to the invasion from Point Isabel to Monterrey and beyond. He also had made a study of the equipment and supplies he thought necessary to capture the seaport Vera Cruz and stage an invasion along the old Camino Real via Jalapa, Perote, Puebla, and the City of Mexico. Scott therefore opted for this latter route of invasion when the President called on him for recommendations. Scott's suggestions were disapproved by the Administration, probably in order to force the general to resign or otherwise put himself out of the candidacy for commander in chief; but his reply was limited to a statement that "If the soldier's plans were not to be supported by the Administration, success could not be expected."

On May 31, 1846, General Scott was notified that he need not go to Mexico. General Gaines was next in rank, followed by Colonel Whistler, but they were too old and feeble to take the field. General Taylor was evidently no more desirable politically than General Scott. The President then proposed to make Senator Thomas H. Benton a lieutenant general and give him the command, but this was refused by Congress. General Scott remained in command and was sent to Mexico, arriving at Point Isabel late in December 1846.

General Taylor with his little army was already on the way to winning his final victory at Buena Vista in February 1847. General Scott therefore had to issue his orders for a part of General Taylor's force to return to the coast and join his expedition to Vera Cruz, leaving Taylor hardly any regular troops. His victory at Buena Vista was won almost entirely with volunteers, undoubtedly an important factor in Taylor's election to the presidency in 1849. The 4th Infantry was one of the regiments taken away from Taylor's command. It concentrated with the rest of Scott's army on the beach in the neighborhood of the mouth of the Rio Grande for several weeks awaiting the transports to reassemble at Vera Cruz.

On March 9, 1847, the debarkation of the little army took place at Sacrificios Island, three miles south of Vera Cruz. Ten to twelve thousand men had been given General Scott to invade a country with a population of seven or eight million people, a mountainous country of varying terrains and climates. Men, animals, equipment, and supplies had to be landed in lighters or surf boats of some sort, which was difficult because of the rough water. Fortunately the Mexicans were considerate and placed no obstacles in the way of the landing beyond an occasional shot from a nearby fort. Therefore on the same day the investment of Vera Cruz from the Gulf of Mexico south of the city to the gulf on the north was quickly and easily effected. The camps were placed out of range of fire from the city, and regular siege operations were then started. By March 27 a considerable breach had been made in the wall surrounding the city, and the Mexican commander, General Morales, opened correspondence relative to the surrender of the city and the old Fort San Juan De Ulloa. On the twenty-ninth the American army occupied the city. Some 5,000 prisoners, 400 pieces of artillery, and large quantities of small arms and ammunition were surrendered. . . .

And what were the political and military backgrounds that Scott and his men confronted? In August 1846 the not unusual political rivalries in Mexico had produced a relatively bloodless revolution in the capital city, resulting in the resignation of Herrera. General Salas became pro tempore president with the understanding he would work to secure the return to power of Santa Anna, a popular ex-president of some repute. He had successfully defeated the Spanish effort in 1829 to reconquer Mexico, and had taken the Alamo on March 6, 1836, and had executed the captured Texan force under James W. Fannin on March 26, only to be ignominiously defeated and taken prisoner by Sam Houston at the battle of San Jacinto. He was later liberated and permitted to return to Mexico for the purpose of persuading his home government to approve two treaties that he had negotiated with Texas while he was a prisoner of war. But the Mexican Government declared them "null, void and of no effect" and so notified the U.S. Government through Gorostiza, the Mexican minister in Washington. In spite of demands by many influential Texans for the punishment of Santa Anna, Houston, Austin, and a few other cool heads were able to prevent any such act of revenge.

By the time Taylor's army had landed at Corpus Christi, won its two initial victories, and was on its way to Monterrey, Santa Anna had returned and accepted the responsibilities of Commander in Chief of the Mexican Army. He first attempted to stop General Taylor's column, but the two brigades he was sending to save Monterrey learned the city had been captured three days before. Santa Anna gathered what army he could at San Luis Potosí on October 8, combining there General Ampudia's force from Saltillo with the garrison of the City of Mexico, and finally meeting a disastrous defeat by Taylor in the battle of Buena Vista on February 22 and 23, 1847. After this Santa Anna was able to collect again a considerable force and march it to confront General Scott at Cerro Gordo.

Meanwhile, Scott knew the importance of starting for Mexico City as soon as practicable, in order to protect the command against yellow fever and other tropical diseases. It was known that Jalapa in the foothills to the Great Plateau of Mexico was out of the torrid zone and enjoyed a pleasant climate generally free from yellow fever. So as soon as transportation could be prepared, General Scott started his three divisions—under Generals Twiggs, Patterson, and Worth—along the Camino Real with Twiggs in advance. About fifty miles west of Vera Cruz this leading division encountered a strongely entrenched enemy in a pass, Cerro Gordo, and went into camp at Plan Del Rio about three miles east of the enemy's fortifications. General Patterson soon reached this camp after Twiggs had arrived. They remained there until April 18 without being molested by the enemy.

General Scott had remained at Vera Cruz to hasten preparations for the movement, but left on April 12, when he learned of the enemy's occupying a strongly fortified position. Upon his arrival with his army he started his engineers on a thorough reconnaissance of the terrain with a view to finding some way of circumventing the enemy's fortified position without too great losses. The engineering team was made up of Captain Robert E. Lee, assisted by Lieutenants P. G. T. Beauregard, Isaac I. Stevens, Z. B. Tower, G. W. Smith, George B. McClellan, and J. G. Foster—all of the Corps of Engineers and officers who attained considerable fame during the Civil War. The reconnaissance was eminently successful and resulted in the strategic location of certain American batteries and positions. This was accomplished by very unusual handling of the artillery guns, moving them by hand and by rope up the steep sides of the pass, where the walls were so steep that men could climb them only with difficulty and animals could not ascend them at all.

Roadways had been extemporized to the north of the enemy's main defensive position, and the Mexicans were quite unaware of their occupation during the night. A brigade under General Pillow made a formidable demonstration against the enemy's fortified front, but when the Mexican commanders discovered American troops behind their positions, they quickly retired, abandoning their very strong position with the loss of some 3,000 prisoners, a large amount of ordnance, and ordnance stores. The prisoners were paroled, and captured artillery was parked, and the small arms and ammunition were destroyed. So hasty was the retreat of the Mexican forces that General Santa Anna's carriage and camp equipment, including his artificial leg and other personal possessions, were captured. Poor Santa Anna! He had hurried to meet Taylor and had been overwhelmingly defeated at Buena Vista; then he had marched his remaining troops, with what reinforcements he could gather on the way, some 800 or 900 miles by road to meet defeat again in Cerro Gordo, which had seemed to him an impregnable position.

The victorious U.S. Army moved on to Jalapa, in beautiful and healthful country above the fevers of the seacoast but still in mountainous terrain, with the snow-capped peak of Orizaba in plain view, rising to a height of 18,700 feet, the highest point in Mexico. The service of a large number of General Scott's troops was to expire shortly, and he decided to discharge them all then and there, before moving farther into the country. When this administrative action had been completed, he moved his army forward toward Puebla on the way to the capital. A picturesque and somewhat historical site on the march was the Castle of Perote. The following two letters to his fiancée will give some account of the march as Lieutenant Grant saw it:

Castle of Perote Mexico
April 24th 1847

My Dear Julia,

You see from the above that the great and long talked of Castle of Perote is at last in the hands of the Americans. On the 13th of this month the rear Division of Gen Scott's Army left Vera Cruz to drive Santa Anna and his army from the Strong Mountain passes which they had fortified, with the determination of driving back the Barbarians of the North, at all hazards. On the morning of the 17th our Army met them at a pass called Cierra Gorda [Cerro Gordo] a mountain pass which to look at one would suppose impregnable. The road passes between mountains of rock the tops of which were all fortified and well armed with Artillery. The road was Barricaded by a strong work with five pieces of Artillery. Behind this was a peak of the Mountains much higher than all the others and commanded them so that the Enemy calculated that even if the Americans should succeed in taking all the other heights, from this one they could fire upon us and be out of reach themselves. But they were disappointed. Gen. Twiggs' Division worked its way around with a great deal of labor and made the attack in the rear. With some loss on our side and great loss on the part of the enemy the highest point was taken and soon the White flag of the enemy was seen to float. Of Generals and other Officers and soldiers some Six thousand Surrendered as prisoners of war. Their Artillery Ammunition supplies and most of their small arms were captured. As soon as Santa Anna saw that the day was lost he made his escape with a portion of his army but he was pursued so closely that his carriage, a splendid affair, was taken and in it were his Cork leg and some Thirty thousand dollars in gold. The pursuit was so close that the Mexicans could not establish themselves in another strong pass which they had already fortified, and when they got to the strong Castle of Perote they passed on leaving it too with all of its Artillery to fall into our hands. After so many victories on our part and so much defeat on the part of the Mexicans they certainly will agree to treat. For my part I do not believe there will be another fight unless we should pursue with a very small force.—From Vera Cruz to this place it is an almost constant rise, Perote being about Eight thousand feet above the ocean. Around us are mountains covered with eternal snow and greatly the influence is felt too. Although we are in the Torrid Zone it is never so warm as to be uncomfortable nor so cold as to make a fire necessary. From Vera Cruz to this place the road is one of the best and one that cost more labor probably than any other in the world. It was made a great many years ago when Mexico was a province of Spain. On the road there are a great many specimens of beautiful table land and a decided improvement in the appearance of the people and the style of building over any thing I had seen before in Mexico. Jalapa is decidedly the most beautiful place I ever saw in my life. From its low Latitude and great elevation it is never hot nor never cold. The climate is said to be the best in the world and from what I saw I would be willing to make Jalapa my home for life with only one condition and that would be that I should be permitted to go and bring my Dearest Julia.—The 5th Inf'y, Fred's Reg.t was not present at the fight of Cierra Gorda. A few days before we left Vera Cruz the 5th Inf'y was ordered down to the coast to Alvardo [sic] to procure horses and mules for the use of the Army, and when we left they had not returned. My dearest Julia how very long it seems since we were together and still our March is onward. In a few days no doubt we will start for Puebla and then we will be within Eighty to a Hundred miles of the City of Mexico; there the March must end. Three years now the 4th Inf'y has been - - - - the tented field and I think it is high time that I should have a leave of absence. Just think Julia it is now three long years that we have been engaged. Do you think I could endure another year's separation loving you as I do now and believing my love returned. At least commission and all will go in less time or I will be permitted to see the one I have loved so much for three long years. My Dearest don't you think a soldier's life a hard one? But after a storm there must be a calm. This War must end some time and the Army scattered to occupy different places and I will be satisfied with any place where I can have you with me. Would you be willing to go with me to some out-of-the-way post Dearest? But I know you would for you have said so so often. Your next letter will probably reach me in Puebla the 3d City in size in the Republic of Mexico. Write to me often Julia I always get your letters. I will write again as soon as the army makes another halt. Has your pa ever said anything more about our engagement? You know in one of your sweet letters you told me something he had said which argued that his consent would be given. Remember me affectionately to your father and mother, Miss Ellen & Emmy.

Ulysses.

P.S. Among the wounded on our side was Lt. Dana very dangerously. In the Rifle Reg't one Officer, Lt. Ewell, was killed, Mr. Maury lost his hand, Mason and Davis a leg each. A great many Volunteer Officers were killed and wounded. I have not had a letter from you since the one I answered from Vera Cruz but there have been but few Mails arrived since. I hope to get one soon.

U.

City of Mexico
September 1847

My Dearest Julia:

Because you have not heard from me for so long a time you must not think that I have neglected to write or in the least forgotten one who is so ever dear to me. For several months no mail has gone to Vera Cruz except such as editors of papers send by some Mexican they hire and these generally fall into the hands of the enemy who infest the whole line from here to the Sea Coast. Since my last letter to you four of the hardest fought battles that the world ever witnessed have taken place, and the most astonishing victories have crowned the American Arms. But dearly have they paid for it! The loss of officers and men killed and wounded is frightful. Among the wounded you will find Fred's name but he is now walking about and in the course of two weeks more will be entirely well. I saw Fred a moment after he received his wound but escaped myself untouched. It is to be hoped that such fights it will not be our misfortune to witness again during the war, and how can it be? The whole Mexican Army is destroyed or disbursed, they have lost nearly all their artillery and other munitions of war. We are occupying the rich and popular valley from which the great part of their revenues are collected and all their seaports are cut off from them. Everything looks as if peace should be established soon; but perhaps my anxiety to get back to see again my Dearest Julia makes me argue thus. The idea of staying longer in this country is to me insupportable. Just think of the three long years that have passed since we met. My health has always been good, but exposure to weather and a Tropical Sun has added ten years to my apparent age. At this rate I will soon be old.

Out of all the officers that left Jefferson Barracks with the 4th Infantry but three besides myself now remain with us; besides this, four or five who joined since are gone. Poor Sidney Smith was the last one killed. He was shot from one of the houses after we entered the City.

Mexico is one of the most beautiful cities in the world and being the capital no wonder that the Mexicans should have fought desperately to save it. But they deserve no credit. They fought us with every advantage on their side. They doubled us in numbers, doubled us and more in artillery, they behind strong breast-works had every advantage and then they were fighting for their homes. It is truly a great country. No country was ever so blessed by nature. There is no fruit nor no grain that can't be raised here, nor no temperature that can't be found at any season. You have only to choose the degree of elevation to find perpetual snow or the hottest summer. But with all these advantages how anxious I am to get out of Mexico. You can readily solve the problem of my discontent Julia. If you were but here and I in the United States my anxiety would be just as great to come to Mexico as it now is to get out.

Oct. 25th. At last a mail is to leave here for the U. States. I am glad at finally having an opportunity of letting you hear from me. A train is going to

Vera Cruz and with it many of the wounded officers and men. Fred is getting too well to be one of them. I am almost sorry that I was not one of the unfortunate so that now I could be going back. It is to be hoped that in future mails will be much more frequent though in fact it is generally believed that as soon as Congress meets the whole Army will be ordered from this valley of Mexico. There is no use of my telling you any more that I will take the first opportunity of getting back to Mo. for I have told you that so often and yet no chance has occurred. At present Gen. Scott will let no officer leave who is able for duty not even if he tenders his resignation. So you see it is not so easy to get out of the war as it is to get into them.

Write to me often dearest Julia so if I can't have the pleasure of sending letters often to you let me at least enjoy the receipt of one from you by every mail coming this way.

No doubt before this the papers are teeming with accounts of the different battles and the courage and science shown by individuals. Even here one hears of individual exploits (which were never performed) sufficient to account for the taking of Mexico throwing out about four-fifths of the Army to do nothing. One bit of credit need not be given to accounts that are given except those taken from the reports of the different commanders.

Remember me my Dearest Julia to your father & mother and the rest of the family and pray that the time may not be far distant when we may take our walks again up and down the banks of the Gravois. Truly it will be a happy time for me when I see that stream again.

Farewell my Dearest Julia,

U. S. Grant

The interruption of mail to the United States, mentioned at the end of the last letter, was probably the period during which Hannah Grant's hair turned gray from the anxiety at not hearing from her son in Mexico. This was evidence of her concern, even though she did not give any other demonstration or expression of her distress. He had taken effective part in the battles that resulted in the capture of the Mexican capital, as evidenced by his brevets to first lieutenant, September 8, 1847, "for gallant and meritorious conduct in the Battle of Molino del Rey" and to captain, September 13, 1847, "for gallant conduct at Chapultepec."

The incident which brought him the brevet at the Battle of Molino del Rey was described by him in later years as follows:

I was with the earliest of the troops to enter the mills. In passing through to the north side, looking toward Chapultepec, I happened to notice that there were armed Mexicans still on top of the building, only a few feet from many of our men. Not seeing any stairway or ladder reaching to the top of the building, I took a few soldiers, and had a cart that happened to be standing near brought up, and, placing the shafts against the wall and chocking the wheels so that the cart could not back, used the shafts as a sort of ladder, extending to within three or four feet of the top. By this I climbed to the roof of the building, followed by a few men, but found a private soldier had preceded me by some other way. There were still quite a number of Mexicans on the roof, among them a major and five or six officers of lower grades, who had not succeeded in getting away before our troops occupied the building. They still had their arms, while the soldier before mentioned was walking as sentry, guarding the prisoners he had *surrounded* all by himself. I halted the sentinel, received the swords from the commissioned officers, and proceeded, with the assistance of the soldiers now with me, to disable the muskets by striking them against the edge of the wall, and threw them to the ground below.

Molino del Rey was now captured; and the troops engaged, with the exception of an appropriate guard over the captured position and property, were marched back to their quarters in Tacubaya. The engagement did not last many minutes, but the killed and wounded were numerous for the number of troops engaged.

Circumstances attending the brevet assigned for meritorious fighting at Chapultepec are described in General Grant's *Memoirs:*

General Quitman, a volunteer from the State of Mississippi, who stood well with the army both as a soldier and as a man, commanded the column acting against Belen. General Worth commanded the column against San Cosme. When Chapultepec fell the advance commenced along the two aqueduct roads. I was on the road to San Cosme, and witnessed most that took place on that route. When opposition was encountered our troops sheltered themselves by keeping under the arches supporting the aqueduct, advancing an arch at a time. We encountered no serious obstruction until within gunshot of the point where the road we were on intersects that running east to the city—the point where the aqueduct turns at a right angle. I have described the defenses of this position before. There were but three commissioned officers besides myself, that I can now call to mind, with the advance when the above position was reached. One of these officers was a Lieutenant Semmes, of the navy. I think Captain Gore and Lieutenant Judah, of the 4th Infantry, were the others. Our progress was stopped for the time by the single piece of artillery at the angle of the roads and the infantry occupying the housetops back from it.

West of the road from where we were stood a house occupying the southwest angle made by the San Cosme road and the road we were moving upon. A stone wall ran from the house along each of these roads for a considerable distance, and thence back until it joined, inclosing quite a yard about the house. I watched my opportunity and skipped across the road and behind the south wall. Proceeding cautiously to the west corner of the inclosure, I peeped around, and, seeing nobody, continued, still cautiously, until the road running east and west was reached. I then returned to the troops and called for volunteers. All that were close to me, or that heard me,—about a dozen—offered their services. Commanding them to carry their arms at a trail, I watched our opportunity and got them across the road and under cover of the wall beyond before the enemy had a shot at us. Our men under cover of the arches kept a close watch on the intrenchments that crossed our path and the housetops beyond, and whenever a head showed itself above the parapets they would fire at it. Our crossing was thus made practicable without loss.

When we reached a safe position I instructed my little command again to carry their arms at a trail, not to fire at the enemy until they were ordered, and to move very cautiously, following me, until the San Cosme road was reached; we would then be on the flank of the men serving the gun on the road, and with no obstruction between us and them. When we reached the southwest corner of the inclosure before described I saw some United States troops pushing north through a shallow ditch near by, who had come up since my reconnaissance. This was the company of Captain Horace Brooks, of the artillery, acting as infantry. I explained to Brooks briefly what I had discovered and what I was about to do. He said, as I knew the ground and he did not, I might go on and he would follow. As soon as we got on the road leading to the city the troops serving the gun on the parapet retreated, and those on the housetops near by followed; our men went after them in such close pursuit—the troops we had left under the arches joining—that a second line across the road, about half-way between the first and the *garita,* was carried. No reinforcements had yet come up except Brooks's company, and the position we had taken was too advanced to be held by so small a force. It was given up, but retaken later in the day with some loss.

Worth's command gradually advanced to the front now open to it. Later in the day, in reconnoitering, I found a church off to the south of the road, which looked to me as if the belfry would command the ground back of the Garita San Cosme. I got an officer of the voltigeurs, with a mountain howitzer and men to work it, to go with me. The road being in possession of the enemy, we had to take the field to the south to reach the church. This took us over several ditches breast-deep in water and grown up with water-plants. These ditches, however, were not over eight or ten feet in width. The howitzer was taken to pieces and carried by the men to its destination. When I knocked for admission a priest came to the door, who, while extremely polite, declined to admit us. With the little Spanish then at my command I explained to him that he might save property by opening the door, and he certainly would save himself from becoming a prisoner, for a time at least; and besides, I intended to go in whether he consented or not. He began to see his duty in the same light that I did, and opened the door, though he did not look as if it gave him special pleasure to do so. The gun was carried to the belfry and put together. We were not more than two or three hundred yards from San Cosme. The shots from our little gun dropped in upon the enemy and created great confusion. Why they did not send out a small party and capture us I do not know. We had no infantry or other defenses besides our one gun.

The effect of this gun upon the troops about the gate of the city was so marked that General Worth saw it from his position. He was so pleased that he sent a staff-officer, Lieutenant Pemberton—later lieutenant-general commanding the defenses of Vicksburg—to bring me to him. He expressed his gratification at the services the howitzer in the church steeple was doing, saying that every shot was effective, and ordered a captain of voltigeurs to report to me with another howitzer, to be placed along with the one already rendering so much service. I could not tell the general that there was not room enough in the steeple for another gun, because he probably would have looked upon such a statement as a contradiction from a second lieutenant. I took the captain with me, but did not use his gun.

Simultaneously the castle on Chapultepec Hill and the Mexican Military Academy there were captured by volunteers under General Pillow and General Quitman. Without attempting to describe in any detail the military operations that led to the capture of the City of Mexico by General Scott, it is interesting to notice the participaion in these operations of John C. Pemberton (later to be a lieutenant general in the Confederate Army), Thomas J. Jackson, and Major Robert E. Lee (later destined to gain world-wide fame as the Commander of the Army of Northern Virginia). Also participating were Joseph Hooker and George Gordon Meade, future commanders of the Army of the Potomac, and Captain Charles F. Smith, who had been Commandant of Cadets at West Point when many of the young officers in Mexico were still working for their commissions. Then there was also Lieutenant George H. Thomas, later to be the Commander of the Army of the Cumberland in the Battles of Chattanooga and Nashville. Sitting on a parapet, while Bragg was handling his guns superbly at the investment of the Black

Fort, Thomas was asked what he thought of the way they were serving their cannons. "Service?" he had asked. "Excellent, but I am thinking we will need, after a while, the ammunition you are throwing away." Lieutenant Meade, later to be the Union commander at the Battle of Gettysburg, was displeased that the southern slaveholders among the volunteers, and only common soldiers, expected the regulars to carry water and firewood for them. And among the illustrious names was Congressman Thomas L. Hamer, who had raised a regiment of volunteers for the war in Ohio. He refused to command it because he did not feel confident of sufficient military knowledge to fill the position, but the President overruled him, and Hamer joined General Scott's force as a brigadier general. Unhappily he died of dysentery, greatly to the chagrin of all those who had served with him. "His death is a loss to me which no words can express," General Taylor lamented. General Hamer had done much to pacify the vehemence of the volunteers and to keep them in some sort of order.

General Garland and Colonel Graham had agreed during the campaign that Lieutenant Grant should be named regimental quartermaster as well as commissary, it being agreed, as Henry Coppée of the 1st Artillery observed, that "He had system and patience and was a solid, energetic, painstaking officer, who would be expected to remain on guard with the camp equipage and pack train during battle." However, Lieutenant Grant objected to the assignment when it came to him. "I respectfully protest against being assigned to a duty that removes me from sharing in the dangers and honors of service with my company at the front and respectfully ask to be permitted to resume my place in line." But he was told officially that his protest was not considered since he had been assigned to duty as quartermaster and commissary because of his observed ability, skill, and persistency in the line of duty, and that he could best serve the country in this assignment. Lieutenant Grant had this to say:

> I should be permitted to resign the position of Quartermaster and Commissary. Why should I be required to resign my position in the Army in order to escape this duty? I *must* and *will* accompany my regiment in battle, and I am amenable to court-martial should any loss occur to the public property in my charge by reason of my absence while in action.

While he does not appear to have kept away from the fighting, as he feared he might have to do, he did perform some very valuable service in his new capacity, for the army was in great need of clothing, harness, and forage for horses and mules. It was also necessary to procure fruit, green vegetables, and fresh meat to guard against scurvy and other sicknesses. To meet these necessities of the army he set up a tailor shop to make uniforms, a cobbler's shop, and a harness-repair shop while in Puebla. Presumably he carried along some of the essential equipment to set these shops up again at other places where an appreciable halt was made. Manifestly, the clothing and shoes obtainable in Mexico and manufactured for the local population were much too small for the large American soldiers. In addition the making of clothing and harness, and repairs required the finding and assembling of whatever materials were necessary. This seems to have been done without Grant's missing any battles. Pertinent to his performance as a supply officer, Lieutenant Alexander Hays is reported to have said: "There was no road . . . so obstructed . . . but that Grant, in some mysterious way, would work his train through and have it in the camp of his brigade before the campfires were lighted." Then would follow the required inspection of mules for sore spots and other injuries, together with first-aid treatment. There was also the constant need to find animals to replace those injured or worn out.

In the meantime Santa Anna, who had refused to discuss peace terms, was somehow maneuvered out of his position as head of state for the drafting of a peace treaty. On January 12, 1847, Secretary of State Buchanan had reported to the Cabinet in Washington that he had talked with Colonel Atocha of Mexico and that Atocha had undertaken to expound the views of Santa Anna and his desires in favor of peace. President Polk had in the meantime sent N. P. Trist, who had been chosen by the Cabinet, to General Scott's headquarters with plenipotentiary powers to draft a peace treaty. Satisfactory terms were finally agreed upon. Negotiations were considerably delayed by the introduction in the U.S. Congress of a bill containing the Wilmot Proviso, an amendment that prohibited the introduction of slavery in any states formed out of territory obtained from Mexico. The bill passed the House but was rejected by the Senate.

The terms of a peace treaty were finally agreed upon and the treaty was signed at Guadalupe Hidalgo February 2, 1848, ceding to the United States an immense territory in the West in consideration of a payment of $15,000,000 and assumption of payment of claims against the Mexican Government, which was very much in need of cash at the time. The treaty was ratified by the U.S. Senate March 10, 1848, and finally by the Mexican Legislature on May 25.

While the army waited, the papers at home kept talking up the merits of Generals Scott and Taylor as presidential candidates. An altercation between General Scott in opposition to Worth, Pillow (who made claims of having saved the army from Scott's mistakes), and Duncan resulted in their arrest and a board of inquiry, which resulted in their release. A messenger arrived on February 13 from President Polk, ordering Scott home and replacing him by General Butler. Grant, in his *Memoirs,* says of Scott:

> It had been a favorite idea with General Scott for a great many years before the Mexican war to have established in the United States a soldiers' home, patterned after something of the kind abroad, particularly, I believe, in France. He recommended this uniformly, or at least frequently, in his annual reports to the Secretary of War, but never got any hearing. Now, as he had conquered the country, he made assessments upon the different large towns and cities occupied by our troops, in proportion to their capacity to pay, and appointed officers to receive the money. In addition to the sum thus realized he had derived, through capture at Cerro Gordo, sales of captured government tobacco, etc., sums which swelled the fund to a total of about $220,000. Portions of this fund were distributed among the rank and file, given to the wounded in hospital, or applied in other ways, leaving a balance of some $118,000 remaining unapplied at the close of the war. After the war was over and the troops all home, General Scott applied to have this money, which had never been turned into the treasury of the United States, expended in establishing such homes as he had previously recommended. This fund was the foundation of the Soldiers' Home at Washington, and also of one at Harrodsburg, Kentucky. The latter went into disuse many years ago. It never had many inmates, and was, I believe, finally sold.

During this period of waiting the U.S. Army was not uncomfortable in the Mexican capital or in not too distant cities where some of the units were quartered, largely because of the healthier conditions; but naturally the U.S. soldiers in Mexico were generally champing at their bits to go home, and no one more than Lieutenant Grant, as indicated in the following letter:

Tacubaya, Mexico
January 9th, 1848

Miss Julia Dent
Sappington Post Office
St. Louis County, Mo.

My dear Julia,

Since I wrote to you last our Brigade has moved to this place which is about four miles from the City of Mexico and from being so much higher than the City is much more healthy. One Brigade has gone to Toluca and it is rumored that before a great while we will move to some distant part, either Queretero, Zaceticus, San Louis Potosi, or Guernivaca unless there is a strong probability of peace. It is now however strongly believed that peace will be established before many months. I hope it may be so for it is scarcely supportable for me to be separated from you so long my Dearest Julia. A few weeks ago I went to the Commanding Officer of my Regiment and represented to him that when the 4th Infy. left Jefferson Barracks, three years ago last May, I was engaged, and that I thought it high time that I should have a leave of absence to go back. He told me that he would approve it but I found that it would be impossible to get the Comdg. Gen. to give the leave so I never made the application. I have strong hopes though of going back in a few months. If peace is not made it is at all events about my turn to go on recruiting service. As to getting a sick leave that is out of the question for I am never sick a day. Mexico is a very pleasant place to live because it is never hot nor never cold, but I believe every one is heartily tired of the war. There is no amusement except the Theatre and as the actors & actresses are Spanish but few of the officers can understand them. The better class of Mexicans dare not visit the Theatre or associate with the Americans lest they should be assassinated by their own people or banished by their Government as soon as we leave. A few weeks ago a Benefit was given to a favorite actress and the Governor of Queretero hearing of it sent secret spies to take the names of such Mexicans as might be caught in indulging in amusements with the Americans for the purpose of banishing them as soon as the magnanimous Mexican Republic should drive away the Barbarians of the North. I pity poor Mexico. With a soil and climate scarcely equaled in the world she has more poor and starving subjects who are willing and able to work than any country in the world. The rich keep down the poor with a hardness of heart that is incredible. Walk through the streets of Mexico for one day and you will see hundreds of beggars, but you never see them ask alms of their own people, it is always from the Americans that they expect to receive. I wish you could be here for one short day then I should be doubly gratified. Gratified at seeing you my Dearest

Julia and gratified that you might see too the manners and customs of these people. You would see what you never dreamed of nor can you form a correct idea from reading. All gamble, Priests & civilians, male & female and particularly so on Sundays. But I will tell you all that I know about Mexico and the Mexicans when I see you which I do hope will not be a great while off now. Fred [Dent] is in the same Brigade with me. I see him every day. He like myself is in excellent health and has no prospect of getting out of the country on the pleas of sickness. I have one chance of getting out of Mexico soon besides going on recruiting. Gen. Scott will grant leaves of absence to officers where there are over two to a Company. In my Regt. there are three or four vacancies which will be filled soon and will give an opportunity for one or two now here to go out. Give my love to all at White Haven and do not fail to write often Dearest Julia. I write but seldom myself but it is because a mail but seldom goes from here to the Sea Coast. Coming this way it is different for the volunteers are constantly arriving.

When you write next tell me if Mrs. Porter and Mrs. Higgins are married or likely to be.

Adieu my Dearest Julia,

Ulysses

During the waiting for the peace treaty to be signed, Lieutenant Grant, like most of the other officers, was interested in seeing more of the country. He made an attempt with a small party to climb to the top of Popocatepetl, but they were forced by a violent and cold storm to descend again before reaching the top.

The party then divided into two parts. Lieutenants Anderson, Stone, and Buckner decided to go to the top of the mountain and actually reached the crater edge. They afterward wrote accounts of the excursion which were published.

Lieutenant Grant and other members of his party decided to go south and west and attempt to visit the caves of Mexico and, as the descent had been so gradual, they were surprised to find a substantial change in the climate upon reaching Cuautla. There they found an almost tropical climate, with orange, banana, and coffee trees and sugar cane flourishing. As the party approached Cuautla, bugles sounded the assembly, soldiers rushed from the guardhouse on the edge of town, and Lieutenant Grant tied a handkerchief on a stick as a flag of truce and advanced with Captains Sibley and Porter a hundred or so yards behind. They were detained at the guardhouse until a messenger could go to the commanding general and return with permission for Lieutenant Grant to be conducted to him. He was followed by the other two officers. The Mexican general reminded them that it was a violation of the terms of the truce to be outside the limits agreed upon. Of course, they had never been informed of any such limits. They were permitted to occupy a vacant house for the night and were promised a guide to put them on the road to Cuernavaca the next morning. This is a town west of Cuautla, with a tropical climate and beautiful scenery.

In a low pass over some mountains they found a very "quaint old town, the inhabitants of which at that date were nearly all full-blooded Indians. Very few of them even spoke Spanish. The houses were built of stone and generally only one story high. The streets were narrow, and had probably been paved before Cortes visited the country. They had not been graded, but the paving had been done on the natural surface." The party had a cart with it, probably the first field vehicle that had ever passed through the town.

The U.S. soldiers ascended the nearby mountain and surveyed a tomb that had been erected there in memory of a ruler venerated by the inhabitants. The next day they went into Cuernavaca. After a day's rest, the party set out again on its march to the great caves of Mexico. As before, they were stopped by a guard. On convincing the guard that they were pleasure seekers trying to visit great sights of the country before their departure, they were conducted to a large hacienda nearby and directed to wait there until the department commander could be consulted and render his decision as to whether they would be permitted to pursue their journey. After waiting a whole day they found out that no messenger had been sent to the commanding general; they decided to go on unless stopped by force. As they proceeded a similar interruption occurred at another village, but the party was conducted around the village and put on its way again. This was the last interruption they suffered.

That night they rested at a large coffee plantation only about eight miles from the cave they were seeking. The next day they visited the cave, accompanied by guides provided with candles and rockets. The inside of the cave seems from the descriptions to be very much like some in the United States. With this visit the party returned to their camps without further adventure.

Grant also attended a bull fight which he describes in some detail in his *Memoirs*. But the spectacle disgusted him by its cruelty to both bulls and horses, and he left before the performance was over.

Naturally, experiences of the Mexican War became a subject of most interesting and emphatic discussion in later years when Grant met a fellow officer of that war. And many officers told of their impressions of U. S. Grant. It is gratifying to note that General Worth in his report made his "Acknowledgments to Lieutenant Grant and the 4th Infantry for distinguished services" in connection with the Battle of Chapultepec; and that Captain Brooks of the 2nd Artillery, under whom he led a fragment of the 4th Regiment, also noted: "I succeeded in reaching the Fort with a few men. Here Lieutenant U. S. Grant and a few others of the 4th Infantry found me. By a joint movement after an obstinate resistance the strong field-work was carried, and the enemy's right was completely turned."

Major Lee in the report of his operations against the same fortress "makes acknowledgments to Captain Brooks of the 2nd Artillery, Lieutenant Grant of the 4th Infantry, and a few men of their respective regiments, for pushing up within short musket range of the barrier, and turning the right flank of the enemy." Lee added, "Lieutenant Grant behaved with distinguished gallantry on the 13th and 14th."

It is pertinent to add the following comment of Colonel Garland: "I must not omit to call attention to Lieutenant Grant, who acquitted himself most nobly upon several occasions under my observation."

Colonel Floyd-Jones recorded the following in connection with his service in Mexico:

Yes, I was with Grant in Mexico; belonging to the same regiment. He was a fine soldier and a singular character, but showing in those early days none of the superior traits that made him famous as a general. He was quiet and reserved, simply attended to his duty without ostentation, and went into a fight without ado. I remember one very interesting occurrence which happened just after we had captured the city of Mexico. Our regiment was ordered to take quarters at the Isabel Convent. Colonel Lee, our Commander, applied for admission, but the priest shut the door in his face. [This having been repeated, Colonel Lee brought up some pioneers who broke in the door.]

Both the priest and the sisters soon recognized that our presence was not only agreeable but a protection to them. Grant, being Quartermaster of the regiment, was one of the first to get on friendly terms with the priest. He had a nephew, a bright young Mexican, who also became attached to Grant and used to go about with him frequently.

Unhappily, this young Mexican was most anxious to ride a magnificent horse which belonged to Captain Prince. After a dinner to which Lieutenant Grant had invited him, the horse was saddled for the young man, together with Lieutenant Grant's horse, but ran away with him when something frightened the high-strung horse. Dashing down the causeway at breakneck speed, the horse jumped a wide ditch and threw the young man off against the trunk of a tree, killing him instantly. "Grant immediately raised the body up and carried it home, and his picture of its reception by the mother was one of the most touching things I ever heard," said Prince, in writing of the sad occurrence in later years. Many of the officers attended the funeral services.

Colonel Floyd-Jones continued:

Sometimes during the Mexican war he was doing double duty as Adjutant and Quartermaster of the regiment, and amidst the bustle of moving onwards, in the heat of an engagement or in the quiet of the camp, he was ever the same good-natured, unenvious and resolute man. He had a very keen idea of the humorous, and among his companions would talk freely and interestingly. His penchant for horses was very marked. He was one of the leaders in making a race-course for the pastime of the officers after we had captured the city of Mexico. He was always fond of a good anecdote, and he frequently regaled us with tales of happenings to him in the discharge of his duties. I remember one day his coming into the quarters and telling a story to illustrate the toughness of the Mexican burro. He said he had been out with a heavy quartermaster's wagon to the outskirts of the city, and in coming in one of the little jackasses that act as beasts of burden in the land of Guadalupe and Hidalgo, laden with a quantity of stone, laid down in the road to rest. The teamster not seeing him, the heavy army wagon passed directly over his body. The little beast got up, shook himself, looked around with a sort of disgusted air and passed on as though nothing had happened.

Another anecdote about Lieutenant Grant concerns a visit one day, to Lieutenant Colonel Joshua Howard of the 15th Infantry, who was in command of Chapultepec. Lieutenant Grant failed to leave his horse at the high breastworks surrounding the office and rode his horse down the long steep flight of stone steps which led to Howard's door. Tying the animal outside, he went in. When the visit was concluded and the two officers emerged, Howard inquired, "How in the world did you get your horse in here?" "Rode him in, sir." "How do you expect to get him out?" "Ride him up the steps instead of down." Mounting, with his usual agility, Lieutenant Grant turned his horse up the stairs. The horse climbed up like a cat, and his rider turned with a wave of his hat and disappeared over the breastworks.

It was an old white mule that Lieutenant Grant probably remembered best, from the trip up Popocatepetl. On the first day's ascent the mule, carrying straw in huge sacks for the officers' horses, struck his head against the ledge, tumbled down a steep mountain slope, and disappeared in the rocks and bushes hundreds of feet below. "We supposed, of course, the poor animal was dashed to pieces," Grant said. But that night the mule came into the party's bivouac, sound and apparently unhurt. Its driver had stayed behind and hunted up his mule in the depths of the gorge; somehow he managed to bring him up again to the path above.

While playing his part in the military operations and while awaiting his return to the States, Grant had the time and will to consider the Mexican War from the standpoint of the commanders and what they might have done. Of his thoughts on this subject he wrote in after years:

Whether General Scott approved of the Mexican war and the manner in which it was brought about I have no means of knowing. His orders to troops indicate only a soldierly spirit, with probably a little regard for the perpetuation of his own fame. On the other hand, General Taylor's, I think, indicate that he considered the administration accountable for the war, and felt no responsibility resting on himself further than for the faithful performance of his duties. Both generals deserve the commendations of their countrymen and to live in the grateful memory of this people to the latest generation.

Earlier in this narrative I have stated that the plain reached after passing the mountains east of Perote extends to the cities of Puebla and Mexico. The route traveled by the army before reaching Puebla goes over a pass in a spur of mountain coming up from the south. This pass is very susceptible of defense by a smaller against a larger force. Again, the highest point of the road-bed between Vera Cruz and the city of Mexico is over Rio Frio Mountain, which also might have been successfully defended by an inferior against a superior force. But by moving north of the mountains, and about thirty miles north of Puebla, both of these passes would have been avoided. The road from Perote to the city of Mexico by this latter route is as level as the prairies in our West. Arriving due north from Puebla, troops could have been detached to take possession of that place, and then, proceeding west with the rest of the army, no mountain would have been encountered before reaching the city of

Mexico. It is true this road would have brought troops in by Guadalupe,—a town, church, and detached spur of mountain about two miles north of the capital, all bearing the same general name,—and at this point Lake Texcoco comes near to the mountain, which was fortified both at the base and on the sides; but troops could have passed north of the mountain and come in only a few miles to the northwest, and so flanked the position, as they actually did on the south.

It has always seemed to me that this northern route to the city of Mexico would have been the better one to have taken. But my later experience has taught me two lessons: first, that things are seen plainer after the events have occurred; second, that the most confident critics are generally those who know the least about the matter criticized. I know just enough about the Mexican war to approve heartily of most of the generalship, but to differ with a little of it. It is natural that an important city like Puebla should not have been passed with contempt; it may be natural that the direct road to it should have been taken; but it could have been passed, its evacuation insured, and possession acquired without danger of encountering the enemy in intricate mountain defiles. In this same way the city of Mexico could have been approached without any danger of opposition except in the open field.

But General Scott's successes are an answer to all criticism. He invaded a populous country, penetrating two hundred and sixty miles into the interior, with a force at no time equal to one half of that opposed to him; he was without a base; the enemy was always intrenched, always on the defensive; yet he won every battle, he captured the capital and conquered the government. Credit is due to the troops engaged, it is true, but the plans and the strategy were the general's.

One of the lessons learned by the officers in Mexico was that disease rather than bullets was the real killer in war. For every man killed by gunfire six men had died of disease. Out of 59,000 volunteers in the U.S. Army, 1,500 had been killed by enemy gunfire, 6,400 lost by disease or accident, 9,200 discharged for disability, and 3,900 deserted. Of the 31,000 regulars, 4,900 had died from disease or accident and 930 from enemy fire, while 4,149 were sent home for disability and 2,850 deserted. The losses of the Mexican Army apparently were not authoritatively reported.

With the peace treaty signed and the military campaigns successfully completed, a number of officers in Mexico City decided to follow the example of the Revolutionary Army and form a hereditary society to provide for the young officers a social center within their means. The Aztec Club of 1847 was founded on October 13 of that year; it occupied the mansion of Señor Bocanegra, a former Mexican minister to the United States. The membership of the founders included General Franklin Pierce, Lieutenants John Magruder, Henry Coppee, and Charles P. Stone, Captain Charles F. Smith, and Colonel John B. Grayson. Many of the officers in General Scott's army joined the club, including Lieutenant Grant, and it still exists, with the descendants of the later Blue and the Gray armies meeting together as they did in Mexico in 1847 and 1848.

The 4th Regiment with General Worth's division evacuated the Mexican capital on June 12, 1848. Both the Mexican and American batteries fired salutes when the Stars and Stripes were lowered and the Mexican flag run up on the National Palace. On June 28 the regiment halted at Jalapa where the division waited above the yellow-fever area for orders to march down to Vera Cruz to be loaded on transports. The last of the U.S. Army in Mexico turned Vera Cruz over to the Mexicans on July 30, 1848.

Peace had made Lieutenant Grant's brevet captaincy merely a complimentary honor on his record. Of his 33 classmates still in service, only one, Rufus Ingalls, had a captain's commission in the regular army, 7 had gone back to second lieutenant's rank, and 25 to first lieutenancies, Grant among them.

IV

The Return Home and Marriage

THE 4th Infantry was sent to Pascagoula, Mississippi. Upon arrival there Brevet Captain Grant lost no time in obtaining leave of absence for four months, and proceeded to St. Louis. On August 22, 1848, he was married to Miss Julia Dent, in the Dent house at Fourth and Cerre streets. Sixteen years later Julia Grant was to ask her husband on what day they had been married, saying that "it was just such a day as this." To this he answered, "On August twenty-second, but I was so frightened that I did not notice what kind of a day it was, whether bright sunshine or snowing." According to all accounts the wedding was a very successful party and quite a social event in St. Louis. Captain Longstreet, later to become lieutenant general in the Confederate Army and one of General Lee's most trusted and effective lieutenants, was one of the ushers.

The family and some of his old friends in St. Louis noted that Grant was no longer "pretty as a doll," as Emmy Dent had once remarked, but was now much sturdier and reserved in manner, with a complexion considerably tanned and weathered by the sun of Mexico. His beard, which he had of necessity grown in Mexico, was shaved off before leaving Pascagoula. In fact a daguerreotype which he gave his wife on their first wedding anniversary shows him very much as he appeared in an earlier one taken in the summer of 1843.

After a few days in St. Louis the couple went to Bethel, Ohio, to visit the bridegroom's father and mother. Ulysses found that none of the letters mailed in Mexico during the previous six months had reached their destination in the United States. Naturally Jesse and Hannah Grant were greatly delighted to have their oldest son back and welcomed him as a hero after his service in the war. According to biographer Lloyd Lewis the captain's Mexican boy, Gregory, made quite a hit with the people in the little Ohio town; he was considered quite a wonder by Uncle Samuel Simpson because of his skill in roping horses, dogs, calves, pigs, and even small boys. Jesse Grant had provided his son a horse to ride to visit relatives. Ulysses called the animal Aqua Nova, a name associated with the Battle of Buena Vista.

On their return to St. Louis, Ulysses and Julia Grant had an opportunity to renew friendship with many old friends and met General Longstreet's bride, whom he had married on March 8. Naturally Mrs. O'Fallon entertained for Julia. She had given the bride her wedding gown, and one of her daughters had been a bridesmaid.

On September 12, Lieutenant Grant asked his regiment for four months' additional leave, but on November 17 he had to report in Detroit. Old Colonel Whistler had returned to active command, now that the war was over and no field service involved, and he had established his headquarters there with two companies. The other companies of the regiment were scattered along the northern frontier of the United States.

The house in which the Grants lived in Detroit, for which they paid a rent of $250 per annum, has since been taken over by the Detroit Historical Society and is preserved in the Fairgrounds. It was located at 1369 (old number 253) East Fort Street, from which location it was moved because of the changed character of the immediate vicinity. It was her Detroit home that Julia Grant left in the spring of 1850 to return to St. Louis and await the birth—on May 30—of her first child, Frederick Dent Grant. He was to become a major general in the Regular Army.

During Grant's tour of duty in Detroit, the Lieutenant had an encounter with one Zachariah Chandler, the Whig candidate in January 1851 for the office of mayor in Detroit. Chandler had established himself as a very prosperous merchant and businessman with a gross income approximating $50,000 a year. He was fearless, contributing openly to the Underground Railroad for escaping slaves, speaking vehemently against slavery, etc. On March 10 he was brought into court by Lieutenant Grant for disobeying the city ordinance requiring home owners to clear the ice and snow off the sidewalks in front of their property. For twenty-five days the officers at the post had suffered from Chandler's neglect, and one night Lieutenant Grant, returning from headquarters, had slipped and sprained a leg. Chandler was found guilty and let off with a fine of six cents and costs. Chandler's animosity melted away with the winter snow and ice when the 4th Infantry was transferred from Detroit to Madison Barracks, Sackett's Harbor, New York.

In Detroit amateur horse racing, either on horseback or trotting races with buggies, seems to have been one of the main amusements. One citizen, H. C. Kibbee, was never to forget the day Lieutenant Grant agreed to buy (for $200) a mare named Nelly of a Mr. Cicotte if it would make a mile, carrying both of them, down Jefferson Avenue in less than three minutes. Grant bought the mare, which afterward won $1,000 on a race in St. Louis and later was sold for $1,400.

Colonel Whistler's daughter, Louise, described as "a sparkling and vivacious beauty," had moved to Madison Barracks with her father. She caused Sam Grant much discomfort by having the regimental band serenade her every evening. He fled from the band concerts, which were painful to him, to seek peace in chess and whist games behind closed doors in the village.

It was at Sackett's Harbor that Lieutenant Grant became acquainted with Charles W. Ford, a young lawyer who was also fond of horses and who later was entrusted with much of the business of the future General Grant. There were, according to Lloyd Lewis, some obstinately pursued games. The lieutenant did not like to be beaten even at chess or checkers, and at the end of one prolonged sitting, when his adversary was tired out, he offered to settle the game by running a race across the public square. Grant won.

Captain and Mrs. John Gore were the Grants' near neighbors at Sackett's Harbor and the two couples became good friends. Gore had participated in the attack on Mexico City and was to die of cholera later in Panama. A Dr. Tripler, just back from Mexico, and his wife, Eunice, were also part of this social group. Mrs. Tripler's reminiscences were in later years to be of some interest, as her friendship with the Grants continued for a long time.

In April 1852 the entire 4th Infantry was ordered to the Pacific Coast. They were assembled at Governors Island, New York Harbor, where a number of recruits joined them. Eight companies sailed for Aspinwall on July 5, numbering a little over seven hundred persons, including the families of officers and soldiers. (Mrs. Grant did not make that journey.

She went instead to Bethel, Ohio, to await the birth of her second son, Ulysses, Jr., on July 22, 1852.) They were assigned to the old steamer *Ohio,* commanded by Captain Schenck of the U.S. Navy. As the assignment to this ship had been made only a day or two before it was to depart and other passengers had previously secured passage on it, the ship was uncomfortably crowded, especially for a trip to the tropics. It took eight days to reach Aspinwall, and the streets of that city (it was the rainy season) were found to be eight or ten inches under water, so that foot passengers had to step from place to place on raised footwalks.

The Panama Railroad had been completed only to the point where it was to cross the Chagres River. The passengers were then transferred to boats to go as far as Cruces, where they were supposed to obtain mules for the ride to Panama City, twenty-five miles farther. Grant wrote in his *Memoirs:*

> Those who traveled over the isthmus in those days will remember that boats on the Chagres River were propelled by natives not inconveniently burdened with clothing. These boats carried thirty to forty passengers each. The crews consisted of six men to a boat, armed with long poles. There were planks, wide enough for a man to walk on conveniently, running along the sides of each boat from end to end. The men would start from the bow, place one end of their poles against the river-bottom, brace their shoulders against the other end, and then walk to the stern as rapidly as they could. In this way from a mile to a mile and a half an hour could be made against the current of the river.

Three companies of the regiment had been sent around Cape Horn by sea but the remainder made the trip across the Isthmus.

As regimental quartermaster, Lieutenant Grant's duties now became most important and tested to the utmost his resourcefulness and readiness to assume responsibility. The contract made in New York with the steamship company ceased to be effective in Panama and the mules contracted to meet the party at Gorgona or Cruces were nowhere to be found. The local resident who had undertaken to furnish the mules had been entirely unable to do so. Under the circumstances, the regiment—except one company, left behind as guards for the public property, and the soldiers with families—marched to Panama City across the Continental Divide. The young quartermaster succeeded in finding mules to carry the camp equipage and baggage and remaining personnel at a cost twice that of the original contract price. This was quite a feat because some of the civilian passengers on the ship were now competing with the 4th Infantry for mules in a limited market. Some of them paid as much as $40 for the use of a mule to ride twenty-five miles, when the mule would have sold for $10 at other times.

Lieutenant Henry Wallen, in after years, remembered that

. . . the ladies, wives of the officers, etc., had been sent forward in the boat under the escort of an officer. While we were preparing to follow the report came back that a boat had capsized and those on board had been drowned. This naturally caused a great deal of anxiety, and Grant, myself and my company were detailed to go up the Chagres River and investigate. We had not proceeded far, however, before we ascertained that the boat which had turned over contained a number of citizen passengers, and we sent back the pleasing intelligence that none of our party were injured. But we pushed on until we reached the ladies, where Grant in his capacity as Quartermaster immediately perfected arrangements for sending them across the Isthmus. This had to be done on hammocks thrown on the shoulders of men, with relays provided at convenient distances along the two day journey. Before we reached our destination on the other side the rumor came to us that cholera had broken out there, and when we arrived at Panama we found that it was true. We were placed on the steamer "Golden Gate" immediately after her arrival, and that night one of my men was taken with the cholera, and by daylight the next morning there were several cases on board. In the two weeks we remained in Panama Bay we lost 110 out of 700 men, the deaths one day amounting to 37.

The doctors desired Captain Patterson, of the "Golden Gate," to pull up anchor and start for San Francisco; but he, having been in the Asiatic country and knowing more of the peculiarities of the disease than they, said that he would not do so, but would put everybody on shore, fumigate his vessel, and then would take the well and convalescent and proceed to San Francisco. The next day we were all landed on the island of Flamenco, and camp was established. Not a single case occurred after we reached the land. This proved that the captain was right; he thoroughly disinfected his vessel, then started for San Francisco, and the cholera was at an end. This Captain Patterson whom Grant met during that trying ordeal he afterwards made chief of the coast survey when he became President of the United States.

Grant was one of the coolest men in all these trying emergencies I ever saw. I remember during that dismal time in Panama Bay that he, a Major Gore and myself sat playing a friendly game of euchre, when Major Gore suddenly dropped his hand, turned pale and said:

"My God, I have got the cholera!" Grant, in the most nonchalant way, undertook to quiet his fears by saying:

"No, major, you have only eaten something that does not agree with you." But the doctor was summoned, and although everything possible was done, Gore died before morning, the only officer we lost.

Our destination on the Pacific coast was Fort Vancouver in Washington Territory, about 110 miles from the mouth of the Columbia river—a beautiful place, which was occupied by the Hudson Bay Company. Here Lieutenant Grant continued his duties as quartermaster for a year or more, and the service was pleasant. Our relations were quite intimate, and I had some very amusing speculations with him during that time.

It will be evident from the foregoing that Lieutenant Grant was left with the public property, the enlisted men and their families, and the one company for guard. To reduce the number of persons exposed to the epidemic, he permitted the company to proceed to Panama and join the rest of the regiment. Its captain and the doctor accompanied the company. The sick and the soldiers who had families remained with the property. It was about two weeks before enough mules had been gathered together and the party could continue on its way to Panama City. New cases of cholera, of course, continued to break out.

The *Golden Gate* started for San Francisco early in September, the cholera epidemic having subsided sufficiently, and arrived when the gold rush was still at its height. San Francisco was a very hectic place at that time, with all sorts of adventurous people who had come to make their fortunes in a hurry.

The regiment spent a few weeks at Benicia Barracks and then went to Fort Vancouver on the Columbia River near where Portland, Oregon, now is. During the winter of 1852–53, Oregon Territory was divided; all north of the Columbia River was taken to make the Washington Territory, and the part south of the Columbia River was left later to become the state of Oregon.

The reminiscences of Delia B. Sheffield, who as a bride went to the Oregon Territory with her husband, a sergeant in the 4th Infantry, help to complete the story of life at Fort Vancouver. A few quotations are pertinent and of interest:

On September 18th, 1852, the regiment was ordered to Fort Vancouver, Oregon Territory. We took passage on the *Columbia,* and after a very rough voyage, during which we encountered heavy gales, which caused almost everyone to be seasick, we landed at Vancouver on September 20th. . . . How glad we were, after our dreadful experience with the cholera at Panama, and our almost equally dreadful experience of seasickness, to find ourselves safely and permanently once more on terra firma.

Vancouver was then a very small hamlet, consisting mostly of the buildings of the Hudson Bay Company's trading post and the barracks and other buildings of the United States military post. There were besides these buildings about a dozen small log cabins, belonging to the Indian and half-breed employees of the Hudson Bay Company. . . .

Life at Vancouver in 1852 and for several years later was of a very simple and primitive sort. Luxuries were not to be had and the necessities of life were costly; eggs cost a dollar and a half a dozen, potatoes nine dollars a sack, and flour twenty-four dollars a barrel. Carpets were unobtainable, all furniture was rude and home-made, and fortunate were those who could secure pieces of furniture that had been brought across the plains, or around by the Isthmus. The easy chair that Captain Wallin made out of a barrel and upholstered with calico and stuffed with moss, was the envy and admiration of the whole garrison. . . .

Early in the spring of 1853, Captain Grant came to my husband and myself and asked that we take the house in which he, Captain Brent, Lieutenant Phil Sheridan [sic], Captain George B. McClellan [sic] and Mr. Eastman, Captain Grant's clerk, had been keeping bachelor's hall all winter, and let them board with us. My husband told him that he thought I was too young and inexperienced to undertake the responsibilities of so large a household. "Oh!" said Captain Grant, "that can be easily managed. I will detail one of the soldiers who is a good cook, to do the cooking, and besides I have an excellent cook-book and am a pretty good cook myself, and I am sure that we shall manage very well."

The Captain was very fond of beef a-la-mode, and he took great pains in instructing the cook how to prepare it. We had always relied on the half-breed wives of the Hudson Bay Company employees for our butter, but one day Captain Grant asked me if I could make some butter, as he was hungry for some sweet home-made butter. So I saved the cream and churned it, and thinking to please the Captain, I put sugar into it instead of salt, as he wanted some *sweet* butter. At dinner, that evening, I displayed it with great pride. I noticed a smile appearing on their faces, and finally Captain Grant said, "Mrs. Sheffield, is this some of our home-made butter?"

"Yes, Captain, how do you like it?"

"Well, it is the sweetest butter that I ever tasted," he remarked, with a twinkle in his eye.

He was very fond of wild game, and whenever we had any, he would put it in a bucket and let it hang in the well for three or four days, before it was cooked. I remember one day a farmer brought to the house a large swan that he had killed and which he wanted to present to Captain Grant, but he would not let any of us look at it, until the Captain came in. Captain was delighted with it, and it also went into the well, and hung there for several days. He said he wanted to cook it himself, and donning a big apron and rolling up his sleeves, he took possession of the kitchen and baked it to perfection.

Occasionally we would have parties, the dining room would be cleared for dancing, and to the music of the 4th Infantry band, we would dance until the wee small hours of the morning. Our guests would come from far and near. General Adair's three daughters, would come from Astoria, and Governor Abernathy's daughter would come from Oregon City; among the young ladies who came from Portland, was Miss Hamilton, who was considered one of the belles of that town. Captain Grant would never take any part in the dancing, but would come in and look on for a while, then go upstairs to his room and remain there all evening smoking. He felt keenly the separation from his wife and family. Oftentimes, while reading letters from his wife, his eyes would fill with tears, he would look up with a start and say, "Mrs. Sheffield, I have the dearest little wife in the world, and I want to resign from the army and live with my family." He would then walk back and forth, on the porch, thinking and smoking, for hours at a time, or he would order his horse and ride for a half day in the woods or along the Columbia river. Often, of a winter's night, when we were seated around the fire, he would tell me of his wife and children and how he missed them. I never saw him angry, but when occasion demanded it, he was very firm. His manners, dress and style of living were simpler than those of any other officer in the garrison. In manner he was unassuming and approachable, and his language was always plain and straightforward.

On one occasion we were having some private theatricals, in our little theatre at the post, when a drunken man, the purser on the *Eagle,* a small boat running between Vancouver and Portland, was disturbing the audience, Captain Grant walked to where he was sitting, and taking him firmly by the collar, marched him out of the hall. He had a true soldier's love of order.

. . . Captain Grant grew restless and wanted to engage in some enterprise from which he could make a little money, so he and Captain Wallin had my husband act as agent for them, and buy up all the chickens within twenty miles of Vancouver. They chartered a small vessel and shipped them to San Francisco. Nearly all the chickens died on the voyage, and they lost the money they put into the enterprise. . . .

In September, Captain Grant was ordered to report at Humboldt, California. It was a more desirable station, but he wanted to resign and go into the lumber business. We bade him goodbye, knowing we were losing an agreeable companion and a true friend.

He gave me his famous cook-book, his feather pillows and a number of other small articles.

During his one year at Vancouver he had not made an enemy and he was kind and considerate to all.

He gained the friendship and good-will of his men by a constant and watchful care of their interests.

During all the early years of my life there, not one word did I ever hear against his character; he was one of nature's noblemen.

Fort Vancouver proved a quite agreeable station, and Lieutenant Grant found plenty of activity in his duties as commissary and quartermaster. However, prices were very high and the cost of living beyond what an officer's pay could provide for, had the army men not been authorized to buy commissary supplies for the prices prevalent in New Orleans. A cook could not be hired for the pay of a captain, flour was 25¢ a pound; potatoes 16¢; beets, turnips, and cabbage 6¢; onions 37½¢; meat and other articles in proportion. The officers whose wives were not present were prone to join, two or three of them, in occupying a set of quarters and running a small mess. Lieutenant Grant was fortunate in having the services of a married noncommissioned officer and his wife, whose wages were of course divided among the three officers in the same house. Many officers whom he had known in Mexico or elsewhere—such as Lieutenant George B. McClellan—passed through Fort Vancouver, and had to be fitted out for an exploring expedition on the Pacific Coast.

In order to help meet the high expenses of living on the Pacific Coast, many of the officers engaged in some sort of business during their spare time, what has come to be called "moonlighting." Lieutenant Grant, always thinking of providing financially for his growing family, was much impressed with this possibility. On August 20 he wrote to his wife back in the United States:

There is no reason why an active, energetic person should not make a fortune every year. For my part I feel that I could quit the army today, and in one year go home with enough to make us comfortable in Gravois all our life. Of course I do not contemplate doing anything of the sort, because what I have is a certainty, and what I might expect to do, might prove a dream. . . .

I can not hope to hear from you after your confinement, for at least a month yet. It distresses me very much. I am almost crazy sometimes to see Fred. I can not be separated from him and his Ma for a long time.

From this point, Lieutenant Grant's letters to his wife are perhaps the best existing record of his life on the Pacific Coast. They will be quoted in so far as they throw light upon what he and others were doing. Being a man of very strong family affection and having had such a short period of service when he could be with his family, their absence, thousands of miles away, became a serious hardship for him and he suffered from the separation.

On October 7 he wrote from Fort Vancouver:

Not a word since the first of last July. I have made on one speculation $1,500 since I have been here and have every confidence I shall make more than $5,000 within the year. . . . I think now that I shall be promoted this winter, and when I am promoted I will apply for orders to go to Washington to settle my accounts. If I am not promoted by spring, I will resign my quartermaster appointment and make the application.

On October 26, 1852:

Another mail has arrived and not a word do I get from you. . . . Our youngest is at this moment probably over three months of age and yet I have never heard a word from it or you, in that time. . . .

There was a marked change on December 3, 1852, when he could write:

How happy this mail's arrival has made me. It not only brought me a letter from you, but four letters, and two more from Clara written at your request. . . . Why did you not come with your brother? I think, however, it was better that you did not come, for in crossing the Isthmus you would have run great risks of losing Ulys. . . . I am better off than ever before, if I collect all that is due me and there are about $1,800 that there is but little doubt about. . . . I have got a farm of about 100 acres all cleared and enclosed, about one mile from here.

This was to be the farming effort of which he speaks in his *Memoirs* and which became economically disastrous because unusually high water in the Columbia River flooded the farm and destroyed most of the crop. Evidently her brother Fred did not come (he was on duty with the 5th Infantry on the Brazos River, Texas; not until 1856 was he sent to Fort

Vancouver, Washington, as captain in the 9th Infantry), for on December 19 he wrote:

> If your brother does not come out there is no telling when I am to see them [the two sons] and you. It cannot be a great while, however, because *I would prefer sacrificing my commission* and trying something [else] to continuing this separation. My hope is to get promotion and then orders to Washington to settle my accounts. . . .

This matter of settling his accounts as regimental quartermaster during the Mexican War and subsequently was very much on his mind, whereas the accounts had been approved but he was apparently never told.

A letter dated February 15, 1853, while repeating the previous statements, does introduce a new consideration relative to Mrs. Grant's coming to the Pacific coast:

> I am now so glad that you could not come. As it is Fred is a strong healthy boy. Had you come [with me] he no doubt would now be in his grave. I believe there were some twenty or more children of his age, and younger came across the Isthmus with us. Out of that number seventeen died on the Isthmus and all the others contracted diseases so that I believe there is not a single one left. Mrs. Wallen's little boy that she lost a few weeks ago, I believe, was the last survivor. . . . I loaned $200.00 to an officer, who was going to San Francisco some two months since on the solemn promise that he would return it by the next mail. He has not paid and from what has transpired since I know he never will. . . . Has Capt. Calender commenced paying you yet? If he has not I must, not withstanding my necessities here, send you some money. Mr. Camp owes me $1,500.00 on a note I hold against him, but it is not due for some time yet. . . .

Evidently, Fort Vancouver was a very busy place. As depot quartermaster and commissary the brevet captain had very onerous duties and not much time in which to brood over the separation from his loved ones; however, that the ache never left him is shown by his correspondence. There were minor exploring expeditions and some expeditions against local Indians to be fitted out, and there was plenty of company—among others his classmate and onetime West Point roommate, Captain Rufus Ingalls.

On May 20, Grant was in San Francisco as a witness for the trial of Lieutenant Scott, and noted that "Stevens is rich; Dodge, Gladwin and

Mrs. Gladwin are doing a good business here." He sends his wife "a deed for the land located with my land warrant for you to sign before a Commissioner. . . . It is very hard to be separated so long, but until I am better off it cannot be helped. If I can get together a few thousand dollars, I shall most certainly go home." However, he was never able to accumulate the nest egg he felt was needed. The farming enterprise, successful in raising a crop estimated to bring in $1,800.00, failed because by June 15 the Columbia was "far over its banks, and has destroyed all the grain, onions, corn and about half the potatoes upon which I had expended so much money and labor." Several sums otherwise earned had to be put in the hands of others to earn an income, and those to whom the jobs were entrusted were either unfortunate or proved to be dishonest. For instance, "Mr. Camp could not stand prosperity. He quit and went home with about $8,000.00, deceiving me as to the amount of money he had and owing me about $800.00." In this same letter of June 15, 1853, he says: "When they [his two sisters, Jenny and Mary] wrote father had not yet returned and of course I heard nothing of the proposition to have me resign that you spoke of. I shall weigh the matter well before I act." So here was his resignation being considered by his family at home, and apparently with some favor, before he mentioned it to anyone but his beloved wife!

The death of Captain William W. S. Bliss on August 5, 1853, brought to Capt. Grant the vacancy for his promotion to rank of captain in the Regular Army and resulted in his assignment to command a company of the 4th Infantry stationed at Fort Humboldt, California. In considering the possibility of this assignment he had spoken of it as "a detestable place where the mails reach occasionally (only)." Moreover, the officer in command was Brevet Lieutenant Colonel Robert C. Buchanan, a martinet and busybody, with whom Lieutenant Grant at Jefferson Barracks had twice had incidents that laid the basis for the senior's strong personal dislike of the younger officer. Of Buchanan, his adjutant, Lewis C. Hunt, had written, "well but heartily tired of Humboldt Bay, or rather of the Commanding Officer there."

After a few days in San Francisco waiting for a ship, the new captain finally got to Fort Humboldt by January 18, 1854, and in his first letter home wrote:

I cannot say much in favor of this place. It is about what I expected before my arrival. . . . Getting here a distance of but little more than 250 miles we were two days in coming. No mail is going, but Mr. Hunt is just starting for S. Francisco and I must avail myself of this occasion of getting a letter to where it can be mailed.

His next letter, on February 2, 1854, starts:

You do not know how forsaken I feel here! . . . I do nothing but sit in my room and read and occasionally take a short ride on one of the public horses. There is game here such as ducks, geese, etc., which some of the officers amuse themselves by shooting, but I have not entered into the sport. Within eight or ten miles deer and occasionally elk and black bear are found. Further back the grisley bear are quite numerous. . . . The quarters are comfortable frame buildings, backed by a dense forest of immense trees. In front is the Bay. We are on a bluff which gives us one of the most commanding views. . . . I got one letter from you since I have been here but it was some three months old. I fear very much I shall lose some before they get in the regular way of coming. There is no regular mail service between here and San Francisco, so the only way we have of getting letters off is to give them to some Captain of a vessel to mail them after he gets down [to San Francisco]. This makes it very uncertain as to the time a letter may be on the way. Sometimes, owing to adverse winds, vessels are 40 to 60 days making the passage, while at others they make it in less than two days.

In 1912, Clara McGeorge Shields rounded up what information could still be gotten from persons who had personally known Captain Grant in those days and published it in the *Humboldt Times* of Sunday, November 10, 1912. Among the reminiscences of such eyewitnesses she quotes an old friend and admirer of Grant, who owned a sawmill, lodginghouse, and store, as saying:

Grant's relations with his commanding officer were inharmonious, to say the least. Colonel Buchanan was extremely punctilious and something of a martinet. Grant was a plain, practical, thoroughly drilled soldier, and he had little use for the fuss and frills of military etiquette. His easy methods and carelessness of dress were constant sources of irritation to his superior officer. Little inconsequent trifles of dress and ceremony became ever recurring causes for remarks and unpleasantness. Yet whatever faults the critical colonel may have found, neglect of duty was not one of them. . . . The welfare of the men was ever kept in view; he made frequent visits to their quarters, tasting their food and inspecting sanitary conditions. The men felt free to go to him with complaints and grievances, knowing that they would be given a hearing and their claims considered with fairness.

That the captain did not lose interest in his military duties, even though they did not keep him as busy as he had been when post quartermaster at Vancouver Barracks, is shown by the following in his letter of February 6, 1854:

I am very much pleased with my company. All the men I have are old soldiers and very neat in their appearance. The contrast between them and the other company here is acknowledged as very great by the officers of the other company. I have however less than a third of the complement allowed by law and all of them will be discharged about the same time. I wish their times were out now so that I could go on recruiting service if no other way.

This same letter of February 6, 1854, begins:

A mail came in this evening but brought me no news from you or anything in reply to my application for orders to go home. I cannot conceive what is the cause of the delay. The state of suspense that I am in is scarcely bearable. I think I have been from my family quite long enough and sometimes I feel as though I could almost go home "nolens volens". I presume, under ordinary circumstances, Humboldt would be a good enough place, but the suspense I am in would make paradise from a bad picture. . . . I have been suffering for the last few days most terribly. That tooth I had set in Watertown (you remember how much I suffered at the time) has been giving me trouble again. Last evening I had it drawn and it was much harder to get out than any other tooth would have been. My face is swollen until it is as round as an apple, and so tender that I do not feel as if I could shave. . . . Has Capt. Calender continued to send you money? Some three or four months ago I bought two land warrants, one of which I want to send you, but when I got to San Francisco I found they were not negotiable on account of not having on the transfer the seal of the County Clerk. I sent them back to Vancouver to have this fixed. . . . They are worth about forty dollars more there than I gave for them. . . . Living here is extravagently high besides being very poor. . . . I believe I told you that Mrs. Wallen has lost another child. . . .

On March 6 he wrote:

I have only one letter from you in three months, and that had been a long time on the way. I know there are letters for me in the Post Office somewhere, but when shall I get them? I sometimes get so anxious to see you, and our little boys, that *I am almost tempted to resign and trust to Providence, and my own exertions, for a living where I can have you and them with me.* It would only require the certainty of a moderate competency to make me take this step. Whenever I get to thinking upon the subject however *poverty,*

U. S. Grant at the age of 21: a brevet second lieutenant in the Fourth Infantry. The photograph was taken shortly after his graduation from West Point in 1843.

Jesse R. Grant and Hannah Simpson Grant, parents of Ulysses S. Grant.

Julia Dent Grant, Ulysses's wife. This photograph was taken when Grant was in the White House.

The Dent home on Gravois Creek outside St. Louis.

"Hardscrabble," the log house Grant built after he resigned from the Army in 1854 on property given his wife by her father.

Library of Congress

Library of Congress

General Grant with his horse Cincinnati.

A sketch of Grant's headquarters before Vicksburg.
Grant sits in front of his tent reading a letter from General Pemberton proposing a meeting to discuss the surrender of the city and its fortifications. The boy with the pony is Frederick D. Grant, the General's oldest son and the author's father. Although he was only twelve years old, Frederick went through the entire Vicksburg campaign with his father and was wounded in the leg at the crossing of the Big Black River. Sitting in the foreground is Charles Dana, Assistant Secretary of War.

Library of Congress

The Union Army crossing the Rapidan River near Germanna Ford, Virginia, by means of a ponton bridge.

An engraving showing Grant's army building a corduroy road in the woods.

U. S. Signal Corps Photo (Brady Collection)

The waterfront at City Point, Virginia, from which Grant's army was supplied.

Grant during the Battle of the Wilderness.

U. S. Signal Corps Photo (Brady Collection)

Library of Congress

General Grant with his Chief of Staff, Maj. Gen. John A. Rawlins, on his right and his Assistant Adjutant General, T. S. Bowers, on his left.

The McLean House at Appomattox, Virginia, where Grant accepted the surrender of General Lee's Army of Northern Virginia.

U. S. Signal Corps Photo (Brady Collection)

General William Tecumseh Sherman.
U. S. Signal Corps Photo (Brady Collection)

General Philip H. Sheridan.
National Archives

Major General Henry W. Halleck, who was superseded by Grant as Commander of the Union forces.

Library of Congress

Major General John A. McClernand.

U. S. Signal Corps Photo (Brady Collection)

Major General John C. Fremont.

U. S. Signal Corps Photo (Brady Collection)

Major General William Rosecrans.

U. S. Signal Corps Photo (Brady Collection)

U. S. Signal Corps Photo (Brady Collection)

Major General Lew Wallace.

President and Mrs. Lincoln receiving General and Mrs. Grant at a reception at the White House.

U. S. Signal Corps Photo (Brady Collection)

President Andrew Johnson.

President Grant and his Cabinet.

From left to right: Jacob D. Cox, Hamilton Fish, John A. Rawlins, John A. J. Creswell, George S. Boutwell, Adolph E. Borie and Ebenezer Hoar.

National Archives

This statue was erected by the Portuguese in the main square of Bolama City, Portuguese Guinea, in memory of Grant's decision in favor of Portugal in that country's dispute with Britain over title to the colony. Grant acted as arbitrator of the question in 1870.

The reception for Grant in Chicago on his return from the trip around the world.

A. Currier & Ives portrait of the Grant family in 1867.
From left to right: General Grant, Jesse Root Grant, Ulysses Simpson Grant, Jr., Frederick Dent Grant, Ellen Wrenshall Grant, Mrs. Grant.

A family portrait taken in June, 1885, a month before Grant's death.
From left to right: U. S. Grant, Jr.; Mrs. Grant; Mrs. Algernon Sartoris, the General's daughter; Julia Grant, the General's granddaughter and the author's sister; General Grant; Ulysses S. Grant, 3rd, the author; Mrs. Frederick Dent Grant (Ida Honore); Colonel Frederick Dent Grant; Nelly Chapman Grant; Mrs. Jesse Root Grant; Jesse Grant.

Frick Art Reference Library

The Healy portrait of Ida Honore Grant, the author's mother.

Frick Art Reference Library

The Healy portrait of Frederick Dent Grant, the General's eldest son and the author's father.

poverty, begins to stare me in the face and then I think what would I do if you and our little ones should want for the necessaries of life. . . . I would be contented at Humboldt if it was possible to have you here but it is not. . . . I get so tired and out of patience with the loneliness of this place that I feel like volunteering for the first service that offers. . . . Wallen has made up his mind to resign. Mrs. Wallen has declared she would not go back to Vancouver, that if he went he would go without her. W. has gone into the coal business.—Stevens is going ahead at a rapid stride. A recent decision of the Courts in a land case made him one hundred thousand dollars better off than before. . . . I have some land warrants one of which I want to send you but I am afraid to trust it to the mail. I will send it by the first favorable opportunity. They are worth about $180.00 in New York: I do not know what you will be able to get in St. Louis.

And from a letter begun on March 25, 1854:

I have had just one solitary letter from you since I arrived at this place and that was written about October of last year. I cannot believe that you have neglected to write all this time but it does seem hard that I should not hear from you. I am afraid too many of my letters do not reach you. The only way of mailing them is to give them to a captain of a vessel to put them in the Post Office in San Francisco, which, if he does, they are all safe, but I have no doubt but that many times they never spend a second thought about letters entrusted to them.

After getting as far as I have done in this I was interrupted [he wrote on April 3] by the entrance of some officers, from continuing for the evening and as the bar at the outlet of the bay was so rough as to prevent vessels from going out for some days I have not taken it up until now. There has been no vessel going out since. The irregularity of the mails is an annoyance which can only be appreciated by those who suffer from it. . . . How very anxious I am to get home once again. I do not feel as if it was possible to endure this separation much longer. But how do I know that you are thinking as much of me as I of you? I do not get letters to tell me so. But you write, I am certain, and some day I will get a big batch all at once. Just think by the time you receive this Ulys will be nearly two years old and no doubt talking as plainly as Fred did his few words when I saw him last. . . . Do you ever hear anything from Ohio? I have not had a letter from there since last October. . . . I am enjoying good health but growing more lazy every day for want of something to do. When the mountain streams dry up a little more however I will find something to do for, if we do not move to the interior, I at least have to go there with a party of men which will take up one month.

The department had not bothered to make any reply to his request for orders to go to Washington to settle his Mexican War and subsequent property and disbursing accounts, a settlement that weighed on his mind. He did not feel free to resign or otherwise push a claim for transfer out of Buchanan's jurisdiction as long as his accounts had not been approved—as they had, but he had not been so informed.

Finally, April 11, 1854, his commission as captain in the 4th Infantry arrived. Here was the official certificate of honorable service. Now he could resign, rid himself of Buchanan's petty persecutions and the dull military routine, return to his family, and face the problems of supporting his dear ones by his own efforts as an independent American citizen. He would not delay but must accept the commission—and, we must presume, be sworn in with his new rank—that very day and at the same time submit his resignation from the army to take effect July 31, 1854. His request for leave of absence was approved by Brevet Lieutenant Colonel Buchanan for sixty days (the limit of his authority as post commander) and by headquarters in San Francisco, with permission to apply for an extension of four months on his arrival in New York. Like all his decisions, it was made with the promptness which later distinguished his effective decisions when in higher command during the Civil War. And he came to decisions without sharing his problems in advance with any one else, so that they came as a surprise to associates.

A small army post was in those days a hotbed for gossip and rumor. What a windfall for the post gossips this sudden resignation of the second in command at Fort Humboldt must have been. Naturally those in lonely stations on the Pacific Coast found all sorts of explanations for it. But "gossip which is written down is no more veracious than gossip which flies current" (Bishop Creighton quoted by Logan Pearsal Smith). What more natural than that Captain Buchanan (the complimentary title of lieutenant colonel was but a brevet) should have maliciously given it to be understood that he had somehow forced the resignation by a threat of charges for drinking? This version was generally accepted by the army at that time, but lacks confirmation by any evidence of a contemporaneous eyewitness the writer can find. Even Captain Grant's classmate and onetime roommate at West Point, Rufus Ingalls, believed it, as did then 2nd Lieutenant Henry C. Hodges. Both of them were at Columbia Barracks, Vancouver, about that time, but neither of them was at Fort Humboldt nor could testify from personal knowledge as an eyewitness. All the evidence for the story seems to be hearsay evidence such as no court would admit.

In her 1912 research among the survivors of the old days at Fort Humboldt, Clara McGeorge Shields had opportunities to interview A. P. Marble, who had been Captain Grant's striker, crossed the Isthmus with him, and could speak from personal knowledge. Marble denied that "there was any special cause for Grant's resignation, other than that he was not satisfied with existing conditions. Cognizant of his own power and ability, he felt that his life was being wasted. His military ambitions were being blasted and his captain's pay was inadequate for the support of his family. Besides his environment was decidedly unpleasant."

Mrs. Shields also refers to a letter from S. S. Todd published in a Kansas City paper in April 1895 which "hints at pressure being brought to bear on Grant to wring from him his commission. This theory is, in the opinion of the writer, erroneous as the most careful investigation among those associated with him at Fort Humboldt, fails to find causes other than those herein ascribed."

She further quotes reminiscences of F. S. Duff and Dr. Jonathan Clark of Eureka, who on occasion performed the duties of surgeon at Fort Humboldt when the army surgeon was away. Both had much to say about their recollections of the captain, whom they liked and admired, but no suggestion of his alleged inclination to drink too much. Dr. Clark had treated him for two illnesses: "it was after recovery of the first illness that he tendered his resignation"—probably the trouble with his tooth mentioned in the letter of February 6 quoted above—"and he had just recovered from the second when the knowledge of its acceptance reached him."

Frank A. Burr states in his life of Grant that "one of the officers of the old regiment now writes thus about his [Grant's] retirement":

> I remember meeting Grant after his resignation, and although our conversation was a short one, it left the impression on my mind that he had become disgusted with army life as he found it at his new post, and had left it without giving the step careful consideration. He spoke of his earnest longing for the quiet life of a farmer. It was apparent to me then that his boyhood ambition to be a tiller of the soil had returned, and, being irritated by the petty annoyances about an unpleasant post, with a captious commander who did not like him, he had resolved to return home. There was a story

about charges against him; but, if there were any, I do not believe they would have had any such effect as to have induced him to resign. He had no reason to care for any allegations that could be trumped up against him by any one. He knew there were none that touched his moral character, or that would have diminished confidence in his integrity and value as an officer, which was then fully established in all army circles. The worst charge that ever I heard suggested would have resulted, if proved, in no inconvenience to him. It might possibly have subjected him to a reprimand from the colonel of the regiment, yet even this would have taken the form of a handsome compliment to his well-known traits of character and conduct. I never knew a man better than I have known Grant, and I never knew a better man.

There is no firsthand evidence that shows he was aware of the story about his drinking until later, during the Civil War, when it was dug up by his enemies and used against him. Even when it was referred to by General Halleck, in a telegram to McClellan after the capture of Fort Donelson, Grant did not know of this exchange of correspondence until the war was over and one of his staff found copies of it in an office vacated by Halleck's staff in the Winder Building in Washington!

In any case it was a matter of principle with Grant throughout his life not to reply to criticisms or allow his friends to attempt a defense of his actions. Thus he later stopped his father, by his letter of August 3, 1862, from defending him against criticism. Therefore, if he was aware, at the time of his resignation, of gossip about him, it is not surprising that he entered no denial. It is pertinent that Miss Helen Nicolay, a very conscientious researcher, in her *Boys' Life of Ulysses S. Grant,* testifies: "There is nothing in the official correspondence to show his motive for resigning, or to cast one breath of scandal upon his name."

Indeed, the letters quoted show conclusively that resignation was not a new idea forced on him at the moment because of misbehavior; rather it was part of a matured plan which he had postponed executing until a suitable opportunity arose. It is also evident that he kept delaying his resignation in the hope of making money that would be a basis for a new start in civil life; and this had become hopeless with his transfer to Fort Humboldt. The internal evidence of his correspondence with his wife does not suggest alcoholism. The letters show sustained clarity of thought, concern for his dear ones, absence of querulousness, and calmness of judgment, in spite of his agony over the continued separation.

In his debate with Douglas on August 21, 1858, Lincoln noted that "a man cannot prove a negative, but he has a right to claim that when a man makes an affirmative charge, he must offer some proof to show the truth of what he says . . . ; it is not satisfactory to me that he may be 'conscientious' on the subject." The writer can find no such evidence that is reliable, namely that of an eyewitness who gave testimony before he had become confused by the generally accepted myth.

To the writer it is evident that this story of Grant's drinking to excess is just one of the lies of history to be attributed to what Ruskin called the "spendid mendacity of man," one of "the lies agreed upon" referred to by Napoleon. It must seem to any fairminded person, to quote from Byron's "Lara," a case

> Where history's pen its praise or blame supplies
> And lies like truth, and most truly lies.

The trip to San Francisco was uneventful.

When Grant arrived there, he found that the orders giving him leave had not provided transportation for his return to the Atlantic Coast, nor had he enough cash to purchase his transportation himself. The following recollection of Mrs. Grant will explain the shortage of cash which has been so overemphasized by some of the biographers:

> I cannot refrain from making mention just here of a person who behaved in a most craven manner. It is rather strange too, for the mother and sisters of this person were unusually refined and cultivated. It was really for their sake that the officers stationed at Madison Barracks elected him post storekeeper, and again induced Capts. Grant and Hunt to commute their servant's transportation to California, to which they were entitled and giving it to this young man. Thus not only securing transportation all the way to California (then a most expensive journey) but securing for him a first class cabin passage with themselves. On arriving in San Francisco, this young man proposed starting at once in some business, a sort of general store (that is, every sort of thing). He asked Capt. Grant to join him in this and help with any means he might have. The Captain gladly joined him, handing him all of his pay that had accumulated since he left New York and for a month or so, every one thought and was told that this fellow was coining a fortune, when suddenly the man said he was losing money in place of making any, though all this time, there was no decrease of custom. This complaining went on until he one day told the Captain that he would feel better if he had the business all to himself; that he would not like to be the cause of any harm

coming to the Captain, etc. The Captain told him if it would make him (the merchant) any happier, that he would take what money he had put in (fifteen hundred dollars) and retire from business entirely. So it was arranged, the man giving the Captain three notes of five hundred dollars each; he even after this prevailed upon the captain to destroy these three notes before his own eyes, saying he could not sleep at nights about these notes for fear the Captain would come on him for the money, when he did not have it to give him, etc. How I chided Ulys when he told me this, telling him that the Vicar of Wakefield's Moses was a financier beside him. He should have given him something to make him sleep, the poker. When I chided him thus, he said: "I believe you are right, for when I resigned and arrived in New York with but little means, I thought of this debtor who had returned to Sacketts Harbor and I borrowed sufficient from a friend, Major Simon B. Buckner (afterwards General and Governor), to pay my expenses there, having notified C. of my coming and for what I was coming (the amount of his debt to me). On arriving at Sackett's Harbor, to my dismay, I found the fellow had gone on his yacht (he kept a yacht now), the day before and no one knew when he would return." Ulys turned to me and said: "You know I had to wait in New York until I heard from you."

I think just here is a good place for me to reply to an article I read in some Western paper which relates most circumstantially the facts of Capt. U. S. Grant procuring through the quartermaster (Allen, I think), transportation from California to New York. General Grant has told me and more than one, of how he had deposited about two thousand dollars with an acquaintance who was on leave of absence (or may be temporarily suspended from his ship) and trying like every one else out there, to turn an honest penny, had started a small banking business. The Captain told me of his depositing his little all with this man *declining* the two percent a month, the bank offered, saying, "I wish this as a *special* deposit for *safe* keeping *until* I *want* it."

So when the Captain resigned and was on his way home, he called on S. for his money, and was both surprised and disappointed when the banker told him that just then he could not pay it, but if the Captain could wait over for the next steamer, he would surely have it for him. And it was with much inconvenience, the Captain did wait. He had to, as he had little other means and besides, wishing to bring his money home with him. He then went on a visit to my brothers at Knight's Ferry, for the two weeks between steamers. Returning to San Francisco the day before the steamer sailed, he again called on S. and was told the banker was out of the city and so, I suppose, this is how it happened that Captain Grant had to depend on the quartermaster for transportation to New York.

Upon making inquiry in regard to this statement, I learn that it was customary *then* for the Steamship Company which was doing a great deal of carrying for the army, to give *all* officers on leave for home, complimentary passes, the officers only paying for their meals en route and, perhaps, for passage across the Isthmus.

From New York he hurried to St. Louis to see his family. His wife remembered that her oldest son, Fred, then just over four years old, told her there was a man outside White Haven with a large beard—this proved to be his father whom he had not seen for over two years. There was a happy family reunion that night and the father was able to make the acquaintance of his second son whom he had never seen. Again quoting from Mrs. Grant's recollections:

After an absence of over two years, Captain Grant, to my great delight, resigned his commission in the U.S. Army, and returned to me, his loving little wife. How very happy this reunion was! One great boy by his knee, one curly-headed blue-eyed Cupid on his lap, and his happy proud wife nestled by his side.

We cared for no other happiness. I have been both indignant and grieved over the statement of pretended personal acquaintances of Captain Grant at this time, to the effect that he was dejected, low-spirited, badly dressed and even slovenly.

Well, I am quite sure they did not know *my* Captain Grant, for he was always perfection, both in manner and person, a cheerful, self-reliant, earnest gentleman. His beautiful eyes, windows of his great soul, his mouth so tender, yet so firm. One must not deem me partial if I say General Grant was the very nicest and handsomest man I ever saw, and I have seen his (—that) great army of one million men, all brave, all handsome, gallant soldiers. May I confess right here, and tell of how my loving heart swelled with pride and gratitude, to know that my own beloved General was Commander of this grand, victorious army?

Ulys always wished to farm, and as my father gave me about one hundred acres, he decided to become a farmer. Our home for the first two years, was at Wishtonwish, a pretty villa erected by my brother Louis, on a hill about one and a half miles south of White Haven, in a magnificent forest of oaks. The Captain's farm lay about a mile north of our old home.

This place, as well as Louis Dent's, was a part of the old farm.

How happy I was at having my beloved one near me again, to have him hold my hand in his and feel his warm breath on my cheek.

On the farm Colonel Dent gave his daughter, Captain Grant built a house with his own hands and some farm labor. It was a two-story double house with rooms on each side of a central hall. When the house was ready for the raising of the ridgepole, neighbors attended in considerable numbers. Because of the work that had been put in on it the captain called it "Hardscrabble." Since his farm was largely in forest, it had to be cleared to make room for the house; at the same time this provided material for building the house, with considerable wood left over. Consequently, the cut wood was the first cash crop available, and the captain frequently drove a team to St. Louis to dispose of fuel wood and timbers for lining mines. He made a lasting impression on his neighbors and the people of St. Louis.

As he states in his *Memoirs,* he lacked the cash to stock the farm and to provide the most essential equipment. Some biographers have been prone to describe this period as one of extreme poverty and considerable privation. However, as Walter B. Stevens says in his book, *Grant in St. Louis:*

> No member of the Grant family looked back upon that farm life as it has been presented by some of the biographers. There was none of that poverty which has been pictured to heighten the contrasts with the fame that came later. There was plenty to eat. There was social life. The Captain and Mrs. Grant went out to the neighborhood gatherings; they had no light vehicle but both were good riders and each took a child on a horse. Grant did not dance but he played cards well. Checkers was his favorite game. At the shooting matches of the neighborhood, the Captain held his own and got the prize, a quarter of beef, about as often as any of the neighbors. Grant was popular with his neighbors along the Gravois Road. He had no quarrels. To this day is remembered the way in which his sense of justice settled the difference between two neighbors. Soon after Grant went on the farm there was a misunderstanding as to the amount he was to pay Trip Reavis and Jonah Sappington for a quantity of cordwood. The two neighbors claimed more was due than Grant thought he was to pay. The captain proposed arbitration; Sappington and Reavis to appoint one arbitrator; he to appoint the other; the cost of the decision of the arbitrators to be paid by the loser. Reavis and Sappington named Ben Lovejoy as their arbitrator. The captain immediately said Lovejoy would suit him, too, and that whatever the decision he would accept it. Lovejoy decided that Reavis and Sappington were right. Grant at once paid the bill. (Could this have been the occasion that suggested to him the peaceful settlement of the Alabama Claims, later when President?)
>
> There is a sequel to this incident. Most of those who were neighbors to Grant in his farming days owned slaves or from old associations sympathized

with the South. In the settlement was formed an organization to extend aid to Confederates. Grant came up to St. Louis in January, 1862, and in accordance with his custom went out to the farm to see his father-in-law. He went about among the neighbors. Someone proposed that the organization kidnap him and take him South a prisoner. The suggestion was promptly vetoed by the leaders.

On August 22, 1857, the captain wrote his sister the following account of his farming:

. . . I am glad to hear that mother and Jennie intend making us a visit. I would advise them to come by the river if they prefer it. Write to me beforehand about the time you will start, and from Louisville again, what boat you will be on, direct to St. Louis,—not Sappington, P.O.—and I will meet you at the river or Planter's House, or wherever you direct.

We are all very well. Julia contemplates visiting St. Charles next Saturday to spend a few days. She has never been ten miles from home, except to come to the city, since her visit to Covington.

I have nothing in particular to write about. My hard work is now over for the season with a fair prospect of being remunerated in everything but the wheat. My wheat, which would have produced from four to five hundred bushels with a good winter, has yielded only seventy-five. My oats were good, and the corn, if not injured by frost this fall, will be the best I ever raised. My potato crop bids fair to yield fifteen hundred bushels or more. Sweet potatoes, melons and cabbages are the only other articles I am raising for market. In fact, the oats and corn I shall not sell. . . .

Your affectionate Brother.

Ulyss.

P.S. Tell father that I have this moment seen Mr. Ford, just from Sacketts Harbor, who informs me that while there he enquired of Mr. Bagley about my business with Camp, and learns from him that the account should be acted upon immediately. Camp is now at Governors Island, N.Y., and intends sailing soon for Oregon. If he is stopped he may be induced to disgorge. Tell father to forward the account immediately.

U.

Again in writing to his sister Mary (Mrs. M. J. Cramer) on March 21, 1858, he has this to say about farming:

This Spring has opened finely for farming and I hope to do well; but I shall wait until the crops are gathered before I make any predictions. I have now three negro men, two hired by the year and one of Mr. Dent's, which, with my own help, I think, will enable me to do my farming pretty well with assistance in harvest. I have however a large farm. I shall have about twenty acres of potatoes, twenty of corn, twenty-five of oats, fifty of wheat, twenty-five of meadow, some clover, Hungarian grass and other smaller products, all of which require labor before they are got into market, and the money realized upon them. You are aware, I believe, that I have rented out my place and have taken Mr. Dent's. There are about two hundred acres of ploughed land on it and I shall have, in a few weeks, about two hundred and fifty acres of woods pasture fenced up besides. Only one side of it and a part of another has to be fenced to take the whole of it in, and the rails are all ready. . . .

In spite of his father's refusal to advance him money with which to purchase farm equipment that he felt necessary to make the farm produce a substantial income, the captain was justified in feeling that he had "managed to keep along very well until 1858, when I was attacked by fever and ague. I had suffered very severely for a long time from this disease while a boy in Ohio. It lasted now over a year, and while it did not keep me in the house, it did interfere greatly with the amount of work I was able to perform."

Indeed, this was a year of much sickness on the family farm, summarized in Ulysses' letter of September 7, 1858, to his sister, Mary:

I thought then to wait for two or three weeks; by that time there was so much sickness in my family, and Freddy so dangerously ill, that I thought I would not write until his fate was decided. He was nearly taken from us by the bilious, then by the typhoid fever; but he is now convalescing. Some seven of the negroes have been sick. Mrs. Sharp is here on a visit, and she and one of her children are sick; and Julia and I are both sick with chills and fever. If I had written to you earlier it would have been whilst Fred's case was a doubtful one and I did not want to distress you when it could have done no good to anyone.

Accordingly, he and Mr. Dent decided, as Ulysses wrote his father on October 1, 1858, to:

make a sale this fall and get clear of all the stock on the place and then rent out the cleared land and sell about four hundred acres of the north end of the place. As I explained to you this will include my place. I shall plan to go to Covington towards spring, and would prefer your offer to anyone of mere salary that could be offered. I do not want any place for permanent stipulated pay, but want the prospect one day of doing business for myself. There is a pleasure in knowing that one's income depends somewhat upon his own exertion and business capacity, that cannot be felt when so much and no more is coming in, regardless of the success of the business engaged in or the manner in which it is done.

This referred to his father's offer to associate him in the partnership with his brothers in Galena, which he was to accept in 1860.

In the meantime he had some correspondence with Washington University as to the possibility of his being appointed as professor of mathematics; but the position was filled or had been filled. Isaac F. Quinby, best mathematician in the class of 1843 at West Point, was also a contender for this place and was not given the job.

Ulysses, following his father-in-law's advice, next entered into a St. Louis real estate firm with Harry Boggs, a cousin of his wife, in the beginning of 1859. Desk room was taken in the law offices of McClelland, Hillyer and Moody, on the first floor of a building that had been a residence, located on Pine Street midway between Second and Third.

On March 12, 1859, Grant wrote his father: "I can hardly tell how the new business I am engaged in, is going to succeed, but I believe it will be something more than a support." His letter went on:

> We are living now in the lower part of the city full two miles from my office. The house is a comfortable little one, just suited to my means. We have one spare room, and also a spare bed in the children's room, so that we can accommodate any of our friends that are likely to come to see us. I want two of the girls, or all of them for that matter, to come and pay us a long visit.

On the subject of his going into the real estate business, his widow in after years had the following to say:

> I cannot imagine how my dear husband ever thought of going into such a business, as he never could collect a penny that was owed to him, if his debtors, and he had several, only expressed regret, and said "Grant, I regret more than you do, my inability to pay you." He always felt sorry for them and never pressed them again, saying "I am sure they will send to me, knowing now as they do, how much I need it, all they owe me as soon as they possibly can." We never heard from these debtors again. On the contrary they were persistent in their demand for favors later.

Indeed, he soon found that the profits of the firm were hardly enough to maintain two families, and he resigned from the firm.

He made application for the position of county engineer, which became vacant; but for political reasons the board of commissioners, charged with the selection of the engineer, did not give his appointment a majority vote and he did not get the position.

The commissioner responsible for the failure to give Captain Grant the position of county engineer was Dr. William Taussig of Carondelet, Missouri, who in later years stated he had not been entirely sure of the Captain's Union sentiments because of the Dent connection; but in after years General Grant, meeting Dr. Taussig toward the end of the Civil War, thanked him for having prevented his obtaining this position. Grant explained that if he had been appointed he might still be performing the not too important duties of county engineer and would have missed the opportunity for doing more effective service toward the re-establishment of the Union.

In this year of 1859, conditions were rapidly crystallizing into inevitable civil war. On March 7 the Fugitive Slave Act was passed and declared constitutional by the Supreme Court. On July 5 the Kansas Constitutional Convention convened at Wyandotte, Kansas, the chief issue being whether the state should be free or slave. On October 4 an Anti-slavery Constitution was ratified by a vote of 10,421 to 5,530, and on October 16 John Brown seized the arsenal at Harpers Ferry, West Virginia. He was subsequently captured by Colonel Robert E. Lee and on December 2 was hanged at Charlestown for murder, conspiracy and treason. And *Dixie* was composed by Dan Emmett, becoming definitely identified with the Confederacy.

But the year seemed to bring no answer to Grant's employment problems. In a letter written to his father on September 23, 1859, he said:

> Next month I get possession of my own house, when my expenses will be reduced so much that a very moderate salary will support me. If I could get the $3000 note cashed, which I got as the difference in the exchange of property, I could put up with the proceeds two houses that would pay me, at least, $40 per month rent. The note has five years to run, with interest notes given separately and payable annually. . . .
>
> You may judge from the result of the action of the County Commissioners that I am strongly identified with the Democratic Party. Such is not the case. I never voted an out and out Democratic ticket in my life. I voted for Buchanan for President to defeat Fremont, but not because he was my first choice. In all other elections I have universally selected the candidates that, in my estimation, were the best fitted for the different offices, and it never happens that such men are all arrayed on one side. The strongest friend I had in the Board of Commissioners is a Free Soiler but opposition between parties is so strong that he would not vote for any one, no matter how friendly, unless at least one of his own party would go with him. The Free Soil party

felt themselves bound to provide for one of their own party who was defeated for the office of County Engineer; a German who came to the West as an assistant surveyor upon the public lands, and who has held an office ever since.

Captain Grant applied for a position in the Custom House and actually was given temporary appointment which lasted about a month, but it was not a satisfactory permanent solution of his problem. His wife reminded him that some years before his father had offered him partnership with his brothers in the leather store in Galena, and that he might very well now accept such a position, especially in view of the continuing illness (consumption) of his brother, Orvil. Accordingly, Grant moved to Galena with his family in May 1860, and joined his two brothers in the management of the store, accepting his father's plan.

The arrangements for his partnership with his brothers have been too frequently misunderstood and misstated by his biographers. Accordingly, it is pertinent to give the following description by Ulysses S. Grant's eldest son, Frederick Dent Grant, of the actual arrangements made for the Galena business:

My grandfather, Jesse R. Grant, was then living in Covington, Ky. He owned tanneries at Portsmouth on the Ohio River, had a large leather store at Galena, in Illinois; a branch store at LaCrosse, in Wisconsin, and, I think, another store somewhere in Iowa. My Missouri grandfather—and he owned an estate of many hundreds of acres himself—thought my Ohio or Kentucky grandfather a rich man. "Old Mr. Grant," I once heard him say, "must be worth $150,000." Anyway my Grandfather Grant was advancing in years and wanted to distribute his property. It was arranged that my father and his two brothers should manage the tanneries and stores, each to be paid $60 a month for his services, and place the profits of the business in a trust fund for their three sisters. When the accumulated profits amounted to the value of the tanneries and stores the brothers were to have the physical property and the sisters the income from the money in trust. We moved to Galena and took a good house. I recall that I was disgusted because I couldn't go barefooted like other boys and that instead of a hickory shirt and one suspender I had to wear a waist which I buttoned to my short trousers. The store building in Galena was four stories high, and was packed with goods. Behind it was the harness factory which extended to the next street. There was also a large stock of carriage hardware. Father has said that he was a clerk in those days, but he was much more; in time he would have been a partner in the business. I recollect that his salary of $60 a month was less than he really required, and that several gifts of money to my mother from her family in St. Louis helped him considerably. The largest, I think, was about $100. Grandfather Grant was at no time a liberal man. We lived in Galena eleven months and then my father went away to the war. He talked rather freely in the family as soon as it was known that Lincoln had been elected, and he predicted that some of the Southern states would secede. The Dents in St. Louis were rebels. He wrote to them, expressing his sympathy, regretting the coming conflict, but telling them that the South would be whipped. In the evening of the day on which Lincoln made his first call for troops, a public meeting was held in Galena, at which father presided. He never went to the leather store after that meeting to put up a package or do any other business. . . . The war interfered with the plan of partnership. In 1866 Jesse Root Grant was ready to distribute a considerable part of his estate, about $100,000, among his children. General Grant refused to take his share saying he had helped to make none of his father's wealth. The general's children were given $1000 each by their grandfather.

V

Civil War Breaks Out

WHEN the English colonies began to coalesce into one nation preparatory to the American Revolution, the subject of slavery was a matter of contention. In the drafting of the Constitution the question was not definitely decided. The Act of 1807, strengthened by that of 1820, prohibited the slave trade after 1808. But the ownership of slaves was continued without comment. At first the thoughtful and practical people in the country probably felt on the subject very much as George Washington did when on September 9, 1786, he wrote: "I never mean, unless some particular circumstance should compel me to it, to possess another slave by purchase, it being my first wish to see some plan adopted by which slavery in this country may be abolished by law." In 1792, he wrote to Governor Pinckney, of South Carolina, on the same subject: "I was in hopes that motives of policy, supported by the dire effects of slavery, would have operated to produce a total prohibition of the importation of slaves, whenever the question came to be advocated in any state that might be interested in the measure."

Thomas Jefferson appears to have had very much the same attitude and the matter drifted along until the prohibitionists, largely in the northeastern states, became active in pushing for the prohibition of slavery everywhere in the country. The question did not become very acute until the Mexican War added an immense territory to the country, land which was probably well adapted to the use of slaves in its agricultural development. There resulted the debates and public differences of opinion in connection with the Fugitive Slave Bill of September 18, 1850, and the subsequent similar Act of March 7, 1859, which was declared constitutional by the Supreme Court. Finally, public attention throughout the country was focused on the subject by the Lincoln-Douglas debates in 1858.

Without repeating the details of these years of discussion both from the angle of the legality of slavery and also from the point of view of its moral iniquity, the matter seems to have been fairly summarized by the following statement of General Grant:

> In the case of the war between the States it would have been the exact truth if the South had said, "We do not want to live with you Northern people any longer; we know our institution of slavery is obnoxious to you, and, as you are growing numerically stronger than we, it may at some time in the future be endangered. So long as you permitted us to control the government, and with the aid of a few friends at the North to enact laws constituting your section a guard against the escape of our property, we were willing to live with you. You have been submissive to our rule heretofore; but it looks now as if you did not intend to continue so, and we will remain in the Union no longer." Instead of this the seceding States cried lustily, "Let us alone; you have no constitutional power to interfere with us." Newspapers and people at the North reiterated the cry. Individuals might ignore the Constitution; but the nation itself must not only obey it, but must enforce the strictest construction of that instrument—the construction put upon it by the Southerners themselves. The fact is, the Constitution did not apply to any such contingency as the one existing from 1861 to 1865. Its framers never dreamed of such a contingency occurring. If they had foreseen it, the probabilities are that they would have sanctioned the right of a State or States to withdraw rather than that there should be war between brothers.
>
> The framers were wise in their generation, and wanted to do the very best possible to secure their own liberty and independence, and that also of their descendants to the latest days. It is preposterous to suppose that the people of one generation can lay down the best and only rules of government for all who are to come after them, and under unforeseen contingencies. At the time of the framing of our Constitution the only physical forces that had been subdued and made to serve man and do his labor were the currents in the streams and in the air we breathe. Rude machinery, propelled by water-power, had been invented; sails to propel ships upon the waters had been set to catch the passing breeze; but the application of steam to propel vessels against both wind and current, and machinery to do all manner of work, had not been thought of. The instantaneous transmission of messages around the world by means of electricity would probably at that day have been attributed to witchcraft or a league with the devil. Immaterial circumstances had changed

as greatly as material ones. We could not and ought not to be rigidly bound by the rules laid down under circumstances so different for emergencies so utterly unanticipated. The fathers themselves would have been the first to declare that their prerogatives were not irrevocable. They would surely have resisted secession could they have lived to see the shape it assumed.

I traveled through the Northwest considerably during the winter of 1860–61. We had customers in all the little towns in southwest Wisconsin, southeast Minnesota, and northeast Iowa. These generally knew I had been a captain in the regular army and had served through the Mexican war. Consequently, wherever I stopped at night, some of the people would come to the public house where I was, and sit till a late hour discussing the probabilities of the future. My own views at that time were like those officially expressed by Mr. Seward at a later day—that "the war would be over in ninety days." I continued to entertain these views until after the battle of Shiloh. I believe now that there would have been no more battles at the West after the capture of Fort Donelson if all the troops in that region had been under a single commander who would have followed up that victory.

It has become more or less a habit of modern historians of the Civil War to assume that the outcome was inevitable and merely a question of the larger population of the North and its greater industrial capacity to produce arms and equipment. Certainly it was some such estimate of the situation which prompted General Grant and others to expect and hope for a quick conclusion of the War of the Rebellion. However, the task was not so easy; in fact the North had to conquer the southern states to bring them back into the Union.

Jomini, the accepted military authority of that day, had written: "War once decided upon, it will be necessary to make if not *a complete plan of operations, which is always impossible,* at least a system of operations in which an objective is proposed and a base secured." The invention of the telegraph made the overall control of armies in different and widely separated theaters of operation possible, and the railroad made the shifting of considerable bodies of troops from one theater to another practicable. These two factors proved during the Civil War that such a general strategic plan as Jomini had thought impossible was not only possible but necessary, and that the present recognition of the need for such a plan became a tenet of the art of war. Indeed, this was one of the major lessons that came out of the Civil War. We can hardly blame the commanders in general for not having anticipated this lesson, and must give credit to the one who did appreciate it and by its successful application finally brought the war to a close.

Moreover, military strategy must necessarily, especially in a republic, follow the political objectives and policies. It can hardly anticipate them, and for the first year, at least, these political objectives were gradually changing and developing. As the threat of war grew, the political objectives of the slave states were to obtain possession of the federal arsenals and war equipment and arms, and of the coast forts. Appreciating this, General Scott as early as October 29, 1860, recommended a reinforcement of the coast garrisons and even insisted upon a personal interview with President Buchanan; but he was prevented from securing an interview by Secretary of War Floyd.

It is pertinent that General Scott greeted the new President on March 4, 1861, with a letter discussing the situation, and stating the alternative political strategic courses open to him. He estimated that to reconquer the seceded states would require a force of at least 300,000 men, which, maintained at that strength for two or three years, would involve the loss of a third that number, and would cost $250,000,000. In view of this, he rather favored letting the "wayward sisters" go. It must be admitted that the old Commander of the Army made a pretty sound but very conservative strategic estimate in spite of his physical afflictions.

While Fort Sumter was being bombarded, April 12 and 13, and before Virginia had seceded, President Lincoln summarized his political strategy to a Virginia delegation:

> In every event I shall, to the extent of my ability, repel force by force. In case it proves true that Fort Sumter has been assaulted. . . . I shall perhaps cause the U.S. Mails to be withdrawn from all the States which claim to have seceded, believing that the commencement of actual war against the Government justifies and possibly demands this. I scarcely need to say that I consider the military posts and property situated within the states which claim to have seceded as yet belonging to the Government of the United States as much as they did before the supposed secession. Whatever else I may do for this purpose, I shall not attempt to collect the duties and imposts by any armed invasion of any part of the country; not meaning by this, however, that I may not land a force deemed necessary to relieve a fort upon a border country. I shall feel myself at liberty to repossess, if I can, like places which had been seized before the Government devolved upon me.

It is noteworthy that there was no threat of invasion or violation of the territory of the seceded states, beyond the recovery of Federal property.

But all efforts at reconciliation failed, and the opening gun of a shooting war was fired April 12 at Fort Sumter in Charleston Harbor by order of General Beauregard. It is worth recording that the Confederate Secretary of State, Robert Toombs, at the Confederate Cabinet meeting to consider the Charleston situation, had warned: "The firing upon that fort will inaugurate a civil war greater than any the world has yet seen. . . . You will wantonly strike a hornet's nest which extends from mountains to ocean, and legions now quiet will swarm out and sting us to death. It is unnecessary; it puts us in the wrong; it is fatal."

One can but sympathize with President Lincoln at this time. He had to determine what he should do and what he legally could do to save the Union, while distracted by the time-consuming and agonizing job of organizing his new administration under the spoils system and providing immediately for the protection of a capital located in the enemy's country, after the riots in Baltimore cut communications with the North and Virginia seceded. He described the situation without exaggeration when he said he felt like a man letting lodgings in the front of his house when the back was on fire. Moreover, the Treasury was empty and the country broke. The Buchanan Administration's last effort to raise a loan had failed miserably. The offers received were economically unacceptable. We can understand Lincoln's plaint, "Why don't they come? Why don't they come?" when the troops ordered to the capital were trying to reach there in spite of cut rail and telegraph communications. But he proved equal to the emergency.

April 15, 1861, he issued a proclamation, under authority of the 1795 Act, calling on the states for 75,000 militia for three months and convoking Congress for the following July 4. The response was almost embarrassingly enthusiastic. As Emerson wrote: "At the darkest moment in the history of the Republic, when it looked as if the nation would be dismembered, pulverized into its original elements, the attack on Fort Sumter crystallized the North into a unit and the hope of mankind was saved." The President took advantage of the enthusiasm and on May 3 issued a proclamation calling into service 64,748 three-year volunteers for the army and 18,000 for the navy, bringing the aggregate force proposed, including an increase in the Regular Army, to 181,461 men of whom 75,000 were to serve only three months.

Things were happening fast. The following list of certain important dates will help the reader to fit the events that follow into their proper chronological order:

(1) *April 17:* Virginia seceded.

(2) *April 18:* Confederate volunteers occupied Harpers Ferry. Five companies of Pennsylvania volunteers from Harrisburg reached Washington.

(3) *April 20:* Colonel Robert E. Lee was given, and accepted, command of Virginia's troops. (Three months before, on January 23, 1861, he had written his son: "Secession is nothing but revolution. The framers of our Constitution never exhausted so much labour, wisdom, and forbearance in its formation, and surrounded it with so many guards and securities, if it was intended to be broken by every member of the Confederacy at will. It was intended for 'Perpetual Union,' so expressed in the preamble, and for the establishment of a government, not a compact, which can only be resolved by revolution or the consent of all the people in convention assembled.")

(4) *April 21:* Confederate volunteers occupied the Norfolk Navy Yard.

(5) *April 22:* At the request of the War Department, Illinois militia was hurried to Cairo and garrisoned.

(6) *April 24:* General Lee writes to General Ruggles on the Rappahannock: "You will act on the defensive"; and on the 26th to Cocke on the Alexandria line: "It is important that conflict be not provoked until we are ready."

(7) *April 25:* 7th New York reached Washington.

(8) *April 26:* 21,000 stands of arms; 110,000 musket cartridges; and 2 fieldpieces shipped from the St. Louis Arsenal to Alton, Ill.

(9) *April 27:* McClellan, not yet back in Federal service, proposed to Scott a double invasion in the Western Theater of Operations with 80,000 men from Gallipolis via the valley of the Great Kanawah on Richmond, with a right flank guard left at Ironton and a prompt movement on Louisville or the heights opposite Cincinnati. As an alternative, he proposed crossing "the Ohio at Cincinnati or Louisville with 80,000 men, march straight on Nashville, and thence act according to circumstances."

(10) *April 30:* Lincoln authorized Colonel Lyon to muster in 10,000 men for the protection of citizens and U.S. property in St. Louis, and to proclaim martial law.

(11) *May 3:* The Department of the Ohio (Illinois, Indiana and Ohio) was established with McClellan in command.

(12) *May 3 and 21:* Scott in two letters to McClellan proposed his Anaconda plan, establishing a cordon of posts along the Ohio and a moving column of 60,000 regular and especially instructed volunteers to start down the Mississippi, partly marching and partly by boat, to extend the cordon there and so blockade the principal seceding states by land! To this he added, "The greatest obstacle in the way of this plan—the great danger now pressing upon us—is the impatience of our patriotic and loyal Union friends. They will urge instant and vigorous action, regardless, I fear, of consequences . . ."

(13) The enthusiasm in response to Lincoln's action and the assurance that the administration was bent upon re-establishing the Union solved the economic problem for the time being, and Secretary Chase was able by May 8 to have a loan of $10,000,000 financed and then an additional $23,000,000.

(14) *May 10:* General Lee given command of all Confederate troops in Virginia, and Colonel Lyon captures the Confederate militia in Camp Jackson, St. Louis.

(15) *May 13:* Queen Victoria's declaration of neutrality.

(16) *May 14:* Eads sent to McClellan with design for river gunboats.

(17) *May 16:* Commander John Rodgers sent to Cincinnati "to establish naval armament on Mississippi and Ohio Rivers."

(18) *May 24:* Arlington Heights and Alexandria occupied by Union troops.

We have seen that on April 18, 1861, a public meeting was held in Galena at which Captain Grant was prevailed upon to preside. John A. Rawlins, an elector on the Douglas ticket, B. B. Howard, the postmaster and a Breckinridge Democrat, and E. B. Washburne made patriotic speeches. This meeting resulted in the decision to raise a company of volunteers in Galena, which was later known as the Joe Davis Guards. Captain Grant was offered command of the company, but refused it as a lesser command than he felt his military service and experience justified. However, he promised to drill it and give it instruction and actually went to Springfield with the company to carry out his promise. The ladies of Galena were as patriotic and as anxious to "do their bit" as the men; so they decided that the Galena company should go to Springfield to be mustered in fully uniformed. To accomplish this, they organized sewing circles to tailor and sew the uniforms for their men.

On April 21, 1861, Captain Grant wrote to his father from Galena as follows:

We are now in the midst of trying times when every one must be for or against his country, and show his colors too, by his every act. Having been educated for such an emergency, at the expense of the Government, I feel that it has upon me superior claims, such claims as no ordinary motives of self-interest can surmount. I do not wish to act hastily or unadvisedly in the matter, and as there are more than enough to respond to the first call of the President, I have not yet offered myself. I have promised, and am giving all the assistance I can in organizing the company whose services have been accepted from this place. I have promised further to go with them to the State capital, and if I can be of service to the Governor in organizing his state troops to do so. What I ask now is your approval of the course I am taking, or advice in the matter. A letter written this week will reach me in Springfield. I have not time to write to you but a hasty line, for, though Sunday as it is, we are all busy here. In a few minutes I shall be engaged in directing tailors in the style and trim of uniform for our men.

Whatever may have been my political opinions before, I have but one sentiment now. That is, we have a Government, and laws and a flag, and they must all be sustained. There are but two parties now, traitors and patriots, and I want hereafter to be ranked with the latter, and I trust, the stronger party. I do not know but you may be placed in an awkward position, and a dangerous one pecuniarily, but costs cannot now be counted. My advice would be to leave where you are if you are not safe with the views you entertain. I would never stultify my opinion for the sake of a little security.

I will say nothing about our business. Orvil and Lank will keep you posted as to that.

Write soon and direct as above.

When the Galena company had been mustered into the United States service as part of the 11th Illinois Volunteer Infantry, Captain Grant felt that his duties in Springfield were over. He was preparing to start home by the evening train when Governor Yates accosted him and asked him to stay over in the capital that night and to call at the Executive Office the next morning. As the governor had been staying at the same hotel, he knew the captain by sight and addressed him by his old army title, "Captain." Of course Grant complied with the request and the next day was assigned to the adjutant general's office, the governor saying that his army experience should be of great use at that time, as indeed it proved to be. Although not considering himself at all qualified as a clerk, Captain Grant had been quartermaster, commissary, and adjutant in the field and was therefore familiar with the forms and could give instructions as to how to make them out. He was assisted by a Mr. Loomis, who proved to be an expert accountant and remained in this position until the end of the war, having a great reputation for accuracy.

Captain Grant was also appointed mustering officer for the ten additional regiments authorized by the Illinois Legislature. While he was assisted by some other officers in carrying out this mission, he mustered in three of the regiments himself in the southern point of the state. One of these regiments was to assemble at Belleville, about eighteen miles southeast of St. Louis. Finding upon his arrival at Belleville that only a few of the companies had arrived and there was no probability of the regiment being assembled in less than five days, he decided to go to St. Louis for those days. A considerable part of the Missouri State Militia had been assembled at Camp Jackson on the outer limits of St. Louis, and it was generally understood that Governor Claiborne F. Jackson intended to use them to seize the United States Arsenal and the city of St. Louis for the Confederate cause. F. P. Blair, a St. Louis political leader of strong Union sentiments, raised a regiment for Federal service and reported with it to Captain Nathaniel Lyon, who was commanding the arsenal and had under him a guard of two companies. Lyon and Mr. Blair and their troops captured Camp Jackson by a surprise attack and saved the arsenal with its arms and ammunition and the important city itself for the Union cause. It was a bold, effective and important strategic action, which Captain Grant was able to witness. He also saw the confusion of the population's loyalties resulting from the action. It was now the time for the Union men in St. Louis to become aggressive and throw their weight around, while the Confederate sympathizers became less active although resentful and abusive.

On May 24, 1861, Captain Grant addressed the following letter to U.S. Adjutant General Lorenzo Thomas, offering his services in the emergency:

Sir: Having served for fifteen years in the Regular Army, including four years at West Point, and feeling it the duty of every one who has been educated at the government expense to offer their services for the support of that government, I have the honor, very respectfully, to tender my services until the close of the war in such capacity as may be offered. I would say, in view of my present age and length of service, I feel myself competent to command a regiment if the President, in his judgment, should see fit to intrust one to me. Since the first call of the President, I have been serving on the staff of the Governor of this State, rendering such aid as I could in the organization of our State militia, and am still engaged in that capacity. A letter addressed to me at Springfield, Illinois, will reach me.

After completing the mustering in of the Illinois regiments, there was not very much for Captain Grant to do, and he obtained leave of absence to visit his parents in Covington, Kentucky, opposite Cincinnati on the Ohio River. George B. McClellan had been commissioned major general and had established his headquarters in Cincinnati. Captain Grant had in mind that it would be easy to visit him there, and hoped that when the general saw him he would remember their service together at West Point, in Mexico, and in California, and would perhaps offer him a position on his staff. But after calling on him two days in succession and failing to see him on either occasion, Grant returned to Springfield.

Earlier, on May 2, in a letter to his father he had written from Springfield of the enthusiasm to volunteer for service in the war. "I should have offered myself for the Colonelcy of one of the regiments, but I find all those places are wanted by politicians who are up to log-rolling and I do not care to be under such persons. . . . I am serving on the Governor's staff at present at his request, but suppose I shall not be here long."

On May 6 he wrote to his father that owing to the rainy weather, drills were suspended at the Springfield camp and he was about to go home when Governor Yates asked him to remain; he thought it would not be for long, and for several days at least he was in command of the camp. However, the 21st Regiment of Illinois Volunteers, which Captain Grant had mustered in at Mattoon, refused to go into the service with the colonel they had elected. Governor Yates appointed Grant colonel of this troublesome regiment on June 15. His predecessor had been unsuccessful in establishing any sort of discipline. The regiment soon recognized that in Grant it had a commanding officer from whom they could expect human understanding, justice, and discipline. On June 28, after listening to the reasoned and persuasive speeches of two Illinois Democratic Congressmen, John A. Logan and John A. Mc-

Clernand, 603 members of the regiment volunteered to enter the U.S. service.

Knowing that there is no better way of breaking in new troops than giving them necessary training, Grant—when his regiment was ordered to go to Quincy, on the Mississippi River—proposed to march the men there and refused to ask for railroad transportation. When the regiment had reached Naples on foot, its orders were changed to go by steamer to Ironton. These orders in turn were amended, calling for the regiment to go to relieve a regiment reported surrounded at Palmyra, Missouri. Grant recounts his feelings in the *Memoirs*:

> My sensations as we approached what I supposed might be "a field of battle" were anything but agreeable. I had been in all the engagements in Mexico that it was possible for one person to be in, but not in command. If some one else had been colonel and I had been lieutenant-colonel I do not think I would have felt any trepidation. Before we were prepared to cross the Mississippi River at Quincy my anxiety was relieved, for the men of the besieged regiment came straggling into town. I am inclined to think both sides got frightened and ran away.

In a few days he took his regiment from Palmyra to Salt River, where the railroad bridge had been destroyed by the enemy. Colonel John M. Palmer, commanding the 14th Illinois, was guarding the workmen engaged in rebuilding the bridge, and, being senior, commanded the two regiments while they were together. The 21st Illinois was ordered, upon completion of the bridge in about two weeks, to move against Colonel Thomas Harris, alleged to be in camp at the little town of Florida about 25 miles to the south. Characteristic of American armies in the beginning of hostile operations, the regiments at Palmyra had no transportation, and because of the country's being sparsely settled it took several days to secure teams and drivers enough to haul the regiment's camp and garrison equipage with a week's supply of provisions and some ammunition. On the march south to Colonel Harris's encampment, no person was encountered and every house appeared to be deserted. Grant wrote in the *Memoirs:*

> As we approached the brow of the hill from which it was expected we could see Harris's camp, and possibly find his men ready formed to meet us, my heart kept getting higher and higher, until it felt to me as though it was in my throat. I would have given anything then to have been back in

Illinois, but I had not the moral courage to halt and consider what to do; I kept right on. When we reached a point from which the valley below was in full view, I halted. The place where Harris had been encamped a few days before was still there, and the marks of a recent encampment were plainly visible, but the troops were gone. My heart resumed its place. It occurred to me at once that Harris had been as much afraid of me as I had been of him. This was a view of the question I had never taken before, but it was one I never forgot afterward. From that event to the close of the war I never experienced trepidation upon confronting an enemy, though I always felt more or less anxiety. I never forgot that he had as much reason to fear my forces as I had his. The lesson was valuable.

Major General John C. Frémont was in command of the Western Department with headquarters in St. Louis, and the strange changes of orders given to Colonel Grant show the lack of any general plan of operations and a certain tendency to try and meet all rumored enemy action. During this period the 21st Illinois was moved first from the Salt River Bridge to Mexico, Missouri. The colonel of the regiment noted on the regiment's march back to Salt River Bridge from the town of Florida that the citizens living on the line of march had returned to their houses and, finding everything in good order, were at their front doors ready to greet the regiment. The idea that national troops carried death and devastation with them had proven untrue. However, other regiments had not been so carefully supervised, and upon reaching Mexico and taking general command of the subdistrict embracing the troops in the immediate neighborhood (some three regiments of infantry and a section of artillery), Colonel Grant promptly issued orders prohibiting soldiers from going into private houses except when invited by the inhabitants, from appropriating private property to their own or to government uses, and from carrying muskets out of camp. Consequently he received very marked courtesy from the citizens of the town of Mexico while there.

During his stay there the regiment was camped near open ground where regimental drill was practicable. The new colonel himself had had nothing other than company drill under the new Hardee tactics. He therefore began a study of the new regulations. When after an evening's study, he rode out in front of his regiment the following morning, he realized that if he attempted to follow the lesson he had studied, he would have to clear away some of the houses and garden fences to make room for the maneuver. It was soon obvious, however, that the French tactics, which Hardee had translated, were an application of common sense to the old Scott system, which called for a halt before almost every change in the formation. With the new tactics these changes could be made without stopping a movement. There seemed to be no difficulty in finding commands that would permit the colonel to lead the regiment wherever he wanted it to go.

After he had been in the town of Mexico several weeks, Colonel Grant noticed in a St. Louis newspaper that the President had recommended him for promotion to brigadier general on the unanimous recommendation of the Illinois delegation in Congress. The presidential appointment was of July 31, 1861, and confirmed by the Senate on August 5, but the commission was dated May 17.

This presented for him the problem of constituting the prescribed small brigade staff. Thinking that he should have one staff officer from his original regiment, he selected Lieutenant C. B. Lagow for one of his aides. Another, Captain William S. Hillyer, he selected from the law firm of McClelland, Moody and Hillyer; he had known Hillyer in St. Louis. Wishing also to take one staff member from his home in Galena, he asked for an eloquent and locally respected lawyer, who had been an elector on the Douglas ticket. He had proved enthusiastically loyal, however, when word came of the firing on Fort Sumter, and had participated in the first war meeting in Galena. This man was John A. Rawlins. Neither Lagow nor Hillyer developed any particular taste or special qualifications for their duties as aides. Lagow resigned during the Vicksburg campaign and Hillyer was relieved soon after the Battle of Chattanooga. Rawlins remained with his new chief as long as he lived and rose to the rank of brigadier general and Chief of Staff to the General of the Army, an office created for him before the end of the war.

Shortly after Grant's promotion he was ordered to Ironton, Missouri, to command a district in that part of the state. He took the 21st Illinois with him. Several other regiments were ordered to the same destination at about the same time, and when General Grant reached Ironton around August 8, Colonel B. Gratz Brown, later to be governor of the state and in 1872 vice-presidential candidate, was in command. Some of his troops, who were ninety-day men and whose time had expired, had no clothing but what they had volunteered in, and much of this was so worn it hardly hung together.

General William J. Hardee, author of the tactics, was at Greenville, some 25 miles south, with 5,000 Confederate troops. Under the circumstances, Colonel Brown's command was much demoralized; and the Colonel himself was very happy to see and be relieved by General Grant, who sent all the former's men home within a few days to be mustered out of service. General Grant felt ready, within ten days of reaching Ironton, to take the offensive against the enemy at Greenville, and made various dispositions for this purpose. He was expecting to take personal command of the movement, but on the eve of this, General B. M. Prentiss arrived with orders to take command of the district. His orders did not relieve General Grant of the command, which the latter held by seniority that no authority at that time could disregard. So Grant started for St. Louis the same day, after giving General Prentiss a description of the situation of the troops and general condition of affairs. The expedition was abandoned by General Prentiss.

From St. Louis General Grant was ordered to Jefferson City, capital of the state, to take command there. The Confederate general, Sterling Price, was thought to be threatening the capital, Lexington, Chillicothe, and other large towns in the central part of Missouri. A good many Federal troops were in Jefferson City but in great confusion, and nobody knew who was there. Colonel James A. Mulligan was supposedly in command, but although he was a gallant officer he lacked knowledge and experience to handle the situation. Many of the volunteers claimed to have obtained permission from the department commander to raise regiments, battalions, or companies; commissions were to be issued according to the number of men each brought in for the service. Soldiers were also being recruited for different terms of service, in spite of the law requiring them to serve for three years or the duration of the war. The confusion was enhanced by Union fugitives driven from their homes by Confederate irregulars. Many of the fugitives were in deplorable condition and on the verge of starvation. General Grant soon restored order, stopping the recruiting business and disposing the troops about the outskirts of the city so as to guard all approaches.

He had been in Jefferson City only a few days when he was directed by department headquarters to fit out an expedition to go to Lexington, Boonville, and Chillicothe to take all funds the banks had and send them to St. Louis. Since the western army had no transportation, it was necessary to secure teams from sympathizers with the rebellion or to hire them from Union men, with the opportunity of giving employment to such refugees as had teams suitable for the purpose. Within eight days General Grant had all the troops from Jefferson City (except a small garrison) in an advanced position; he expected to rejoin them the next day. While waiting in his office before starting for the front, Grant saw an officer of rank approaching. He proved to be Colonel Jefferson C. Davis, bearing an order for himself to proceed to Jefferson City to relieve General Grant of command, and directing Grant to report at department headquarters in St. Louis without delay, to receive important special instructions. As the regular daily train would depart in an hour, Grant turned over to Colonel Davis his orders and hurriedly explained to him the preparations made to carry out the department commander's wishes. Within the hour he was on the train to St. Louis, leaving a single staff officer to follow the next day with horses and baggage.

The "important special instructions" proved to be his assignment to command the district of southeast Missouri, embracing territory south of St. Louis in that state, as well as all of southern Illinois. At first he was to take personal command of a combined expedition to capture Colonel Jeff Thompson, a more or less independent partisan commander who was disputing possession of southeast Missouri with the Union troops. Some of the troops had been ordered to move from Ironton to Cape Girardeau on the Mississippi River, some seventy miles to the south; the forces at Cape Girardeau had been ordered to move west to Jackson (on the road to Ironton); and the troops at Cairo and Bird's Point in Illinois were to hold themselves in readiness to move down the Mississippi to Belmont, about eighteen miles downstream, to be moved west from there when General Grant took command of them. His headquarters were to be at Cairo, but in pursuance of these orders he established temporary headquarters at Cape Girardeau and sent instructions to the commanding officer at Jackson, Missouri, to inform him of the approach of Prentiss from Ironton.

Neither Prentiss nor Marsh, in command at Jackson, knew his destination. General Grant had drafted instructions for the contemplated move but kept them in his pocket until he heard of the junction of his troops in Jackson. A few days after his arrival at Cape Girardeau he heard that General Prentiss was approaching Jackson and planned to meet him there and give him his orders. But Prentiss directly arrived in Cape Girardeau. He was given his orders, but seemed much aggrieved at being placed under another brigadier general to whom he believed himself superior.

Prentiss had been in command at Cairo when Grant had been mustering officer for the state and without Federal military status. The commissions of both, as brigadier generals, had been dated May 17, 1861; but Grant by virtue of his army rank and previous service was a senior under the existing law.

General Prentiss failed to get orders to his troops to remain at Jackson, as he had been instructed, and they were reported approaching Cape Girardeau. General Grant then ordered him to take his command back to Jackson. He obeyed, but bade his command good-by when he reached Jackson and then proceeded to St. Louis, which broke up the expedition. However, this was without important consequences, since Jeff Thompson had no fixed place for even nominal headquarters and was as much at home in Arkansas as in Missouri; he could therefore be depended upon to avoid any meeting with a superior force. Prentiss was sent to another part of the state.

General Grant regretted General Prentiss' action. It kept Prentiss out of the following campaign, and as a result he did not receive promotion that would have come to him had he remained second-in-command in the district of southeast Missouri.

Early in September 1861 General Grant moved his headquarters to Cairo, Illinois. A few days later a man representing himself as a scout of General Frémont reported to Grant. He said that he had come from Columbus, a point on the Mississippi in Kentucky, twenty miles below Cairo. Confederate troops from Columbus were planning to seize Paducah, at the mouth of the Tennessee River. Telegraphing the department commander this news, Grant reported that he planned to leave that night and secure this strategic point before the enemy could reach it. Boats were available and troops loaded; the expedition started before midnight and arrived early the morning of September 6, anticipating the enemy by six or eight hours. There was great astonishment among the people of Paducah, who were expecting Confederate forces to take possession that day; and in fact there were 4,000 men from Columbus, already within ten or fifteen miles of Paducah and intent on occupying that town. Although the Union force was but two regiments of infantry and one battery, the enemy did not know this and returned to Columbus.

After stationing his troops to guard the roads leading into the town and leaving some gunboats to police the river front, General Grant issued a proclamation to the people of Paducah, assuring them that only persons in rebellion against the Federal Government and their abettors need fear any interference by the Union force, which had come in their midst only to preserve the peace and prevent their city's take-over by the enemy. This proclamation, written in a hurry by the young brigadier general, proved strangely in accord with the principles laid down by the War Department in General Orders No. 100 of 1863, which was the first codification of the laws and customs of civilized warfare attempted. After issuing this proclamation, which relieved the fears of the population and prevented any violence or disorder, the commanding general returned to his headquarters in Cairo.

In a letter to his sister, Mary, dated September 11, 1861, General Grant told of the taking of Paducah and then explained his refusal to get a position for someone recommended by his father.

> I receive letters from all over the country for such places, but do not answer them. I never asked for my present position, but now that I have it I intend to perform the duties as rigidly as I know how without looking out for places for others. I should be very glad if I had a position within my own gift for Al. but I have not.
>
> My duties are very laborious and have been from the start. It is a rare thing that I get to bed before two or three o'clock in the morning and am usually wakened in the morning before getting awake in a natural way. Now, however, my staff are getting a little in the way of this kind of business and can help me.

At this time Brigade Surgeon John H. Brinton reported for duty and has left the following personal description:

> Of the many who have written of him, made speeches about him, applauded him, and flattered him, few, very few are left who saw him, and watched him, and studied him as I did. From the very first, he attracted me, and I felt very soon, and indeed at the time of the battle of Belmont, Mo., wrote home, that the man had come who would finish this war, should he have the chance.
>
> I first saw General Grant at the dinner table, when I was introduced to him by Dr. Simons, receiving from him a friendly nod. On the same evening I went into the bank. Behind the counter, the general and his assistant

adjutant general, Jno. A. Rawlins, or Captain Rawlins, as he was then, were seated at a little round table. I fancy that I wanted to write a letter home, for I remember that the general very kindly asked me to sit down, and continued his work with Rawlins. I had then a good opportunity to observe him, and I did so very closely. He was then a very different looking man from the General Grant, or the President of after days. As I first saw him, he was a very short, small, rather spare man with full beard and moustache. His beard was a little long, very much longer than he afterwards wore it, unkempt and irregular, and of a sandy, tawny shade. His hair matched his beard, and at first glance he seemed to be a very ordinary sort of man, indeed one below the average in most respects. But as I sat and watched him then, and many an hour afterwards, I found that his face grew upon me. His eyes were gentle with a kind expression, and thoughtful. He did not, as a rule, speak a great deal. At that time he seemed to be turning matters over in his mind, and to be very much occupied indeed with the work of the hour. He did nothing carelessly, but worked slowly, every now and then stopping and taking his pipe out of his mouth.

But this reminds me, that I have not yet spoken of his pipe. The man in after days became so thoroughly identified with the cigar, that people could scarcely believe that he was once an assiduous smoker of the pipe. Well, the pipe which he first used was a meerschaum with a curved stem eight or ten inches long, which allowed the pipe to hang down. He smoked steadily and slowly and evidently greatly enjoyed his tobacco.

Dr. Brinton was sent to St. Louis on September 16, 1861, in charge of some sick. Upon his return he was assigned to supervising the establishment of what came to be called the Mound City Hospital. For this purpose some buildings at Mound City were purchased which had been constructed for warehouses, but never so used.

The establishment of this first military hospital in the West proved to be quite a job and called for all the resourcefulness and energy of Dr. Brinton. There was a considerable wave of patriotic volunteering of women as nurses, but when it came to finding people to scrub the floors and make the beds and wash the linen, the response was far from adequate. Obtaining people to perform such chores proved a serious problem. Naturally the soldiers—big, husky, western farmhands, miners, and such—considered this woman's work and claimed that they had volunteered to fight, not wash and scrub. Many women volunteer nurses were a problem because they expected furnished quarters with mirrors, china, and other items hardly obtainable. However, apparently at Dr.

Brinton's suggestion to some of the Roman Catholic religious orders, six sisters of the Holy Cross from St. Mary's Academy, Notre Dame, Indiana, presented themselves at Cairo along with their mother superior, Mother Angela Gillespie, and asked to be assigned to duty. They were followed by others and, although, belonging to a teaching order, they fitted in very well. The Holy Cross Sisters eventually numbered 80 volunteers. They served on the Red Rover, the Navy's first hospital ship, and staffed 12 military hospitals: 3 in Paducah, 3 in Memphis, 1 each in Mound City and Cairo, Illinois, St. Louis and Franklin, Missouri, Louisville, Kentucky and Washington, D. C.

About November 1, General Grant was directed from department headquarters to make a demonstration on both sides of the Mississippi River, for the purpose of keeping the rebels at Columbus within their fortified line. Before the troops could be sent on this mission, information was received of the location of 3,000 of the enemy on the St. Francis River southwest of Cairo; Grant was directed to send another force against them. On November 5 word came that the rebels were about to detach a considerable force to be moved from Columbus in boats down the Mississippi and up the White River in Arkansas, in order to reinforce General Sterling Price, and this was to be prevented if possible.

The directions thus received presented a rather complicated problem of distribution of his command to the young brigadier general. He designated a regiment under Colonel W. H. L. Wallace from Bird's Point to overtake and reinforce Colonel Oglesby with orders to march to New Madrid, some distance below Columbus on the Missouri side of the river. At the same time General C. F. Smith was ordered to move from Paducah all the troops he could spare in a demonstration against Columbus. Finally, General Grant gathered up all the troops at Cairo and Fort Holt, Kentucky, except necessary guards, and moved them in steamboats down the river, with two wooden gunboats (*Tyler* and *Lexington*) convoying them, and accompanying them himself in command.

This last force consisted of some 3,000 men, embracing five regiments of infantry, two guns, and two companies of cavalry. On the sixth this latter force went downstream to within about six miles of Columbus, dropping off a few men on the Kentucky side to establish pickets to make connections with General C. F. Smith's troops when they arrived from Paducah. The gunboat *Tyler* was below the transports preparatory to opening fire on Fort Columbus at daylight, when at 2 A.M. the situation changed abruptly with the arrival of a special courier from Colonel Wallace. The courier brought the wholly unexpected message that a reliable Union man had reported the enemy crossing troops from Fort Columbus with a view to cutting off Colonel Oglesby's column. This seemed likely enough to General Grant. In addition to the mission of preventing troops' going to Price, Grant now had the problem of protecting his western column.

The following quotation from the third volume of Kenneth P. Williams' *Lincoln Finds a General* is a vivid account of the test presented to General Grant:

It was an hour heavy with destiny for the United States. Grant faced a quick decision. The decision would show the kind of general that he was; and on that would depend the future of the nation. The stage was appropriate to the importance of the act that was being played: the great river lapping against the vessels; the quiet, darkened boats, barely visible in the moonless night; the sentinels on the decks; some men sleeping easily, others restless; the protecting gunboats with their alert watches peering into the night, waiting for an hour to pass before they would drop down to engage the forts; a mist rising from the broad waters and slowly gathering into fog; and in the lighted cabin of the *Belle Memphis* the general who had read the unexpected message. The very hour was chosen to make the test more searching; for it was one when resolution often wanes. Napoleon was wont to speak of "three-o'clock-in-the-morning courage."

Grant decided that he would change the demonstration into an attack. He would do more than "menace Belmont"; he would throw everything he had into a sharp blow against the enemy regiments reported to have crossed the river. That would keep them from cutting off Oglesby; and it would give his regiments the battle that they wanted, and his battery the opportunity to see what it could do. Rawlins, with eight weeks of schooling behind him, already devoted to his chief, wrote the order. He set down the hour as "2 o'clock a.m."; the decision had been made as quickly as that. Then followed the sentence, "The troops composing the present expedition from this place will move promptly at 6 o'clock this morning." In a slight reorganization of the force, Colonel Henry Dougherty was given command of a small brigade consisting of his own Twenty-second Illinois and the Seventh Iowa; he was to follow McClernand's brigade. At a place beyond the range of enemy guns, to be selected by Commander Walke, the expedition was to debark upon the Missouri shore. It was an adequate order, with no waste of words.

It is hardly necessary to give the details of the battle that followed, except that orders were sent to Colonel Oglesby to retire toward Belmont, probably as a reserve in case the attack decided on was not entirely successful. General Grant wrote the following letter to his father on November 8 after returning to Cairo. It gives a clear statement of the way he viewed the action and its success:

It is late at night and I want to get a letter into the mail for you before it closes. As I have just finished a very hasty letter to Julia that contains about what I would write, and having something else to do myself, I will have my clerk copy it.

Day before yesterday, I left here with about 3000 men in five steamers, convoyed by two gun boats, and proceeded down the river to within twelve miles of Columbus. The next morning the boats were dropped down just out of range of the enemy's batteries and the troops debarked.

During this operation our gun boats exercised the rebels by throwing shells into their camps and batteries.

When all ready we proceeded about one mile towards Belmont opposite Columbus; then I formed the troops into line, and ordered two companies from each regiment to deploy as skirmishers, and push on through the woods and discover the position of the enemy. They had gone but a little way when they were fired upon, and the *ball* may be said to have fairly opened.

The whole command with the exception of a small reserve, was then deployed in like manner with the first, and ordered forward. The order was obeyed with great alacrity, the men all showing great courage. I can say with gratification that every Colonel without a single exception, set an example to his command that inspired a confidence that will always insure victory when there is the slightest possibility of gaining one. I feel truly proud to command such men. From here we fought our way from tree to tree through the woods to Belmont, about two and a half miles, the enemy contesting every foot of ground. Here the enemy had strengthened their position by felling the trees for two or three hundred yards and sharpening the limbs, making a sort of abattis. Our men charged through making the victory complete, giving us possession of their camp and garrison equipage, artillery and everything else.

We got a great many prisoners. The majority however succeeded in getting aboard their steamer and pushing across the river.

We burned everything possible and started back, having accomplished all that we went for and even more. Belmont is entirely covered by the batteries from Columbus and is worth nothing as a military position. It cannot be held without Columbus.

The object of the expedition was to prevent the enemy from sending a force into Missouri to cut off troops I had sent there for a special purpose, and to prevent reinforcing Price.

Besides being well fortified at Columbus their numbers far exceed ours, and it would have been folly to have attacked them. We found the Confederates well-armed and brave. On our return, stragglers that had been left in our rear, *now front,* fired into us, and more recrossed the river and gave us battle for fully a mile and afterwards at the boats when we were embarking. There was no hasty retreating or running away. Taking into account the object of the expedition the victory was most complete. It has given me a confidence in the officers and men of this command, that will enable me to lead them in any future engagement without fear of the result. General McClernand—(who by the way acted with great coolness throughout, and proved that he is a soldier as well as statesman)—and myself each had our horses shot under us. Most of the field-officers met with the same loss, besides nearly one third of them being killed or wounded themselves. As nearly as I can ascertain our loss was about 250 killed, wounded, and missing.

I write in great haste to get this in the office tonight.

It will be noted that in the fifth paragraph in the above letter General Grant says: "The whole command with the exception of a small reserve, was then deployed in like manner with the first, and ordered forward. The order was obeyed with great alacrity, the men all showing great courage." This extended-order formation was an innovation on the prescribed tactics then in use, and as the only time that General Grant was in immediate tactical control of his troops during the Civil War it is of interest that he instinctively put his attacking force in extended order. Apparently he did not realize the importance of this innovation sufficiently to require its adoption in his larger commands. In fact, it was not until the Boer War that the necessity for open-order formation was recognized; but Grant had more or less done it instinctively in this one case when he was in immediate contact and prescribing in person the attack formation. The adoption of open order in attack in both armies might have saved many lives in the Civil War.

The day after the battle General Grant went, by arrangement with some of General Polk's officers, to bury the dead at Belmont and to exchange prisoners. In his *Memoirs* he relates another incident:

While on the truce-boat I mentioned to an officer whom I had known both at West Point and in the Mexican War, that I was in the corn-field near their troops when they passed; that I had been on horseback and had worn a soldier's overcoat at the time. This officer was on General Polk's staff. He said both he and the general had seen me, and that Polk had said to his men, "There is a Yankee; you may try your marksmanship on him if you wish"; but nobody fired at me.

Although the results were favorable insofar as they developed the closer organization and co-operation of the troops when under fire and accomplished the mission assigned, there was a great newspaper argument and quite a fuss—both on the Union side and Confederate sides—over whether this was a victory. But the unprejudiced reader today will probably be convinced by the fact that the Union column's mission was accomplished to the satisfaction of its commander and the rebel move to send an expedition westward into Missouri was prevented.

Late in October, Dr. Brinton was appointed acting medical director in the absence of Surgeon James Simons. It was during this period that the doctor in a letter said: "General Grant (an old regular) is very kind to me and helps me out of many a tight place, so also does Captain Hawkins (regular). We are quite intimate. Grant is a plain, straightforward, peremptory and prompt man. If I ask for anything it is done at once, the great secret in all military matters." Brinton got up from a sick bed to accompany the Belmont expedition.

Two days after the Battle of Belmont, General Frémont was relieved of command of the department and was succeeded by Major General H. W. Halleck. The latter was a well-known officer in the army, nicknamed "Old Brains" probably because he had qualified as a lawyer after resigning from the army and was practicing law in San Francisco. He had also made a translation of Jomini's works that had been studied at West Point. Halleck was the author of *Elements of Military Art and Science* (1846) and other books of professional interest, such as *International Law, or Rules Regulating the Intercourse of States in Peace and War* (1861). Although undoubtedly well versed in the literature of military operations, he seems to this writer to have shown lack of decision and stamina as a commanding general.

VI

Fort Henry and Fort Donelson

IN an article published in *McClure's Magazine* in 1895, Colonel John M. Thayer described a meeting—in 1861—with General Grant at Pilot Knob, Missouri. He found the General immersed in maps and studying the general military situation. While at that time he could hardly have decided on the best line of attack against the Confederate forces, he must have made up his mind that the most inviting way to break the Confederate line of defense—which extended from Columbus on the Mississippi in the west to eastern Kentucky and the general vicinity of Cumberland Gap—would be to move his army by boat up the Tennessee River, capture Fort Henry, and then send the fleet around to the Cumberland and up that river to capture Fort Donelson.

He thought so well of this plan, and was so anxious to have his men actively engaged in opposition to the enemy, that he obtained a somewhat grudging consent to visit St. Louis in order to lay the matter before General Halleck. However, he received no encouragement whatever from Halleck and returned to Cairo much crestfallen. Grant's next military move was a maneuver in January, 1862, intended to help Brigadier General Don Carlos Buell. Buell was in command of the Department of the Ohio with headquarters at Louisville, and he was confronted by Simon B. Buckner, who commanded a larger Confederate force at Bowling Green. Grant's demonstration was successful in preventing the sending of reinforcements to Bowling Green and in giving General George H. Thomas an opportunity to fight and win the Battle of Mill Springs.

General Grant was encouraged by General C. F. Smith's agreeing with him cordially as to the possibility of capturing Fort Henry and perhaps Fort Heiman, which stood on higher ground across the river from Fort Henry. Quite a number of steamers, suitable for use as transports, and some gunboats had been gathered at Cairo. The little fleet of gunboats was under command of Flag Officer Andrew H. Foote, with whom General Grant was fortunate in establishing cordial relations for co-operation and mutual support. On January 28, General Grant telegraphed the department commander that he could take and hold Fort Henry if permitted, and Flag Officer Foote sent a similar telegram. On February 1 this was answered with full instructions to move on Fort Henry and the expedition started on the second.

As the number of boats available was not enough to carry at one time the 17,000 men he proposed to move up the Tennessee River, General Grant loaded the boats with more than half his force and sent General McClernand in command. Grant then followed with a boat that had arrived later; he found McClernand had stopped about nine miles below Fort Henry. The seven gunboats under Flag Officer Foote had accompanied the advance force. The transports were unloaded and sent back to Paducah to bring another division with General C. F. Smith in command. General Grant accompanied them, to hurry the reloading.

Because the river was swollen, part of the ground on which Fort Henry stood was as much as two feet under water. Fort Heiman, on high ground, commanded Fort Henry entirely. Because of the importance of Fort Henry and Fort Donelson, only eleven miles distant, it was to be expected that the enemy would throw reinforcements in from wherever obtainable; therefore prompt action on the part of the Union commander was evidently called for. Orders were issued at 11 A.M. on February 6 to start the troops and gunboats at the same time, the troops to invest the garrison and the gunboats to attack the fort at close quarters. General Smith, meanwhile, was to have arrived and landed a brigade on the west bank to get in the rear of Fort Heiman. Brigadier General Lloyd Tilghman, who was commanding Fort Henry, had sent his entire command, except about a hundred men to man the guns in the fort, to the outworks on the road to Dover and Donelson. He and staff were captured with ninety men, as well as the armament of the fort, ammunition and stores. The Union cavalry pursued the retreating column toward Fort Donelson, picking up two guns and a few stragglers. The gunboats had been hit many times but no serious damage had been done, except

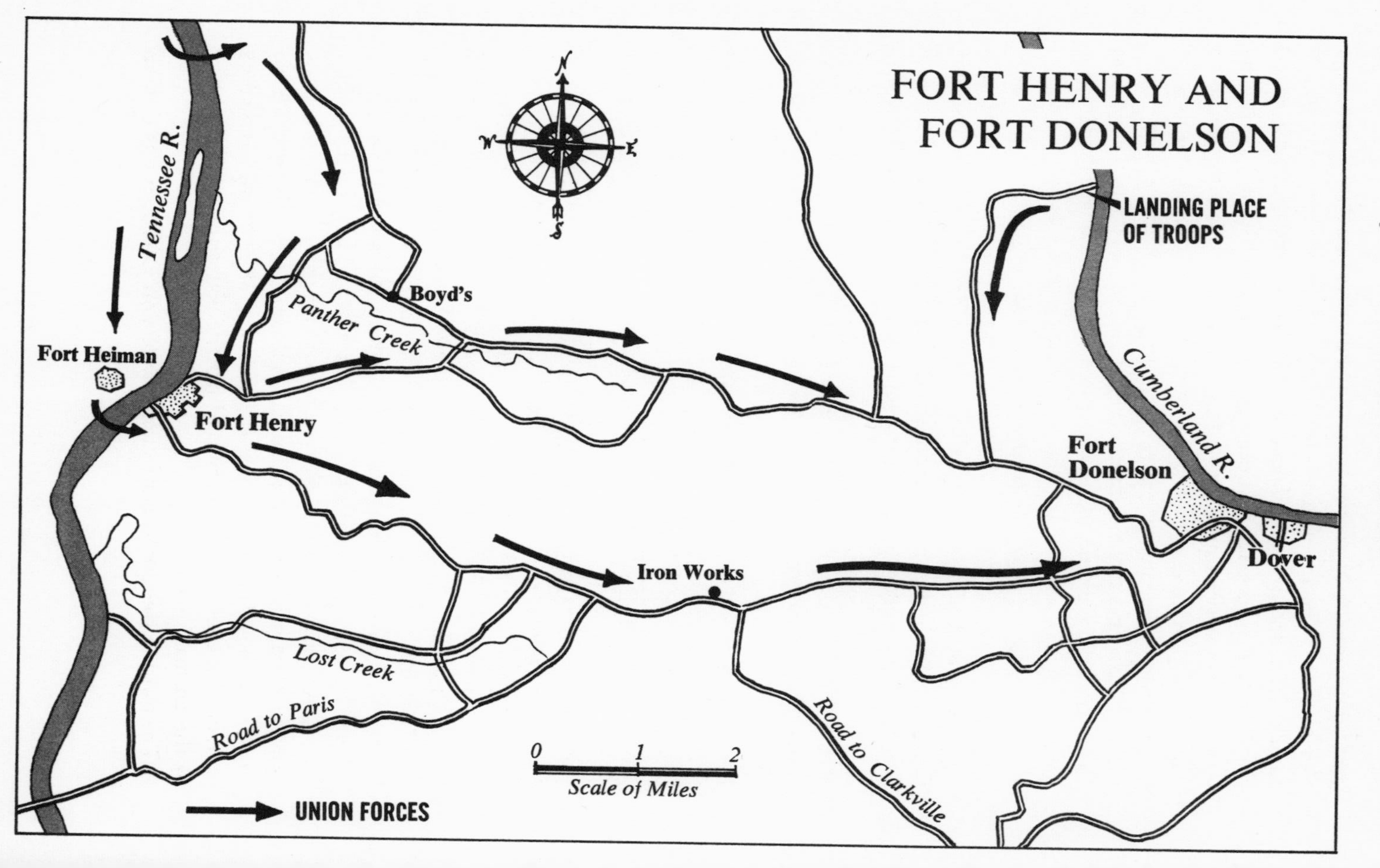

FORT HENRY AND
FORT DONELSON
N
W
E
S
LANDING PLACE
OF TROOPS
Tennessee R.
Boyd's
Panther Creek
Fort Heiman
Fort Henry
Cumberland R.
Fort
Donelson
Dover
Iron Works
Lost Creek
Road to Paris
0
1
2
Scale of Miles
Road to Clarkville
UNION FORCES

to the *Essex.* A shell had penetrated its boiler and exploded, killing and wounding forty-eight men. This is one of the very few occasions on which a land fortification, adequately manned, has been captured by the fire of a fleet alone. Of course in this case there were troops on land ready to take possession of Fort Henry, and General Smith had found Fort Heiman evacuated.

In reporting the capture of Fort Henry to the Department Commander Halleck, General Grant expressed the intention of taking Fort Donelson on the eighth; but continuing rain made the roads impassable for artillery and wagon train, and in addition it was prudent not to start the column on its march until the gunboats had neared Fort Donelson and the latter fort could simultaneously be invested from the land side.

On February 7, General Grant with his staff and part of a cavalry made a reconnaissance to the vicinity of Fort Donelson. General Floyd commanded the garrison. He had been secretary of war in the Buchanan Administration and active in transferring arms and munitions from the arsenals in the North to those in the South, where they could easily be taken by the Confederates when the time came. It was General Floyd, too, who had refused to arrange for General Scott to have an interview with President Buchanan when the question of the harbor forts became critical.

Floyd's second-in-command was General Pillow, who had had some experience in the Mexican War and had considerable confidence in his own military judgment.

Grant never had a high opinion of Pillow, a former law partner of James K. Polk who had been given a brigadier's commission in the Mexican War by his friend the President. He had amused the regular officers by digging a trench on the wrong side of the parapet and had been nicknamed "Polk's spy." Subsequently, he had been criticized for the claim to a wound of dubious character which nonetheless brought him a major generalcy from the White House. Now in the Confederate service, he was mentioned by Grant in a letter to his father: "valiant Pillow" had planned an attack on Cairo, but would desist on learning that the place was garrisoned and had a ditch filled with water *on the outside* of the parapet. Grant also wrote that Pillow might irritate a superficial scratch "until he convinced himself that he had been wounded by the enemy."

The third in the Confederate hierarchy of Fort Donelson was General

Simon B. Buckner, who had been at West Point three years with his opponent and had befriended the latter when he arrived in New York from California.

The reconnaissance showed that there were two roads that might be used in approaching the fort from Fort Henry—one leading to the village of Dover, two miles upstream, thence to the fort, and the other leading directly to Fort Donelson. The fort, occupying about a hundred acres of land, was well constructed, equipped with heavy guns, and protected by an abatis.

The march to Fort Donelson was started only on February 12. Up to that time General Grant and his staff had occupied quarters on the steamer *Tigress*. Dr. Brinton, a member of the staff as chief surgeon, gives the following condensed chronology of the campaign:

> We occupied the headquarters house on the afternoon of the 12th of February and here we remained until after the capture of Fort Donelson and of the little town of Dover, which was included within the enemy's line of defense. . . . On the 13th, I was busy fixing my hospitals and doing the best I could. The whole of this day was employed in establishing the positions of our forces, and in strengthening their lines. We threw up no breastworks but depended upon the natural strength of the ground, and its "lay" for our protection should the enemy attempt any sortie. . . .
>
> February 14th (Friday), there was little fighting, with an attack by a gunboat fleet under Commander Foote, which failed. February 15th (Saturday), the enemy made a fierce sortie and are repulsed, and retire into the Fort. General Grant visits the fleet. February 16th (Sunday), surrender of Fort Donelson to the Union forces under General Grant.

In the attack of the river forts by the fleet on the fourteenth, Commodore Foote had been wounded and his flagship badly damaged, as were several others. Here the conditions, which had been so favorable to the Union fleet at Fort Henry, were reversed. The enemy batteries on higher ground had a plunging fire on the gunboats, whereas at Fort Henry the gunboats, because of high water in the river, had been above the parapet of the fort and had had the advantage. The department commander, and especially his chief of staff, Brigadier General George W. Cullum, became active in trying to send reinforcements to the expedition, and the first installment under General Thayer arrived near Fort Henry on the twelfth. The fleet was starting its trip around by the

Ohio up the Cumberland to Fort Donelson, and Thayer was ordered to accompany it.

It may be of interest to interpolate the following description by Chief Surgeon Brinton of the march across the neck of land between the Tennessee and the Cumberland rivers:

> We marched in battle order, ready for action. The actual luggage of the staff was represented by a few collars, a comb and brush and such toilet articles, contained in a small satchel belonging to me. General Grant had only a tooth brush in his waistcoat pocket, and I supplied him with a clean white collar. Of whiskey or liquor, of which so much has been said, there was not one drop in the possession of any member of the staff, except that in my pocket, an eight-ounce flask, which I was especially requested by the General to keep only for medical purposes, and I was further instructed by him not to furnish a drink under any pretext to any member of the Staff, except when necessary in my professional judgment.

Special attention was given to locating first-aid stations and field dressing stations or temporary places for the most urgent hospital treatment. There was no serious fighting except for an assault made by General McClernand in order to capture an enemy battery that was annoying his troops. As the battery was a part of the Confederate defensive line, the assault was naturally repulsed with considerable loss. The wounded found their way to one of the hospitals and it was soon filled.

In regard to the Union line, General Grant in his *Memoirs* wrote:

> The troops were not entrenched, but the nature of the ground was such that they were just as well protected from the fire of the enemy as if rifle-pits had been thrown up. Our line was generally along the crest of ridges. The artillery was protected by being sunk in the ground. The men who were not serving the guns were perfectly covered from fire on taking position a little back from the crest. The greatest suffering was from want of shelter. It was midwinter, and during the siege we had rain and snow, thawing and freezing alternately. It would not do to allow camp fires, except far down the hill out of sight of the enemy, and it would not do to allow many of the troops to remain there at the same time. In the march over from Fort Henry, numbers of the men had thrown away their blankets and overcoats. There was therefore much discomfort and absolute suffering.

On February 15, before broad daylight, a messenger from Flag Officer Foote handed General Grant a note expressing a desire to see him on the flagship, and explaining that his wounds prevented him from calling on the army commander. Leaving word with the adjutant general to notify each of the division commanders of his absence and instructing them to do nothing to bring on an engagement until receipt of further orders, Grant proceeded to visit Foote. The heavy rains of the preceding few days and the constant use of the roads by the troops had made the roads almost impassable. The intense cold of the preceding night had frozen the ground and made travel on horseback slow and slippery. When he finally reached the fleet, having made the best time he could under the circumstances, the flagship was anchored in midstream and a small boat had been left to transport him to the flagship. Foote explained the harm done his fleet by the previous day's engagement and recommended that the troops be entrenched while he returned to Mound City with his disabled boats; he believed they could be repaired and he could be back in ten days. General Grant saw the absolute necessity for the boats to go back for repairs, but was distressed by the prospect of possibly having to settle down to a siege. However, the enemy relieved him of this necessity.

When he had left to visit Flag Officer Foote, he had not expected any attack by the enemy. For two days there had been no move on their part, while he was before Fort Donelson with only 15,000 men of all arms; and now he had been reinforced by 2,500 men brought from Fort Henry by General Smith, and he also had a fleet of six naval vessels with a large division under General Lew Wallace. However, just as Grant landed, Captain Hillyer of his staff met him and reported the enemy had attacked in great force and scattered McClernand's division, which was in full retreat. In spite of the condition of the roads, Grant hastened to his right wing as rapidly as possible, passing some four or five miles north of his left wing. He saw no evidence of excitement in the portion of the line commanded by General Smith; but he found that General Wallace, nearer the scene of conflict, had sent Thayer's brigade to the support of McClernand and thereby contributed to holding the enemy within his lines. When he reached the extreme right, Grant found that the enemy had issued forth in full force to cut its way out and escape. McClernand's division had had to bear the brunt of the attack from the combined enemy force. His men had resisted gallantly until the ammunition in their cartridge boxes gave out. There was an abundance of ammunition in boxes lying on the ground, but in those early days of the war few commanders of regiments, brigades, or even divisions were experienced enough to see that their men were supplied with ammunition during an engagement. When McClernand's men found themselves without ammunition and attacked by an enemy who seemed to have plenty, the division broke and a portion fled; but as they were not pursued most of them just fell back out of range of the enemy's fire. At about this time, Thayer pushed his brigade in between the enemy and those of McClernand's men who had no ammunition, and that is where General Grant found him.

In his *Memoirs* he describes the scene:

> I saw the men standing in knots talking in the most excited manner. No officer seemed to be giving any directions. The soldiers had their muskets, but no ammunition, while there were tons of it close at hand. I heard some of the men say that the enemy had come out with knapsacks and haversacks filled with rations. They seemed to think this indicated a determination on his part to stay out and fight just as long as the provisions held out. I turned to Colonel J. D. Webster, of my staff, who was with me, and said: "Some of our men are pretty badly demoralized; but the enemy must be more so, for he has attempted to force his way out, but has fallen back; the one who attacks first now will be victorious, and the enemy will have to be in a hurry if he gets ahead of me." I determined to make the assault at once on our left. It was clear to my mind that the enemy had started to march out with his entire force, except a few pickets; and if our attack could be made on the left before the enemy could redistribute his forces along the line, we would find but little opposition, except from the intervening abatis. I directed Colonel Webster to ride with me and call out to the men as we passed, "Fill your cartridge-boxes quick, and get into line; the enemy is trying to escape, and he must not be permitted to do so." This acted like a charm. The men only wanted some one to give them a command. We rode rapidly to Smith's quarters, when I explained the situation to him and directed him to charge the enemy's works in his front with his whole division, saying at the same time that he would find nothing but a very thin line to contend with. The general was off in an incredibly short time, going in advance himself to keep his men from firing while they were working their way through the abatis intervening between them and the enemy. The outer line of rifle-pits was passed, and the night of the 15th General Smith, with much of his division, bivouacked within the lines of the enemy. There was now no doubt but that the Confederates must surrender or be captured the next day.

Inevitably this resulted in the exchange of correspondence with General Buckner, who had been left holding the bag by his two superiors, which concluded with General Grant's soon famous "unconditional surrender" message. Buckner did surrender on the morning of February 16. This was not only the first important Union victory, with decisive strategic results, but also the largest capture of men and arms that had occurred on this continent. In addition to 65 guns and 17,600 small arms, the number of prisoners surrendered was 14,623 and the killed and wounded estimated at over 2,500, while apparently some 4,000 escaped along the river during the night of February 15–16, making the total rebel force at the beginning of the siege 21,123.

The North was tremendously enthused over the victory. The Southern line had definitely been broken in its center, and General Albert Sidney Johnston, who had inherited the Confederate command at Bowling Green, felt it necessary to retire his line, giving up the position at Columbus and even abandoning Nashville, while the Union forces found the Cumberland River open as far as Carthage and the Tennessee River eventually open to Savannah and Pittsburg Landing.

Colonel Fiebeger, professor of engineering and military art at West Point, said of this campaign in his *Campaigns of the American Civil War:* "The capture of Fort Donelson by raw troops in midwinter was one of the most remarkable events of the war and reflected great credit on Grant to whose energy it was due. His promptness in closing the gap made by Pillow's attack sealed the fate of the Confederate garrison."

At this time President Lincoln was greatly disturbed, not only by his anxiety about Fort Donelson but also about the illness of his son William Wallace, who died on February 20. This was a terrible blow to the President and Mrs. Lincoln, but even during his deep family distress he was able to join in a congratulatory order to General Grant and Flag Officer Foote and the forces under their command for the victories on the Tennessee and the Cumberland.

Congratulations from all over the country came in in a flood, but nothing of the sort came from General Halleck directly. He had telegraphed to Washington that the victory was due to General C. F. Smith, and recommended his promotion. On the other hand, General Cullum wrote Grant a very cordial congratulatory letter. Of course, General Grant approved strongly the promotion of General Smith, as he did all the other promotions made at the time. He was of the opinion that immediately after the fall of Fort Donelson the Union Army might have invaded the area south without meeting much effective resistance; that if a general who was willing to take the responsibility had been in command of all the troops west of the Alleghenies, he could have marched to Chattanooga, Corinth, Memphis, and Vicksburg with the troops then available. As volunteering was rapidly progressing in the north, there would have been force enough at all these centers to operate offensively against any forces the enemy could have found near them. However, no such movement was undertaken. The troops available were used to take possession of an area of territory evacuated by the Confederates.

Grant had offered to take possession of Clarksville on February 21 and Nashville on March 1, both places on the Cumberland River, unless ordered not to do so. Having had no such message, he sent General Smith to Clarksville, which he found evacuated. He would have sent troops to take possession of Nashville, except that he assumed erroneously that Buell had followed the retiring Confederates from Bowling Green to Nashville. It is not possible here to go into the details of the minor operations that now took place, beyond pointing out that an opportunity had been lost and that General Grant was reprimanded for having gone outside the limits of his own command to confer with Buell at Nashville, even after he had been given general instructions to co-ordinate his movements with General Buell. Here was a case in which the rigid adherence to the boundaries of territorial departments and districts prevented proper and prompt military action.

At this time there was also apparently an interruption of communications from General Grant's headquarters to General Halleck; a rebel sympathizer was in charge in the telegraph office through which messages had to pass, and he finally deserted his post, carrying off many of the messages he had received and not transmitted. Finally, a telegram was received by General Grant from General Halleck, accusing him of not obeying orders and not reporting the strength and location of his troops. The matter was settled between the two generals and so reported to the War Department—but not until General Halleck had put General C. F. Smith in command of a force being moved to the neighborhood of Pittsburg Landing and Shiloh Church on the Tennessee River, leaving General Grant in what President Cleveland would have called "innocuous desuetude."

Before we leave the campaign that ended with the capture of Fort Donelson, it may be of interest to mention that a newspaper artist had published a drawing, widely circulated, of General Grant on horseback with a cigar in his mouth. It so happened that at the conclusion of lunch on the flagship on February 15, Flag Officer Foote had given a cigar to his guest who put it into his mouth without lighting it. Then on hearing of the rebel outbreak on the right flank, Grant had let it go out or forgotten to light it and had ridden with it in his mouth most of the day. The publicity given the picture resulted in many people sending him boxes of cigars; he had a tentful of them for some time and made a practice of giving a box to any visitor. In making an effort to do his own part in consuming these cigars he became addicted to their use rather than the pipe he had been accustomed to before.

VII

Shiloh and Corinth

GENERAL Albert Sidney Johnston, the Confederate commander, had a great advantage: he was in command of all Confederate troops west of the Appalachian Mountains and east of the Mississippi River, and it was possible for him to make a sound strategic plan after his line of defense from the Mississippi to Cumberland Gap had been broken in the center by the capture of Forts Henry and Donelson. His plan was obviously to concentrate his available forces farther west near the road and railroad center of Corinth, Mississippi, and then attack the troops gathering under General Smith at Pittsburg Landing and Shiloh before the arrival there of reinforcements from General Buell. After defeating the Army of the Tennessee under Smith, he could then turn on Buell and defeat him, being superior in numbers to each of the Union commanders. However, the Union commanders did not know just what his plan was and General Smith continued to gather his forces at Pittsburg Landing, while Buell was directed to march to join him there.

When General Grant was told to resume command of his troops, he found that General Smith was suffering from an injury, which proved fatal, and was living in the Cherry House in Savannah. As troops arrived General Smith had sent them to Pittsburg Landing to await further orders. General William Tecumseh Sherman was the senior officer on the spot for a time and, taking a position for his division in the neighborhood of Shiloh Church (from which the subsequent battle was to take its name), he assigned other divisions as they arrived to camp grounds in the vicinity. An exception was General Lew Wallace's division, which he placed at Crump's Landing, a landing on the west bank of the Tennessee River a little over four miles north of Pittsburg Landing, but on a road leading directly to Corinth, where the Confederates were known to be gathering. There were many estimates of the number of men the Confederates might have, varying from upwards of 20,000 to 40,000. There was also a report that some heavy artillery had arrived in Corinth. On March 18, Sherman's adjutant had addressed a message to General Grant, to which General Sherman, himself, added a postscript at 4 P.M.: "Magnificent plain for camping and drilling, and a military point of great strength. The enemy has felt us twice, at great loss and demoralization; will report at length this evening; am now much worn out." The next day Sherman's division had landed and joined Hurlbut's division. McClernand's division had preceded both.

General Grant visited the troops at Pittsburg Landing on March 19 and the day before had acknowledged a dispatch from Halleck, dated the sixteenth, to the effect that he believed the enemy to be in strong force and that his instructions against bringing on an engagement "must be strictly obeyed." General Grant personally remained at Savannah to be on hand for Buell's arrival, expected almost any time. The Pittsburg position had not been occupied without any resistance on the part of the Confederates, as Beauregard had sent a battery there to sweep the river from the high bluff. Lieutenant Gwin at Savannah and some 32nd Illinois sharpshooters had steamed upstream on March 1 and been fired on by some six guns which Gwin and Lieutenant Shirk, commanding the Lexington, were sure included one rifled cannon. The fire of the two gunboats forced the battery to retire with insignificant loss.

Early in August there had been gathered in this way five Union divisions, mostly raw recruits who had never been in battle, but there were a few organizations—such as McClernand's and Lew Wallace's divisions—that had served at Fort Donelson and Fort Henry. Because of General C. F. Smith's illness, his division was commanded by General W. H. L. Wallace. These five divisions were encamped in a roughly triangular space bounded by the Tennessee River, Snake Creek, Owl Creek, Shiloh Branch, and Lick Creek. There was a dearth of habitations, the local landmarks being limited to the arrangements at Pittsburg Landing for loading and unloading boats, a log cabin near the landing (which played an important part as a receiving point for the first treatment of seriously wounded), and Shiloh Church near the left center of the Union line of camps about four miles from the landing. General Sherman later wrote of the situation:

> I always acted on the supposition that we were an invading army; that our purpose was to move forward in force, make a lodgment on the Memphis & Charleston road, and thus repeat the grand tactics of Fort Donelson, by separating the rebels in the interior from those at Memphis and on the Mississippi River. We did not fortify our camps against an attack, because we had no orders to do so, and because such a course would have made our raw men timid. The position was naturally strong, with Snake Creek on our right, a deep, bold stream, with a confluent (Owl Creek) to our right front; and Lick Creek, with a similar confluent, on our left, thus narrowing the space over which we could be attacked to about a mile and a half or two miles. At a later period of the war, we could have rendered this position impregnable in one night, but at this time we did not do it, and it may be it is well we did not. From about the 1st of April we were conscious that the rebel cavalry in our front was getting bolder and more saucy; and on Friday, 4th of April, it dashed down and carried off one of our picket guards, composed of an officer and seven men, posted a couple of miles out on the Corinth road . . . but thus far we had not positively detected the presence of infantry, for cavalry regiments generally had a couple of guns along, and I supposed the guns that opened on us on the evening of Friday, April 4th, belonged to the cavalry that was hovering along our whole front.

In the meantime, General Albert Sidney Johnston was gathering his troops at Corinth. Among the latter there were two full Confederate generals and a third officer, Bragg, who was later to be one; and there were two who would become lieutenant generals. Thus there were five distinguished soldiers to co-ordinate and direct the reserve and three corps of the rebel army, which consisted of four actual and two virtual additional divisions. They were concentrated and concealed in the woods about two miles from the Union camps. It had been General Johnston's expectation that he would arrive in time to launch an attack against the army under General Grant on April 5, but due to delays and muddy roads and greenness of his troops he did not arrive until the evening of the fifth. There was a Confederate council of war that night to consider the advisability of giving up the contemplated attack and returning to Corinth, but General Johnston insisted upon carrying out the original plan on the morning of the sixth.

General Nelson with his division of Buell's army had arrived in Savannah on April 5, and so did General Buell in person fairly late in the evening. But he did not report to General Grant who, he knew, was waiting for him.

On April 5, General Sherman reported that the enemy had reached Pea Ridge the day before with a brigade of two regiments of infantry, one of cavalry, and a battery of field artillery, halting about five miles from his front. General Sherman had sent a force to rescue if possible the picket captured by the rebels, and he ended his report:

> Our cavalry drove them back upon their artillery and Infantry, killing many, and bringing off ten prisoners, all of the First Alabama Cavalry, whom I send to you. We lost of the pickets one first lieutenant and seven men of the Ohio Seventieth Infantry (list enclosed); one major, one lieutenant, and one private of the Seventy-second Ohio, taken prisoners; eight privates wounded. . . . We took ten prisoners, and left two rebels wounded and many killed on the field.

Evidently, General Sherman knew of the presence of the enemy in force in his vicinity but probably still was of the opinion, stated previously, that "the enemy is saucy, but . . . I do not apprehend anything like an attack on our position."

The decision to attack on April 6 led to the issue of a formal order by command of General Johnston and prepared by General Jordan, Beauregard's adjutant, with General Bragg's assistance. General Jordan wrote: "As I framed the order, I had before me Napoleon's order for the battle of Waterloo, and in attention to ante-battle details, took those of such soldiers as Napoleon and Soult for model." In somewhat the same spirit of the two French commanders mentioned by Jordan, General Johnston made an eloquent appeal to his men for "a decisive victory over agrarian mercenaries, sent to subjugate and despoil you of your liberties, property, and honor. . . . The eyes and hopes of 8,000,000 of people rest upon you. . . ."

After the battle much was written and said about the Union Army having been surprised. It is desirable in the interest of historic truth to note that, in addition to General Sherman's contact with the reconnaissance by the enemy near Pea Ridge, Colonel Everett Peabody, commanding the 1st Brigade of Prentiss' division, astride the eastern branch of the road from Corinth to Pittsburg Landing, felt that trouble might be gathering in the woods to the south and sent his brigade officer of the day, Major James E. Powell, out on a reconnaissance at 3 A.M., April 6, with three companies of the 25th Missouri.

Powell led his reconnaissance party through the woods over Shiloh

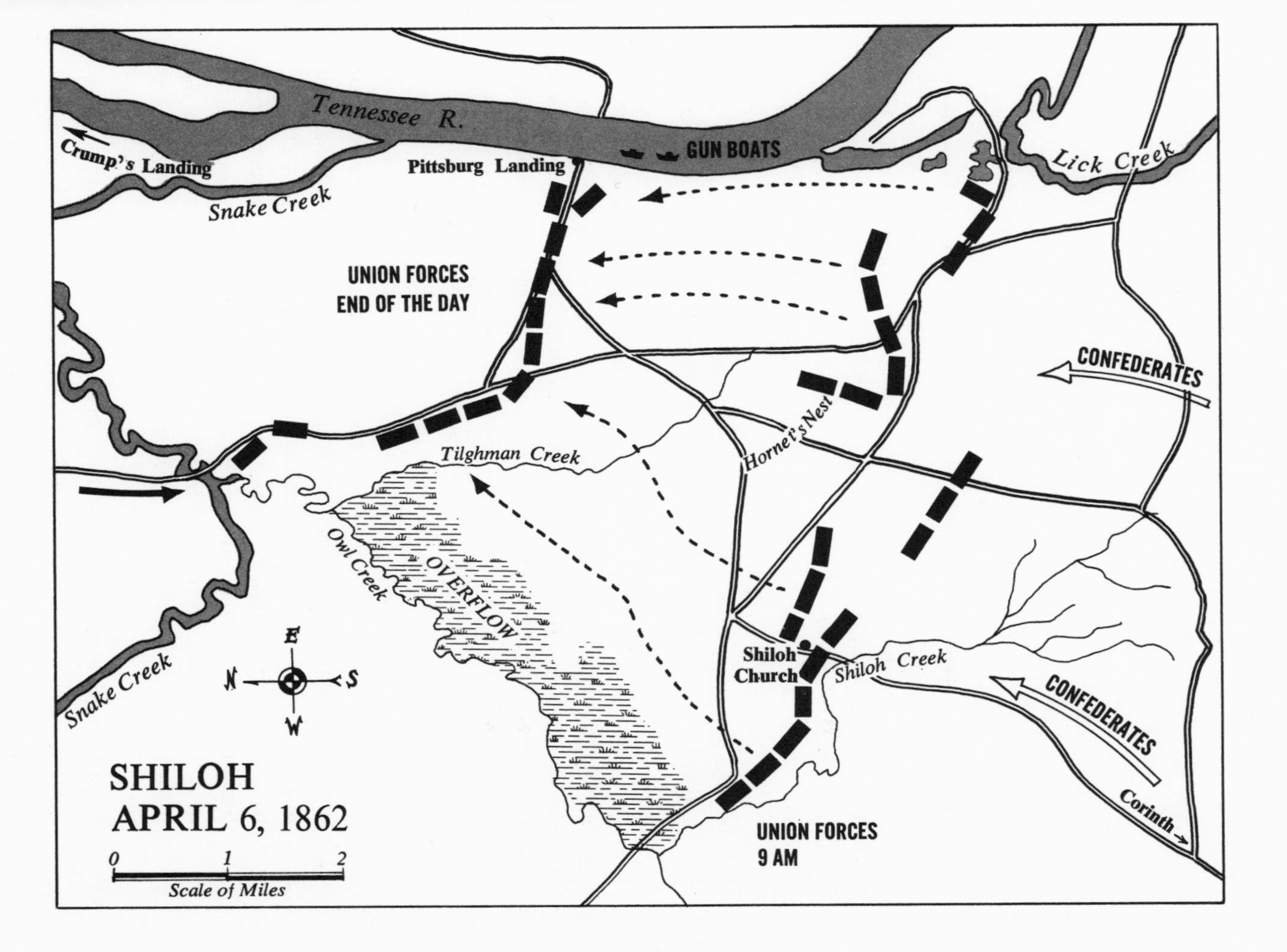
Tennessee R.
Crump's Landing
GUN BOATS
Pittsburg Landing
Snake Creek
Lick Creek
UNION FORCES
END OF THE DAY
CONFEDERATES
Hornet's Nest
Tilghman Creek
Owl Creek
OVERFLOW
E
N
S
W
Snake Creek
Shiloh
Church
Shiloh Creek
CONFEDERATES
Corinth
UNION FORCES
9 AM
SHILOH
APRIL 6, 1862
0
1
2
Scale of Miles

Creek and to the Corinth road branch that ran past the little church, whence he turned to the left. As Powell and Peabody were killed on the first day of the battle, we must turn to a report by Major A. B. Hardcastle, commanding the 3rd Mississippi Infantry Battalion, to determine just where the battle of Shiloh began: "About dawn the cavalry vedettes fired three shots, wheeled, and galloped back." Evidently, the Union reconnoitering party had flushed the rebel horsemen and pressed forward only to encounter infantry and to be forced to fall back. Hardcastle says, "We fought the enemy an hour or more without giving an inch." Finally at about six-thirty Hardcastle fell back upon his brigade and Powell had to retire before the heavy advancing column from the Confederate line of battle. He was met by a reinforcing party of five companies of the 21st Missouri under command of Colonel David Moore, which Peabody had sent. Thus the Battle of Shiloh began with the driving in of a cavalry outpost by the reconnoitering party sent out by a regiment in General Prentiss' division and finally driven back after nearly an hour's fighting.

The Confederate attack struck the Union forces at about 6:30 A.M. on April 6. This attack was successful in pushing the Union line back on Pittsburg Landing about two miles before it was stopped, largely by the splendid resistance put up by Prentiss' division at what came to be called the "Hornet's Nest."

The noise of the guns was heard at Savannah, Missouri, where General Grant was having breakfast at six o'clock. He promptly boarded the *Tigress,* with the members of his staff who were present, to go upstream, stopping at Crump's Landing across the river to direct General Lew Wallace to hold his command in readiness to move as soon as he received orders. Before leaving Savannah, an order had been sent to General Nelson to march his division down the east bank of the Tennessee River to a point opposite Pittsburg Landing and have his division transferred from there in the boats available at that point.

Unfortunately, General Nelson thought that he should have the order confirmed by his army commander, General Buell, and this took until 1:30 P.M., when he moved up the east bank. He did not reach the battlefield until evening, just in time to take position in the last line formed.

As soon as he reached Pittsburg Landing and disembarked, General Grant realized from the situation visible that the entire Confederate

Army was apparently engaged in the attack on his army and that he need not fear a flank attack on Lew Wallace at Crump's Landing. He gave orders to General Rawlins, his adjutant general, to send word to General Lew Wallace to march his command to the battlefield by the *river road.* Several hours passed and General Wallace did not appear. An aide, sent to locate him and start him in the right direction, found him on a back road going west, almost parallel with the line of battle. He had to countermarch and did not reach the battlefield until the situation had been settled for the night.

Some of the units, somewhat surprised by the violence and determination of the enemy's attack, did more or less dissolve, and a number of stragglers collected at Pittsburg Landing. Some of the organizations that had left the field in the morning were gathered together again in the late afternoon and under proper leadership played their part in stopping the enemy's last attack. The enemy attacked again at about 2 P.M. with renewed force and determination, and a similar effort two hours later was rewarded with the driving back of the Union troops on both sides of Prentiss' division. This forced his surrender, with about 2,000 of his men. However, the resistance that his division had put up for so long had had a very salutary effect.

General Grant visited all the different division commanders and personally insured their supporting one another as far as possible. Buell, according to his own account, came on the battlefield at about 1 P.M. when he asked General Grant: "What are you going to do to save your army if you are beaten?" General Grant said they would "retire to the other side of the river." General Buell then pointed out that he didn't have boats enough to transport more than 10,000 men, to which General Grant replied that, if he were beaten, he would not have more than 10,000 men. In any case, General Buell does not seem to have offered any explanation for General Nelson's failure to have reached the battlefield by that time. Nelson later reported that it was 1:30 P.M. when he left Savannah in compliance with Grant's order.

However unfavorable things looked to the Union commander, he probably would have been cheered to know the situation on the enemy's side. General Breckinridge, who commanded what reserve General Johnston had, committed his first brigade to the action by 9:30 A.M. and the second brigade of his reserve before noon, its commander writing, "We were led by General A. S. Johnston, who told us a few more charges and the day was ours." General Johnston seems to have played a part of inspirational leader and to have left the co-ordinating of action in the Confederate force to his second-in-command, General Beauregard.

The Confederate attack had originally been organized with the different corps in line, each covering the whole front and attacking in parallel lines. This inevitably resulted in the mixing of units, as the second line under Bragg came up and merged with Hardee's first line, both to be followed by Polk with Breckinridge in reserve in the rear. To avoid further confusion, each general was assigned a part of the line, Hardee having the left, Polk a small section on Hardee's right, Bragg having the center, and Breckinridge the extreme right.

At 3 P.M., General Grant was again on the right flank with General Sherman. During a slight lull that followed Generals Sherman and McClernand selected a new line of defense, with its right covering the bridge by which General Wallace was expected. The fighting began again in earnest, but Sherman was able to find a clear field about two hundred yards wide in his immediate front and succeeded in keeping the enemy's infantry at that distance during the rest of the day. His troops rested in that position for the night. General Prentiss held on until about 5:30 P.M. when with ammunition exhausted he surrendered with about 2,200 men. The battery of the 5th Ohio, under command of Captain A. Hickenlooper, had limbered up its four guns and withdrawn to join General Sherman after having played a very effective role with Prentiss. With the end of the day, General Grant had personally, with his staff, formed a concentration of artillery and infantry from Hurlbut's, McClernand's, and Sherman's divisions which repulsed the final attacks of the Confederates decisively and actually countercharged successfully, thus ending the day's fight. Lew Wallace finally reached the field and was placed on Sherman's right.

General A. S. Johnston had received a wound in his leg at about 2:30 P.M. He died soon after, but General Beauregard was already handling the battle as far as it could be controlled for the Confederates. General Johnston received his wound in a personal effort to organize a charge he thought would win the battle. While there is no question of his popularity with his troops, it is doubtful whether his death really affected the outcome of the battle to any great extent.

It rained hard during the night, which put out some minor fires that had started in the woods and threatened such wounded as had been left there. At the log cabin near Pittsburg Landing the seriously wounded were operated on as fast as possible, and thus there was extemporized the handling of wounded in three stages: (1) first aid and removal to a dressing station; (2) dressing-station treatment for those not too seriously wounded; and (3) field-hospital treatment pending removal to hospitals behind the lines. The three steps improvised on the field of battle were copied and more carefully organized by Surgeon Letterman of the Army of the Potomac. They have since been the adopted procedure in all subsequent wars, with the removal of wounded much facilitated and speeded up by new kinds of transportation.

As Nelson's division—followed later by those of Crittenden and Alexander M. McCook—arrived, they were placed on the Union left and, being comparatively fresh, played an important part in attacking and driving the Confederates off the battlefield the next morning. After directing each division commander to start the attack early the next morning, General Grant first sought shelter in the log cabin at Pittsburg Landing, but was driven from it by the groans and distress of the wounded who were being operated on. He spent the night in the rain under a tree.

By two-thirty in the afternoon of April 7, the enemy had been thrown back; it was in full retreat by 4 o'clock. Author Kenneth Williams pictures that retreat rather vividly with the help of General Bragg:

> After a night of tribulations of a weary general retreating in the dark through rain and deep mud, Braxton Bragg's morale hit a new low; and at 7:30 on April 8, still ten miles from the food and comfort of Corinth, he wrote to Beauregard: "Our condition is horrible. Troops utterly disorganized and demoralized. Road almost impassable. No provisions and no forage; consequently everything is feeble. Straggling parties may get in tonight." He had ordered Breckinridge to hold on with the rear guard until pressed by the enemy, and he asked if fresh troops with five days' rations could not be sent to his relief. "It is most lamentable to see the state of affairs," said the discouraged general, "but I am powerless and almost exhausted." Wood with his two brigades and Sherman with two—including Hildebrand's—and some cavalry did do some pressing. Clear evidence of the haste of the Confederates was found: hospitals with wounded, artillery ammunition, abandoned equipment of all sorts, including Johnston's field desk with its interesting papers. Sherman was satisfied that the enemy's artillery and infantry had crossed Lick Creek—nearly five miles from Shiloh Church—during the night and early morning. That there was still fight in the cavalry covering the enemy's retreat

Sherman learned when a sharp charge caused one of his infantry regiments to break, though it later reformed and advanced again. Wood's third brigade, just off the boats, came puffing up through the mud, got fired at a little, and evinced an eagerness—according to Wood—"to engage the enemy." But the Battle of Shiloh was over.

There can be no doubt that the Battle of Shiloh, which was the bloodiest and hardest-fought battle up to that time, was a definite Union victory. The Confederate attack, delivered with surprising intrepidity and vigor, had been stopped before dark on April 6, and fresh troops, brought in during the night, drove the Confederate Army off the field decisively the next day. It is necessary to make this clear because of the conflicting reports and claims made after the battle.

Considerable difference of opinion exists as to the exact strength of the two commands engaged in this two-day battle; but for the first day it is fairly safe to claim that the Confederates had about 42,000 men available and General Grant, without Lew Wallace's division, had about 35,000. This was a decided superiority in force for the Confederates. With the addition of the units from Buell's army and Lew Wallace's division, the advantage of numbers was reversed on the second day. Even so, the units of Buell's army had been marching for a considerable length of time in order to reach the battlefield, and the Army of the Tennessee had certainly been exhausted by the fighting on the first day. No pursuit to the bitter end was attempted.

The *New York Herald* carried what seems to have been the earliest news of the Battle of Shiloh, stating that the battle was begun by a party of the 25th Missouri attacking "the advance guard of the rebels" and that the Federal troops were promptly formed. For some reason this very good piece of reporting was superseded in public notice by a quite erroneous one.

It happened that a newspaperman, later of some prominence, came to Pittsburg Landing on April 6, 1862. His name was Whitelaw Reid. Sick upon his arrival, it is doubtful that he ever got to the level of the battlefield; but he wrote a very unfavorable account of the battle and emphasized the skulkers who had gathered at the landing, without giving credit to the men who were fighting and who had maintained their organization and discipline through the morning of the sixth. This caused quite a hullabaloo in the press, as well as in army circles, and started arguments about the Battle of Shiloh that have not been concluded even today. I have a letter from General Sherman, in his own handwriting, to General Grant, in which he says that the account of the battle as written by my grandfather in the article for the Century Company is exactly correct according to his records and recollection. Maybe we can leave it there, with the testimony of the two most important commanders in the battle on the Union side. Evidently there were many officers who resented the successes that had been gained by this little-known West Point graduate who had resigned his commission to go to farming in Missouri. Tales and accusations were carried to Mr. Lincoln but he refused to give them consideration with the statement: "I can't spare this man Grant, he fights."

Almost simultaneously with the Battle of Shiloh, Island No. 10 near New Madrid on the Mississippi River was being captured by a combined land and naval force under General John Pope. As a result of this success, he was ordered to Virginia and given command of the army being formed there (while McClellan and his army were being retired from the Peninsula), and he was soon ignominiously defeated by General Lee in the second Battle of Bull Run, August 30, 1862. However, before this misadventure, General Pope brought his troops from Island No. 10 to join the force which General Halleck was concentrating for the march on and capture of Corinth, Mississippi. Altogether General Halleck assembled about 120,000 men for this adventure and assigned, on the last day of April, the 2nd, 4th, 5th and 6th divisions of Grant's old Army of the Tennessee and a division of George H. Thomas' to constitute the right wing of the new force. Thomas, now a major general, was given command. Buell's Army of the Ohio, reduced to Nelson's, McCook's, and Wood's divisions, became the center; and Pope's Army of the Mississippi, consisting of four infantry divisions and one cavalry division, became the left wing. A reserve, under McClernand, was formed of his old division and the divisions of Lew Wallace and Crittenden. General Grant was assigned as second-in-command, but in the course of the campaign found he had no responsibilities and no command and was rarely consulted by General Halleck. He naturally became discontented and felt humiliated. He was about to insist on being relieved and sent elsewhere, when General Sherman persuaded him to stick it out for a while.

From April 30 this grand army started its advance from Shiloh upon

Corinth, moving forward with all the hesitation and caution that would be usual in siege operations. On the twenty-eighth of May, General Sherman's division carried two Confederate positions some distance out from the main works and thus completed investment of the city. On that same day General Logan, whose command was then on the Mobile and Ohio Railroad, told General Grant that the enemy had been evacuating Corinth for several days; he believed that he could take his brigade into Corinth if permitted to do so. Trains were heard coming in and going out of the city, and experienced railroad men with the army claimed that they could tell by putting their ears to the rail which trains were loaded and which were not. They claimed that loaded trains had been going out for several days and empty ones coming in, and subsequent events confirmed their judgment.

General Halleck had his whole army drawn up in battle array on May 30, and published in orders his belief that the Union left would be attacked that morning. However, Corinth had already been evacuated and the National troops marched in without meeting any opposition and took possession. Everything had been destroyed or carried away, while arriving trains had been cheered by the Confederate soldiers in order to create the impression on the Yankees that reinforcements were arriving rather than the garrison being removed. The leaving to the Union forces of this important strategic, fortified road and railroad center, without even a gesture of opposition, was very different from Beauregard's message to the Confederate adjutant general claiming a great victory at Shiloh and the retirement to Corinth, "*which could be held.*" The fact was that the Confederate Army had been so shaken by the Battle of Shiloh, and its retreat from there, that it had no heart for resistance at Corinth. It seems an irony of history that the Confederate order for the Battle of Shiloh should have been modeled on Napoleon's order for the Battle of Waterloo, where the French army's initial attacks on the English position met with some early success but the arrival of Blücher on the battlefield turned the scales and started the repulse and dissolution of Napoleon's army.

It is evident, from what actually occurred, that the Confederate Army had been so thoroughly beaten at Shiloh that it was not prepared to put up a fight for Corinth, in spite of Beauregard's assurance to the secretary of war on April 8 that he could and would hold Corinth. Perhaps it was Beauregard who was beaten in spirit. By June 15 he asked to be

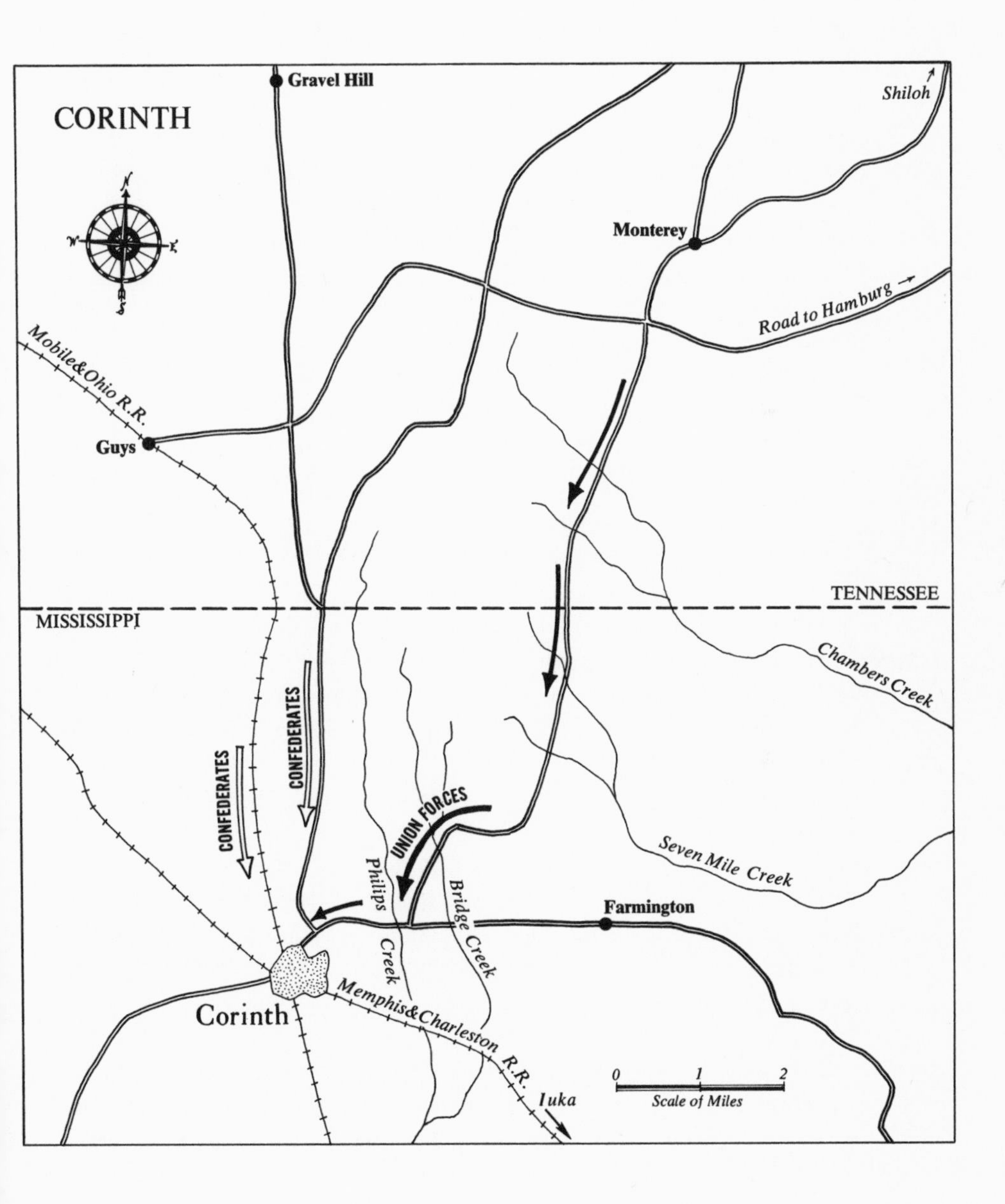
CORINTH
Gravel Hill
Shiloh
Monterey
Road to Hamburg
Mobile&Ohio R.R.
Guys
TENNESSEE
MISSISSIPPI
Chambers Creek
CONFEDERATES
CONFEDERATES
UNION FORCES
Seven Mile Creek
Philips Creek
Bridge Creek
Farmington
Corinth
Memphis&Charleston R.R.
Iuka
0 1 2
Scale of Miles

relieved from duty on account of ill health, attested to by two doctors, and sought two months' rest.

One of the results of the Shiloh campaign and the march on Corinth, which was to have a very important effect on the military situation during the rest of the war, was that General Grant was touched and impressed with the help Sherman had given during the Donelson Campaign in the forwarding of troops to him. He was further impressed with Sherman's skillful and determined resistance in the Battle of Shiloh. And finally, he was undoubtedly appreciative of Sherman's arguments against his asking to be relieved and sent elsewhere during Halleck's slow and too systematic advance on Corinth. Grant and Sherman established a close friendship based on mutual admiration and confidence, and from then on they were to constitute an almost unbeatable team.

After the capture of Corinth, General Grant believed that "A movable force of 80,000 men, besides enough to hold all the territory acquired, could have been set in motion for the accomplishment of any great campaign for the suppression of the rebellion. In addition to this, fresh troops were being raised to swell the effective force." But it was characteristic of General Halleck that, having concentrated a force of between 100,000 and 120,000 men for this capture without bloodshed of Corinth, a point of strategic importance, he would not pursue the success. On the contrary, he scattered the troops in various ways and left the army, at the point where the successes had been won, too weak to accomplish very much further against an enemy whose activity was reviving under the command of generals less afflicted with illness than Beauregard.

General Buell with the Army of the Ohio was sent east, following the line of the Memphis and Charleston Railroad and repairing it as he advanced—giving the enemy's guerrillas the pleasant occupation of destroying it again in their leisure. General Grant believed that if he had been sent direct to Chattanooga, as fast as he could march, he could have reached that city without any serious fighting and saved the lives lost in retaking Chattanooga later. Bragg would not have had time to raise an army to contest possession of middle and east Tennessee and Kentucky; the battles of Stone River and Chickamauga could have been avoided. However, these possibilities were not seen by his superiors. Accepting the situation, he obtained permission to move his headquarters to Memphis and on June 21 started with his staff and a cavalry escort of part of one company. He proceeded to Memphis by way of La Grange, where he found General Hurlbut and dined with him and with a fine old southern gentleman who told them all he was doing for the Confederate cause. On the evening of June 23 General Grant reached Memphis.

General Grant did not remain very long in Memphis, where for the first time he had the experience of administering a department in which the rebel population had remained. There had been no population at Pittsburg Landing, and the town of Dover had practically been within the limits of Fort Donelson. On July 11, General Halleck was ordered to Washington to be Commander in Chief of all the armies. His orders urged him to repair to Washington as rapidly as possible, and he telegraphed his orders to General Grant at Corinth. When General Halleck left on July 17, he left General Grant in command of the District of West Tennessee. Since there was no department commander over him, he had practically all the responsibilities and authority of a department commander.

Presumably the Administration was not satisfied with General McClellan as Commander in Chief. The feeling was that commanding the Army of the Potomac was really a full-time job by itself and could not effectively be combined with the job of Commander in Chief. It is interesting to read in his *Personal Narrative* General McClellan's opinion of the officer chosen to succeed him: "Of all men whom I have encountered in my position Halleck was the most hopelessly stupid. It is more difficult to get an idea through his head than can be conceived by anyone who never made the attempt. I do not think he ever had a correct military idea from beginning to end." This was a direct reversal of his opinion implied in a letter of the previous January to General Halleck, namely, "I like your views as to the future."

One of the first things Grant had to see to was putting smaller fortifications around Corinth. In this way it could be occupied and held, under the changed circumstances, by a smaller garrison. On July 30, General Grant learned from Colonel P. H. Sheridan (who had been some distance south) that Bragg was in Rome, Georgia, with his troops moving by rail by way of Mobile to Chattanooga; his wagon train was marching overland to join him at Rome. Price was at Holly Springs,

Mississippi, with a large force, and occupied Grand Junction as an outpost. General Grant, accordingly, asked Commander in Chief Halleck permission to drive him away, but was informed that while he had to judge for himself, the best use to make of his own troops was *not to scatter them.*

The rebel General Van Dorn with a force of 35,000 to 40,000 men was south of the Army of the Tennessee and confronting it. This was an anxious time for General Grant. Memphis was somewhat isolated from the rest of the army because there was no direct telegraph to it, but it was in Sherman's reliable hands. There was considerable fighting between small bodies of troops unexpectedly coming in contact. On August 2, General Grant received orders from Washington to live upon the country—on the resources of citizens hostile to the government so far as practicable. He was also directed to handle the rebels within Union lines "without gloves"—to imprison them or expel them from their homes and from Union lines. (Grant later did not remember having arrested or confined any civilian during the entire rebellion. He was aware, however, that a great many were sent to northern prisons by some of his subordinates, with the statement that it was by his orders. He had all such prisoners released the moment he learned of their arrest and finally sent a staff officer north to release every prisoner said to have been confined by his orders.)

On August 14 he was called on to send two more divisions to General Buell. On the twenty-second, Colonel Rodney Mason surrendered Clarksville with six companies of his regiments. Colonel Mason was one of the officers who had led their regiments off the field at almost the first rebel fire at Shiloh. He came to the general with tears in his eyes and begged to be allowed to have another trial. Grant felt great sympathy for him and sent him to garrison Clarksville and Donelson. On being allowed to count the enemy, Colonel Mason surrendered to a guerrilla force and advised his subordinate at Donelson to do the same. However, the latter did not surrender but marched out and put the guerrillas to flight.

Very careful arrangements were made to catch any Confederate force that might attempt to recapture Corinth or Iuka. In an effort to get troops into Tennessee to reinforce General Bragg's campaign there, General Sterling Price on September 13 entered Iuka, a town about twenty miles east of Corinth on the Memphis and Charleston Railroad.

Colonel R. C. Murphy, who commanded the garrison there, simply evacuated the town on the approach of the enemy without making any resistance. General Grant did not feel he had force enough at hand to attack Price, but he moved the forces at Bolivar and Jackson to Corinth, which they reached within twenty-four hours. They were commanded by General E. O. C. Ord. Rosecrans commanded the district of Corinth with a movable force of about 9,000, independent of the garrison.

It was known that General Van Dorn was about four days' march south and might co-operate with Price in an attack on Corinth. General Grant wished to attack Price before Van Dorn could reach Corinth or go to his relief. It was proposed to transport General Ord's command by rail to Burnsville, a village on the railroad about seven miles west of Iuka. From there his troops were to march and attack Price from the northwest while Rosecrans was to move eastward by way of the Jacinto road, where a small force was to be left while the main force moved on the Fulton road.

On September 18, General Ord had moved by rail to Burnsville. He left the cars there and moved out to perform his part of the program: to get as near the enemy as possible during the day and entrench himself to hold the position until the next morning. He successfully repelled the enemy with considerable loss to the latter and was ready to attack on schedule. Rosecrans was to be on Jacinto and Fulton roads by the morning of the nineteenth, and the attack was to be made from all three quarters simultaneously. Enough troops had been left at Jacinto and Rienzi to prevent a sudden dash into Corinth by Van Dorn. General Grant remained at Burnsville, and kept sufficient cars and locomotives to transport the whole of Ord's command at once. If Van Dorn, then, had moved against Corinth instead of Iuka, General Grant could have thrown in reinforcements in the number of 7,000 or 8,000 before Van Dorn's arrival.

Disappointingly, Rosecrans sent a dispatch after midnight from Jacinto that the rear of his column had not yet reached Jacinto; he expected to reach Iuka by two o'clock the next day. This seemed impracticable because of the distance and the condition of the roads. General Grant had in mind, in addition, that troops after a forced march of twenty miles are not in good condition to fight immediately. Ord was accordingly sent a copy of Rosecrans' dispatch and ordered to be in readiness to attack the moment he heard the sound of guns from the south or southeast, and to have his officers on the alert for any indications of a battle. However, the wind blew in the wrong direction to transmit any sound to Ord or to the department commander in Burnsville.

A couple of hours before dark on the nineteenth, Rosecrans arrived with the head of his column at Barnett's, the point where the Jacinto road to Iuka leaves the road going east. He here turned north without sending any troops to the Fulton road. After moving in column up the Jacinto road, he met a force of the enemy and had his advance badly beaten and driven back upon the main road. In this brief engagement his loss was considerable for the number engaged, and one battery was taken from him. After the engagement a dispatch announcing the result was brought from Rosecrans by courier. There was no road between Burnsville and the position occupied by Rosecrans, and the way across country was impassable for a man on horseback. The courier had to move west nearly to Jacinto to find a road leading to Burnsville, and it was a late hour of the night before the commanding general at Burnsville knew about the battle.

Ord was ordered to attack in the early morning, and Rosecrans himself renewed the attack and entered Iuka with but little resistance. Ord also went into the town without hearing a gun from the south of the town; he supposed the troops from the southwest must be up by then; but *Rosecrans had put no troops on the Fulton road* as directed, and the enemy had taken advantage of this neglect to escape during the night. On hearing that our troops were in Iuka, General Grant immediately rode into town and found the enemy was not being pursued even by the cavalry. He ordered the pursuit to be taken up by the whole of Rosecrans' command and went with him several miles. After he had left Rosecrans, the latter continued the pursuit only a few miles and then went into camp. General Grant was greatly disappointed at the failure either to defeat or definitely capture the enemy force, but having a high opinion of General Rosecrans and assuming there must be some explanation, he found no fault with him at the time.

General George H. Thomas was ordered east on September 19 to reinforce General Buell. This put the army under General Grant still more on the defensive and necessitated the abandonment of the Memphis-Charleston Railroad except at Corinth, with small forces at Chewalla and Grand Junction. Soon afterward the latter of these two places was given up, and Bolivar became the Union's most advanced position on the Mississippi Central. The Union cavalry was kept well to the front, and frequent expeditions were sent out to watch the movements of the enemy. In a country where nearly all the people, except the Negroes, were friendly to the Confederate men, it was easy for the latter to get early information of the Union Army's moves, and it was hard for the Union authorities to keep informed as to the rebel moves.

On the twenty-second Bolivar was threatened by a large force from south of Grand Junction, reported to be twenty regiments of infantry with cavalry and artillery. General Grant reinforced Bolivar and went in person to Jackson, Tennessee, to superintend the quick movement of troops to wherever the attack might be made. Troops from Corinth were brought in time to repel the threatened movement without a battle. The Union cavalry followed the enemy south to Davis' Mills in Mississippi. On the thirtieth it was apparent that Van Dorn was endeavoring to strike the Mississippi River above Memphis. At the same time other points within General Grant's command were under such a threat that he could not concentrate a force to drive Van Dorn away. At this juncture there was a large Union force in Helena, Arkansas; had it been within Grant's command he could have ordered those troops across the river to attack and break up the Mississippi Central far to the south, which would not only have forced Van Dorn to retire, but would have compelled the retention of a large rebel force far to the south to prevent a repetition of such raids on the enemy's line of supplies. The geographical lines between command jurisdictions during the Civil War were not always well chosen or were too rigidly adhered to for the convenience of military operations.

Van Dorn did not attempt to get on the line above Memphis, as he had apparently intended. He was simply covering a deeper design—one more important to his cause. By the first of October it was fully apparent to General Grant that Corinth was to be attacked with great force and determination, and that Van Dorn, Lovell, Price, Villepigue, and Rust had joined their strength for this purpose. There was some skirmishing before Corinth on October 3, with the rebels massed in the northwest angle of the Memphis and Charleston and the Mobile and Ohio railroads, thus interposed between the Union troops at Corinth and all possible reinforcement. Fresh Union troops would have to come by a circuitous route.

Accordingly, that night General Grant ordered General McPherson, who was at Jackson, to join Rosecrans at Corinth with reinforcements equal to a brigade picked up along the line of the railroad. Hurlbut had been ordered from Bolivar to march for the same destination; and as Van Dorn was coming upon Corinth from the northwest, some of his men fell in with the advance from Hurlbut's, some skirmishing ensuing therefrom. On the fourth, Van Dorn made a dashing attack, hoping no doubt to capture Rosecrans before his reinforcements could reach him. Under these conditions Confederate forces could have occupied the defenses at Corinth and held at bay any Union troops that arrived; in fact the rebels could have taken the offensive against reinforcements of three or four times their number and still have left a sufficient garrison in Corinth to hold it. The enemy almost succeeded in doing this, as some Confederate troops penetrated the National lines at least once; but the works built after Halleck's departure enabled Rosecrans to hold his position until both McPherson's and Hurlbut's troops approached the rebel front and rear.

The enemy was finally driven back with great slaughter; their charges made with great gallantry were repulsed. The Union loss was heavy, but nothing compared to Van Dorn's. McPherson had come up with a train of cars carrying his command as close to the enemy as was prudent, and debarked on the rebel flank getting into the support of Rosecrans just after the repulse. His approach, as well as Hurlbut's, was known to the enemy and had a moral effect. General Rosecrans, however, *failed to follow up the victory although he had been definitely ordered in advance* of the battle to pursue the moment the enemy was repelled. He did not do so, and the order was repeated after the battle. In the first order he had been cautioned that the 4,000 men coming to his assistance would be in great peril if the enemy was not pursued.

These two battles (Iuka and Corinth) were victories for the Union forces, but they might have been a decisive defeat or capture of the enemy forces at hand had Rosecrans carried out his instructions. General Grant had almost made up his mind that he would have to relieve General Rosecrans, when on October 23 General Rosecrans was ordered to succeed General Buell in command of the Army in Middle Tennessee with quite a number of troops from the Army of the Tennessee.

The general's wife, Julia, remembered that Grant was greatly relieved and pleased with General Rosecrans' transfer to independent command in another area. He had hated to relieve him and perhaps end the career of a general with considerable promise who, in a position of independent command, would probably not make the mistakes he had made as a subordinate.

During these months of trying to protect a large enemy area with a sadly reduced force, General Grant felt compelled to set up an information center, which he wisely confided to General Grenville M. Dodge. Dodge proved a remarkably effective collector of information and organizer of military intelligence. He rather too modestly gives the following account of his efforts:

From the beginning of the war I had made considerable use of spies and scouts within the enemy's lines, and had obtained a very reliable force, mostly Southern men living in Northern Alabama and Mississippi. They had relatives enlisted in the First Alabama Cavalry, a regiment I raised while in command at Corinth. These scouts were instructed how to obtain the number of troops in any command, company, regiment, brigade, division or corps, and I placed them at Chattanooga, Atlanta, Selma, Montgomery, Mobile, Meridian, Jackson and Vicksburg, for the purpose of watching the movements of the enemy, and especially to report any force that should move towards Vicksburg, and, after Vicksburg was invested, to report the force sent to Johnston, who was moving an army to relieve Vicksburg. It is a singular fact that from their reports *Grant was notified of every movement in his rear,* and he ordered reinforcements from the North, of as many men as were sent to Johnston, and placed them under Sherman on the Big Black, ready to meet Johnston.

These secret-service men never gave a larger force than 30,000 men with Johnston, which was about the size of Johnston's army. These spies never left their stations. They communicated with me through their relatives, often through their wives, who would come into Corinth to see their relatives in the Alabama Cavalry, and thus throw off suspicion. In one or two cases of emergency they reported directly to Grant.

General Frederick D. Grant tells of one who reported to General Grant on the morning of the Battle of Champion Hill, giving General Grant, General Johnston's position and force, and General Grant said he could attack and defeat Pemberton and reach Vicksburg before General Johnston could aid or reinforce Pemberton. General Grant acted on their information, and speaks of it in his dispatches and Memoirs, and as I take the Rebellion Records and read my dispatches to Hurlbut at Memphis, who sent them by boat to Grant, I am surprised at the accuracy of the reports of these scouts. Of course they were often detected and lost their lives, but there were always others ready to take their places.

General McClernand had in the meantime been authorized by the President to go north and organize new units to be used in opening the Mississippi. These new levies with other reinforcements now began to come in. On October 25, General Grant was placed in command of the Department of the Tennessee, and by November 2 felt himself strong enough to take the initiative. This was a great relief to him after his two and a half months of continued defensive operations over a large area where nearly every citizen was an enemy, ready to give information of every move made by Union troops.

VIII

The Vicksburg Campaign

VICKSBURG was very important strategically as the connecting link between the eastern and western Confederate States. A railroad located across the river from Vicksburg extended westward to Shreveport, and the Vicksburg-Jackson Railroad made the connection cross-country to the east. Situated on a bluff commanding several miles of the Mississippi River, Vicksburg blocked passage on the river and was fortified by the Confederates with all their skill and armament, much of the latter from the Federal forts on the Gulf Coast. Admiral Farragut had taken New Orleans on April 25, 1862, and had actually made a run up to Vicksburg, but he had had to retire to the neighborhood of Baton Rouge.

The first Union attempt to reach Vicksburg began with a movement on Grand Junction by three divisions from Corinth and two from Bolivar. The commanding general was leaving the next evening (November 3) from Jackson, Tennessee, to take command in person of the expeditionary force, which he estimated to have a strength of 30,000 men, and he thought the rebels under General John C. Pemberton had about the same number. General McPherson commanded the left wing of the Union force, General C. S. Hamilton the center, and Sherman, who was still at Memphis, the right wing. Pemberton was in a fortified position on the Tallahatchie River but occupied Holly Springs and Grand Junction on the Mississippi Central Railroad. On November 4 the Union forces occupied Grand Junction and La Grange, throwing a considerable force seven or eight miles to the south along the railroad. The road from Bolivar forward was repaired and put in running order as the troops advanced. General Grant felt confident that the railroads and various junction points, which his troops had been holding with so much anxiety against the raiding operations of the Confederates, could be left more lightly guarded as soon as he began moving his force in offensive operations against the enemy, pre-empting their attention. All the forage within reach was collected under the army quartermaster and the provisions under the chief commissary, receipts being given when there was anyone to take them and the supplies being accounted for as government stores.

It was at this time that the escaped slaves, who gathered in great numbers from the plantations as the force advanced, became a real problem. It was not only that they had no sources of supply and could not be allowed to starve, but also because with inadequate shelter and clothing they were afflicted with various diseases and a danger to the army's health. This was the sort of problem that General Grant enjoyed solving. Accordingly, after getting recommendations, he selected Dr. John Eaton, chaplain of the 27th Ohio, to be in command of the slaves and their families, with the promise that he would support him and help him in every way possible. The idea was to provide work for those who could work, and pay them a reasonable amount for their labor, using the funds earned to supply food and other necessities. Edward E. Hale in after years wrote to General Eaton: "I have said a hundred times in public that Grant never showed his knowledge of men more distinctly than when he chose you for the important duty which you assumed in the West under his direction."

Dr. Eaton's account of his first interview with General Grant offers a vivid picture of the general.

I dismounted, hitched my horse, and approaching a sentry who paced in front of a large house, I inquired of him where General Grant was to be found. He directed me to enter the house, and, pointing to the passageway, told me that I should find the General's orderly at his door and that he would direct me. My heart was thumping violently, but I found the orderly, and asked to have him announce that Chaplain Eaton had come to report in accordance with orders. To my surprise he said,—pointing to the door before which we were standing,—"Tap on the door and he'll tell you to come in." This seemed very different from my previous experiences at headquarters. I rapped, and a voice said very quietly, "Come in." Upon entering the room the same quiet voice said to me, "Have a seat, and I'll talk with you in a few moments." Then, as I announced my name, the General added, "Oh, you are the man who has all these darkies on his shoulders."

I saw at a glance that I had interrupted a council of the various generals in Grant's command, and I felt distinctly out of place. Grant, who was seated at the centre-table, was distinguished from his officers only by the shoulder-straps of a Major-General. My eyes were alert for the signs on his face of the dissipation with which rumor charged him, but I saw at once that no such signs were there. Everything about him betokened moderation and simplicity. His simplicity was no less obvious than the respect which his associate generals manifested for him. I felt my preconceived notions of headquarters and the atmosphere surrounding them undergoing a change. . . . The officers soon filed out, and as they passed me, one and another threw me a glance of amused comprehension, as if they had some suspicion of what my duties were to be. When the last one had left the room, Grant turned to me, and pointing to the table at which he was seated said, "Sit up, and we'll talk." I drew my chair to his table, hardly knowing whether I was the same man who had ridden into camp with such unpleasant memories of former experiences with our commanders and such dark forebodings of the experience before me.

An earnest conversation followed, which, though it involved me in great responsibilities, relieved my mind once and for all of my anxiety concerning the man to whom I had come to report. At first I exerted myself to the utmost to have the order which had brought me revoked. I described the situation in the brigade, where, in the absence of so many of the chaplains, I had been able to become active and helpful among a large body of soldiers. I emphasized my inability, lacking as I was in commanding rank, to enforce the orders I should find it necessary to issue. To take the colored people out of the camps would bring me into conflict with all the officers now making personal use of their services; to set them at work in the cotton fields, the product of which was to be turned over to the Government, would bring me into conflict with all the speculators in the cotton interest. The price of cotton was then mounting, and speculation ran high. I felt so intensely my own inability to meet the situation that I put forward all the energy I could summon to get the order revoked. All that I said had no more effect upon that quiet, attentive face than a similar appeal might have had upon a stone wall. When my arguments were exhausted, the General simply remarked, "Mr. Eaton, I have ordered you to report to me in person, and I will take care of you." And so he did.

This is no place to attempt a discussion in detail of the pertinent factors in this problem. Dr. Eaton had been interested in the subject for some time but had not found anyone ready to offer a solution. As he said later:

The whole question of methods of dealing with the Negro had scarcely as yet been faced by the National Government. Congress had emancipated the slaves of the District of Columbia, which fell directly under its jurisdiction. General Butler had cut the knot of tangled relationship between the army and the blacks by declaring the slaves of those in rebellion against the Government to be contraband of war, and hence liable to retention within the lines of the Union forces as a means of crippling the Confederates. . . . Difficult as the question was, Grant had boldly undertaken to solve it within the limits of his own command. Nor had he waited for instructions from Washington before outlining his plans. The order to me was issued . . . on November 11th. It was not until four days later that he sent the following message, dated from LaGrange, to General Halleck: "Citizens south of us are leaving their homes and Negroes coming in by wagon loads. What will I do with them? I am now having all the cotton still standing out picked by them." To this inquiry, General Halleck replied: "The Secretary of War directs that you employ the refugee negroes as teamsters, laborers, etc., so far as you have use for them, in the Quartermaster's department, on forts, railroads, etc.: also in picking and removing cotton on account of the Government. So far as possible subsist them and your army on the rebel inhabitants of Mississippi.

In his first interview with General Grant, Dr. Eaton found that he had already grappled with the problem and had gotten beyond these instructions, which he had not yet received. But General Halleck's reply had authorized the kind of solution Grant had in mind. According to Dr. Eaton, General Grant had explained the necessity for action as follows:

It would not do, he said, for him to pass these problems indifferently; they must be met and solved, and he had undertaken the responsibility, as his order indicated. He had been compelled, he said, to take this step from two considerations; first, that of military necessity,—the obligation of protecting his troops against the diseases and demoralization to which contact with this body of disorderly people subjected them; second, the dictates of mere humanity demanded that these helpless people should be themselves protected, so far as possible, and spared all possible suffering. The need for action was especially urgent as winter was coming on and the Negroes were incapable of making any provision for their own safety and comfort.

The commanding general and Chaplain Eaton together fixed the price to be paid for the Negro labor, whether rendered to the government or to individuals. The cotton was to be picked from abandoned plantations, the laborers to receive a stipulated price. The quartermaster would ship the cotton north to be sold for the benefit of the government. Those citizens who remained on their plantations were permitted to have the properties worked by their former slaves under government control. The freedmen, as they were later to be called, became self-sustaining almost immediately. They were not paid directly, but the money earned was expended judiciously for their benefit and they gave no trouble afterward.

During the latter part of 1862 the commanding general was very much disturbed by the operations of commercial agents carrying an authority from the Treasury Department to collect and purchase cotton in the southern states and bring it north for sale, presumably to the government. Inevitably, the usual irregularities of a black market made themselves felt. Not only was speculation in cotton facilitated by the officers of the army, but the cotton agents themselves were going from behind the Union lines to the Confederate areas and coming back, certainly spreading information that should not have been put in the hands of the enemy. These agents seem to have been mostly Jews and to have been generally spoken of as such, although there were undoubtedly some who were not Jews. In any case, an order reading as follows was published from General Grant's headquarters:

HEADQUARTERS, 13th ARMY CORPS
DEPARTMENT OF THE TENNESSEE
December 17, 1862

The Jews, as a class violating every regulation of trade established by the Treasury Department and also department orders, are hereby expelled from the Department within 24 hours from the receipt of this order.

Post commanders will see that all of this class of people be furnished passes and required to leave, and any one returning after such notification will be arrested and held in confinement until an opportunity occurs of sending them out as prisoners, unless furnished with a permit from headquarters.

No passes will be given these people to visit trade headquarters for the purpose of making personal application for trade permits.

BY ORDER OF MAJ. GEN. U. S. GRANT
John A. Rawlins, Assistant Adjutant-Gen.

As General Grant had no prejudice against Jews, as such, it is obvious that this order as published went beyond his intentions. In enforcing it, long-time residents in Mississippi were removed from their homes, which of course he never intended. The writer has always believed that advantage was taken of verbal instructions in which the reference was to Jews, a general term then in use, rather than to the cotton brokers carrying on a trade that was a military menace. Simon Wolf has shown in his book, *Presidents I Have Known,* that this was the case. In any case, the order caused quite a rumpus in Washington and was countermanded by the secretary of war.

Holly Springs had been selected for the chief depot of supplies and munitions of war, all of which at that time came from Columbus, Kentucky, except what had been collected about La Grange and Grand Junction. This involved the maintaining of a very long line of supply in the enemy's country. On November 15, General Grant sent word to Sherman to meet him in Columbus. After discussion of general plans for the future, he ordered Sherman with two divisions to march down the Mississippi Central Railroad if he could. By the twenty-ninth Sherman was at Cottage Hill, ten miles north of Oxford, and he had brought three divisions with him, leaving a garrison of only four regiments of infantry, a small detachment of cavalry, and a couple of pieces of artillery. An expedition under Generals Hovey and C. C. Washburn was sent to cut the road in Pemberton's rear, but the damage done to the railroad was only negligible and was soon repaired. The Tallahatchie River, which was in front of General Grant and his forces, was very high and the railroad bridge had been destroyed. Pemberton had strongly fortified himself on the south side of the river. Crossing in the presence of the enemy would have been impracticable, so the cavalry was sent upstream and secured a crossing. This caused the enemy to evacuate his position, possibly accelerated by the expedition of Hovey and Washburn. The enemy was followed as far as Oxford by the main body of troops and seventeen miles farther by McPherson's command. The repair of the railroad bridge on the piles that had been left standing was a short matter and later rails were obtained for cars.

On December 18 orders were received to divide the command into four army corps, with General McClernand commanding one of them, to be assigned to the part of the army operating down the Mississippi. This would interfere somewhat with General Grant's plans, but the difficulty was later overcome by his taking personal command of the operation down the Mississippi.

In the meantime he had established his headquarters at Oxford, where it happened his wife and youngest son, Jesse, came to visit him. They had stopped on the way at Holly Springs but left on the nineteenth to go to Oxford. There, as my grandmother remembered, they found considerable activity engendered by a report from Colonel Dickey. He had come in from a reconnaissance only half an hour before her arrival and had reported that at a considerable distance he had seen a column of troops, said to be Van Dorn's, and that it was striking for the railroad over which she had passed shortly before. The general had been busy telegraphing orders all evening to various local commanders to be on the lookout for Van Dorn and give his force a warm reception. The next morning a knock at the door announced important telegrams, with the bad news that Colonel Murphy, in command at Holly Springs, had surrendered with 2,300 officers and men, that the hospital and commissary stores had been burned, and that Van Dorn had paroled the prisoners, thus making them useless for the present, and then dashed on to do further mischief.

Of course, Mrs. Grant and Jesse had to return via Holly Springs. While passing through there they were told that the house in which she had so recently stopped momentarily had been visited by Van Dorn's staff officers. They insisted that Mrs. Grant was there, and wanted to capture her and her baggage, horses, and carriage. But her hostess of two nights before had insisted that she had left, and was able to keep them from getting the carriage and baggage "by her earnest and personal request." She also learned that Colonel Murphy had received the warning telegrams from headquarters, quietly put them in his pocket, and then gone out to dine, so that the Union troops were surprised.

By contrast, General Morgan of the Union Army, stationed at an old mill with a small detachment, on receiving the notification from headquarters of Van Dorn's proximity was ready for him. When summoned to surrender, he replied tersely, "Come and take me," at which Van Dorn rode on to larger and easier conquests if he could find them.

The following quotation from General Grant's *Memoirs* is pertinent:

> The capture of Holly Springs was a disgraceful one to the officer commanding, but not to the troops under him. At the same time Forrest got on our line of railroad between Jackson, Tennessee, and Columbus, Kentucky, doing much damage to it. This cut me off from all communication with the North for more than a week, and it was more than two weeks before rations or forage could be issued from stores obtained in the regular way. This

demonstrated the impossibility of maintaining so long a line of road over which to draw supplies for an army moving in an enemy's country. I determined, therefore, to abandon my campaign into the interior with Columbus as a base, and returned to LaGrange and Grand Junction, destroying the road to my front and repairing the road to Memphis, making the Mississippi River the line over which to draw supplies. Pemberton was falling back at the same time.

Obviously General Grant was unable to give the expected support to Sherman in his attack on Vicksburg. This attack was made from Chickasaw Bluffs, the only high ground north of Vicksburg. But Pemberton had gotten back to Vicksburg first and was ready to meet Sherman's attack. The attack was made under great difficulties because of the high water and general flooding of the country; Sherman was unable to use more than one quarter of his force. The assaults were repulsed on December 29, and after suffering 1,776 casualties, General Sherman was convinced that he was unable to force an entry into Vicksburg. On the way back, at the mouth of the Yazoo, he was met by McClernand, who by seniority and previous designation took command of the force. He persuaded General Sherman to make a diversion and attack Arkansas Post, about 50 miles up the Arkansas River, adding 12,000 men from Helena to his force on the way. Rear Admiral David D. Porter was in command of the fleet, and after a bombardment of three days by the navy a combined assault was made and the place captured with 5,000 prisoners and 17 guns. McClernand then returned with his entire force to Napoleon at the mouth of the Arkansas River. From there General Sherman and Admiral Porter both sent messages to General Grant urging him to come and take command in person.

Accordingly, General Grant visited McClernand at his command at Napoleon, where he was satisfied that both the army and navy were so distrustful of McClernand's capabilities for the command that it would have been criminal to send troops on so dangerous an expedition under these circumstances. In his *Memoirs,* General Grant says, "By this time I had received authority to relieve McClernand, or to assign any person else to the command of the river expedition, or to assume command in person. I felt great embarrassment about McClernand. He was the senior major-general after myself within the department. It would not do, with his rank and ambition, to assign a junior over him. Nothing was left, therefore, but to assume the command myself."

On January 20, General McClernand with the entire command was ordered to proceed to Young's Point and Milliken's Bend, both in Louisiana, while General Grant returned to Memphis to complete arrangements for the campaign against Vicksburg and to make sure that the territory left behind was reasonably protected. General Hurlbut with the XVI Corps was left in command. The Memphis and Charleston Railroad was held, while the Mississippi Central was abandoned. Columbus, Kentucky, was the only point on the river between Cairo and Memphis left with a garrison. All the troops and guns from posts on the abandoned railroad and river were sent to the front. On January 29, 1863, General Grant arrived at Young's Point and assumed command the next day. General McClernand took exception to this in a way characteristic for him, his correspondence on the subject being in the nature of a reprimand rather than a protest. However, his insubordination was overlooked, in the belief that this was for the good of the service.

By this time there was much discouragement in the North. The 1862 election had gone against the party which favored a vigorous prosecution of the war to save the Union. Voluntary enlistments had ceased throughout most of the North, and the draft, which had to be enforced, had met with considerable opposition. The Union commander was convinced that retirement to Memphis and an attempt to reach Vicksburg along the railroad to Jackson, back of the flooded land, would appear a retreat, and he would again have to depend upon a long line of supply almost impracticable to maintain. He was convinced that activity by the army under his command must be evident to the public and that a new approach by river to high land south of Vicksburg was the only solution that would satisfy public opinion. From Memphis to Vicksburg there is no high land at the water's edge. The intervening land is cut up with bayous filled from the river during high water.

It was essential to keep the army busy during the high-water season and to keep it healthy and engaged in some undertaking aimed at successfully reaching Vicksburg. Accordingly, various projects were undertaken, such as the completion of the canal cutoff across the bend in front of Vicksburg, development of a water route by Lake Providence, and access to the city through the Yazoo River and its contiguous bayous. I am convinced that General Grant did not have much confidence in the success of any of these projects, but in any case they kept the army busy, and the people in the North were aware that something was being done.

Mrs. Annie Wittenmyer, who was with the army near Vicksburg during this campaign, gives an interesting and vivid picture of some of the conditions at that time in her book *Under the Guns, A Woman's Reminiscences of the Civil War:*

In digging the ship canal across the point opposite Vicksburg, hundreds of men were killed or wounded in the great trench. By long practice the gunners on the bluffs of Vicksburg acquired the ability to drop a shell into the great ditch, causing terrible slaughter. The heavy guns of the Union forces answered the enemy's batteries, but failed to silence them. "Whistling Dick," as we all soon learned to call one great cannon used by the enemy, kept the music going night and day. The loud, clear, musical whistle which accompanied every discharge won for that gun the attention of all. "Whistling Dick" was a gun of long range, and was effective in execution, especially along the canal. But one day, after a loud, sharp whistle, there was an explosion, and "Whistling Dick" was heard no more. The work of death went on, however; for there were other effective guns, and the most determined resistance to the project of the Union troops was shown.

The wounded soldiers were taken to a hospital hastily improvised at a point just opposite Vicksburg, where, although more than a mile nearer the enemy, with only the Mississippi River between them, they were nevertheless comparatively safe, being protected by a high embankment. I had been sending supplies to this little hospital with lavish hand. It seemed dreadful that wounded men should lie there night and day under the guns of two armies, the battle always on, the shriek and thunder of shell and shot over them, and all around them, and shaking the very earth on which they lay. Weary, homesick, and suffering, they were isolated from the army and from all other companionship, except that of the surgeon and his force of detailed soldiers. But this surgeon (I have forgotten his name, or I would mention it with the highest respect) was a thoughtful and kind-hearted man, who desired the best for his men and heartily sympathized with them. One day he came into my quarters on the Sanitary boat with radiant face. He had thought of something which would please his "boys," and that was that I should visit them. At first the thing seemed impossible. The distance was many miles. I could not go in an ambulance, or on foot, and the dangers of the journey were appalling. But he had thought of all that, and explained the whole scheme. He could get a good, safe horse, and I could ride on a cavalry saddle; and although there was some water in the canal, and the banks were steep, the crossing was entirely safe, and there were places where the horse could climb.

I could not refuse to go to the men who had faced the cannon, and gone down wounded and helpless to the gates of death for my country and my flag. General Cyrus Bussey, who was afterwards the Assistant-Secretary of the Department of the Interior, and his plucky, lovely little wife, who is now among the glorified in heaven, volunteered to accompany me. Mrs. Bussey had her own horse and a side-saddle. I had a great raw-boned animal, which looked as though he had been in several wars, with a good new cavalry saddle which some officer had kindly lent for the occasion. "This horse is good and safe," the surgeon explained, by way of apology; "they say he wouldn't shy or jump if a shell burst just before him."

The guns of two armies were screaming over us when we reached the point which our guide designated as "the safe place to cross the canal." He did not know that some of the barriers at the mouth of the canal had given way, and that the water in the canal was several feet deeper than when he had crossed that morning. The tide was swift and turbulent; but the surgeon said cheerfully, "It's perfectly safe; just follow me." The next moment his horse went down into the muddy, swirling flood, and, struggling heroically, swam to the opposite shore.

The surgeon called back to us that he had missed the crossing, and designated a point a little higher up, which, as he said, "was perfectly safe." I had misgivings, but, settling myself well to the saddle, gave the horse loose rein. He marched bravely in, and went down into the flood with a plunge. General Bussey, fearing I would be drowned, spurred his horse in after me, and the two brave animals struggled together until we reached the opposite shore. Thanks to my Kentucky training, I kept the saddle, and the only damage done was a good drenching.

As General Bussey expressed a wish that Mrs. Bussey should not attempt to cross, she remained at a cabin near by, which was somewhat protected, till we returned.

Reaching the embankment opposite Vicksburg we scattered, the surgeon taking the lead. I followed about fifty yards behind him, and General Bussey about fifty yards behind me. The road was fair, and we flew over that stretch at a full gallop. My shaggy, raw-boned steed made good time. It was a wild ride. We were surrounded by batteries. The mortar boats of the Union army, placed as near to Vicksburg as possible, were sending their uncertain shells thundering over our heads into the doomed city with deafening fury. The heavy guns along the heights of Vicksburg were answering the long line of batteries and heavy mounted guns on our side of the river; and only the river lay between us and the enemies' works. Shot and shell screamed over us. Sometimes it seemed as if the sky was torn to pieces above us; but my horse did not flinch. On and on we went, in a full gallop. If a gun was levelled at us that day from any of the near batteries, we were not in range when the shot came over, and so we reached the hospital in safety. . . .

The return trip was safely made. Again we swam the canal; Mrs. Bussey joined us, and we returned to camp. The next morning I called on General Grant, and reported the condition of these wounded men. General Grant was most thoughtful and careful of his sick and wounded. He took in the situation at once. Calling Rawlins, he said, "Those wounded men must be moved from the Point right away. Send an order to the medical director to that effect." And that night, under the cover of the darkness, they were removed to hospitals at Milliken's Bend, twenty-five miles away from the belching batteries.

While the water level was too high to permit starting what was to be the real campaign to capture Vicksburg, great criticism of General Grant was expressed in the newspapers, and prominent citizens told Lincoln that Grant drank too much and was incompetent. The President continued to have faith, and must have noted the reports of Charles Dana, who was sent to join headquarters early in April. Dana had been managing editor of the *New York Tribune* for thirteen years, but resigned because of disagreements with Horace Greeley and was later made assistant secretary of war under Edward M. Stanton. At first Mr. Dana was investigating the cotton business and looking into the payment of troops and so forth. He had first seen General Grant as the latter was leaving Memphis, and later joined his headquarters and remained with him until after the capture of Vicksburg. It is likely that his favorable reports had much to do with satisfying the President and Stanton that General Grant was doing his job with thoroughness and efficiency.

There is also the record of Lincoln's interview with General John M. Thayer, a caller at the White House, just in from Vicksburg:

"General," asked the President, "you have a man down there by the name of Grant, have you not?"

"Yes, sir, we have," was the reply.

"What kind of fellow is he?" asked the President.

Thayer replied that Grant was an excellent and popular commander with the army and had a stubborn determination to win under all circumstances.

"Does Grant ever get drunk?" asked Mr. Lincoln bluntly.

"No, Mr. President," replied Thayer, "Grant does not get drunk."

"Is he in the habit of using liquor?" pressed the President.

"I have seen him often, sometimes daily," was the reply, "and I have never noticed the slightest indication of his using any kind of liquor. . . . The charge is atrocious, wickedly false. I saw him repeatedly during the battles of Donelson and Shiloh, on the field, and if there were any sober men on the field, Grant was one of them. . . . I am glad to bring this testimony to you in justice to a much maligned man."

Mr. Lincoln then said: "What I want is generals who will fight battles and win victories. Grant has done this and I propose to stand by him. . . . Somehow I have always felt a leaning toward Grant. Ever since he sent that message to Buckner, 'No terms but unconditional surrender,' I have felt that he was the man that I could tie to, though I have never seen him."

General Grant was back in Memphis on January 19 and forwarded from there to General Halleck a message he had written on the eighteenth, in which he said: "What may be necessary to reduce the place [Vicksburg] I do not yet know, but since the late rains think our troops must get below the city to be used effectively." This seems to have been an indication of his final conclusion that the capture of Vicksburg could be accomplished only by getting below the city, landing there on high ground, and attacking it from the south.

On January 25, Halleck telegraphed Grant: "Direct your attention particularly to the canal proposed across the point. The President attaches much importance to this." Grant remained in Memphis until the twenty-seventh and wired the War Department: "News just received from Vicksburg says water in old canal, and rising rapidly." However, General Grant had realized that the canal (started previously by someone else) would be under fire from Vicksburg and that the head of this canal was located where there was an eddy in the river; the river, then, could hardly be expected to pour a sufficient stream into the canal bed to wash it out and deepen it as had been hoped. He, therefore, had considered as a possible solution of his problem the digging of a canal elsewhere that did not have these disadvantages. But he abandoned all thought of this for the more risky but less time-consuming running of the batteries by his gunboats and transports some night.

It is also of interest that he pointed out the advantage in having the troops on the west bank of the river placed under the commander of the expedition against Vicksburg, at least during the present operation. Grant modestly said that he would co-operate to the best of his ability with whoever was put in the over-all command.

It is not necessary here to go into details of General McClernand's resistance to General Grant's taking over-all command of the expedition, as he had been authorized to do by General Halleck. McClernand wrote protests to the President, but by that time the President and General Halleck must have realized that McClernand was a troublemaker, and while answering him evasively but politely, they apparently decided to leave his position to General Grant's discretion and good judgment.

General Pemberton, commanding the Vicksburg garrison, had met various Union attempts to reach Vicksburg promptly and cleverly. Other attempts were frustrated by the weather and the changing height of the water in the Mississippi River. Finally, on April 20, 1863, conditions had changed sufficiently to permit General Grant to issue his order for the guidance of the "Army in the Field" in its movement "to obtain a foothold on the east bank of the Mississippi River, from which Vicksburg can be approached by practicable roads." The troops were marched down the west bank, while the gunboats and transports made their dramatic running of the batteries of the fortress, and Sherman's Corps distracted the enemy's attention by a feint north of the city in the direction of Haines' Bluff, and then followed McPherson's XVII Corps on May 1.

April 17, Colonel Grierson, commanding a cavalry force of 1,700 men, had started from La Grange, Tennessee, on a raid to Baton Rouge, Louisiana, which surprised the enemy, destroyed his railroads, screened Grant's move into position south of Vicksburg, and collected in pursuit all of Pemberton's cavalry and all the irregular mounted forces that the Confederates could gather. Pemberton then was without "eyes" to discover just what was going on; he could not concentrate on preventing the landing of Union troops at Bruinsburg April 30. Having detached Hatch with part of his command to destroy the railroad between Columbus and Macon and return to La Grange, Grierson successfully reached Baton Rouge May 2 with about 1,000 men. Perhaps this was the one big cavalry raid during the war that had a really important strategic effect, and it was led by a music teacher who hated horses; when a boy he had been kicked in the forehead by one.

Descriptions of the Vicksburg campaign in detail would require more space than allowable here, and they have been amply narrated in standard works on the war. But it must be noted that Grant defeated Pemberton in decisive battles at Champion's Hill and Big Black River.

* * *

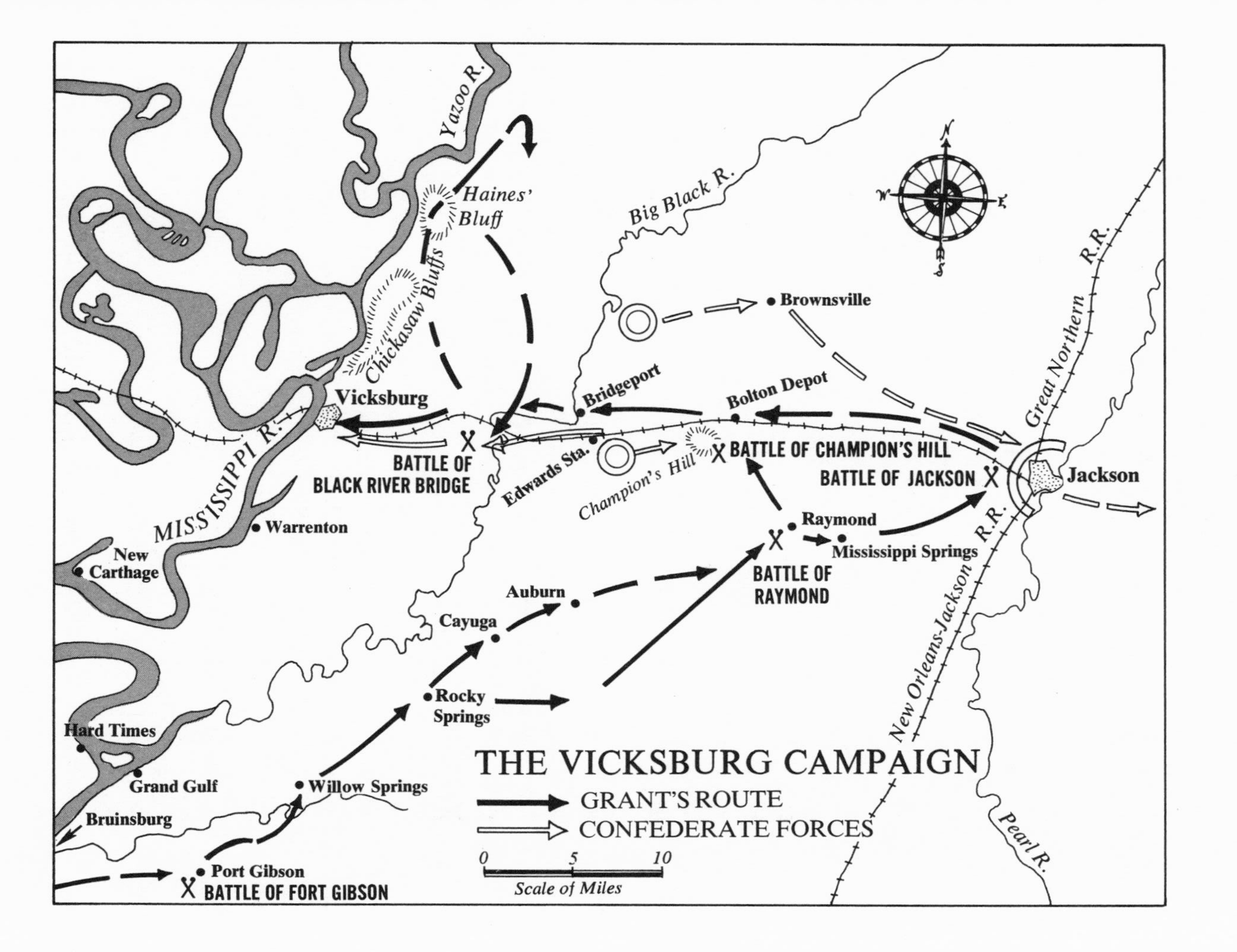
THE VICKSBURG CAMPAIGN
GRANT'S ROUTE
CONFEDERATE FORCES
0 5 10
Scale of Miles
Yazoo R.
Haines' Bluff
Chickasaw Bluffs
Big Black R.
Brownsville
Great Northern R.R.
Vicksburg
Bridgeport
Bolton Depot
MISSISSIPPI R.
BATTLE OF BLACK RIVER BRIDGE
Edwards Sta.
Champion's Hill
BATTLE OF CHAMPION'S HILL
BATTLE OF JACKSON
Jackson
Warrenton
Raymond
Mississippi Springs
BATTLE OF RAYMOND
New Orleans-Jackson R.R.
New Carthage
Auburn
Cayuga
Rocky Springs
Hard Times
Grand Gulf
Willow Springs
Bruinsburg
Port Gibson
BATTLE OF FORT GIBSON
Pearl R.

After its defeat at Champion's Hill (on May 16), the Confederate army retired in haste to the Big Black River, planning to make an effort to stop the Union army's advance there. However, the Confederates were forced to retire again and take refuge within the defenses of Vicksburg. In this engagement the general's son, Fred Grant, was following his father and observing carefully the action of the enemy, when suddenly he felt a bullet penetrate his right thigh. Apparently he turned pale from the shock and when one of the staff officers came up and asked him what was wrong he replied briefly, "I'm killed." The staff officer did not take this seriously and said to him, "Wiggle your toes." He did wiggle his toes and was pronounced to be still alive and not too badly hurt.

However, after he reached the position before Vicksburg the wound began to fester, and it gave him quite a good deal of trouble. The boy was very anxious to bathe the wound and cool it, but the doctors would not permit it. After they left his tent, he heard them discussing whether they would have to amputate his leg. Feeling that anything would be better than that, the lad, approaching the age of thirteen, sneaked out the back of his tent, when the doctors were well out of the way, and sat himself on a stone in a little stream, letting the water of the stream pour over his wound. After he had sat there for a time, he got up, went back to his tent, and lay down again. The wound was very much better the next day and continued to improve.

The Union army arrived in front of Vicksburg and invested it on May 18. I quote Dana and Wilson's *Ulysses S. Grant:*

> Within these eighteen days, Grant had won five battles, taken 40 field guns, many colors and small arms, and nearly 5,000 prisoners; killed and wounded 5,200 of the enemy; separated their armies, in the aggregate, nearly 60,000 strong; compelled the abandonment of the strong positions of Grand Gulf and Haines' Bluff, with their armament of 20 heavy guns; destroyed the railroads and bridges; and made the investment of Vicksburg complete. In doing this McPherson's and McClernand's corps has marched an average of 156 miles; while Sherman's had marched 175 miles. During this time the united strength of these three corps did not exceed 45,000 men. The limits of this work will not permit us to dwell upon the brilliancy of this campaign nor to descant upon the surpassing boldness and vigor of the generalship displayed by Grant, in conducting it. There is nothing in history since Hannibal invaded Italy to compare with it.

The assault on the Confederate works at Vicksburg took place on May 19 and 22. It was repulsed with great loss to the Union forces, convincing everyone that a protracted siege would be necessary, always a tedious and slow operation. It was an interesting coincidence that the siege lasted forty-seven days, and that when General Grant had been a cadet at West Point, Professor Dennis Hart Mahan had prepared a day-by-day account of the steps of a siege of a fortified place which would force the place to be captured or to surrender in forty-seven days. General Grant remembered years afterward that after an excellent recitation on the subject by one cadet the professor asked the class: "Now, young men, if any of you were in command of such a fortress, how would you proceed?" Cadet "Squibob" Derby, an inveterate joker, held up his hand in token that he had the answer, and when called on said: "I would march out, let the enemy in, and at the end of forty-five [sic] days I would change places with him." Thus the siege of Vicksburg followed a textbook prescription.

Vicksburg surrendered on July 4, 1863, and instead of making prisoners of the garrison which had put up such a heroic defense, General Grant proposed to parole both officers and men to take no further part in the war, for which measure of mercy and economy he was criticized by the War Department.

New Orleans had been captured April 25, 1862. Port Hudson surrendered four days after Vicksburg. As General Fuller says: "The South had been cleft in twain. Vicksburg, not Gettysburg, was the crisis of the Confederacy." The seceded states east of the Mississippi River were now blockaded both east and west, and were deprived of food and supplies from west of the Father of Waters. The only hope left the Confederacy was foreign intervention or to continue the struggle until the North was discouraged of eventual success and agreed to a negotiated peace.

Of his Vicksburg campaign General Grant afterward said to John Russell Young: "If the Vicksburg campaign meant anything, in a military point of view, it was that there are no fixed laws of war which are not subject to the conditions of the country, the climate and the habits of the people. The laws of war in one generation would insure defeat in another. I was well served in the Vicksburg campaign."

President Lincoln graciously thanked the commanding general and his troops for this signal victory in the following letter:

My dear General: I do not remember that you and I ever met personally. I write this now as a grateful acknowledgment for the almost inestimable service you have done the country. I wish to say a word further. When you first reached the vicinity of Vicksburg, I thought you should do what you finally did—march the troops across the neck, run the batteries with the transports, and thus go below; and I never had any faith, except a general hope that you knew better than I, that the Yazoo pass expedition and the like could succeed. When you got below and took Port Gibson, Grand Gulf and vicinity, I thought you should go down the river and join General Banks; and when you turned northward, east of the Big Black, I feared it was a mistake. I now wish to make a personal acknowledgment that you were right and I was wrong.

Even before the surrender of Vicksburg had been completed, instructions were given General Sherman to drive Johnston from the Mississippi Central Railroad and destroy bridges as far north as Grenada: "I want you to drive Johnston out in your own way, and inflict on the enemy all the punishment you can. I will support you to the last man that can be spared." Ord and Steele were both notified to move the moment Vicksburg had surrendered, and Sherman was assured he would be informed as soon as Pemberton's final answer was received.

Thus General Sherman's men were not to rest and enjoy their victory but to return to the area they had successfully fought over, and where the water supply in most localities had either been exhausted or contaminated by the Confederates. However, General Johnston's troops suffered from the same heat and the same thirst. He had no heart to attack Sherman, and after the capture of Jackson for the second time on July 17, General Sherman decided that he had fulfilled his mission.

To mitigate the suffering consequent on military operations, on August 1, 1863, General Grant published his General Orders No. 50, appointing commissaries "within the county of Warren laid waste by the long presence of contending armies" to issue "articles of prime necessity to all destitute families calling for them," and added "conduct disgraceful to the American name has been frequently reported to the Major General Commanding. . . . Summary punishment will be inflicted upon all officers and soldiers apprehended in acts of violence or lawlessness." It is perhaps pertinent in this connection that, in his book *Destruction and Reconstruction,* The Confederate General Richard Taylor says: "Genius is God-given, but men are responsible for their acts; and it should be said of General Grant that, as far as I am aware, he made war in the true spirit of a soldier, never by deed or word inflicting wrong on non-combatants."

A further depletion of the force before Vicksburg was made on August 7 by sending the XIII Corps under General Ord to General Banks at New Orleans. In addition orders had been received by General Grant to co-operate with Banks in movements west of the Mississippi. Upon receipt of this order he went to New Orleans to discuss the proposed movement with General Banks. On September 4 he reviewed General Bank's army, riding a large and somewhat wild and nervous horse, loaned him by General Banks. An accident occurred, which Grant described in his *Memoirs*.

> The horse I rode was vicious and but little used, and on my return to New Orleans ran away and, shying at a locomotive in the street, fell, probably on me. I was rendered insensible, and when I regained consciousness I found myself in a hotel near by with several doctors attending me. My leg was swollen from the knee to the thigh, and the swelling, almost to the point of bursting, extended along the body up to the armpit. The pain was almost beyond endurance. I lay at the hotel something over a week without being able to turn myself in bed. I had a steamer stop at the nearest point possible, and was carried to it on a litter. I was then taken to Vicksburg, where I remained unable to move for some time afterward.

While he was still there, Halleck on September 13 telegraphed him to send all available forces to Memphis and thence to Tuscumbia, to co-operate with Rosecrans for the relief of Chattanooga. Another telegram—slow in arriving because addressed to Hurlbut in Memphis—ordered all available forces to go to Rosecrans. In the meantime, Rosecrans had been disastrously defeated September 19–20 at Chickamauga.

Still unable to rise from his bed without assistance, General Grant gave orders in compliance with the telegram, providing for four divisions to start on their way to Chattanooga. The Administration in Washington was naturally very much wrought up about the situation in Chattanooga, and Mr. Charles A. Dana was sent to Rosecrans' headquarters. Under date of October 3 Grant received a message saying the secretary of war would like Grant, as soon as he could take the field, to go to Cairo and report by telegraph. In spite of his lameness he started immediately. Arriving at Columbus (Kentucky) on the sixteenth he reported that: "Your dispatch from Cairo of the 3d directing me to report from Cairo was received at 11:30 on the 10th. Left the same day with staff and headquarters, and am here *en route* for Cairo."

IX

The Victory of Chattanooga

A REPLY to General Grant's October 16 telegram from Cairo came the next morning and directed him to proceed immediately to the Galt House, Louisville, where a War Department officer would meet him with instructions. Grant left Cairo within an hour or two by rail, via Indianapolis. At the station there a messenger arrived and stopped the train, saying that Secretary of War Stanton was just coming into the station and wanted to see the general.

This was their first meeting, and the secretary was accompanied by Governor Brough of Ohio, who had been a friend of old Jesse Grant. Stanton dismissed the special train that had brought him to Indianapolis and accompanied the general into Louisville. Soon after the train had started, Stanton handed Grant two orders and told him he could choose between them. Both created the Military Division of the Mississippi, composed of the Departments of Ohio, the Cumberland, and the Tennessee, and all the territory from the Alleghenies to the Mississippi except Banks's command in the Southwest; one of the orders left the department commanders as they were, and the other relieved Rosecrans and assigned Thomas in his place. The general chose the latter.

They reached Louisville after nightfall in a cold drizzling rain, and from this the secretary of war caught a bad cold from which he never recovered. However, he spent the next day in consultation about the military situation. When all the questions seemed to be settled, General and Mrs. Grant, who had accompanied him, left the hotel to spend the evening with relatives in Louisville. A message to Mr. Stanton from Mr. Dana, then in Chattanooga, informd Stanton that, unless prevented,

Rosecrans was going to retreat. Dana recommended peremptory orders to prevent his doing so.

After the surrender of Vicksburg, General Grant had urged on General Halleck a movement against Mobile. The latter city was important to the enemy and in the absence of a threatening force had little but artillery to defend it. If threatened by land and water simultaneously, it was sure to fall into Union hands, and troops would have to be detached by General Bragg for the defense of Mobile. However, General Grant was overruled in this; Rosecrans was left to be beaten at Chickamauga and besieged in Chattanooga by General Bragg, his army flushed by the victory at Chickamauga. The threat of Rosecrans' retreat would have brought on another disaster, and General Grant telegraphed to Chattanooga, relieving Rosecrans and ordering General Thomas to take command.

After his defeat at Chickamauga, Rosecrans had apparently overlooked the necessity for keeping direct contact open with Bridgeport. General Bragg had stationed his army—from the northern end of Missionary Ridge along the ridge, then westward on Lookout Mountain—so as to control the railroad and the river road all the way to Bridgeport. This station, then, was the farthest to which supplies could be sent by train for the army in Chattanooga. The only other road to the city was through the hills and about sixty miles long. This is the way General Grant rode on horseback to reach his destination.

He was still very lame from his accident and had to be assisted in mounting and dismounting his horse. The road he traversed was strewn with the bodies of horses and mules, dead from starvation. Supplies to the army in Chattanooga were limited to food only, and the soldiers were living on "half rations of hard bread and beef dried on the hoof," as the soldiers called the emaciated cattle that were brought in. There was little or no fuel left within the Union lines, and even the stumps of trees had been used for cooking.

On October 20, Grant and his staff had gone as far as Nashville. As it was then not prudent to travel beyond Nashville by night, he remained there until the next morning. There he met for the first time the military governor of Tennessee, Andrew Johnson, who delivered a speech of welcome which was evidently not a maiden effort. It was long and the general was in torture while it was being delivered, fearing that some response would be required from him; but this demand did not occur.

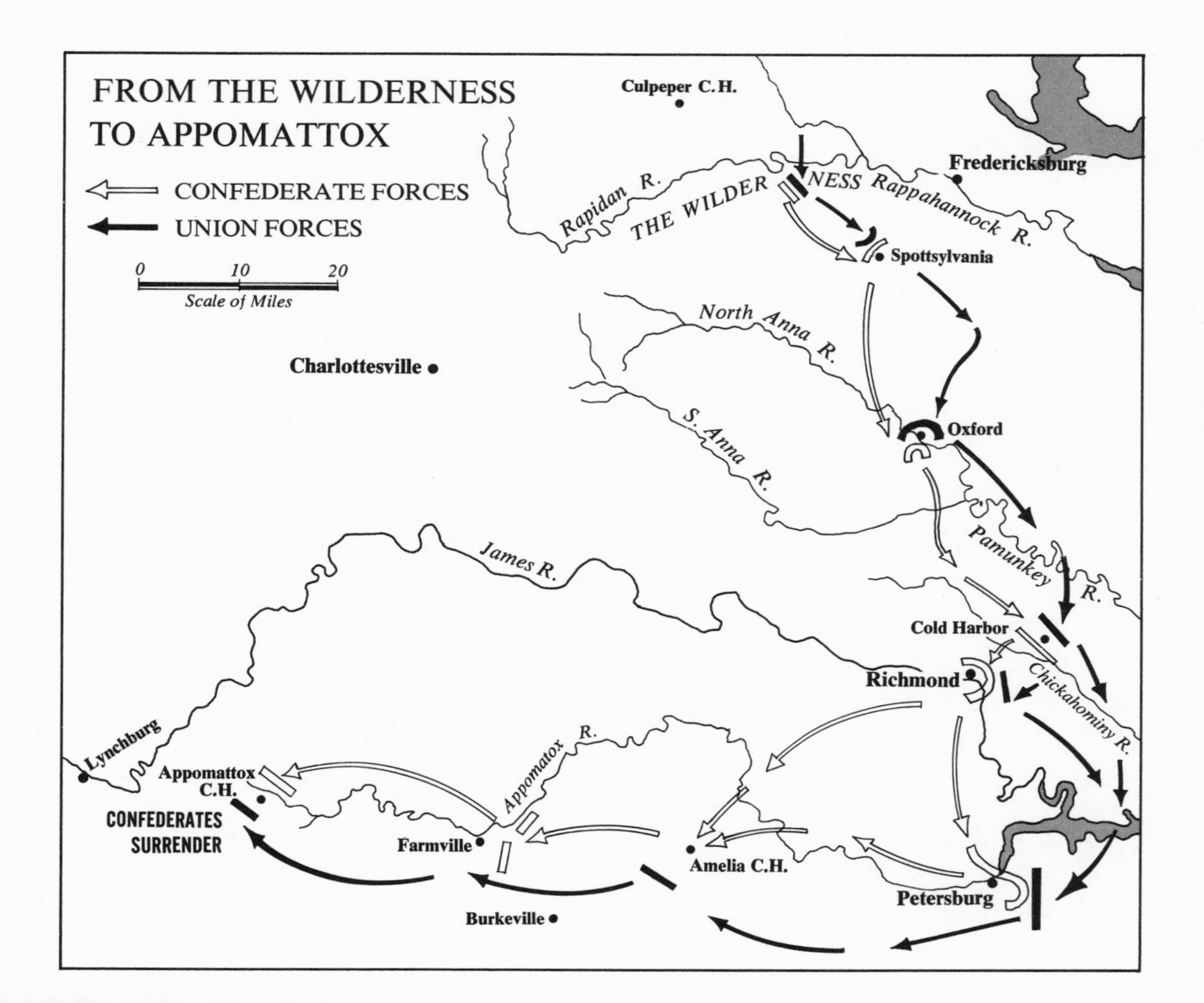
FROM THE WILDERNESS
TO APPOMATTOX
CONFEDERATE FORCES
UNION FORCES
0
10
20
Scale of Miles
Culpeper C.H.
Fredericksburg
Rapidan R.
THE WILDER NESS
Rappahannock R.
Spottsylvania
North Anna R.
S. Anna R.
Charlottesville
Oxford
Pamunkey R.
James R.
Cold Harbor
Richmond
Chickahominy R.
Appomatox R.
Lynchburg
Appomattox C.H.
CONFEDERATES SURRENDER
Farmville
Amelia C.H.
Petersburg
Burkeville

From Nashville the general sent three telegrams: to Burnside at Knoxville, telling him to fortify important points in his department so that they could be held with the least number of men; to Admiral Porter at Cairo, telling him that Sherman's first elements had passed Eastport, Mississippi, that rations were doubtless on their way from St. Louis by boat to supply his army, and that Porter should send a gunboat to convoy them; and to Thomas, suggesting a large party be put to work on the wagon road back to Bridgeport.

On the morning of the twenty-first, the general's party boarded a train, reaching Stevenson, Alabama, after dark. They met Rosecrans on his way north, and he described to General Grant briefly but very clearly the situation at Chattanooga. He made some good suggestions as to what should be done, without any explanation of why he had not done it.

General Grant spent the night at Bridgeport and from there, taking horses, proceeded via Jasper over Waldron's Ridge to Chattanooga. Mud was knee-deep in some places and the roads hardly passable because of washouts on the mountainsides. General Grant had to be carried when it was not safe to move on horseback. The party stopped for the night at a small hamlet some ten or twelve miles beyond Jasper. The next day General Grant and his staff reached Chattanooga a little before dark and went directly to General Thomas' headquarters, where they remained three days until Grant's own headquarters could be established.

Assistant Secretary of War Charles A. Dana was in the room with General Thomas and other general officers when Grant arrived. The next morning he sent a dispatch to the War Department beginning, "Grant arrived last night, wet, dirty, and well." Indeed, the rain had been pouring down for two days. When a staff officer called attention to his clothes being soaking wet, the general refused at the moment to accept the loan of a change of clothing; he insisted on remaining seated in front of the fire and obtaining the views of the general officers present as to what might best be done to relieve the threat of starvation, both for animals and men. He was very much impressed by the plan which General W. F. (nicknamed "Baldy") Smith, chief engineer of the Army of the Cumberland, proposed and seemed to have worked out in detail.

The next morning, the twenty-fourth, General Grant, with Smith, Thomas, and others, was on his way on horseback to see for himself whether General Smith's somewhat complicated plan was feasible. General Smith had cut timbers and established a sawmill on the bank of the Tennessee River, extemporized with an old engine found in the neighborhood; had cut from the logs rafted downstream from above Chattanooga lumber for pontoons and railroad plank for a second bridge (a flying bridge was already there); and had materials for a third bridge. Then he had partly constructed a steamer to ply between Chattanooga and Bridgeport as soon as the Union troops had possession of the river.

Apparently, General Bragg's army considered the Army of the Cumberland as already condemned to starve or surrender, and there seemed to be little animosity between the two armies. The Grant reconnaissance party crossed the river to the north side and reached it again at Brown's Ferry about three miles below Lookout Mountain, unobserved by the enemy. Leaving their horses concealed, back from the river, they approached the river on foot. An enemy picket station of about twenty men in full view was within easy range; but it did not fire at Grant's party or seem disturbed by their presence.

The reconnaissance on the twenty-fourth was convincing, and that evening General Grant gave the necessary orders for carrying out General Smith's plan. He placed General Smith in command of a task force to execute the project, a somewhat unusual placing of a staff officer in command of troops; but so many engineer officers were already in command of different units that at the time this did not seem to be any exception to general practice.

At midnight of October 26, General Smith began his march down the north bank of the river with 2,800 men. At 3 A.M. of the thirty-seventh, Hazen started silently down the stream with his pontoons carrying 1,800 men; by 5 o'clock he was at Brown's Ferry, completely surprising the guard at that point and taking most of them prisoners; by 7 o'clock Smith's force had been ferried across and had begun to fortify the position; and by 10 A.M. the bridge had been completed.

Hooker with XI and XII Corps had been sent from the east and was waiting in the vicinity of Bridgeport for the road to Chattanooga to be opened. Sherman was already on his way to join the army at Chattanooga. Now that the road from Bridgeport to Chattanooga on the south bank of the river had been opened for use by the Union troops, "the Cracker Line" (as it was called by the soldiers) was reopened and the fear of starvation of both men and animals was dispelled, giving a strong uplift to the morale of the besieged army. Why Rosecrans, who was familiar with Smith's plan and had approved it, had done nothing about it, has never been explained.

In the meantime, on the twenty-sixth General Grant had made a careful reconnaissance of the position of the Union troops and, as far as visible, of the Confederate troops. It was during this reconnaissance that the following incident occurred.

When in sight of Chattanooga Creek, by which the pickets of the two armies were separated, General Grant again left his staff. Supposing that the enemy would not fire at one sole officer, which would have been a breach of the truce the pickets on both sides were observing, he stepped out in the place where apparently the men of both armies were in the habit of getting water without exchanging any shots. A sentinel of the Union picket guard recognized General Grant as he approached and as customary cried, "Turn out the guard—commanding general!" The enemy on the opposite side of the creek heard this call and one of his sentinels cried out, "Turn out the guard—General Grant!" The Confederate guard accepted the joke, formed promptly facing the Union line, and presented arms. The general returned the salute by lifting his hat, the guard was dismissed, and he continued on his way. Of this incident, General Horace Porter remarked, "We knew that we were engaged in a civil war, but such civility largely exceeded our expectations."

One of the special events of General Grant's arrival at Thomas' headquarters on October 23 had been the presence of Captain Horace Porter in the room with General Thomas' staff. There began between Grant and Porter a very sincere friendship and a mutual admiration and confidence in one another which lasted until General Grant's death. After Captain Porter had served a short period as acting chief of ordnance, General Grant succeeded in having him assigned as aide-de-camp with the rank of lieutenant colonel, in which capacity he performed outstanding services in all the battles of the following year in Virginia.

The enemy was evidently surprised at the activity of the Union Army under the "new management." When Bragg recovered from his surprise, he sent Longstreet to retrieve the lost ground if possible. Reaching Wautatchie during the night of October 28, he made an attack on Geary's division of Hooker's forces. Geary was able to hold his ground against greatly superior numbers for about three hours. Geary's teamsters were apparently scared and deserted their teams. Equally scared by the noise of battle, the mules stampeded, broke loose, and ran away. It was for the benefit of their reputation and the safety of the command that they headed toward the enemy, heads down and tails up, with trace chains rattling and whiffle trees snapping on the stumps of trees. They charged upon Longstreet's bewildered men. Assuming this to be an organized cavalry charge, the rebel infantry took to their heels. Convinced that such distinguished service should be rewarded, the quartermaster in charge of the animals sent in the following communication: "I respectfully request that the mules, for their gallantry in this action, may have conferred upon them the brevet rank of horses." With all the brevets handed out to various officers, this recommendation was thought to be a good joke and afforded much amusement to the commanding general. The Union loss of killed, wounded, and missing in this engagement was only 422 men. The enemy never made a further attempt to interrupt the newly established line of supply.

However, it took several weeks for the Army of the Cumberland, both men and animals, to recover strength enough to assume the offensive. But preparations were made for the coming battle, such as placing 116 pontoon boats in the North Chickamauga Creek, with material for the roadway over the bridge deposited near the Tennessee River a few hundred yards away (out of sight of the enemy) to indicate where the north end of the bridge was to rest.

Nothing was heard from Burnside, but messages were received indicating the distress in Washington on his account. The commanding general therefore decided to launch a limited attack on November 23. The position that had been occupied for several months by the Army of the Cumberland had been strongly fortified for defense. It was about a mile from the town and extended from Citico Creek—a small stream running near the base of Missionary Ridge and emptying into the Tennessee about two miles below the mouth of the South Chickamauga—on the left to Chattanooga Creek on the right. One of the elevations especially fortified was called Fort Wood, and owed its importance largely to the fact that it lay between the city and Missionary Ridge. It had twenty-two pieces of artillery, most of which could reach points in the enemy's line.

The attack was made by Granger's Corps of two divisions, Sheridan's and T. J. Wood's. Howard's Corps was placed in support in rear of the center. By 2 o'clock in the afternoon all were ready to advance, and the clouds had lifted so that the enemy could see what was going on. The rebel pickets were driven back on the main guards and these were also carried without a stop, before the enemy had time to reinforce its advance guards. The Union loss was approximately 1,100 killed and wounded, while the Confederates probably lost as many, including prisoners captured. Except for artillery fire from Missionary Ridge and Fort Wood this ended the first day's battle.

By that night Sherman was in position on the Union left except for Osterhaus' division which had not yet crossed at Brown's Ferry. Because the river was continuously rising, the bridge at that point was not safe for use by troops; therefore Osterhaus was ordered to report to Hooker if unable to cross by 8 o'clock on the morning of the twenty-fourth.

Giles A. Smith's division was pushed out from the North Chickamauga Creek by 2 o'clock in the morning of November 24 with 30 brave and well-armed men in each of his 116 boats. The boats dropped downstream noiselessly with the current until they arrived at the mouth of the South Chickamauga. Here a few boats were landed, the troops disembarked, and a rush made on the picket guard known to be at that point. The guard was surprised and 20 of their number captured. The remainder of the troops landed with equally good results at the site of the future bridge.

The ferrying of Sherman's command from the north side of the Tennessee in the pontoons had immediately begun. A steamer from the city was brought up to assist, and the divisions of M. L. Smith and John E. Smith were successfully landed and started entrenching their position. By daylight two entire divisions were across and well protected. Shortly after noon two bridges had been completed. At one o'clock Sherman's troops (preceded by skirmishers) attacked and, by 3:30 P.M., gained possession of the heights without much loss. A drizzling rain and low clouds obscured Lookout Mountain and the top of Missionary Ridge from the view of persons in the valley. However, with the taking of the hill the enemy evidently became aware of what was happening and opened fire on their assailants, but without avail. Later in the day a more determined attack was made, this also without success. Sherman's cavalry was on the march soon after one bridge had been completed, and by half-past three the whole of it was over both bridges and on its way to attack the enemy's communications at Chickamauga Station. During the afternoon General Giles A. Smith had been severely wounded and had been carried from the field.

Thomas having accomplished on the twenty-third the mission to be assigned to him for the twenty-fourth had nothing to do on the latter day; but Howard had slipped across Citico Creek and achieved a junction with Sherman, having been directed in the morning to report to him.

In the meantime, Hooker on the west of the line had three divisions: Osterhaus' of the Army of the Tennessee, Geary's of the Army of the Potomac, and Cruft's of the Army of the Cumberland—all west of Lookout Creek. Early in the morning of the twenty-fourth Hooker had crossed the creek, captured the picket, and then commenced ascending the mountain in his front. By 11 o'clock the bridge across the creek was completed and Osterhaus was across, driving the enemy and inflicting considerable loss. During the action at the bridge Geary was pushing with his division up the hill, surmounting important obstacles and opposed by the enemy directly in his front and the guns on top of the mountain. But the enemy, seeing its left flank threatened, gave way and the whole command pushed up the hill. By noon Geary gained the open ground on the north slope of the mountain, but there were strong fortifications in his front. As the rest of the command came up, a line was formed from the upper palisade to the mouth of Chattanooga Creek.

Generals Grant and Thomas from the top of Orchard Knob could see the continuous Union line now formed from the Tennessee River, where Sherman had crossed, up the Chickamauga Creek to the base of Missionary Ridge and over the top of its northern end to Chattanooga Valley, and then parallel to the ridge a mile or more across the valley to the mouth of Chattanooga Creek, thence up the slope of Lookout Mountain to the top of the palisade. Because of clouds that obscured the top of Lookout Mountain as seen from the valley, Hooker's fight there came to be known as the "Battle above the Clouds."

General Grant was able to telegraph to Washington: "The fight today progressed favorably. Sherman carried the end of Missionary Ridge, and his right is now at the tunnel and his left at Chickamauga Creek. Troops from Lookout Valley carried the point of the mountain, and now hold eastern slope and a point high up. Hooker reports 2,000 prisoners taken, besides which a small number have fallen into our hands from Missionary Ridge." To this the President replied the next day: "Your dispatches as to fighting on Monday and Tuesday are here. Well done. Many thanks to all. Remember Burnside." Halleck also telegraphed and after congratulations expressed his concern about Burnside.

At midnight General Grant began issuing his orders for the next day, beginning with a telegram to Orlando B. Willcox, one of Burnside's division commanders who was in position up the valley but still in communication with the north. He wanted Willcox to inform Burnside, if practicable, that the attack on Bragg would commence the next morning; this should relieve the pressure on Burnside, if he could hold. Grant had been reassured by a previous message saying that Bragg was to be attacked and Longstreet would find the country very bare and would probably lose his transportation before reaching Kentucky.

Orders were sent to Sherman to attack at daylight and to Hooker to move at the same hour and endeavor to intercept the enemy's retreat if still there; if he had gone, then Hooker was to move directly to Rossville and operate against the left and rear of the force on Missionary Ridge. Thomas was not to move until Hooker had reached Missionary Ridge.

November 25 opened clear and bright, and from the top of Orchard Knob the whole field was visible. It remained so all day. Bragg's headquarters were in full view, and officers were seen coming and going constantly.

The point of ground which Sherman captured the day before was disconnected from the ridge by a low pass, over which a wagon road crossing the ridge intervened between the two hills, with a railroad tunnel near it. The problem now was for Sherman to get on the main ridge and attack the enemy, well fortified there, and back still farther on higher ground was a second fortification. The Union troops engaged advanced rapidly and carried the extreme end of the rebel works. Morgan L. Smith had reached a point which cut the enemy off from the railroad bridge and from the means of bringing up supplies from their main depot at Chickamauga Station. Brave and strenuous but unsuccessful efforts were made to drive Union troops from the position they had gained. From where he was the Commander in Chief could see Confederate column after column moving against Sherman. Every Confederate gun that could be brought to bear was concentrated on him. J. E. Smith with two brigades charged up the west side of the ridge to support Corse's command over open ground and in the face of a heavy fire of both musketry and artillery. He reached the enemy's parapet but after a short time was driven back by a heavy enemy force on his right flank, only to re-form his men in a wood and drive the attacking party back to its entrenchments. Viewing this action, General Grant directed Thomas to send a division to reinforce J. E. Smith. Baird's division was assigned this mission, which required their marching a considerable distance in full view of the enemy. Bragg at once commenced marching his men in the same direction. This was just what Grant wanted, since Hooker was expected soon to cross the ridge in the neighborhood of Rossville, compelling Bragg to send troops in that direction also.

Unexpectedly, Hooker was detained four hours crossing Chattanooga Creek, and the Union forces lost the immediate tactical advantage that had been expected. Hooker's appearance on Bragg's flank was to be the signal for Thomas' assault on the center of the ridge, but Sherman's situation was getting so critical that the assault for his relief could no longer be delayed. Sheridan's and Wood's divisions had been waiting to move the instant the signal was given. General Thomas was ordered to have them charge at once, but, seeing no signs of this, Grant turned to inquire of Thomas what caused the delay. He was surprised to see him talking to General Thomas J. Wood, one of the division commanders who was to make the charge. Asked why he was not making the charge, Wood replied that this was the first he had heard of it. He was told to charge at once, departed directly, and in an incredibly short time loud cheering was heard. He and Sheridan were driving the enemy's advance before them toward Missionary Ridge.

The Confederates were strongly entrenched on the crest of the ridge, with a second line halfway down and another at the base. Union men drove the troops in the lower line of rifle pits so rapidly and followed them so closely that Union and Confederate troops went over the first line of works almost simultaneously. Rebels who were not captured and sent to the rear retreated and were pursued. Without awaiting further orders or stopping to re-form, northern troops captured the second line of works and then rushed on to the crest—thus effectually carrying out the orders of the eighteenth for the action intended on the twenty-fourth. The fire from the rebel line was terrific, cannon and musket balls filling the air; but the damage done was small because of the steep slope, and in order to avoid shooting their own men, the rebels had to shoot high. The safest place for the Union soldiers, strangely, was in the front line commingling with the retiring Confederates. The retreat of the enemy along its line on top of the ridge was so precipitate and the panic so great that Bragg lost control over his men. Thousands were captured, many throwing away their guns in their flight.

Sheridan pushed forward with his division until he reached the Chickamauga Creek at a point above the place the enemy crossed. He met some resistance from the troops on the second hill in the rear of Missionary Ridge, probably intended to cover the retreat of the main body and the artillery and trains. Sheridan pushed his men forward up the second hill slowly and without attracting attention of those intended to defend it, while he detached forces to the right and left to surround the position. The enemy, discovering this before the dispositions were complete, retreated hastily, leaving artillery, wagon trains, and many prisoners to Sheridan's troops. Except for his prompt pursuit the capture of prisoners, artillery, and small arms that day would have been much less.

The moment the troops of General Gordon Granger's command were seen to be crossing the defenses at the top of Missionary Ridge, General Grant mounted his horse and rode to the front. General Thomas left Orchard Knob at about the same time, and General Sheridan on the right was already in full pursuit of the enemy east of the Ridge. General Wood had accompanied his division to the left of Sheridan on horseback in the charge but did not join in the pursuit. On the Union's left—where Bragg's troops had been massed against Sherman—the resistance was more stubborn and the contest lasted longer. Granger was ordered to follow the enemy with Wood's division, but he was so excited and kept up such a roar of musketry in the direction taken by the enemy that by the time the firing could be stopped the enemy had gotten well out of reach. The rebels who had been fighting Sherman fled on seeing everything to their left giving way. Sherman, however, was not aware of the extent of the Union Army's success until after nightfall, when he received orders to pursue at daylight the next morning. As soon as Sherman discovered that the enemy had left his front, he sent his reserves, Davis' division of the Army of the Cumberland, to hasten over the pontoon bridge at the mouth of the Chickamauga and to move toward Chickamauga Station.

Hooker, detained by the destruction of the bridge at Chattanooga

Creek, got his troops across, with the exception of the artillery, by fording the stream a little after 3 o'clock. Leaving his artillery to follow when the bridge had been reconstructed, he pushed on with the remainder of his command. He encountered a division of the enemy at Rossville, and they retired along the ridge, which threw them on Palmer. Thus they were caught between two Union forces, and many were captured. During the night of the twenty-fifth, Hooker's position was near Rossville, extending east of the ridge.

During the night General Grant telegraphed Willcox that Bragg had been defeated and that immediate relief would be sent Burnside if he could hold out. To General Halleck he sent announcement of the victory and informed him that forces would be sent immediately to relieve Burnside. Before the Battle of Chattanooga began, he had taken measures for the relief of Burnside as soon as practicable. Directions were given Thomas to have the little steamer built at Chattanooga loaded with rations and ammunition. Granger's Corps was to move by the south bank of the Tennessee River to the mouth of the Holston and from there to Knoxville, accompanied by the boat. In addition to the supplies on the boat the men were to carry forty rounds of ammunition in their cartridge boxes and four days' rations in their haversacks.

It may be noted that as General Sherman's troops came in to Chattanooga and marched to their position on the left of the Union line, an officer of the Army of the Cumberland had commented on the fact that the Army of the Tennessee did not have any corps insignia visible. To this General Sherman replied, "Oh yes they have! Their insignia is their cartridge box with 'forty rounds' of ammunition."

In his *Memoirs* General Grant called attention to the fact that:

> The accidents growing out of the heavy rains and the sudden rise in the Tennessee River so mingled the troops that the organizations were not kept together, under their respective commanders, during the battle. Hooker, on the right, had Geary's division of the Twelfth Corps, Army of the Potomac; Osterhaus's division of the Fifteenth Corps, Army of the Tennessee; and Cruft's division of the Army of the Cumberland. Sherman had three divisions of his own army, Howard's corps from the Army of the Potomac, and Jefferson C. Davis's division of the Army of the Cumberland. There was no jealousy—hardly rivalry. Indeed, I doubt whether officers or men took any note at the time of the fact of this intermingling of commands. All saw a defiant foe surrounding them, and took it for granted that every move was

intended to dislodge him, and it made no difference where the troops came from so that the end was accomplished.

The troops, however, seem to have operated satisfactorily under the various corps and army commanders, without any confusion resulting from the intermingling.

Owing to the advantage the Confederacy had from its position and the terrain, the victory at Chattanooga was won against great odds. The victor attributed his success to certain mistakes which he thought Bragg had made, which we need not repeat in detail here; but it is perhaps of interest that Mr. Jefferson Davis had visited General Bragg on Missionary Ridge a short time before General Grant had come to Chattanooga. It was an accepted rumor that he had come to reconcile a serious difference between Bragg and Longstreet and, finding this difficult to do, had planned the campaign against Knoxville to be conducted by Longstreet.

Bragg was remarkably intelligent and well informed, both professionally and otherwise. He was also thoroughly upright, but possessed of an irascible temper and was innately disputatious. It was an old army story that, when stationed at a post of several companies commanded by a field officer, Bragg himself was commanding one of the companies and acting as post quartermaster and commissary. As commander of the company he submitted a requisition upon the quartermaster (himself) for something wanted for the company. As quartermaster he declined to fill the requisition and endorsed on the back of it his reasons for so doing. As company commander he replied urging that his requisition only called for what he was entitled to, and that it was the duty of the quartermaster to fill it. As quartermaster he still persisted he was right, and under the circumstances referred the whole matter to the commanding officer of the post. When the latter read through the correspondence he exclaimed, "My God, Mr. Bragg, you have quarreled with every officer in the army, and now you are quarreling with yourself!"

Longstreet was an entirely different sort of person. He had been at West Point three years with General Grant and remained a lifelong friend in spite of their being on opposing sides in the Civil War. "He was brave, honest, intelligent, a very capable soldier, subordinate to his superiors, just and kind to his subordinates, but jealous of his own rights, which he had the courage to maintain. He was never on the lookout to detect a slight, but saw one as soon as anybody when intentionally given," Grant wrote of Longstreet.

The victorious commander in his *Memoirs* summarized his conclusions about the battle:

> My recollection is that my first orders for the battle of Chattanooga were as fought. Sherman was to get on Missionary Ridge, as he did; Hooker to cross the north end of Lookout Mountain, as he did, sweep across Chattanooga Valley, and get across the south end of the ridge near Rossville. When Hooker had secured that position the Army of the Cumberland was to assault in the center. Before Sherman arrived, however, the order was so changed as that Hooker was directed to come to Chattanooga by the north bank of the Tennessee River. The waters in the river, owing to heavy rains, rose so fast that the bridge at Brown's Ferry could not be maintained in a condition to be used in crossing troops upon it. For this reason Hooker's orders were changed by telegraph back to what they were originally.

While following the enemy on the twenty-sixth and again the morning of the twenty-seventh, generally on the road to Ringgold, General Grant directed Thomas, verbally, not to start Granger until he received further orders and told him he was going to the front to observe the situation himself. There was a possibility that Bragg's troops might get over their stampede by the time they had reached Dalton and that he might think it well to take the road back to Cleveland and from there go to Knoxville, uniting with Longstreet to make a sudden attack on Burnside. However, when Grant reached Ringgold on the twenty-seventh he saw that the rout was sincere. The rebels had thrown away guns, caissons, small arms, provisions; they were moving like a disorganized mob for Cleburne's division, which was acting as rear guard to cover the retreat.

As Hooker moved from Rossville toward Ringgold, Palmer's division took the road to Graysville and Sherman moved by way of Chickamauga Station toward the same place. As soon as Grant saw the situation at Ringgold, he sent a staff officer back to Thomas with orders to inform him of the state of affairs and direct him to start Granger at once. Confident that the troops were already on the march for the relief of Burnside, General Grant stayed through the day at Ringgold to prepare for the return of his troops. He had arrived just as the artillery left at Chattanooga Creek by Hooker was coming up. Hooker's men were attacking Cleburne's division, which had taken a strong position in adjacent hills to cover the retreat of the Confederate army through a narrow gorge. Just beyond the gorge the valley is narrow and the creek tortuous. Hooker captured three pieces of artillery and 230 prisoners, and 130 rebel dead were left on the field.

General Grant directed Hooker to collect the flour and wheat in the nearby mills for the use of Union troops. He was then to destroy the mills and other properties that might be of use to the enemy, avoiding any wanton destruction.

General Sherman arrived from Graysville with his troops, where he found Palmer had preceded him. The latter had picked up many prisoners and much abandoned property on his way. General Grant went back with Sherman to Graysville where he remained overnight. He returned to Chattanooga the following night, October 29. There he found that Thomas had not yet started Granger and so had lost a full day—an important delay in determining the fate of Knoxville. Both Thomas and Granger were aware that Burnside had telegraphed on the twenty-third that his supplies might last for ten or twelve days, during which time he could hold out against Longstreet; but if he was not relieved within that time, he would be obliged to surrender or attempt to retreat. To effect the latter would have been impracticable. He was already very low on ammunition and with an army pursuing him he would not be able to gather supplies. Granger not only had not started but was very reluctant to go, since he had decided that it was not a wise move. General Grant then directed General Sherman to march to the relief of Knoxville, telling him that he had to solve the problem of Burnside having only four to six days' supplies left and that he must be relieved within that time.

It was with regret that he assigned this job to Sherman, because his men needed rest after their long march from Memphis and the hard fighting at Chattanooga; but it was evident that Burnside would not be rescued if his relief depended on General Granger. Unfortunately Sherman's men had left the north side of the Tennessee River near Chattanooga on the night of the twenty-third with only two days' cooked rations in their haversacks because they expected to be back in their tents by that time. Planning to be engaged in battle, they had not taken overcoats or blankets with them, and the weather was already cold at night. There was very little likelihood of their finding any food in this country, passed over so often by the Confederate troops. However, in the mills they found some flour and a good deal of bran, which they made into bread. In this and other ways they eked out an existence until they reached Knoxville.

To induce him to hold out a little longer, it was important to inform Burnside of the steps being taken. General Grant selected Colonel James H. Wilson of his staff to get to Knoxville and report the situation fully to Burnside, giving him all the encouragement possible. Dana, who had been at Chattanooga, volunteered to accompany Colonel Wilson. Information as to what was being done to relieve Knoxville was put in writing, and Colonel Wilson was told to try to manage that a copy fall secretly into the hands of General Longstreet. The two messengers made the trip safely, General Longstreet learned of Sherman's coming in advance of his reaching there, and Burnside was prepared to hold out longer if necessary.

A boom had been placed across the Holston River by Burnside to catch scows and flats as they floated down. On these, by prearrangement with the loyal people of East Tennessee, flour and corn, forage and provisions generally were placed and thus secured for the use of the Union troops. Cattle was also driven into Knoxville from the east, which side was not invested by the enemy, so that, when relief arrived, Burnside had more provisions on hand than when he had last reported.

General Grant at Chattanooga had about 60,000 men. Bragg had more than three quarters this number, but his position was supposed to be impregnable. And it was his own fault that he had reduced his command by sending Longstreet away, with something over 20,000 men. Furthermore, even after Sherman had arrived and was on the north side of the Tennessee River, Bragg had sent Buckner's division to reinforce Longstreet and started another division a day later. However, the Union attack had commenced before the latter reached Knoxville and Bragg ordered the division back, but it did not return to Chattanooga in time to be of any service. This mistake may have been due to a misconception of what was going on on the Union side. Although Sherman's troops had crossed to the north side of the Tennessee River at Brown's Ferry, in full view of Bragg's troops on Lookout Mountain a few days before the attack, Sherman's men had disappeared behind the foothills and were not visible to the rebels on Missionary Ridge until they assaulted him there. Bragg may have assumed that Sherman had gone on up to Knoxville to defeat Longstreet; but the blunder of detaching Longstreet can hardly be accounted for. If Bragg had captured Chattanooga, East Tennessee would have fallen without a struggle. General Grant could write in later years: "It would have been a victory for us to have our army away from Chattanooga safely. It was a manifold greater victory to drive away the besieging army; a still greater one to defeat that army on his chosen ground and nearly annihilate it."

The victory at Chattanooga received much attention even abroad. The following is a quotation from Judge Louis A. Coolidge's biography of Grant.

> A sense of the inevitable was beginning to pervade the North and to be felt abroad. "Thank Heaven! The coming man for whom we have so long been waiting seems really to have come," wrote Motley from Vienna, "Ulysses Grant is *at least* equal to any general now living in any part of the world and by far the first that our war has produced on either side." A German writer spoke of Chattanooga as "An action which both for the scientific combination and bravery of execution is equal to any battle of modern times from the days of Frederick the Great downward."

President Lincoln recommended a national thanksgiving and telegraphed General Grant:

> Understanding that your lodgment at Chattanooga and at Knoxville is now secure, I wish to tender you, and all under your command, my more than thanks—my profoundest gratitude—for the skill, courage, and perseverance with which you and they, over so great difficulties, have effected that important object! God bless you all!

It was a week after the address at Gettysburg, and within a fortnight a bill was introduced in Congress reviving the grade of lieutenant general. The bill was soon passed with great majorities, and the President indicated he would give the advanced rank to General Grant, making him General in Chief of all the Armies of the United States.

Any fear Mr. Lincoln may have had that he was promoting a possible rival was put to rest by General Grant's letter to Isaac N. Morris, of Illinois, January 20, 1864, part of which follows.

> In your letter you say that I have it in my power to be the next President. This is the last thing in the world I desire. I would regard such a consummation, as highly unfortunate for myself, if not for the country. Through Providence I have attained to more than I ever hoped, and, with the position I now hold in the regular army, if allowed to retain it, will be more than satisfied.

I certainly shall never state a sentiment, or the expression of a thought with the view to being a candidate for office. I scarcely know the inducement that could be held out to me to accept office, and unhesitatingly say that I infinitely prefer my present position to that of any civil office within the gift of the people.

This is a private letter to you, and not intended for others to see, or read, because I want to avoid being heard from by the public except through my acts, in the performance of my legitimate duties.

This was re-echoed in a letter to his father on February 20, 1864, showing that it was not just a political gesture.

After the victory at Chattanooga, General Grant established the headquarters for his now greatly enlarged department at Nashville. Burnside had followed Longstreet only to Strawberry Plains twenty miles or more to the east and then had stopped, believing Longstreet would leave the state; but the latter did not do so, and subsisted the army for the winter off the people of East Tennessee. J. G. Foster now relieved General Burnside, and Sherman made distribution of his troops as ordered along the Tennessee. In his *Memoirs,* General Grant says: "Nothing occurred at Nashville worthy of mention during the winter," but his son has added a footnote to the effect that the citizens of Jo Daviess County, Illinois, had presented to him, their most prominent citizen now, a sword with a gold scabbard, ornamented with a scroll running nearly the entire length with the names of General Grant's battles engraved on it, and with diamonds set in the hilt of the sword; and also that a gold medal was voted to him by Congress for the victories of Vicksburg and Chattanooga. These souvenirs are now in the Smithsonian Institute in Washington.

Many things neglected during the rescue of Chattanooga were now attended to. Plans were made for the coming campaign, which proposed the capture of Mobile. Preparatory thereto, among many operations assigned him, was General Sherman's Meridian Campaign in January and February 1864.

On horseback from Knoxville to Lexington, Kentucky, the nearest place from which he could go back to Nashville by rail, General Grant made a personal exploration of the Wilderness Road over Cumberland Gap. The weather was unusually cold, and the road had been cut into by wagons to considerable depth. The six days' ride from Strawberry Plains to Lexington was remembered as "a very cheerless one and very disagreeable." Grant found many people at home along the route and almost all of them intensely loyal.

They would collect in little places where we would stop of evenings to see me, generally hearing of my approach before we arrived. The people naturally expected to see the Commanding General the oldest person in the party. I was then forty-one years of age, while my medical director was gray haired and probably twelve or more years my senior. The crowds would generally swarm around him, and thus give me an opportunity of quietly dismounting and getting into the house. It also gave me an opportunity of hearing passing remarks from one spectator to another about their general. Those remarks were apt to be more complimentary to the cause than to the appearance of the supposed general, owing to his being muffled up, and also to the travel worn condition we were all in after a hard day's ride. I was back in Nashville by the 13th of January, 1864.

The reconnaissance showed the road over Cumberland Gap was not adequate for the supply of an army.

When I started on this trip it was necessary for me to have some person along who could turn despatches into cipher, and who could also read the cipher despatches which I was liable to receive daily and almost hourly. Under the rules of the War Department at that time, Mr. Stanton had taken entire control of the matter of regulating the telegraph and determining how it should be used, and of saying who, and who alone, should have the ciphers. The operators possessed of the ciphers, as well as the ciphers used, were practically independent of the commanders whom they were serving immediately under, and had to report to the War Department through General Stager all the despatches which they received or forwarded.

I was obliged to leave the telegraphic operator back at Nashville, because that was the point at which all despatches to me would come, to be forwarded from there. As I have said, it was necessary for me also to have an operator during this inspection who had possession of this cipher, to enable me to telegraph to my division and to the War Department without my despatches being read by all the operators along the line of wires over which they were transmitted. Accordingly I ordered the cipher operator to turn over the key to Captain Cyrus B. Comstock, of the Corps of Engineers, whom I had selected as a wise and discreet man who certainly could be trusted with the cipher if the operator at my headquarters could.

The operator refused point-blank to turn over the key to Captain Comstock as directed by me, stating that his orders from the War Department were not to give it to anybody—the commanding general or any one else. I told him

I would see whether he would or not. He said that if he did he would be punished. I told him if he did not he most certainly would be punished. Finally, seeing that punishment was certain if he refused longer to obey my order, and being somewhat remote (even if he was not protected altogether from the consequences of his disobedience to his orders) from the War Department, he yielded. When I returned from Knoxville I found quite a commotion. The operator had been reprimanded very severely and ordered to be relieved. I informed the Secretary of War, or his assistant secretary in charge of the telegraph, Stager, that the man could not be relieved, for he had only obeyed my orders. It was absolutely necessary for me to have the cipher, and the man would most certainly have been punished if he had not delivered it; that they would have to punish me if they punished anybody, or words to that effect.

This was about the only thing approaching a disagreeable difference between the Secretary of War and myself that occurred until the war was over, when we had another little spat. Owing to his natural disposition to assume all power and control in all matters that he had anything whatever to do with, he boldly took command of the armies, and, while issuing no orders on the subject, prohibited any order from me going out of the adjutant-general's office until he had approved it. This was done by directing the adjutant-general to hold any orders that came from me to be issued from the adjutant-general's office until he had examined them and given his approval. He never disturbed himself, either, in examining my orders until it was entirely convenient for him; so that orders which I had prepared would often lie there three or four days before he would sanction them. I remonstrated against this in writing, and the Secretary apologetically restored me to my rightful position of General-in-Chief of the Army. But he soon lapsed again and took control much as before.

X

Commander in Chief and the 1864 Campaign

MARCH 3, 1864, General Grant was ordered to Washington. His arrival there five days later, with his oldest son and two staff officers and without any advance notice or ceremony, was unexpected by the public and caused considerable comment. He went to the Willard Hotel and registered as "U. S. Grant and son, Galena, Illinois." At first the clerk did not recognize him and assigned him a room on the top floor, as the hotel was crowded. However, he was soon recognized, and this caused much disturbance. With profuse apologies he was assigned a much better room by the hotel clerk, and when he entered the dining room the word was evidently passed around among the other guests. While he was eating his dinner, someone recognized him and announced the fact; the guests gave him a cheer. He was embarrassed and retired somewhat abashed.

When the bill to revive the rank of lieutenant general had passed after Grant's victory at Chattanooga, the President had said: "I have never seen Grant. Before I appoint him to the command of the armies, I want to learn all about him. Who of his friends knows him best?" Washburne suggested Joseph Russell Jones, United States Marshal for Illinois, and known to Mr. Lincoln. Jones was, accordingly, summoned to the capital. A few weeks earlier it happened that he had written Grant, asking his views about the presidency, to which letter he had received a reply. When he reported to the White House, Mr. Lincoln asked him a number of questions.

Jones asked the President, "Perhaps you would like to know whether Grant is going to be a candidate for the presidency?" Mr. Lincoln confessed to a little curiosity on the subject. Mr. Jones thereupon produced the letter saying that, although it was a private letter, he felt no impropriety in showing it to Mr. Lincoln and that it would be most satisfactory for the latter to read just what was said. In it, General Grant had said that nothing was further from his wishes than that high office; and that, even if he had been ambitious for it, he would not then permit his name to be used, but was for Abraham Lincoln above all men and under all circumstances. Jones left the letter with Mr. Lincoln, and it is presumably somewhere among his papers.

In the debate in the House on the bill to re-establish the rank of lieutenant general, Mr. Washburne, who had introduced the bill, had said:

> I am not here to speak for General Grant. No man, with his consent, has ever mentioned his name in connection with any position. . . . Every promotion he has received since he first entered the service to put down this rebellion, was moved without his knowledge or consent; and in regard to this very matter of lieutenant-general, after the bill was introduced and his name mentioned in connection therewith, he wrote me and admonished me that he had been highly honored already by the Government, and did not ask or deserve any thing more in the shape of honors or promotion; and that a success over the enemy was what he craved above every thing else.

General Grant was now to satisfy Lincoln's curiosity by attending the reception at the White House to pay his respects to the President and Mrs. Lincoln. The President recognized him as he came to the door of the Blue Room and, walking over toward him, said, "Well, here is General Grant," and shook hands with him very cordially. After he had introduced him to Mrs. Lincoln and such members of the Cabinet as were nearby, the general became the object of special attention of those who could crowd around him, and Mr. Seward, the secretary of state, escorted the distinguished visitor to the East Room where his presence caused a near riot. At Mr. Seward's suggestion he was persuaded to stand up on a sofa so that those at a distance could see him. After considerably more embarrassing attention from the other guests, he at last escaped and returned to his hotel.

On the ninth he went with his oldest son, Frederick, to the White House and was received by the President in the presence of the Cabinet to be given his commission as lieutenant general. Knowing that he was bashful about public speaking, the President had thoughtfully given him in advance a draft of what he expected to say in handing him the commission. Lincoln suggested that Grant would now have time to write out his reply.

The President said:

> General Grant, the nation's appreciation of what you have done, and its reliance upon you for what remains to be done, in the existing great struggle, are now presented, with this commission constituting you Lieutenant-General in the Army of the United States. With this high honor devolves upon you, also, a corresponding responsibility. As the country herein trusts you, so, under God, it will sustain you. I scarcely need to add that, with what I here speak for the nation, goes my own hearty personal concurrence.

To this Grant replied:

> Mr. President, I accept the commission, with gratitude for the high honor conferred. With the aid of the noble armies that have fought in so many fields for our common country, it will be my earnest endeavor not to disappoint your expectations. I feel the full weight of the responsibilities now devolving on me; and I know that if they are met, it will be due to those armies, and, above all, to the favor of that Providence which leads both nations and men.

On March 10 the general visited the headquarters of the Army of the Potomac at Brandy Station, and was much impressed with General Meade's patriotic attitude in suggesting that the new Commander in Chief might wish to replace him with an officer of the western army. On mature consideration General Grant later decided definitely that he would retain General Meade in command of the Army of the Potomac, because of the confidence that army had in him since the victory at Gettysburg. He also realized that the Army of the Potomac would look with some lack of confidence on any other western officer being given command in the eastern army, perhaps because of the disastrous second battle of Manassas when General Pope, after issuing a rather boastful general order, had been so badly defeated by General Lee. In fact, Grant realized that perhaps they might not be too sure of *his* being able to defeat General Lee. This doubt may have persisted until after the Battle of the Wilderness, when General Lee had been driven back into his entrenchments and remained there, and the Army of the Potomac was withdrawn and turned south when it reached the highway to Richmond.

Before leaving Nashville, Grant had written a very complimentary letter to General Sherman and a similar one to General McPherson. Both men acknowledged the letters with gratitude and affection. General Grant was much pleased to find his recommendation for their promotion had been carried out.

On March 12, orders placing General Grant in command of all the armies were published, but he had left the night before to return to his command in the West and to meet Sherman in Nashville. Before leaving on the eleventh, he had received an invitation from Mrs. Lincoln to a military dinner at the White House, given in his honor, at which twelve other prominent generals were expected to be present. He asked to be excused because he had to return immediately to Nashville. Mr. Lincoln is reported to have said, "I don't see how we *can* excuse you. It would be *Hamlet* with the Prince of Denmark left out." General Grant had replied, "I appreciate fully the honor Mrs. Lincoln would do me; but time is precious; and—really—Mr. President, *I have had enough of the show business.*"

Lincoln must have felt in those early days of March that he had found the right man. General Grant had gone to receive his commission with the firm intention, expressed to General Schofield and General Sherman, that he would not accept the increased rank and its responsibilities unless he could obtain the President's personal assurance that he would not be interfered with in his plans or in carrying them out by the secretary of war or General Halleck. The latter was to be left in Washington as chief of staff in the War Department. The following paragraphs from the *Memoirs* seem to be pertinent and to cover the subjects as concisely as possible:

Although hailing from Illinois myself, the State of the President, I never met Mr. Lincoln until called to the capital to receive my commission as lieutenant-general. I knew him, however, very well and favorably from the accounts given by officers under me at the West who had known him all their lives. I had also read the remarkable series of debates between Lincoln and Douglas a few years before, when they were rival candidates for the United States Senate. I was then a resident of Missouri, and by no means a "Lincoln man" in that contest; but I recognized then his great ability.

In my first interview with Mr. Lincoln alone he stated to me that he had never professed to be a military man or to know how campaigns should be conducted, and never wanted to interfere in them; but that procrastination on the part of commanders, and the pressure from the people at the North and Congress, *which was always with him,* forced him into issuing his series of "Military Orders"—one, two, three, etc. He did not know but they were all wrong, and did know that some of them were. All he wanted or had ever wanted was some one who would take the responsibility and act, and call on him for all the assistance needed, pledging himself to use all the power of the government in rendering such assistance. Assuring him that I would do the best I could with the means at hand, and avoid as far as possible annoying him or the War Department, our first interview ended.

The Secretary of War I had met once before only, but felt that I knew him better.

While commanding in West Tennessee we had occasionally held conversations over the wires, at night, when they were not being otherwise used. He and General Halleck both cautioned me against giving the President my plans of campaign, saying that he was so kind-hearted, so averse to refusing anything asked of him, that some friend would be sure to get from him all he knew. I should have said that in our interview the President told me he did not want to know what I proposed to do. But he submitted a plan of campaign of his own which he wanted me to hear and then do as I pleased about. . . .

I did not communicate my plans to the President, nor did I to the Secretary of War or to General Halleck. . . .

My general plan now was to concentrate all the force possible against the Confederate armies in the field. There were but two such, as we have seen, east of the Mississippi River and facing north. The Army of Northern Virginia, General Robert E. Lee commanding, was on the south bank of the Rapidan, confronting the Army of the Potomac; the second, under General Joseph E. Johnston, was at Dalton, Georgia, opposed to Sherman, who was still at Chattanooga. Besides these main armies the Confederates had to guard the Shenandoah Valley, a great storehouse to feed their armies from, and their line of communications from Richmond to Tennessee. Forrest, a brave and intrepid cavalry general, was in the West with a large force, making a larger command necessary to hold what we had gained in Middle and West Tennessee. We could not abandon any territory north of the line held by the enemy, because it would lay the Northern States open to invasion. But as the Amy of the Potomac was the principal garrison for the protection of Washington even while it was moving on Lee, so all the forces to the west, and the Army of the James, guarded their special trusts when advancing from them as well as when remaining at them. Better, indeed, for they forced the enemy to guard his own lines and resources at a greater distance from ours, and with a greater force. Little expeditions could not so well be sent out to destroy a bridge or tear up a few miles of railroad track, burn a storehouse, or inflict other little annoyances. Accordingly I arranged for a simultaneous movement all along the line. Sherman was to move from Chattanooga, Johnston's army and Atlanta being his objective points. Crook, commanding in West Virginia, was to move from the mouth of the Gauley River with a cavalry force and some artillery, the Virginia and Tennessee railroad to be his objective. Either the enemy would have to keep a large force to protect his communications, or see them destroyed, and a large amount of forage and provision, which he so much needed, fall into our hands. Sigel was in command in the Valley of Virginia. He was to advance up the valley, covering the North from an invasion through that channel as well while advancing as by remaining near Harper's Ferry. Every mile he advanced also gave us possession of stores on which Lee relied. Butler was to advance by the James River, having Richmond and Petersburg as his objective.

Before the advance commenced I visited Butler at Fort Monroe. This was the first time I had ever met him. Before giving him any order as to the part he was to play in the approaching campaign I invited his views. They were very much such as I intended to direct, and as I did direct, in writing, before leaving.

What was to happen is perhaps best summarized and clearly stated in the opening paragraph of Kenneth P. Williams' *Lincoln Finds a General, A Military Study of the Civil War,* which this writer has found to be the most thoroughly researched history of the war:

In the early hours of May 4, 1864—at the beginning of the fourth year of the great American Civil War—the Union Army of the Potomac opened a campaign that was in many ways without precedent in the annals of warfare. For almost a year it would be in constant and close contact with its adversary, the Confederate Army of Northern Virginia. There would be day after day of battle, fiercer and more determined than any armies had ever waged before, interspersed with bitter skirmishes. There would be movements the execution of which would test the courage and skill of the ablest commanders and the most seasoned troops; there would be losses in killed, wounded, and missing that would try the souls of the people who sustained the armies. Finally the end would come miles away in the quiet parlor of an unpretentious house in Appomattox, Virginia—a village until then without fame—when the two Generals in Chief of the North and the South, after a handclasp and a reminiscent conversation, put their signatures to documents that have found a permanent place among the cherished possessions of their people.

One of the changes introduced in the reorganization of the Army in the East was the bringing together of the cavalry into a mounted corps under the command of General Philip H. Sheridan. Up to that time the cavalry had been kept busy and had been used almost entirely as protection for the trains, on various local reconnaissance duties, for prisoner guards, and especially as orderlies and messengers. It had not been utilized as a united mobile force moving faster than the infantry and therefore capable of playing an important part in a maneuver as a fast-moving striking force. This was a new idea and was not thoroughly understood by all the unit commanders. In fact, a difference of opinion between General Sheridan and General Meade gave rise to an altercation which was taken to the Commander in Chief. Grant, hearing that Sheridan had said that he could move out with his cavalry and whip Stuart, "remarked quietly that Sheridan generally knows what he is talking about. Let him start right out and do it. So the matter was settled" —in favor of General Sheridan, as the independence of the cavalry corps was an essential part of his strategy.

We have already referred to the strategic importance of Grierson's raid in the Vicksburg campaign, and now such independent use of the cavalry was to become a matter of standard operating practice. In his *Memoirs* General Grant speaks of the first such operation of the newly formed cavalry corps as having:

> . . . attained in its brilliant execution and results all the proportions of an independent campaign. . . . On the 8th of May, just after the Battle of the Wilderness, and when we were moving on Spottsylvania, I directed Sheridan verbally to cut loose from the Army of the Potomac, pass around the left of Lee's army, and attack his cavalry; to cut the two roads—one running west through Gordonsville, Charlottesville, and Lynchburg, the other to Richmond —and, when compelled to do so for want of forage and rations, to move on to the James River and draw these from Butler's supplies. This move took him past the entire rear of Lee's army. These orders were also given in writing through Meade.
>
> The object of this move was threefold. First, if successfully executed—and it was—he would annoy the enemy by cutting his line of supplies and telegraphic communications, and destroy or get for his own use supplies in store in the rear and coming up. Second, he would draw the enemy's cavalry after him, and thus better protect our flanks, rear and trains than by remain-

ing with the army. Third, his absence would save the trains drawing his forage and other supplies from Fredericksburg, which had now become our base. He started at daylight the next morning, and accomplished more than was expected. It was sixteen days before he got back to the Army of the Potomac.

Sheridan passed through the outer defenses at Richmond, and could probably have entered the inner defenses, but could not have maintained himself there without strong support from other troops. He struck out directly for the James River below the city, and after communicating with Butler and resting his men and horses, as well as collecting food and forage, he moved between the Chickahominy and the James until stopped at Mechanicsville on May 12. Turning north to cross the Chickahominy at Meadow Bridge, he found this barred to him and the reorganized, previously defeated cavalry occupying the opposite shore. The panic created by his first entrance within the outer works of Richmond having subsided, troops were sent out to attack his rear. He now had the well-manned defenses of Richmond on his right, the Chickahominy on his left with no available bridge and the opposite bank occupied, and in his rear was a force sent from Richmond. This latter force Wilson's and Gregg's divisions attacked and beat back while Sheridan with the remaining division built a bridge over the Chickahominy under fire, forced a crossing, and soon dispersed the Confederates he found there. On the fourteenth, with his command all across the Chickahominy, he went into camp at Haxall's Landing. Establishing communication with General Butler, the latter directed what supplies he needed to be furnished.

Not knowing where the Army of the Potomac was, having left it at Spottsylvania, great caution was necessary in getting back to the army. By May 22 Sheridan was at Aylett's on the Mattapony, where he learned the location of the two armies, and he joined the Army of the Potomac on its march from North Anna to Cold Harbor. In this memorable raid he had moved entirely around Lee's army, had encountered his cavalry four times and defeated them in each engagement, and he recaptured 400 Union prisoners and killed or captured many of the enemy. He destroyed or used many supplies and munitions of war, tore up miles of railroad and telegraph line, and freed the Union army of annoyance by the enemy's cavalry for more than two weeks.

* * *

General Grant had chosen to move by the enemy's right flank, but recognized that there would be some advantages in moving by the left flank. By the route chosen, the Potomac River, Chesapeake Bay, and many streams would furnish an easy line of supply for the Union army and limit the distance over which supplies would have to be hauled by wagons. On the other hand, the disadvantages were that General Lee could, when he chose, move a large force or even his entire army on a line interior to that of the Union army; and the Union army would have to subsist on supplies and ammunition with which it started or which could follow it. In those days before motor transportation, wagon trains had difficulty moving as fast as the troops, even the infantry. And it was not possible to build up new supply points for an army that kept moving, because the part of Virginia through which the Union army would pass had been denuded to meet the demands of the Confederate army itself. Of the two possible lines of advance the one by the enemy's right flank and the Union army's left flank seemed to offer the best promise of success, and apparently this expectation was realized as the campaign progressed.

The crossing of the Rapidan with such a large army at the various fords seems to have been considered a critical beginning of the campaign, but it was accomplished without any interference by the rebels. General Grant doubtless hoped that he would be able to get the Army of the Potomac through the Wilderness without suffering a flank attack from the Army of Northern Virginia. However, this is just what General Lee decided to do, and it resulted in the Battle of the Wilderness.

The battle was at its height on May 5, and the Confederates were driven back to take shelter behind their entrenchments by the night of the sixth; they remained there during May 7. In this battle the Union army outnumbered the Confederates but could not make full use of its numbers. It suffered the great disadvantage, too, of not being as familiar with the country, where the wooded character of the ground prevented effective use of artillery and a good view of what was going on at a distance.

General Porter noted in his book that General Grant appeared on the morning of May 5 in full uniform with sash and sword and some light lisle thread gloves, given him by his wife. He was obviously under the impression that the Army of the Potomac would expect the commanding

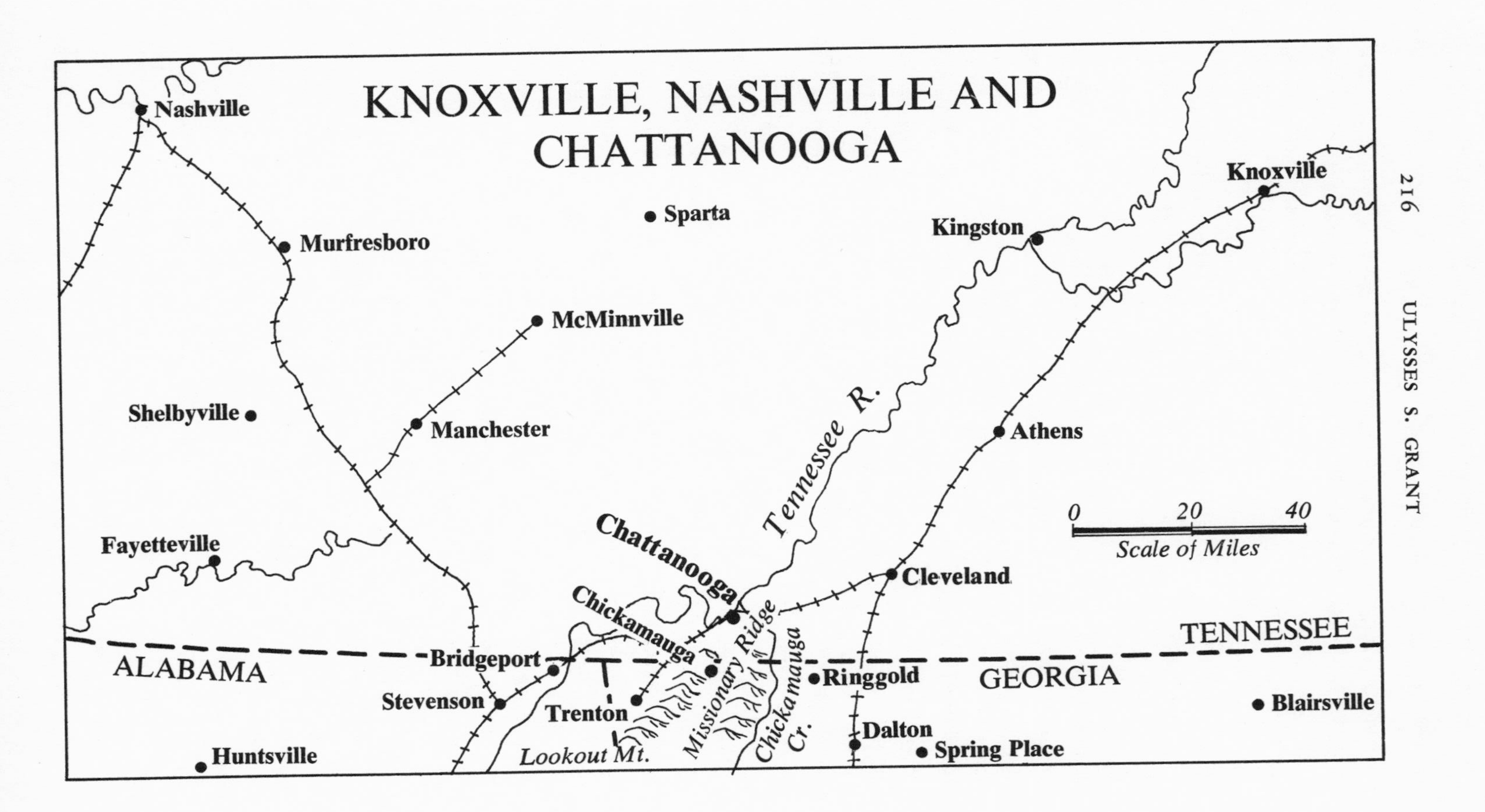
KNOXVILLE, NASHVILLE AND CHATTANOOGA
Nashville
Murfresboro
Sparta
Kingston
Knoxville
McMinnville
Shelbyville
Manchester
Tennessee R.
Athens
0
20
40
Scale of Miles
Fayetteville
Chattanooga
Cleveland
Chickamauga
Missionary Ridge
Chickamauga Cr.
TENNESSEE
ALABAMA
Bridgeport
Stevenson
Trenton
Ringgold
GEORGIA
Blairsville
Dalton
Spring Place
Huntsville
Lookout Mt.

general to be thus attired, but he did not find it necessary to appear in such full dress again.

In speaking of the Vicksburg campaign in later years, Grant observed with feeling that he had been well served in that campaign. The first two days fighting in the Wilderness must have shown him that the Army of the Potomac and its leaders could not be depended upon for the same mutual support and team play as the Army of the Tennessee had achieved the year before. As we go along with the story, we will necessarily be distressed at times by the fact that some corps or division commander failed to carry out his part of a maneuver with the speed and vigor necessary to achieve success.

General Burnside, commanding the Army of the James at Fredericksburg, was hurried to join the Army of the Potomac by a telegram on May 5 and remained with it thereafter. Although regretfully having left the western army to General Sherman, General Grant decided to accompany the Army of the Potomac. He felt that his presence would be necessary to prevent interference with the commander of the Army of the Potomac for political reasons or for other reasons that might seem important to the secretary of war, General Halleck, or even influential members of the Congress.

At a critical moment in the Battle of the Wilderness when Warren's Corps was being driven back on part of his line in front of general headquarters, the enemy's shells were beginning to fall on the knoll where General Grant was seated on a tree stump. It looked for a time as if the tide of battle might sweep over that part of the field. According to General Porter:

> He rose slowly to his feet, and stood for a time watching the scene . . . without making any comments. His horse was in charge of an orderly just behind the hill, but he evidently had no thought of mounting. An officer ventured to remark to him, "General, wouldn't it be prudent to move headquarters to the other side of the Germanna road till the result of the present attack is known." The General replied very quietly, between the puffs of his cigar, "It strikes me it would be better to order up some artillery and defend the present location." Thereupon a battery was brought up, and every preparation made for defense. The enemy, however, was checked before he reached the knoll.

It was toward the end of May 5 that, seated on the ground and looking at a map, he had said:

I do not hope to gain any very decided advantage from the fighting in this forest. I did expect excellent results from Hancock's movement early this morning, when he started the enemy on the run; but it was impossible for him to see his own troops, or the true position of the enemy, and the success gained could not be followed up in such a country. I can certainly drive Lee back into his works, but I shall not assault him there; he would have all the advantage in such a fight.

The next day a really serious attack was made on the Union right, and General Sedgwick received his fatal wound. Then news came that a large force had scattered Sedgwick's entire corps, and it was rumored that both Sedgwick and Wright had been captured. Again according to Porter, a general officer approached the general in chief, and evidently in considerable excitement said:

"General Grant, this is a crisis that can not be looked upon too seriously. I know Lee's methods well by past experience; he will throw his whole army between us and the Rapidan, and cut us off completely from our communications." General Grant rose to his feet, turned to the officer, and taking his cigar out of his mouth said: "Oh, I am heartily tired of hearing about what Lee is going to do. Some of you always seem to think he is suddenly going to turn a double somersault, and land in our rear and on both our flanks at the same time. Go back to your command, and try to think what we are going to do ourselves instead of what Lee is going to do."

General Porter was reminded of a remark General Sherman had made in his presence: "I believe the chief reason why he was more successful than others was that while they were thinking so much about what the enemy was going to do, Grant was thinking all the time about what he was going to do himself."

This had been a particularly long and strenuous day, and it was noted that General Grant, after allowing for those he had given away, figured that he had smoked about twenty strong and large cigars. But this was probably a record not to be equaled again. General Porter goes on to remark that he looked in the commanding general's tent at the end of this day and found him soundly and peacefully asleep. He had to wake the general up to communicate a report, but Grant considered it a gross exaggeration, and since he had made every provision for meeting a renewed attack on the right, he turned over and went to sleep again. Undoubtedly we may assume that his staff officers, who had been kept on the move all day, were well-nigh exhausted and slept equally soundly as did the horses they had been riding.

But on May 7, General Lee did not renew his attack, remaining under cover of his entrenchments and presumably treating the wounded and burying the dead, as far as they could be located in the woods. General Grant consequently started to organize the retirement of the Army of the Potomac from the Wilderness area and from contact with the enemy, a maneuver always recognized by military critics as a most difficult one. However, preparations were made to withdraw from the right the Army of the Potomac and hasten the units as fast as withdrawn toward Spottsylvania under the cover of night. The maneuver was successfully carried out, and when the troops reached the main road behind the line they had been defending and turned south toward Richmond, there was a great cheer given the commanding general, who was on horseback waiting to see the column pass southward. (In fact, I remember very well that Chief Hood, chief engineer of the Southern Pacific at the time, at dinner in the Bohemian Club Grove, was asked by Captain Anderson, president of the California Transportation Company, what he remembered as the most distressing event of his service in the Civil War. Chief Hood, who had been a private in the ranks recently out of Dartmouth College, had no hesitation in replying: "When after having beaten Lee at Gettysburg we had to stand idle and see the Army of Northern Virginia escape across the Potomac River." This started considerable discussion and conversation at the table. When the guests quieted down again, Captain Anderson renewed his attack by asking Chief Hood what was the most inspiring event he remembered in his Civil War service. Again he answered without hesitation, "When we came out of the Wilderness and turned towards Richmond.")

Obviously General Lee had attempted by a bold movement to strike the Army of the Potomac in flank before it could be put in line of battle and be prepared to fight to advantage; but this had failed. However, when he heard that the Union trains were moving eastward, from force of habit he assumed that the army was retiring to the neighborhood of Fredericksburg, as had happened so often in the past, but he was soon apprised of the fact that they were moving southward.

Unhappily, General Lee also saw the strategic advantage of the Spottsylvania position, and as soon as he realized that the Union army was withdrawing he began moving his army to Spottsylvania. As he had the advantage of interior lines to Spottsylvania, some of his troops got there first. General Wilson with his cavalry division had actually arrived there before the Confederates. But the Confederates, with a superior force of cavalry and infantry (Anderson's corps), were able to push Wilson back and to continue entrenchment of the position they had taken near Spottsylvania. Late in the afternoon of May 8, Warren and Sedgwick were ordered to attack with all their forces, but it was nearly dark before the assault could be made and only half of Sedgwick's corps and one of Warren's divisions participated. The result of the day's fighting was inconclusive. Everyone was up at daylight on the ninth, ready for another hard day's work. Hancock was now on the right, Warren next, and then Sedgwick; Burnside was moving to take position on the extreme left of the Union army.

General Grant had indicated his intention of spending the day in reconnoitering the enemy's line and preparing a co-ordinated attack as soon as suitable preparations for it had been perfected. The country was more open than the Wilderness, and four rivers ran through it in a southeasterly direction, namely, the Mat, the Ta, the Po, and the Ny. Together they joined to form the Mattapony. The enemy's movements suggested that General Lee might be contemplating a move toward Fredericksburg to cut off the Union line of supply. If this proved his intention, General Grant proposed to attack Lee's right flank and throw the Army of the Potomac between him and Richmond; but if Lee had any such intention it was abandoned as soon as Burnside was established south of the Ny river. Grant's *Memoirs* record:

By noon of the 9th the position of the two armies was as follows: Lee occupied a semicircle facing north, northwest, and northeast, inclosing the town. Anderson was on his left extending to the Po, Ewell came next, then Early. Warren occupied our right, covering the Brock and other roads converging at Spottsylvania; Sedgwick was to his left and Burnside on our extreme left. Hancock was yet back at Todd's Tavern, but as soon as it was known that Early had left Hancock's front the latter was ordered up to Warren's right. He formed a line with three divisions on the hill overlooking the Po early in the afternoon, and was ordered to cross the Po and get on the enemy's flank. The fourth division of Hancock's corps, Mott commanding, was left at Todd's when the corps first came up, but in the afternoon it was brought up and placed to the left of Sedgwick's—now Wright's—Sixth Corps. In the morning General Sedgwick had been killed near the right of his intrenchments by rebel sharpshooters. His loss was a severe one to the Army of the Potomac and to the nation. General H. G. Wright succeeded him in the command of his corps.

Hancock was now, 9 P.M. of the 9th of May, across the left flank of Lee's army. but separated from it, and also from the remainder of Meade's army, by the Po River. But for the lateness of the hour and the darkness of the night he would have attempted to cross the river again at Wooden Bridge, thus bringing himself on the same side with both friend and foe.

Some maneuvering by Hancock forced Lee to reinforce his left during the night, so that on the morning of the tenth Hancock found himself confronted by some of Early's command (brought from the extreme right of the enemy), and only one of Hancock's brigades was gotten across when he was stopped by finding the enemy entrenched. Because General Lee must have weakened other parts of his line to meet Hancock's movement, on the morning of the tenth orders were issued for Warren's and Wright's corps, under Hancock's command, to join in the attack. Two reconnaissances in force by Warren convinced him to recommend that the assault be made. A reconnaissance by Wright resulted in gaining a considerably advanced position. He organized a storming party of twelve regiments under Colonel Emory Upton of the 121st New York Volunteers.

About 4 o'clock in the afternoon the assault was ordered. The movement was prompt and resulted in one of the fiercest struggles of the war. The battlefield was densely forested; only a little of it could be seen by any one person. Generals Meade and Grant occupied the best position obtainable in rear of Warren who was repulsed with heavy loss but not pursued by the enemy; he therefore found it possible to reorganize his command. The Union success was decisive on the left, but the advantage so gained was sacrificed by Mott's feeble action. Upton pushed forward with his assaulting party and crossed the enemy's entrenchments; then, turning right and left, he captured several guns and hundreds of prisoners. Mott failed to give him effective help as he had been ordered to do. The loss of time in getting troops from the right to reinforce the effort was such that Upton was ordered to withdraw; but his officers and men were averse to giving up what they had so handsomely won and they were allowed to remain. Renewal of the assault was then ordered so as to relieve the pressure on them.

Hancock's corps was then joined to Warren's and Wright's in this last assault. Although many men got to and over the works of the enemy, they were not able to hold their gains and at night were withdrawn. Upton brought his prisoners with him but had to abandon the guns he had captured. He had gained an important advantage, lost by a lack of spirit and dash on the part of others, and had been seriously wounded. Authorized before he left Washington to promote officers in the field for special acts of gallantry, General Grant gave an on-the-spot promotion to Upton for his part in this battle, and the rank of brigadier general was confirmed to him by the President later.

In the meantime, Burnside with the Army of the James had gotten within a few hundred yards of Spottsylvania Court House completely turning Lee's right flank. He was not aware of the importance of the advantage he had gained, and General Grant, with the troops where the fighting was heaviest, did not know of it. Whether General Meade was aware of it, we do not know. But Burnside was moved over to contact with Wright's corps during the night; and this took him back about a mile and lost the advantage he had gained. General Grant states in his *Memoirs:* "I attach no blame to Burnside for this, but I do to myself for not having had a staff-officer with him to report to me his position."

The enemy had not ventured out of his fortified line except in the single instance of his attacks on Barlow. On May 11 there was no battle and but little firing; and the lieutenant general wrote to General Halleck the oft-quoted letter:

We have now ended the sixth day of very hard fighting. The result up to this time is much in our favor. But our losses have been heavy as well as those of the enemy. We have lost to this time eleven general officers killed, wounded, and missing, and probably twenty thousand men. I think the loss of the enemy must be greater—we having taken over four thousand prisoners in battle, whilst he has taken from us but few except a few stragglers. I am now sending back to Belle Plain all my wagons for a fresh supply of provisions and ammunition, and *purpose to fight it out on this line if it takes all summer.*

The arrival of reinforcements here will be very encouraging to the men, and I hope they will be sent as fast as possible, and in as great numbers. My object in having them sent to Belle Plain was to use them as an escort to our supply-trains. If it is more convenient to send them out by train, to march from the railroad to Belle Plain or Fredericksburg, send them so.

I am satisfied the enemy are very shaky, and are only kept up to the mark by the greatest exertions on the part of their officers, and by keeping them intrenched in every position they take.

Up to this time there is no indication of any portion of Lee's army being detached for the defense of Richmond.

The reconnaissance made by General Mott on the eleventh had discovered a salient at the right center of the enemy's line, and an assault at four o'clock the next morning was ordered by Hancock, after moving his command by the rear of Warren and Wright under cover of darkness. Burnside was ordered to attack on the left of the salient at the same time. Warren and Wright were directed to hold themselves in readiness to join in the assault if circumstances made it desirable. General Grant took a central position convenient for the receiving of information from all points.

Fog delayed the start of the attack more than half an hour. Hancock had to pass over heavily wooded and ascending ground. Birney had a marsh in front of him to cross. Undeterred by these difficulties, the troops pushed on without firing a gun and when 400 or 500 yards in front of the enemy's line broke out in loud cheers and rushed over the breastworks, where a desperate hand-to-hand conflict took place. The hand conflict was soon over and Hancock's corps had recaptured some 4,000 prisoners, including a division and a brigade commander, twenty or more guns with their horses, caissons with their ammunition, several thousand stand of arms, and many colors. As soon as possible Hancock turned the enemy's guns around and advanced inside the rebel lines. About 6 o'clock Warren's corps was ordered to support Hancock. On the left Burnside advanced east of the salient to the enemy's parapet, and one of his divisions got over but was unable to stay there.

This victory was important, and General Lee brought up troops from his left and attacked Hancock furiously. Hancock was forced to fall back slowly with his face to the enemy, inflicting heavy loss until he got behind the breastworks he had captured. Wright was ordered to reinforce Hancock and reached him by 6 o'clock. He was wounded soon thereafter but did not give up command of his force. At 8 o'clock Warren was ordered up again but was so slow that his orders had to be repeated frequently. At 11 o'clock Meade was given written orders to relieve Warren of his command if he failed to move promptly. Hancock placed some batteries on high ground in his rear, using them against the enemy by firing over the heads of his own troops.

While Burnside had accomplished little on the left, he kept Lee from reinforcing the center from that quarter. Better results would have been obtained had Warren been as prompt as Wright.

Lee massed his troops heavily from the left flank on to the broken part of his line. During the day he assaulted furiously five times without dislodging Union troops from their new position. In one place a tree, eighteen inches in diameter, was cut down entirely by musket balls, and all the trees between the lines were very much injured by artillery and musketry. Fighting did not cease until 3 o'clock the next morning, May 13. Some Union troops had been under fire twenty hours; but the Union army did not lose a single organization, not even a company, whereas the Confederacy lost one division with its commander, one brigade, and one regiment with heavier losses elsewhere. During the night General Lee had occupied a position in rear of the previous one and entrenched it strongly.

During the thirteenth, General Grant was passing continuously along the line from wing to wing. Near the center his attention was attracted to a house found to be occupied by an old lady and her daughter, both of very strong Union sentiments. She had not seen a Union flag, she said, for so long that it did her heart good to look upon it again. Her husband and son were in the Union army somewhere, if still alive. She was nearly without food, and the commanding general after stopping there ordered some rations issued to her, promising to find out, if possible, the whereabouts of her husband and son.

The lieutenant general sent recommendations to the War Department for the promotion of a number of officers, among them Generals Sherman and Meade, to be major generals in the Regular Army; General Hancock to be brigadier general; Wright, Gibbon and Humphreys to be major generals of Volunteers, and Upton and Carroll to be brigadiers.

Lee moved to cover his new front the night of May 14–15. This left Hancock without any enemy in front of him. He was accordingly brought to the rear of the Union center, ready to be moved in any direction that might be advisable. On the fifteenth news came from Butler and Averell. Butler had captured the outer works of Drury's Bluff on the James River and his cavalry had destroyed railroad and telegraph south of Richmond on the Danville Road. Averell had destroyed a depot of supplies at Dublin, West Virginia, and had broken up the New River Bridge on the Virginia and Tennessee Railroad. The next day news came from Sherman: he had forced Joseph E. Johnston out of Dalton, Georgia, and was following himself. Finally, Sheridan reported his passing through the outer defenses of Richmond. The prospect in Richmond was probably very dismal at this time. General Grant wrote to General Halleck on May 16, at 8 A.M.:

> We have had five days' almost constant rain without any prospect yet of its clearing up. The roads have now become so impassable that ambulances with wounded men can no longer run between here and Fredericksburg. All offensive operations necessarily cease until we can have twenty-four hours of dry weather. The army is in the best of spirits, and feels the greatest confidence of ultimate success. . . .
>
> You can assure the President and Secretary of War that the elements alone have suspended hostilities, and that it is in no manner due to weakness or exhaustion on our part.

Because of the conditions of the roads nothing was attempted on May 17, but that night Hancock and Wright moved their corps by night march to their old positions and attacked at 4 o'clock in the morning. Lee had gotten his troops back in time to protect his old line, so the assault was repulsed. Therefore, on the eighteenth, the news was as discouraging for the Union side as it had been two days before for the rebels: in addition to the repulse of Hancock's and Wright's assault of the night before, news came that Sigel had been badly defeated at New Market and was retreating down the Shenandoah Valley (this resulted in a request for Sigel to be relieved and replaced, for which assignment Hunter was selected); news came from Butler that he had been driven from Drury's Bluff but still held the Petersburg Road; and Banks had been defeated in Louisiana and relieved by Canby.

In spite of the discouraging character of this news, it was no time to repine, and the march by the left flank to Richmond was ordered resumed to commence the night of the nineteenth. Further, the War Department was asked to obtain the co-operation of the navy in changing the army's base of supplies from Fredericksburg to Port Royal.

Up to this time the only reinforcements received had been 6,000 raw troops under Brigadier General Robert O. Tyler. They had not yet joined their command, Hancock's corps, but were on the right of the army. General Lee probably suspected some move on the part of the Union commander and, seeing his right abandoned, moved Ewell's corps about 5 o'clock in the afternoon, with Early's as a reserve, to attack the Union army in that quarter.

Tyler's raw troops received the attack and maintained their position in a manner worthy of veterans. Then they were reinforced. Hancock, in a position to do this quickly, did not delay to make formal dispositions, and Ewell was whirled back speedily with heavy loss. Warren had been ordered to get on Ewell's flank and rear, to cut him off from his entrenchments, but his efforts were so feeble and slow that Ewell got back with the loss of only a few hundred prisoners, besides his killed and wounded. Since the engagement lasted until after dark, the order for the march by the left flank that night was rescinded.

General Grant had been convinced by the battles of Wilderness and Spottsylvania that he had more artillery than could ever be brought into action at any one time. It took up much road space in marching and threw a heavy burden on the wagon train in bringing up forage. While very useful when it can be brought into action, an excess of artillery is a burdensome luxury when the terrain does not allow it to be used effectively. Before leaving Spottsylvania he therefore sent back to Washington more than a hundred pieces of artillery, with horses and caissons, thus relieving the roads over which he had to march of more than two hundred six-horse teams. Another reduction in the strength of the artillery was again made before reaching the James River.

Grant hoped by the exposure of one corps to tempt General Lee to attack it before reinforcements could come up; then when the main army arrived in support, it could attack the Confederates before they had time to entrench. This plan was set forth in directions sent General Meade on May 18, but General Lee did not respond to the opportunity offered him; therefore the left-flank movement was resumed on the night of the twentieth, General Lee having shown no signs of coming out. By the night of the twenty-first, Hancock, who was in the lead, had marched to Guiney's Station on the Fredericksburg Railroad and thence south to Bowling Green and Milford. Here he was met by a detachment of Pickett's division coming from Richmond to reinforce Lee. They were quickly driven away and several hundred of them were captured. Warren followed and reached Guiney's Station the night of the twenty-first without opposition.

Wright and Burnside were left at Spottsylvania to maintain the threat of an intended assault and to hold Lee while Hancock and Warren got start enough to interpose between him and Richmond. Again, General Lee was given an opportunity either to attack Wright and Burnside alone or, by following the telegraph road, to strike Hancock's and Warren's corps (or even Hancock's alone) before reinforcements could come up. He disregarded the opportunity and, moving by interior lines, kept between his capital and the Army of the Potomac. Never again was he given an opportunity to deal the Union army such a heavy blow.

The character of the country had now changed noticeably. The roads were wide and good and the land well cultivated. No men were seen except those with weapons in their hands; even the slaves had been sent away. However, the country was new to the Union army, which had neither guides nor maps to indicate the road. Engineer officers were able to locate all roads near each corps, and since the direction of the advance was southward, roads leading in that direction were used, as long as they did not separate the parts of the army too widely.

Lee had got his entire army south of the North Anna River, and the Union lines covered his front with six miles separating the two wings guarded by only one division. As Lee could reinforce any part of his line by a very short march from any other part of the line, the Union army was practically in the situation of two armies besieging the Confederates. The latter had in the meantime been reinforced by Pickett's division from Richmond, Hoke's brigade from North Carolina, and Breckinridge, making a total reinforcement estimated at 15,000 or more.

Dispatches received on May 22 or 23 from Washington announced that Sherman had taken Kingston, crossed the Etowah River, and was advancing into Georgia. At the time, General Grant was sitting on the porch of a fine plantation house waiting for Burnside's corps to pass. Beside his own staff, Meade and his staff were with the commanding general. The lady of the house, a Mrs. Tyler, and an elderly lady friend were present. Burnside came up on the porch and, saluting the two ladies, remarked that he supposed they had never seen so many "live Yankees" before; but the elderly lady spoke up promptly, saying, "Oh yes, I have; many more," to which Burnside asked, "Where?" The answer was, "In Richmond." That she meant prisoners was, of course, understood.

The general read his dispatch aloud, which drew tears from the younger lady because it refuted information she had received earlier: that Lee was driving Union forces from the state in a totally demoralized condition, and that in the southwest the Union troops were but little better than prisoners of war. In reply to her inquiry as to whether this information from Washington could be true, Grant assured her that there was no doubt about it. The general left a guard to protect the house from intrusion until all the troops had passed.

As General Lee remained behind his entrenchments, there seemed to be nothing that the Union army could do unless General Lee were to assume the offensive. General Grant determined to withdraw his army from its present position and make one more effort to interpose his army between Lee and Richmond. Hardly expecting now to succeed in doing this, he did hope to hold the Confederates far enough west to enable him to reach a point higher up on the James. Sheridan was now again with the Army of the Potomac.

On May 26, General Grant informed the government in Washington of the position of the two armies, of the reinforcements the enemy had received, and of the move he proposed to make, also directing that his base of supplies be shifted to White House on the Pamunkey River. The wagon train and guards moved directly from Port Royal to White House while the supplies were moved by river and guarded by the navy. General Butler was directed to send W. F. Smith's corps to White House; it was to land on the north side of the Pamunkey and march until it joined the Army of the Potomac.

Wilson's division of cavalry was brought from the left and moved to the Union right south to Little River, making a feint of preceding an attack on the left flank of Lee's army. Under cover of night the right wing of the northern army was withdrawn from the north side of the river without difficulty, a rather risky move.

The night of May 30, Lee's position was substantially from Atlee's Station on the Virginia Central Railroad south and east to the vicinity of Cold Harbor. The Union position was with Warren's corps on the left, on Shady Grove Church Road extending to Mechanicsville Road, Burnside on his right, then Hancock, and Wright on the extreme right extending toward Hanover Court House. Sheridan with two divisions of cavalry was watching the Union left front toward Cold Harbor. Wilson with his division on the Union right was directed to strike the Virginia Central Railroad and tear it up as far down the line as possible.

The enemy attacked Sheridan's pickets but was repulsed. Passing by the rear of the army, Wright's corps was expected to arrive by daylight or before at Cold Harbor, but the night was dark and the distance great and it did not reach its destination until 9 o'clock on June 1. Before Wright's arrival Sheridan had been attacked twice, but both assaults were repulsed with heavy loss to the enemy. With the arrival of Wright's corps there was no further assault on Cold Harbor. Smith, supposedly directed to march on Cold Harbor, by some blunder had been directed to New Castle instead; thus he did not reach his destination until 3 o'clock in the afternoon and then with worn-out men.

General Lee discovered that Wright's corps had left his front after dark on May 31 and evidently guessed that he had gone to the Union left. At all events Anderson, soon after light on June 1, commanding the corps on Lee's right, was seen moving along Warren's front. Warren was ordered to attack him vigorously in flank while Wright moved out to get in his front. Warren fired his artillery at the enemy but lost so much time in preparations that Anderson got by and at 3 o'clock he reported the enemy strongly entrenched in his front.

Wright reconnoitered for some distance to his front, but the enemy halted and fortified some distance to the west, after finding Old Cold Harbor had been taken. By 6 o'clock Wright and Smith were ready to launch an assault. Both charged across the open space of several hundred yards and into the woods, capturing and holding the enemy's first line of rifle pits and capturing 700 or 800 prisoners.

In the meantime the Confederate troops charged Warren three times with vigor but were repulsed each time with loss. There was also an attack on Hancock's and Burnside's corps at the same time—feeble and probably intended only to relieve Anderson. During the night Hancock was moved to the left of Wright, and the enemy made frequent but ineffectual attacks in the effort to dispossess the Union army of the important position it had gained. The head of Hancock's column, delayed by the heat, dust, and the difficulty of keeping on the right road in the dark, did not reach Old Cold Harbor until 7:30 A.M., on the left of Wright's; Burnside was moved to Bethesda Church in reserve; and Warren's corps was moved to the left to connect with Smith. While Warren and Burnside were making these changes, the enemy came out several times and attacked them, capturing a number of prisoners. The attacks were repulsed but not pushed as they should have been, and General Meade was directed to instruct his corps commanders that they should seize such opportunities without waiting for orders, as all the maneuvers were made for the primary purpose of getting the enemy out of his cover.

Sheridan was put to work reconnoitering the banks of the Chickahominy to find crossings and learn the conditions of roads. His reports were favorable. During the night General Lee moved his left up to correspond to the Union line; his line extended from the Totopotomoy to New Cold Harbor. The Union line reached from Bethesda Church by Old Cold Harbor to the Chickahominy, with a division of cavalry guarding the Federal right. An assault was ordered for the morning of June 3—to be made by Hancock's, Wright's, and Smith's corps, and to be supported by Warren and Burnside, who were to threaten Lee's left and attack with earnestness if he should reinforce any more threatened point or if a favorable opportunity presented itself.

Wright's corps captured the rifle pits in its front but accomplished nothing more. Smith's corps found a ravine running toward his front deep enough to protect men in it from cross fire and to some extent from direct fire; the men were able to cross the open ground with one division in this ravine and the others in support on each side and also gain the outer rifle pits. But no part of the enemy's fortified position was captured. Warren and Burnside had advanced and gained ground bringing them up on line with the rest of the army. However, Grant recorded that "this assault cost us heavily, and probably without benefit to compensate; but the enemy was not cheered by the occurrence sufficiently to enduce [sic] him to take the offensive."

The commanding general visited the Union corps commanders and found them very dubious of gaining any decisive success. He "concluded, therefore, to make no more assaults, and a little after twelve directed . . . that all offensive action should cease. The remainder of the day was spent in strengthening the line we now held. By night we were as strong against Lee as he was against us."

The enemy during the night quitted the Union right front, leaving some of its wounded and dead on the field. The following message was sent to General Lee on June 5 1864:

> It is reported to me that there are wounded men, probably of both armies, now lying exposed and suffering between the lines occupied respectively by the two armies. Humanity would dictate that some provision should be made to provide against such hardships. I would propose, therefore, that hereafter, when no battle is raging, either party be authorized to send to any point

between the pickets or skirmish-lines unarmed men bearing litters to pick up their dead or wounded, without being fired upon by the other party. Any other method, equally fair to both parties, you may propose for meeting the end desired will be accepted by me.

U. S. Grant,
Lieutenant-General.

In reply General Lee was doubtful that such an arrangement could be carried out without misunderstanding and suggested that when either party wanted to remove their dead and wounded a flag of truce be sent. Considerable correspondence resulted, but the burial of the dead and the rescue of wounded was finally acceded to on June 7, forty-eight hours after the first request. Owing to a misunderstanding of the final arrangements, especially as to time, two officers and six men of the 8th and 25th North Carolina regiments were captured but finally returned.

In his *Memoirs,* General Grant says: "I have always regretted that the last assault at Cold Harbor was ever made. I might say the same thing of the assault the 22nd of May, 1863, at Vicksburg. At Cold Harbor no advantage whatever was gained to compensate for the heavy loss we sustained." In fact the Army of the Potomac was pretty well tired out and had lost the *élan* it had had at Spottsylvania. The Army of Northern Virginia had lost its offensive spirit entirely and evidently preferred to stay in the shelter of its entrenchments. The opportunity for a pitched battle in an open field, which might result in a defeat of General Lee's army such as Bragg's had suffered at Chattanooga or Pemberton's at Champion's Hill, was gone for the present.

It looked like a checkmate. Lee was still champion of those dimensions of war in which he was versed. To his consternation Grant knew a fourth dimension.

As early as June 5, General Grant replied to some suggestions of General Halleck in the following statements:

A full survey of all the ground satisfies me that it would be impracticable to hold a line northeast of Richmond that would protect the Fredericksburg railroad, to enable us to use that road for supplying the army. To do so would give us a long vulnerable line of road to protect, exhausting much of our strength to guard it, and would leave open to the enemy all of his lines of communication on the south side of the James. *My idea from the start has been to beat Lee's army, if possible, north of Richmond; then, after destroying his lines of communication on the north side of the James River, to transfer the army to the south side and besiege Lee in Richmond, or follow him south if he should retreat.*

I now find, after over thirty days of trial, the enemy deems it of first importance to run no risks with the armies they now have. They act purely on the defensive behind breastworks, or feebly on the offensive immediately in front of them, and where in case of repulse they can instantly retire behind them. Without a greater sacrifice of human life than I am willing to make, all cannot be accomplished that I had designed outside of the city. I have therefore resolved upon the following plan:

I will continue to hold substantially the ground now occupied by the Army of the Potomac, taking advantage of any favorable circumstance that may present itself, until the cavalry can be sent west to destroy the Virginia Central railroad from about Beaver Dam for some twenty-five or thirty miles west. When this is effected I will move the army to the south side of the James River, either by crossing the Chickahominy and marching near to City Point, or by going to the mouth of the Chickahominy on north side and crossing there. To provide for this last and most possible contingency, several ferry-boats of the largest class ought to be immediately provided.

Once on the south side of the James River, I can cut off all sources of supply to the enemy except what is furnished by the canal. If Hunter succeeds in reaching Lynchburg, that will be lost to him also. Should Hunter not succeed, I will still make the effort to destroy the canal by sending cavalry up the south side of the river with a pontoon-train to cross wherever they can.

The feeling of the two armies now seems to be that the rebels can protect themselves only by strong intrenchments, whilst our army is not only confident of protecting itself without intrenchments, but that it can beat and drive the enemy wherever and whenever he can be found without this protection.

In a privately printed account by Henry E. Wing, we find the following narrative of his interview with President Lincoln in the latter's private room on June 3, 1864. Mr. Wing had been a senate reporter for the *New York Tribune* and war correspondent with the Army of the Potomac. Later he was an enlisted soldier and the principal in a heroic episode following the first day's Battle of the Wilderness in May 1864, when at great personal risk he carried a personal message from General Grant to Mr. Lincoln.

General Grant's fame as a successful leader had preceded him East and with it had floated many statements derogatory of his private character. Among other faults, was the use sometimes in excess, of spiritous liquors;

indeed a popular current "Lincoln story" was, in effect, that someone reported to the President that Grant was "drunk" on the occasion of one of his brilliant victories, to which Mr. Lincoln made reply that he would be pleased to learn the brand of that whiskey, to prescribe it to some of his other commanders. (Mr. Lincoln made prompt and emphatic denial of this "incident," yet the fabrication is still circulated, by the liquor interests, as an indorsement by the great President of the drink habit.)

These representations had led me to expect to meet a man of a dominating personality, of rough manners and questionable morals. Instead, to my surprise, I was greeted by a mild-mannered, matter-of-fact, sedate gentleman in uniform, who, upon acquaintance, proved to be clean in speech, scrupulous in his observance of the proprieties of life, and, most astonishing of all, a total abstainer from intoxicants.

A night ride and lonely bivouac in the forest with one of his staff afforded an opportunity to seek light on the question: Was there ever any ground for those damaging reports? I learned that the general early in his career as commander was addicted to the moderate use of alcoholic spirits. In one of the great battles in which he won a decisive victory, he was more than ordinarily under the influence of stimulants. That was the end. Realizing, evidently, how nearly he had ventured to the verge of incapacity and disaster, with no avowal of his purpose, he quit. And since that day, without a word of explanation to even his most intimate associates, he had followed his present abstemious course of life. (This is not the story in which some person is exploited as being the "humble instrument" in the reformation of General Grant, but it was related to me by one of his most intimate associates, and is perfectly consistent with the character of the introspective, reticent man whom I knew in 1864.)

I had taken for granted that Mr. Lincoln had heard these damaging reports and that he would be pleased to have them corrected, and he had encouraged me, thus far, by an occasional nod or smile of assent, but it was when I broached the subject of the loyalty of the chief commander toward his immediate subordinates in rank, that my auditor was roused to an attitude of intense interest. (As I write this now, after an interval of nearly fifty years, I can see him sitting opposite me, squarely fronting the flat table, with his long body bent forward in one of his familiar attitudes of attention, his arms stretched out in a great circle, and his rough, bony fingers, gripped together under his rugged face.)

The General gave us an example of this chivalrous regard for the honor and fair fame of his comrades-in-arms at the very beginning of the great Wilderness campaign. After the first day's unpromising struggle in the Wilderness, at a gathering of the chief captains, General Meade and some others favored a retreat across the Rapidan, under cover of the night, and a renewal of the movement by some more feasible route. To this suggestion the Lieutenant General interposed a positive veto. While the meeting was strictly private, every newspaper man at headquarters became possessed of the facts; but this was before the days of "yellow journalism," and none of us felt at liberty to spread before the public what had transpired at a secret council of the men into whose hands had been committed such grave interests. None of us made mention of the affair in our reports—with a single exception. The correspondent of one quite influential paper made a "story" of it, recognizing the significance of the circumstance, that at last a man had control of affairs at the front who would not fall back, in the face of defeat. When this report came to the notice of General Grant, he had the adventurous correspondent arrested, pronounced the story a falsehood, branded the author as a "calumniator," and expelled him from the army.

We understood that this was an example of his loyalty to Meade, and of his patriotism as well, for, however much his reputation might be enhanced by the publication of this incident, the morale of the army certainly just then depended upon the implicit faith of the rank and file in their recognized leaders. This trust, so essential to the *esprit de corps* of the troops, impaired as it had been by fractional jealousies and rivalries, General Grant proceeded to foster and strengthen, even at the cost of possible disparagement of himself. We, whose business it was to look closely into matters, soon discovered that while he directed every important movement, Meade was to be recognized as the ostensible commander, and, with his immediate lieutenants was to have full credit for every achievement. Grant even went so far as to assume responsibility where blame might be attached, as in the last misadventure at Cold Harbor.

It was this that had kept that great army of citizen soldiers—baffled, torn, decimated, but ever pressing on its devious way—in such a spirit of transport as it had never before experienced. They had come to believe in themselves, in each other, in their immediate commanders, and in the final triumph of the cause for which they fought. Every man was doing his best, and no one was making any mistakes, except, possibly, the unobtrusive, self-effacing man, with whom they had no intimate, personal relations.

It was Mr. Charles C. Coffin, the veteran correspondent of the Boston Journal, a man of deep insight into human character, who led me to realize the true meaning of this exceptional course of conduct. General Grant was patriotic enough to sacrifice his reputation, if need be, for the country; and he knew what was due, in propriety, from an officer to his inferior in rank; but neither of these, nor both together, fully explained his conduct and bearing through these trying times. These could be accounted for only in the view of his absolute unselfishness and true nobility of character. I have never known a more unselfish man. He did not have to study to be kind and courteous to his comrades. It was by no effort of his strong will that he evaded deserved recognition for success and invited censure for disaster. It was instinctive with him. To one who knew him, an ignoble act would have been inconsistent with his character. He could be depended upon in any event and through any provocation to act the part of a manly man.

I could realize, as many others could not, what General Grant's example and spirit had wrought in that army. Only a few months before I was a soldier in the ranks. And as I lay, broken and bleeding, upon a battlefield, I had seen the flag, for which I had sworn to die—and for which just then, I wanted to die,—borne off the field, in retreat, in the face of the enemy. And the boys who were bearing it away were as brave as the best, as willing, as anxious to die defending it. There was no panic, no haste. I had a grim satisfaction in that. These comrades of mine were not being driven; they were being led. It was deemed "expedient" that they should "retire." That was only one incident in the experience of the Army of the Potomac. For hundreds of years we descendants of fighting men had been trained—through our ancestors—to face our foes; to stand and take a knockout blow; to get up and take or give another; to die, if we must, in our tracks. Now, for nearly three years, we had been ordered, repeatedly, to take that awkward, unsoldierly, backward step.

It was a gladsome message, a promise of happy reprisal, that I had taken, at the close of that first day in the Wilderness, to my old comrades of the Second Corps; "To hold their lines all night, and to charge the enemy at daylight." With that decision of the great commander was the advent of a new spirit, the birth of a great hope and purpose. Since then, through all the vicissitudes of the campaign, I had noticed the steadily rising tide of robust faith and courage through the ranks. And I had come to realize how certainly—almost entirely—this spirit of conquest was due to the steadfast resolution and the generous patriotism of the modest, silent man whom Providence had placed in chief command.

I sat under the spell of Mr. Lincoln's ardent gaze and rehearsed this story, stimulated by the almost painful interest and quite carried away by my admiration of the man of whom I was speaking. But presently I came to myself and recalled that I was in the presence of a man of large affairs, whose time I had been consuming with what might seem to him like concerns of small importance. I might find a partial excuse in the fact that he had deliberately chosen the topic for my monologue and had encouraged me by his silence and attention. I uttered some words of apology and started to rise to my feet; but with a gesture of his lifted hand, palm downward, he signaled me to be seated. Then, leaning half way across the table, he said in grateful tones, "My boy, you have told me just what I was hungry to hear." And it is no small joy to me now, years afterward, to know that I was privileged, for a brief half hour that summer night, to bring courage and comfort to that burdened, tired, sorrowful spirit.

Mr. Lincoln reached for a sheet of paper, wrote a half dozen or so lines, folded it in an envelope, addressed it and passed it to me. I read the address: "Lieut. Gen'l. U. S. Grant. By the hand of H. E. (not she) Wing."

I noticed that the envelope was open, and, as I moistened and sealed it, I remarked, "General Headquarters these days are a fleeting show. Many things might happen to me before I reach them." He seized the missive, and laid it upon the table, and, covering it with his broad hand, said: "Henry, you will see that this letter is placed in General Grant's own hand." His look and tones sobered me. "Mr. President," I replied, "I can only promise that it shall fall into no other hands than his."

Several hours afterward, on the banks of the James, seizing upon an occasion when General Grant was alone, I handed him the envelope. He opened it in his deliberate manner; but as soon as he scanned the lines his face flushed with surprise and pleasure. Then a "far away" look, such as one may see once or twice in a lifetime, came into his serious face and held his gaze for a single instant. But for that instant he was a seer; he was receiving a revelation. From that moment he carried another secret in his bosom. Recovering himself, he turned to me and, taking my hand in both of his, he said simply, "I thank you," with significant emphasis on the last word. I had never seen him so deeply moved.

On June 13, General Lee reported to the Confederate secretary of war:

At daybreak this morning it was discovered that the army of Genl Grant had left our front. Our skirmishers were advanced between one and two miles, but failing to discover the enemy were withdrawn, and the army was moved to conform to the route taken by him. He advanced a body of cavalry and some infantry from Long Bridge to Riddell's Shop, which were driven back this evening nearly two miles, after some sharp skirmishing.

And again on June 14, Lee wrote President Davis:

I think the enemy must be preparing to move south of James River. Our scouts and pickets yesterday stated that Genl Grant's whole army was in motion for the fords of the Chickahominy from Long Bridge down, from which I inferred that he was making his way to the James River as his new base. I cannot however learn positively that more than a small part of his army has crossed the Chickahominy.

It was General Grant's desire and hope to take Petersburg by surprise and assault; the fortification works were very lightly manned. If this could be done, there might be an opportunity to meet Lee in the open space between Richmond and Petersburg and at last have the desired pitched battle away from prepared entrenchments. A raid toward Lynchburg by Sheridan would distract the attention of the Confederate command. It might deceive them into thinking that the objective was to support Hunter in the Shenandoah Valley, and it would be possible to do great damage to the Confederacy by destroying the Virginia Central Railroad and the James River Canal, as well as some of the factories around Lynchburg making war equipment.

Sheridan had left his camp at New Castle Ferry on June 8, but he was intercepted by Hampton's cavalry, followed by a somewhat indecisive battle after which Sheridan held the field. But learning that a force of infantry was between him and Lynchburg under command of Breckinridge, Sheridan started back, only to find his retreat blocked by Hampton. Repulsed in this action, he left his seriously wounded behind and made his way back to White House. Arriving there on the twentieth he was ordered to conduct the wagon train of the Army of the Potomac to the pontoon bridge across the James. Although tactically not particularly successful, this feint was a strategic victory, as it drew the Confederate cavalry away from the Army of the Potomac and enabled the entire Union army to cross the James River while Lee still believed it was on the north bank.

The attack on the fortifications of Petersburg was entrusted to General W. F. Smith and his XVIII Corps. They marched to White House and then were sent by steamer to City Point, where 6,000 reinforcements, including 3,000 cavalry under General Kautz, were added. Four days previously Kautz had ridden over the fortifications of Petersburg as part of a movement by the X Corps of Butler's army to take the city by surprise; the movement failed because of General Gillmore's timidity. However, although General Smith made a good beginning, he for some reason was delayed or stopped to better inform himself, and General Beauregard was given time to man the fortifications and prevent their capture by a *coup de main.*

General Smith replied to an inquiry by General Butler at midnight

June 15–16; "It is impossible for me to go further tonight, but unless I misapprehend the topography I hold the key to Petersburg. General Hancock not yet up." Hancock was being hurried across the James to act as a reserve for the Army of the James. The failure to get into Petersburg when it was relatively without defense was a real disappointment. General Smith's failure to push on and add to his capture of five redans and two and one half miles of his first line gave rise to a quarrel in official correspondence with General Butler. General Smith asked for an investigation, but General Grant in this moment of emergency said there was nothing to investigate, and he attached no blame to General Smith or General Meade or General Hancock. The fact seems to have been that General Smith, who had made the brilliant and somewhat complicated plan for reopening the "Cracker Line" to Chattanooga and had led a part of the force entrusted with that job, when alone in command in a new situation failed to take advantage—by reason of timidity or indecision—of an unusual opportunity.

General Beauregard performed an extremely clever piece of deception by extending his small number of men over the entrenchments facing the Union advance and by having cannons fired from the works while he was waiting for assistance he had begged of General Lee. On June 14 he telegraphed General Lee: "A deserter from the enemy reports that Butler has been reinforced by the XVIII and a part of the X Army Corps." After Beauregard had sent Colonel Paul, one of his staff, to General Lee to explain the emergency, the latter said that Beauregard must be in error in believing that the enemy had thrown a large force on the south side of the James; the troops referred to must be but a few of Smith's corps going back to Butler's lines. But General Lee finally said he had already ordered Hoke's division to return to Beauregard and would do all he could to expedite it.

Even though these efforts to take Petersburg by surprise were unsuccessful, Colonel Robert McCormick, in his biography of the general, says that:

> Grant's maneuver across the James River and up to the defenses was a triumph of the military art. To its success the Confederate General Alexander attributes the loss of the war. Thus the last, and perhaps the best, chances of Confederate success were not lost in the repulse at Gettysburg, nor in any combat of arms. They were lost during three days of lying in camp, believing that Grant was hemmed in by the broad part of the James below City Point,

and had nowhere to go but to come and attack us. Here at last, literally driven into the location in front of Petersburg, Grant found himself in a position of rare strategic advantage; certain to give him possession of Richmond when properly utilized. Indeed, it seems strange that it had not been realized in 1862, that the position astraddle both rivers at the junction of the James and Appomattox was the key to Richmond. For it would force Lee to hold an exterior line of such enormous length—from the Chickahominy River to the south of Petersburg, nearly thirty miles—that it could not be long maintained.

That the Confederate cause was lost when Grant got across the James River was realized by General Ewell. Lincoln had apparently been mystified by the course the campaign was taking. Then General Grant telegraphed: "Our forces will commence crossing the James today. The enemy shows no signs of yet having brought troops to the south side of Richmond. I will have Petersburg secured, if possible, before they get there in much force." The President replied, "I have just received your despatch of 1 P.M. yesterday. I begin to see it. You will succeed. God bless you all."

There was nothing for General Lee to do but take refuge behind the fortifications of Richmond and Petersburg and subject himself, much against his will, to siege operations on the part of the Union army. Richmond and Petersburg together formed too extensive a fortified area to be completely surrounded and invested, as Vicksburg had been. As it happened, the Union lines were ultimately about 37 miles long. Even with a force of approximately 116,000 men at the opening of the campaign and again brought to that figure toward the close of the campaign, the Union would have only about 1.2 men per yard to hold their lines, assuming that one third of the army was necessarily on special duty protecting the line of supply, drawing supplies and moving them to the army, protecting places between the army and Washington which needed to be protected, and on leave or sick. The Confederate interior lines of fortification were appreciably shorter, but General Lee had reason to be anxious as well, since the Union commander could always concentrate a strong force to break through the Confederate line without the commander of the latter knowing where the blow was going to be struck unless he discovered some concentration of force on the Union side.

While both armies were settling down to make the best possible use of the changed conditions, it may be useful for the writer to call attention to a book not often quoted, namely, *The Life of Ulysses S. Grant* by Charles A. Dana and J. H. Wilson (1868). Mr. Dana was assistant secretary of war; James H. Wilson was an engineer officer on the general's staff and at the end of the war was brigadier general of U.S. Volunteers and a brevet major general of volunteers commanding one of the cavalry divisions in General Sheridan's Cavalry Corps.

Dana had been with General Grant's headquarters during the Vicksburg campaign and was again with him at Chattanooga and much of the time in the last year's campaign in Virginia. It may be assumed that Dana and Wilson knew what they were doing when they wrote the book and that their knowledge of statistics was as accurate as anybody's, based as it was on both then-current official reports and personal observations.

For instance, they state that on the morning of May 5, Grant's army was between 90,000 and 100,000 strong in the Wilderness, whereas many other authors have made the figure larger. An obvious reason for this book's not being used as much as it merits is that, when the two authors afterward became enemies to President Grant, they tried to recover and destroy as many copies of the book as they could. Just why they changed from loyal friends to enemies is not specifically known. But in sending me a copy of the book many years ago, my father spoke of their having become enemies because one of them was disappointed in not being appointed collector of the port of New York and the other disappointed in not being made secretary of war, presumably on the death of General Rawlins. In regard to the New York appointment, Dana in his *Recollections* indicates that he never wanted to be collector of the port of New York, and Dana was certainly "an honorable man" although a vicious enemy.

In connection with the Battle of Cold Harbor they had the following to say:

Grant has been severely criticised for the details of this battle, and it is possible that it should not have been fought at all; but it ought to be remembered that Grant could give only general directions, and that it was Meade's special function to see that the actual dispositions of the troops were made in such a manner as to secure the greatest possible advantage in direction as well as in tactical execution, while it was the privilege and duty of each corps commander, upon that occasion as well as upon all others, to use his discretion in forming his troops for attack, and in selecting or at least suggesting that point in his own front, upon which his efforts should be directed. It seems to be well established, however, that Meade gave his orders in the same general terms as they were couched in when they reached him, and finally ordered the different corps commanders to attack without regard to each other. It was not in the character of General Grant, any more than in the necessities of the case, that he should depart from his well established and judicious practice in such matters; nor was it possible for him to become acquainted so thoroughly with the varied features of the extended battlefield as to be able to designate to the subordinate commanders the points upon which they should move.

It does not appear from any official report or statement yet published, that either Meade or any of the corps commanders, ever proposed a meritorious plan of attack or pointed out a weak place in the enemy's line, without being encouraged by the Lieutenant-General to avail himself of it. Neither does it appear in any official paper, or in any authentic record of military events that General Grant ever ordered an assault or permitted one, either against troops in the open field, or behind breastworks, in opposition to the expressed judgment of Meade or any one of his corps commanders. Those who know him best are well aware of the fact that while he believes celerity and hard fighting to be essential elements in warfare, there is no commander more opposed to hammering without an object, or whose humane heart is more deeply afflicted by the unnecessary effusion of blood. On the other hand it would be injustice to him and an outrage upon common sense to assert that he is a believer in partial or irresolute measures. He knows as well as any man that war can not be made affectionately [sic]; nor can it be made successfully, without loss of human life.

In connection with the failure to capture Petersburg by surprise the joint authors have this to say:

He [W.F.Smith] made a rapid march, and by daylight of the 15th, was confronting the rebel forces near Petersburg. His advance was made in three columns, composed of Kautz's cavalry and the infantry divisions of Hinks, Brooks, and Martindale. Skirmishing began at an early hour, resulting in driving the rebels into the works about Petersburg, with the loss of one gun. It was noon, however, before all the troops were brought up, and nearly sundown before the final dispositions for the attack had been perfected. Smith being an able engineer and a General of fine judgment, did everything with deliberation and precision; his cavalry was posted well out upon the exposed flank, his batteries occupied commanding positions, while his infantry divisions were formed in long but mutually supporting lines. At seven o'clock, when it had begun to grow dusk, the troops, both white and colored, deployed in a heavy line of skirmishers, advanced rapidly to the attack, carrying everything before them, capturing two and a half miles of redoubt and rifle-pits, with 15 pieces of artillery, and taking 300 prisoners. It was an auspicious beginning; Lee had not yet arrived, and the local militia were a different sort of soldiery from that which had been encountered at Cold Harbor; but darkness having set in, Smith suspended further operations in order to reform his troops, although, says Grant: "Between the line thus captured and Petersburg, there were no other works, and there was no evidence that the enemy had re-enforced Petersburg with a single brigade from any source. The night was clear, the moon shining brightly, and favorable to further operations. General Hancock, with two divisions of the Second corps, reached Smith just after dark, and offered the service of these troops, as he (Smith) might wish, waving rank to the named commander, who he naturally supposed, knew best the position of affairs, and what to do with the troops. But instead of taking these troops, and pushing at once into Petersburg, he requested General Hancock to relieve a part of his line in the captured works, which was done before midnight." [Grant's Official Report] The opportunity was deferred, and Petersburg was lost. That night Lee's advance reached the city, and by the next day its enclosing lines were bristling with rebel bayonets. Fortifications arose on every available spot. Grant, who had returned to the Army of the Potomac for the purpose of hurrying it forward, joined Smith at an early hour on the 16th, and was chagrined to see that nothing could be done with the force then at hand. Burnside and the rest of Hancock's corps were hastened forward, and at six o'clock in the afternoon, an attack was made, continuing with intermissions and varying success till six o'clock the next morning. Several more of the enemy's redoubts to the left of Smith were taken, together with several pieces of artillery and about 400 prisoners. On the 17th, the Fifth corps arrived, and during that and the succeeding day, the fighting was renewed, but only forced the enemy to contract his lines, leaving the investing army in possession of much advantageous ground.

The reader will have perceived from the foregoing precise statement of facts, that in the movement upon Petersburg, Grant had clearly outwitted Lee, and had beaten him on the march to the town by an entire day, but through the delay in making the attack, and its untimely suspension by General Smith, the ripest fruits of this superior generalship had not been gathered. A contemporary writer, in discussing this operation has not hesitated to say: "There can be no question as to who is responsible for the failure to take Petersburg. This is no other than the Lieutenant-General himself." [Swinton's *Army of the Potomac,* p. 506] To support this assertion he quotes from a paper said to be on file in the archives of the army, and upon which General Meade has made the following endorsement: "Had Hancock or myself known Petersburg was to be attacked Petersburg would have fallen." It is hard to believe that General Meade could have written such a sentence, for on the day previous to Smith's movement, he was personally directed by General Grant to order Hancock to march directly for Petersburg by the shortest road in order to support the attack to be made there by Smith.

But independent of these orders which were given to him verbally by the Lieutenant-General, as were many of the most important orders up to that epoch of the campaign, both Meade and Hancock must have known that the army landing where it did, must necessarily take possession of and march through Petersburg in order to reach Richmond, or to secure a safe base of operations against the enemy in the field. In truth there was not a lieutenant in the army but knew that the rules of strategy required as much; but the fact that Meade had specific orders from General Grant, and the additional fact that two divisions of Hancock's corps actually joined Smith at Petersburg, settle all discussion upon this point. The failure of Smith to reap the full advantage of the brilliant maneuver by which he carried the outer line of the Petersburg defenses, was a matter which Grant could not possibly control. He had perfect confidence in the judgment and generalship of that officer, but they were both at fault upon this occasion. Without wasting time in vain regrets, Grant set about arranging a plan by which the same or equal advantages might be otherwise obtained. He had sent Wright with a part of the Sixth corps to Bermuda Hundred, to re-enforce Butler, who had moved out and occupied the rebel works on the railroad, which had been abandoned in order to re-enforce Petersburg. Grant directed that General to strengthen his advance and secure his hold upon the railroad, but instead of doing so with the combined forces at his disposal, he [Butler] allowed Wright to halt near the outer lines. As soon as the pressure against Petersburg was relieved, the rebels returned to Butler's front, and before he could take effective measures to avert it drove him back into his fortified line which encircled his camps at Bermuda Hundred.

Since it was not possible for the Union army to entirely surround the Richmond-Petersburg area, it is noteworthy that the only general supply lines left to supply the garrison were the Virginia Central Railroad, partially destroyed and exposed to further interference by the invading army; the Richmond and Danville Railroad, coming into the Confederate capital across the Appomattox River from the southwest; the South Side Railroad, coming into Petersburg from the west and roughly paralleling the Appomattox River for many miles; and, finally, the Weldon Railroad, entering Petersburg directly from the south. General Meade sent Wright with his corps and Birney, temporarily commanding the II Corps, to take the Weldon Railroad and to send Wilson's cavalry from the Army of the James to cut the South Side and Richmond and Danville railroads. Wilson performed this duty with great success. Since Sheridan had cut the Virginia Central a few days before, "Richmond was without supplies and was filled with fugitives joining the army in eating the stores on hand." The infantry was less successful in its efforts to take possession of the Weldon Railroad. The VI Corps and the II, moving westward, gradually moved apart but failed to patrol the area between them. Confederate General Hill moved out with splendid initiative and, holding the VI Corps with one division, passed between the two army corps with his other division and struck three Union divisions one by one from the rear, routing them and capturing men, guns, and flags, on June 22—a brilliant feat of arms which completely repulsed the Army of the Potomac's efforts to reach the Weldon Railroad. Wright seems to have lost his self-possession, and Meade asked General Grant to come to the scene of the battle. According to Colonel McCormick:

> When Wilson's tired but exultant raiders returned to the Weldon Railroad, followed by W. H. Lee's cavalry, they found waiting for them, not the Army of the Potomac, but a trap composed of two infantry brigades from the Army of Virginia, and Hampton's cavalry which had returned from its encounters with Sheridan. Surprised, outnumbered, almost surrounded, most of this force escaped and rejoined the army, after destroying its train. Kautz's artillery was lost. The futility of the Army of the Potomac in the attempt to storm Petersburg and in this move against the railroads under Meade's supervision is sufficient answer to all suggestions that Grant should not personally have conducted the overland campaign. When pressure of other matters compelled him to entrust movements to any of his subordinates except Sheridan, they invariably miscarried.

While these maneuvers and fights were going on between the Army of the Potomac and the Army of Northern Virginia, and while the latter was being forced to take refuge behind the defenses of Richmond and Petersburg, other important events were taking place. These events stemmed from executing the general plan of co-ordinated action by all the armies against the fighting forces of the Confederacy.

General Sherman in the Western Theater of Operations with Armies of the Tennessee and the Cumberland maneuvered against the remnants of Bragg's army and such other Confederate reinforcements as Joseph E. Johnston had been able to assemble in the general vicinity of Dalton,

Georgia. The campaign between Sherman and Joseph E. Johnston resulted in the latter being driven back to Atlanta. Because President Jefferson Davis, who had no special liking for Johnston from the beginning, decided that he had not made the most effective use of his army, he relieved him of command and placed Lieutenant General J. B. Hood in command of the Confederate Army, believing him to be a more energetic and aggressive leader. To fulfill these expectations General Hood, rather than waiting to be cooped up in Atlanta and eventually forced to surrender, decided to take a chance and start north with his army in the general direction of Nashville. He presumed that Sherman would follow with most of his army. However, the latter failed to be enticed into such a stern chase, but turned General Thomas and General Schofield loose with two corps to handle Hood. Sherman returned to the rest of his army, occupied Atlanta, and subsequently obtained permission to march his army through Georgia to Savannah on the Atlantic Ocean and then up the coast to threaten General Lee's army in Richmond.

It had been intended that General Franz Sigel, who was in the northern part of the Shenandoah Valley and was supposed to march up the Valley and dispose of any Confederate troops that might oppose him, should join Hunter, who was to come into the valley from the west and capture Lynchburg. Sigel got only as far as New Market, was defeated, retired down the valley cleverly eluding a pincer movement by Early, and took a position on Maryland Heights back of Harper's Ferry after destroying the bridges. Hunter defeated Confederate General Jones at Piedmont on June 5 and on the eighth joined forces with Crook and Averell at Staunton.

After the repulse of the Army of the Potomac at Cold Harbor and not knowing of the movement to the James, General Lee sent Early in command of General Ewell's Army Corps into the Shenandoah Valley in order to make a diversion there and possibly threaten Washington. He undoubtedly expected that troops would be dispatched in considerable numbers to take care of Early and that the pressure on him in Richmond and Petersburg would be lightened. Near Lynchburg, Hunter, who had energetically taken the offensive and was successful, now came face to face with Early's army. Short of ammunition, he felt forced to leave Lynchburg to Early and retired to Harpers Ferry via the Gauley and Kanawha rivers, the Ohio River and the Baltimore and Ohio Railroad, a time-consuming trip. In the meantime Early carried on a successful campaign in the valley. Because of Sigel's well-chosen position he was constrained to invade Maryland via Frederick and so proceed to the immediate vicinity of the Union capital, which he reached on July 11. General Lew Wallace, in command in Baltimore, with due enterprise and diligence took what troops he could gather together and met Early on the Monocacy River, near Frederick, Maryland, on July 9. Although defeated by Early, General Wallace secured a delay which proved most useful to the Union cause. Of his action General Grant wrote in his *Memoirs,* "General Wallace contributed on this occasion, by the defeat of the troops under him, a greater benefit to the cause than often falls to the lot of a commander of an equal force to render by means of a victory."

Ricketts' division of the VI Corps had been with General Wallace at the Monocacy. The remainder of the VI Corps under General Wright—and the XIX Corps picked up on its way from Louisiana and sent to Washington by river—had reached there the night of the eleventh and the morning of the twelfth, just in the nick of time to meet Early's attack and persuade him that Washington was too strong a place for him to try to capture. General Augur, in command of the Washington garrison, had thrown out a reconnaissance force in the neighborhood of Fort Stevens. The fight there was not too serious, but the Union troops lost 280 killed and wounded, and skirmishing was continued during the whole day, the enemy retiring that night, July 12.

Of historic interest is the fact that President Lincoln was at Fort Stevens while this fight was going on, that he exposed himself to the enemy's fire, and that a future associate justice of the Supreme Court, Captain Oliver Wendell Holmes, was also in Fort Stevens and is reported to have reached up and pulled Mr. Lincoln by the coattail and told him to get down. The President did this, observing, "that's the way you military men treat a poor civilian." This story was told me before Associate Justice Holmes, who nodded his head, and I accepted it as history. However, I afterward was given the recollections in manuscript of another officer who recorded that he was present in Fort Stevens at the time and no such incident happened! Such conflicting evidence is constantly a test of the historian's judgment.

It was Wright's duty to follow Early closely and push his retreat, but due to interference by the War Department Wright did not do so.

When Early got back in the valley at Strassburg and found that he was not being pursued, he returned to Winchester, where Crook was stationed with a small force, and drove him out. He then sent McCausland to destroy Chambersburg, Pennsylvania, an utterly defenseless town, without any garrison or fortifications. The town was burned on June 30, and some 300 families rendered homeless. The outrage gave rise to much discussion in the rebel army; one of its leaders refused to participate and had charges preferred against him. McCausland was met on his return and defeated and driven into Virginia by General Kelley.

The approach of Early to the capital had caused great alarm and confusion, and shown the weakness and ineffectiveness of the territorial districts and departments as the limitations of military commands. Sigel had simply enough been defeated by Early and was relieved and superseded by Hunter (because of Halleck's prejudiced report of him, according to Colonel McCormick).

Thus the valley was left open to the enemy and Early took advantage of the opportunity. To get rid of Early and deny the Shenandoah Valley to Lee as a dependable source of supply of food and forage, General Grant sent orders to Halleck that he wanted Sheridan put in command of all the troops there in the field "with instructions to put himself south of the enemy and follow him to the death. Wherever the enemy goes, let our troops go also. Once started up the Valley, they ought to be followed until we get possession of the Virginia Central Railroad."

The following quotation from a dispatch of Mr. Lincoln of August 3, 1864, is of special interest in this connection:

> I have seen your despatch in which you say, "I want Sheridan put in command of all the troops in the field, with instructions to put himself south of the enemy and follow him to the death. Wherever the enemy goes, let our troops go also." This, I think is exactly right, as to how our forces should move. But please look over the despatches you may have received from here, even since you made that order, and discover, if you can, that there is any idea in the head of any one here, of "putting our army *south* of the enemy," or of "following him to the *death*" in any direction. I repeat to you it will neither be done nor attempted unless you watch it every day and hour, and force it.

To this General Grant replied that he would start for Washington in two hours. He soon got off but went directly to the Monocacy without stopping in Washington. Hunter's army had arrived at the Monocacy with a collection of cars and engines picked up for their safety and availability. In reply to the question of where the enemy was, Hunter said he did not know, that he had been "so embarrassed with orders from Washington moving him first to the right and then to the left that he had lost all trace of the enemy." He was assured by General Grant that the valley was so important to the enemy as to make it certain the enemy would concentrate and shortly be found in front of our troops.

To the suggestion that he select any place of his choice for his department headquarters and turn over his troops to General Sheridan, who was in Washington, Hunter asked to be relieved entirely, adding that he did not want to embarrass the operations in any way and that he felt Halleck did not have confidence in him.

Sheridan hopped on a special train and came at once. He would now have 30,000 men, 8,000 of them cavalry. Early had about the same number. To prevent Lee from sending additional reinforcements to Early, General Grant ordered Meade to threaten an attack on the Richmond works north of the James River for August 13 and 14. No more rebel troops were sent to Early for the time being. Sheridan sent Early whirling up the Shenandoah Valley and started to fullfill his mission to destroy food and other supplies that would help support the rebellion.

The enemy then decided to make one more try to save the supplies not yet destroyed and hold possession of this rich area. General Grant's instructions for General Sheridan were rewritten and materially changed on their way through the War Department so that Sheridan protested against them. He was accordingly summoned to Washington, and the commanding general's wishes were made clear. On the way back he spent the night of October 18 in Winchester, the same night Early started his new offensive. In Sheridan's absence the left flank of his army was defeated and put to flight. Hearing the guns and noise of battle, Sheridan made his famous ride from Winchester to Cedar Creek on his charger, Rienzi, turned his fleeing troops back, and won a dramatic victory which brought much enthusiasm to the people of the North and psychologically doubtless influenced the vote in the presidential election in favor of Mr. Lincoln.

The most exciting event in connection with the siege operations was the preparation of a mine. It was under the works of the Confederates, starting in the side of a ravine at about the center of General Burnside's front and carried for about 500 feet until it was under a formidable rebel fort on Cemetery Hill. This mine was largely the proposal of

Colonel Henry Pleasants of the 48th Pennsylvania, composed mostly of miners. The scheme had been presented to General Meade and General Grant and detailed orders were issued. The work underground was carefully done and successfully carried through without detection. The commanding general hoped that it might be possible to capture Petersburg by attack through the breech, if the mine were a success. In any case it was hoped that the cavalry and Hancock's corps, the movement of which was begun on July 26 under cover of the astonishment caused by the mine, might reach and destroy much of the Virginia Central Railroad; the infantry was posted to secure their retreat.

In spite of the perfection of the arrangements—the special training given the division which was to enter the crater when the mine had been exploded, and other careful preparations—at the eleventh hour the troops to be used were changed. The specially trained division was not permitted by General Meade to go in first, and this critical duty fell by lot to a division with an utterly incompetent colonel. In general, the operation was messed up as much as possible. When the mine exploded at 5 A.M. on July 30—with a crater 600 feet long, 60 feet wide, and 30 feet deep—everything went more or less wrong. The division trained to follow along the edge of the crater jumped in, was followed by others, and the struggling mass of humanity in the crater became a wonderful target for the riflemen and guns of the Confederates, as soon as they had recovered from the first shock and surprise. By noon withdrawal was sounded, but the wounded lay there for thirty-six hours as Burnside's request for a cessation of hostilities to bury the dead and care for the wounded had been sent to Richmond for instructions. The next day a truce of four hours was granted.

To take advantage of the concentration of troops of Lee's army north of the James, General Meade was directed to send one corps and the cavalry next morning to destroy fifteen or twenty miles of the Weldon Railroad. But these orders were rescinded, and it was not until August 18 that the Union army got permanent possession of the Weldon Railroad, after which the Rebels never got it back.

Obviously the outcome of the presidential election in November 1864 would have a decisive effect on the conduct of the war. While the Republicans had nominated Mr. Lincoln, the Democrats had nominated General McClellan on a platform which included a declaration that the war was a failure, although McClellan had personal reservations about this statement. Many of the states had authorized their troops to vote in the field, others had not given any such permission. The following interview with President Lincoln, as reported by A. K. McClure, seems important enough to be repeated here:

His usually sad face was deeply shadowed with sorrow when I told him that I saw no reasonable prospect of carrying Pennsylvania on the home vote, although we had about held our own in the hand-to-hand conflict through which we were passing. "Well, what is to be done?" was Lincoln's inquiry after the whole situation had been presented to him. I answered that the solution of the problem was a very simple and easy one—that Grant was idle in front of Petersburg; that Sheridan had won all possible victories in the Valley; and that if 5000 Pennsylvania soldiers could be furloughed home from each army the election could be carried without doubt. Lincoln's face brightened instantly at the suggestion, and I saw that he was quite ready to execute it. I said to him: "Of course, you can trust Grant to make the suggestion to him to furlough 5000 Pennsylvania troops for two weeks?" To my surprise, Lincoln made no answer, and the bright face of a few moments before was instantly shadowed again. I was much disconcerted, as I supposed that Grant was the one man to whom Lincoln could turn with absolute confidence as his friend. I then said with earnestness: "Surely, Mr. President, you can trust Grant with a confidential suggestion to furlough Pennsylvania troops?" Lincoln remained silent and evidently distressed at the proposition I was pressing upon him. After a few moments, and speaking with emphasis, I said: "It can't be possible that Grant is not your friend; he can't be such an ingrate?" Lincoln hesitated for some time, and then answered in these words: "Well, McClure, I have no reason to believe that Grant prefers my election to that of McClellan."

I must confess that my response to this to me appalling statement from Lincoln was somewhat violative of the rules of courteous conversation. I reminded Lincoln how, in that room, when I had appealed to him to respect the almost universal demand of the country for Grant's dismissal, he had withstood the shock alone and interposed his omnipotence to save Grant when he was a personal stranger. Lincoln, as usual, answered intemperance of speech by silence. I then said to him: "General Meade is a soldier and a gentleman; he is the commander of the Army of the Potomac; send an order to him from yourself to furlough 5000 Pennsylvania soldiers home for two weeks, and send that order with some trusted friend from the War Department, with the suggestion to Meade that your agent be permitted to bring the order back with him." After a little reflection Lincoln answered: "I reckon that can be done." I then said, "What about Sheridan?" At once his sad face brightened up, like the noonday sun suddenly emerging from a dark cloud, as he answered: "Oh, Phil Sheridan; he's all right." Before I left his room that night he had made his arrangements to send messengers to Meade and Sheridan. The order was sent to Meade, and he permitted it to be returned to the President, but Sheridan needed no order. The 10,000 Pennsylvania soldiers were furloughed during the week, and Lincoln carried Pennsylvania on the home vote by 5712 majority, to which the army vote added 14,363 majority. It was thus that Lincoln made his triumph in Pennsylvania a complete victory without what was then commonly called the "bayonet vote," and Lincoln carried New York by 6749, leaving McClellan the worst defeated candidate ever nominated by any of the great political parties of the country.

I left Lincoln fully convinced that Grant was an ingrate, and Lincoln certainly knew that he permitted that conviction to be formed in my mind. He did not in any way qualify his remark about Grant, although it was his custom when he felt compelled to disparage any one to present some charitable explanation of the conduct complained of. The fact that he refused to send his request to Grant, while he was willing to send it to Meade, proved that he was, for some reason, disappointed in Grant's fidelity to him; and the enthusiasm with which he spoke of Sheridan proved how highly he valued the particular quality that he did not credit to Grant. I confess that the conviction formed that day made the name of Grant leave a bad taste in my mouth for many years. I heartily supported his nomination for the Presidency in 1868, and was chairman of the Pennsylvania delegation in the Chicago Convention that nominated him, because I believed that the chivalrous victor of Appomattox would command the highest measure of confidence from the Southern people and hasten the restoration of peace and business prosperity; but Grant and his immediate friends knew that while I earnestly supported his nomination and election, I did not have the confidence in him that he generally commanded. I now believe that Lincoln was mistaken in his distrust of Grant. It was not until after Grant's retirement from the Presidency that I ever had an opportunity to hear his explanation. I remembered that on election night, when Grant was advised at his headquarters in front of Petersburg of Lincoln's election, he sent Lincoln a dispatch heartily congratulating him upon his triumph. I never heard Lincoln allude to the subject again, and I am therefore ignorant as to whether his belief was ever changed. . . . .

I was anxious to learn, if possible, what Grant's feelings were in the Presidential battle of 1864. Without intimating to him that Lincoln had doubted his fidelity, I reminded him that he had maintained such a silent attitude that some of Lincoln's closest friends were at a loss to know his preference in the contest. He answered very promptly that he supposed none could have doubted his earnest desire for the re-election of Lincoln, although he studiously avoided any expression, public or private, on the subject. He said: "It would have been obviously unbecoming on my part to have given a public expression against a general whom I had succeeded as Commander-in-Chief of the army." I do not doubt that Grant declared the exact truth in that statement. Naturally silent and averse to any expressions whatever on politics, he felt that he could not with propriety even appear to assail a man who had failed and fallen in the position that he had won and maintained. Thus for twelve years I cherished a personal prejudice against Grant because of his supposed want of fidelity to Lincoln that I now believe to have been wholly unjust.

The election on November 8, 1864, proved a great victory for Mr. Lincoln, giving him a popular majority of 411,281, and 212 electoral votes as against 21 for McClellan. He could well say:

> The purpose of the people within the loyal States to maintain the integrity of the Union was never more firm nor more nearly unanimous than now. . . . No candidate for any office whatever, high or low, has ventured to seek votes on the avowal that he was for giving up the Union. There have been much impugning of motives and much heated controversy as to the proper means and best mode of advancing the Union cause; but on the distinct issue of Union or no Union the politicians have shown their instinctive knowledge that there is no diversity among the people. In affording the people the fair opportunity of showing one to another and to the world this firmness and unanimity of purpose, the election has been of vast value to the national cause.

Obviously, Sherman's capture of Atlanta, Georgia, and the start of his march to the sea, Farragut's capture of Mobile in August, Sheridan's success in the Shenandoah Valley—all contributed very much to this political success of the Administration. The defeat of Hood by General Thomas at Nashville in December and the capture of Savannah by Sherman on December 22, when he had reached the sea, doubtless further won popular confidence in the ultimate re-establishment of the Union. Thus 1864 ended with the success of the Federal cause evident to all but the most conservative die-hards in the Confederacy.

XI

Appomattox

AS the winter wore on and the advent of spring was at least hoped for, the Confederates made a first attempt to make peace and appointed a peace commission. General Grant tells the story:

On the last of January, 1865, peace commissioners from the so-called Confederate States presented themselves on our lines around Petersburg, and were immediately conducted to my headquarters at City Point. They proved to be Alexander H. Stephens, Vice-President of the Confederacy, Judge Campbell, Assistant Secretary of War, and R.M.T. Hunter, formerly United States Senator and then a member of the Confederate Senate.

It was about dark when they reached my headquarters, and I at once conducted them to the steamer *Mary Martin,* a Hudson River boat which was very comfortably fitted up for the use of passengers. I at once communicated by telegraph with Washington, and informed the Secretary of War and the President of the arrival of these commissioners, and that their object was to negotiate terms of peace between the United States and, as they termed it, the Confederate government. I was instructed to retain them at City Point until the President, or some one whom he would designate, should come to meet them. They remained several days as guests on board the boat. I saw them quite frequently, though I have no recollection of having had any conversation whatever with them on the subject of their mission. It was something I had nothing to do with, and I therefore did not wish to express any views on the subject. For my own part, I never had admitted, and never was ready to admit, that they were the representatives of a *government.* There had been too great a waste of blood and treasure to concede anything of the kind. As long as they remained there, however, our relations were pleasant, and I found them all very agreeable gentlemen. I directed the captain to furnish them with the best the boat afforded, and to minister to their comfort in every way possible. No guard was placed over them and no restriction was put upon their movements; nor was there any pledge asked that they would not abuse the privileges extended to them. They were permitted to leave the boat when they felt like it, and did so, coming up on the bank and visiting me at my headquarters.

President Lincoln and Secretary of State William H. Seward met with the three Confederate peace commissioners aboard a government steamer at Hampton Roads, Virginia. After his return to headquarters at City Point, the President stopped at General Grant's cabin. The General's wife was there, too. The general was in his office, as Mrs. Grant related in after years and, being anxious herself, she asked Mr. Lincoln if any conclusions in the interests of peace had yet been reached.

He hesitatingly replied: "Well, no."

He had evidently come to have a talk with the General, and perhaps thought my questions premature, as they undoubtedly were.

I exclaimed: "No! Why, Mr. President, are you not going to make terms with them? They are our own people, you know!"

Then he answered: "Yes, I do not forget that," and quietly taking from his pocket a large paper, he carefully unfolded it and read aloud the terms he proposed to them, which were most liberal, I thought.

After finishing, he looked up and I said: "Did they not accept those?"

He smiled wearily and said: "No."

Whereupon I wrathfully exclaimed: "Why, what do they want? That paper is most liberal."

He smiled and said: "I thought when you understood the matter, you would agree with us."

I had quite an interview with the [Confederate] Commissioners, telling them they held a brother of mine as a prisoner and that he was a thorough Rebel, if there ever was one. I knew this to be so as I had had many a battle royal with him on this subject.

These gentlemen asked if General Grant could not exchange him.

"Why, of course not," I explained. "My brother is not a soldier." He was on a visit to a friend in Louisiana when he was captured.

I had already approached General Grant on the subject and he had asked me if I thought it would be just for him to give a war prisoner in exchange for my brother, when we had so many brave men languishing in prison, who had fought for the Union.

In his *Memoirs* General Grant explains what Mr. Lincoln told him about the interview:

> He . . . said he had told them that there would be no use in entering into any negotiations unless they would recognize, first: that the Union as a whole must be forever preserved, and second: that slavery must be abolished. If they were willing to concede these two points, then he was ready to enter into negotiations and was almost willing to hand them a blank sheet of paper with his signature attached for them to fill in the terms upon which they were willing to live with us in the Union and be one people. He always showed a generous and kindly spirit toward the Southern people, and I never heard him abuse an enemy.

General Grant always remembered with great satisfaction that three of the last four weeks of Lincoln's life were spent at his City Point headquarters. The President lived on the steamer *River Queen* and conducted the affairs of state from the drawing room of Appomattox Manor, a large white frame house still standing high on the bluff above the Appomattox and James rivers. General Grant used the manor's dining room as his office and communications center.

In the last ten months of the war, the Union Army headquarters was at City Point, the old steamer landing at the confluence of the Appomattox and James rivers which today is part of Hopewell, Virginia.

Twenty-odd miles northwest stood beleaguered Richmond; seven miles southwest lay embattled Petersburg. Out of City Point, the Union's earth-and-log trenches stretched ever longer, covering Richmond and curving around beneath Petersburg like a clenching fist.

One after another, Lee's vital supply roads angling in from the south and west had been chopped off. The Confederate capital itself suffered from shortages of all sorts of supplies. (Two years before General Lee had given his inability to supply his army in Virginia as one of his reasons for the risks of the Gettysburg campaign.)

March wore on. Up from the deep South drove Union Major General William T. Sherman's army, starting from Savannah, Georgia, on February 1 and marching all the way to Greensboro, North Carolina, by March 23. By then, the mauled Confederate forces of General Joseph E. Johnston could do little more than annoy him.

On April 1, 1865, Sherman commanded 81,155 troops and estimated Johnston's force at about 45,000, still widely scattered. Only 120 miles north of Greensboro, Grant with about 100,000 men held Lee's starving

Army of Northern Virginia at bay—an army of more than 75,000 men.

General Lee had for some months appreciated the danger to his army resulting from the defeat of other Confederate armies in other theaters of operation. He was especially aware of the danger of General Sherman's reaching the Atlantic coast and marching north, which could mean an attack on Petersburg and Richmond by the combined armies of General Grant and General Sherman. Of the conclusion of this grand maneuver, General J. F. C. Fuller wrote:

> The one great strategical problem of the North was to manoeuvre in such a way as to create an enemy rear. This was accomplished from the West, the Western Federal forces moving southwards down the Mississippi, eastwards through Chattanooga, Atlanta, to Savannah, and then northwards towards Richmond. A right flank wheel of more than a thousand miles extending in time over three years; a strategical movement compared to which the German right flank wheel in 1914, however powerful, was child's play.

The situation of the Confederacy had been discussed with the President and Cabinet in a conference in Richmond. General Lee's idea that he must withdraw his army from the fortifications of Richmond and Petersburg was approved and President Davis had suggested that he do it right away; but General Lee said his animals were not in condition for lack of forage and his supplies inadequate to start the movement at that time.

It was General Lee's desperate plan to make an attack on the right of the Union line before Petersburg, attempting a breakthrough, which would force the Union commander to weaken his left and concentrate additional forces on his right. This would make it easier for the Army of Northern Virginia to escape to the west or southwest and perhaps unexpectedly attack General Sherman's army and, after defeating it, turn north and attempt to defeat the Army of the Potomac. The point selected for the break-through was Fort Stedman, and the command of the assault was given to General Gordon.

Grant had, with singular prescience, looked for some such movement from Lee a month before. He had ordered Parke, then in command of the IX Corps, to be ready to meet an assault on his center and to let his commanders understand they were to lose no time in bringing all their resources to bear on the point of danger. "With proper alacrity in this respect," he added, "I would have no objection to seeing the enemy get through." This is one of the most characteristic phrases we have met with in Grant's orders. It throws the strongest light both on his temperament and on the mastery of his business at which he had arrived. A month beforehand he foresaw Gordon's attack, prepared for it, and welcomed the momentary success which attended it. Under such generalship an army's lines are a trap into which entrance is suicide.

The attack, very carefully planned and especially prepared, was delivered on March 25 at 4 A.M. and succeeded at first; in fact, the assaulting troops entered Fort Stedman and spread to the right and left. But General Parke counterattacked and in splendid fashion retook all that had been lost, at the same time inflicting a loss of 2,681 on the Confederates—1,600 of them, prisoners, were looked over by President Lincoln at Meade's headquarters that afternoon.

It was an interesting coincidence that the day Gordon was making his preparations for the attack on the Union right (March 24), General Grant issued his order for the movement of his armies around Lee's right flank to start on the twenty-ninth, cutting off his remaining supply lines, the Richmond and Danville Railroad and the South Side Railroad. The Union Commander in Chief was not distracted a moment from his plan, which he knew would force General Lee to abandon his fortified line.

The advance of the Union forces for this movement was confided to General Sheridan, who distinguished himself greatly in the next few days, from Dinwiddie Court House to Five Forks, which was a strategically important road center. March 29–30 brought heavy rains which made the progress of General Sheridan's troops very difficult, the horses in many cases sinking up to their bellies in water and quicksand. Some soldiers called to officers as they passed, "When are the gunboats coming?"

Now began one of the greatest American campaigns, the commanders on both sides being masters of the military art and neither making any serious blunders.

On March 29 the Union army had started its movement around the enemy's right, attacking at Hatcher's Run, leaving a minimum force in front of the Confederate works, under General Weitzel before Richmond and under General Parke before Petersburg, with directions to keep in close touch with the enemy and follow up any indication of his retiring.

When General Sheridan's troops approached Five Forks they found it occupied by Confederate infantry under the command of General Pickett, whom General Lee had sent there to "hold Five Forks at all hazards. Protect road to Ford's Depot and prevent Union forces from striking the South Side Railroad." Sheridan's cavalry was repulsed, and he asked for infantry support. The V Corps under General Warren was accordingly sent by General Grant to support Sheridan, but again because of the condition of the roads and the rain, Warren was very much delayed and some of his troops did not arrive until late afternoon the next day.

Counting on the arrival of the V Corps, on April 1 Sheridan organized his attack, while Pickett, apparently confident of the effective repulse administered the day before, went off to a shadbake provided by General Rosser! General Sheridan at one time exclaimed: "This battle must be fought and won before the sun goes down. All the conditions may be changed in the morning. We have but a few hours of daylight left us. My cavalry are rapidly exhausting their ammunition, and if the attack is delayed much longer they may have none left." At 4 o'clock the formation was completed and the order to assault was given, and in a short time Pickett's entrenched line was broken by a successful attack on his left.

When Ayres' skirmish line seemed to waver while under fire from a dense woods as it crossed an open field, General Sheridan with characteristic dash shouted, "Come on, men, go at 'em with a will! Move on at a clean jump, or you'll not catch one of 'em. They're all getting ready to run now, and if you don't get on to them in five minutes they'll every one get away from you. Now go for them!" Sheridan on his favored horse, Rienzi, which had carried him on his famous ride from Winchester to Cedar Creek, put his spurs to the horse and jumped the Confederate parapet, landing amidst a number of men who had surrendered. They asked, "Where do you want us all to go?" To which Sheridan answered, "Go right over there," pointing to the rear. "Get right along now, drop your guns; you'll never need them any more. You'll all be safe over there. Are there any more of you? We want every one of these fellows." Nearly fifteen hundred were captured at the angle.

Thus was won the victory of Five Forks on April 1. News of it was carried to the Union commander by Colonel Horace Porter, who had been sent to be with Sheridan all that day and to report frequently.

One of his bulletins had stated: "I have noticed among the prisoners and dead many old men whose heads are quite bald." This was in evidence that the enemy in recruiting was "robbing the grave." Ingalls, who was present and quite bald, was cautioned by the commanding general, his classmate and onetime roommate at West Point, to be very careful not to fall into the hands of the enemy for they would be commenting thus on his bald head in their reports.

After Five Forks, Sheridan pushed on toward Jetersville, while General Lee was gathering together the remains of his army at Amelia Court House, hoping to find that rations and forage had been sent there by railroad. However, he was disappointed to find that no such supplies had been received for his famished army; the Danville Railroad was closed to him, and the direct route to the southwest no longer available.

Meanwhile, Petersburg had been evacuated during the night of April 2–3, and directions were sent to General Meade to push westward with all haste. General Grant had telegraphed Mr. Lincoln the good news and invited him to meet him in Petersburg, which the President said he would do. General Grant with his chief staff officers rode into Petersburg and stopped at 21 Market Street, the residence of Mr. Thomas Wallace. They all took seats on the porch where they were joined by President Lincoln, his sons Robert and Tad, and Admiral Porter. The President seemed delighted at the good news and shook General Grant's hand for some time, expressing his thanks and joy at the success gained so far.

Mr. Lincoln talked about the civil complications that would follow the destruction of the Confederate armies in the field. He intimated clearly enough that thoughts of leniency to the conquered were uppermost in his heart. Perhaps it was at this time that he said it would relieve the situation somewhat if some of the rebel political leaders could manage to escape. His son Tad seemed to be unhappy and not much interested; General Sharpe, who apparently understood the boy's mute expression, produced some sandwiches which Tad seized as a drowning man would seize a life preserver. This greatly amused the President and General in Chief. The proprietor of the house invited the general to come into the parlor, but he declined with a, "Thank you, but I am smoking."

After taking his leave of the President, with the latter's good wishes for every success, General Grant received a message from General

Weitzel: "We took Richmond at eight fifteen this morning. I captured many guns. The enemy left in great haste. The city is on fire in two places. Am making every effort to put it out. People received us with enthusiastic expressions of joy." The general expressed his regrets that he had not had this news before parting with the President and then gave directions that it be circulated among the troops as rapidly as possible.

In contrast to the quiet in Petersburg, in Richmond there was great disorder: much looting and stealing and destruction. No police organization had been provided, and violence and disorder prevailed until General Weitzel's arrival put a stop to it. However, Colonel George A. Bruce, approaching the burning city, noticed "a farmer plowing in a field while cinders from the burning capital were falling at his feet!"

That evening, April 3, Generals Grant and Meade both went into camp at Sutherland's Station; but the Army of the Potomac caught only a few hours' sleep and was again on the march at 3 A.M. General Ord with the Army of the James was swinging along toward Burksville to prevent Lee's possible escape to Danville, where he was assumed to be pushing in order to unite with Johnston's army. April 4 was another day of racing westward, and the Union soldiers all seemed to realize that this was a race to end the war and that, if they won the race, the war would be over, at least in the eastern theater.

The night of April 4, General Grant camped at Wilson's Station on the South Side Railroad. A dispatch came from Sheridan, saying he had captured some guns and wagons and intercepted Lee's advance toward Burksville and that Lee himself was at Amelia Court House. A horseman in full Confederate uniform, who had emerged from the woods like an apparition, was about to be seized as a prisoner, when General Horace Porter, one of the aides, recognized him as a Sheridan spy named Campbell. He was brought to General Grant, who also recognized him.

Campbell took a small pellet of tin foil out of his mouth, opened it, and pulled out a sheet of tissue paper on which was written a message to General Grant from Sheridan describing the situation at Jetersville and concluding, "I wish you were here yourself." In response General Grant immediately started to see Sheridan, changing from his black pony, Jeff Davis, to his larger horse, Cincinnati. He told Campbell to lead the way. He was accompanied only by two aides and the headquarters mounted escort of fourteen men, there being no body of cavalry to furnish a more adequate escort. The route led through woods, with indications that Confederate cavalry had been through there recently and with occasional rebel camp fires visible at a distance through the trees. The distance was about twenty miles, and by half-past ten o'clock the party reached Sheridan's pickets, who could hardly believe that the Commander in Chief would be in enemy country with so small an escort. But some of the sleeping men woke up and recognized him with various remarks like, "Great Scott! The Old Chief's out here himself. The Rebs are going to get busted tomorrow"; or, "Uncle Sam's joined the cavalry sure enough. You can bet there'll be lively times here in the morning."

After getting Sheridan's estimate of the situation and learning of his fear that Lee might escape if much of the Army of the Potomac were moved farther to the right as Meade proposed, Generals Grant and Sheridan went over to General Meade's headquarters. Once there, they explained to Meade that it was not desirable to push the enemy and follow him, but to get by him and in front of him and surround him, stopping his advance. Before leaving Sheridan's headquarters directions were sent to General Ord to move westward parallel to the South Side Railroad and especially to prevent General Lee from reaching Burksville or Farmville. General Ord and his Army of the James had marched down from Bermuda Hundred just before the big maneuver started, and had taken an important part in the fight at Hatcher's Run.

Near Summit on April 3, as he was proceeding to Amelia Court House, General Lee received an invitation from Judge James H. Cox for him and Longstreet and their staff officers to dine with him. They were naturally delighted at the prospect of a really good meal. When the welcome mint juleps were served, General Lee hardly touched his and, holding out his glass of ice water, remarked to Miss Kate Cox, "This glass of cold water is, I believe, far more refreshing than the drinks they are enjoying so much." Later, when coffee was served, Miss Cox asked if he took cream with his after-dinner coffee. To which the General replied: "I have not taken coffee for so long that I would not dare to take it in its original strength."

The continued march was saddened for the Confederate commander by news that all but one of the bridges over the Appomattox River, to which he had directed his columns, were not usable and that the pontoon bridge he had ordered had not been sent. There were further discouraging reports of teams unable to advance, men too weak to keep up with their units, and losses from enemy action and the taking of prisoners. By April 4, Lee had the remainder of his army pretty well concentrated at Amelia Court House. Realizing that their case was hopeless, great numbers of the Confederates deserted. On April 6 it was discovered that General Lee, after attempting to gather in food for the remnants of his command, had left Amelia Court House and was marching west, having evidently given up the hope of reaching Danville and supplies there, and was now trying to escape to Lynchburg, crossing to the north side of the Appomattox River.

The Union army continued its pursuit on parallel roads in the effort to interpose itself between Lee and this latest objective. News came of the destruction by Sheridan and Wright of Ewell's command with the capture of six general officers and 7,000 men at Sailor's Creek. General Grant spent that night at Burksville, and started early the morning of April 7 for Farmville. He was cheered lustily by the troops as he made his way on the crowded roads and was amused by such assurances from the men as, "The cavalry's gi'en out, General. Infantry's going to crush the rest of the mud"; or, "We've marched nigh 20 miles on this stretch, and we're good for 20 more, if the general says so." The general raised his hat to acknowledge the cheers, and gave a cordial nod to the men who addressed him.

Finally from Farmville on April 7 General Grant, feeling confident that the line of escape was closed, addressed a note to General Lee calling attention to the hopelessness of the Confederate Army's situation and stating he regarded it as his duty "to shift from myself the responsibility of any further effusion of blood, by asking of you the surrender of that portion of the Confederate States Army known as the Army of Northern Virginia." General Lee replied the same day differing as to the plight of his army but with a request to know what terms might be considered. The next day (April 8) General Grant replied that "peace being my great desire, there is but one condition I would insist upon, namely that the men and officers surrendered shall be disqualified for taking up arms again against the Government of the United States." Grant offered to meet him or appoint officers to meet anyone General Lee might appoint at any point agreeable to him.

General Grant started early in the morning of April 8 to ride toward the head of his army, and so was temporarily out of communication with General Lee. The latter on receiving this last message sent a flag of truce and notified both Sheridan (in his front) and Meade (following him), asking for a cease-fire and saying he was requesting a meeting with General Grant to discuss terms of surrender. At daybreak on April 9, with massive Federal forces having headed off the Confederate army, now at Appomattox Court House, Lee had attempted a last, desperate breakthrough. The Union force in front of him—Ord's army and Sheridan's corps—was too strong. The Confederate General in Chief then sadly said, "There is nothing left me to do but to go and see General Grant, and I would rather die a thousand deaths." As the two Union army commanders "had heard nothing of this until the fighting had got to be severe and all going against Lee," General Grant wrote "both of these commanders hesitated very considerably about suspending hostilities at all. They were afraid it was not in good faith. . . . They, however, finally consented to a suspension of hostilities for two hours, to give an opportunity of communicating with me in that time, if possible. It was found that, from the route I had taken, they would probably not be able to communicate with me and get an answer back within the time fixed unless the messenger should pass through the rebel lines."

General Lee, therefore, sent an escort with the officer (Thomas Goode Jones, later governor of Alabama) bearing his reply through his lines accepting the proposal for an interview with regard to the terms of surrender which had been suggested and seemed acceptable. Receipt of this message acted as an immediate cure of General Grant's sick headache. He was riding toward Appomattox Court House to avoid having to pass through the Confederate force and had been suffering acutely for two days from an attack of migraine, a malady to which he had been subject all his life. (Occasionally the attacks would incapacitate him for hours, a fact which undoubtedly triggered some of the rumors that he drank.)

General Grant answered: "Your note of this date (April 9, 1865) is but this moment (11:50 a.m.) received, in consequence of my having passed from the Richmond and Lynchburg road to the Farmville-Lynchburg road. I am at this writing about four miles west of Walker's Church, and will push forward to the front for the purpose of meeting you. Notice sent to me on this road where you wish the interview to take place will meet me."

He soon reached the place where General Sheridan, with his army barring the road to the Confederate army, was waiting with General Ord and members of their staffs. He found them still excited and fearful that the truce was just a ruse and that General Lee expected to slip out of their grasp and join Johnston in North Carolina. But General Grant had no doubt about the good faith of Lee, and was soon conducted to the house of a Mr. McLean at Appomattox Court House, where General Lee was waiting with Colonel Charles Marshall, one of his staff.

As General Grant came in the front door, General Babcock, who had brought the last message to General Lee, opened the door to the room on the left. On General Grant's entrance General Lee rose and shook hands with the Union commander. General Grant opened the conversation by saying that he remembered General Lee very well in the old army in the Mexican War; he did not expect General Lee to remember him, because of the difference in their rank and age at that time. General Lee said something about remembering meeting him in Mexico but not having been able to recall his features. As the conversation went on, General Grant, although quite jubilant on receipt of Lee's letter, now "felt like anything rather than rejoicing at the downfall of a foe who had fought so long and valiantly and suffered so much for a cause, though that cause was," he believed, "one of the worst for which a people ever fought."

Finally General Lee said, "I suppose, General Grant, that the object of our present meeting is fully understood. I asked to see you to ascertain upon what terms you would receive the surrender of my army." On being assured that they were substantially those outlined in his letter of the day before, General Lee asked that they be reduced to writing so that they could be formally acted upon. In compliance with this wish, General Grant asked General Ely S. Parker, secretary of his staff, for writing materials and wrote out in pencil:

Appomattox C.H., Virginia
April 9, 1865.

General R. E. Lee,
Commanding Confederate States Armies:

General: In accordance with the substance of my letter to you of the 8th inst., I propose to receive the surrender of the Army of Northern Virginia on the following terms, to wit:

Rolls of all the officers and men to be made in duplicate, one copy to be given to an officer designated by me, the other to be retained by such officer or officers as you may designate. The officers to give their individual paroles not to take up arms against the Government of the United States until properly [exchanged,] and each company or regimental commander sign a like parole for the men of their commands.

The arms, artillery, and public property to be parked and stacked, and turned over to the officer appointed by me to receive them. This will not embrace the side-arms of the officers, nor their private horses or baggage. This done, each officer and man will be allowed to return to their homes, not to be disturbed by United States authority so long as they observe their parole and the laws in force where they may reside.

Very respectfully,
U. S. Grant,
Lieutenant-General

On reading over this draft carefully, General Lee noted that the word "exchanged" had obviously been omitted; after asking permission to fill it in, he borrowed a pencil from General Horace Porter for the purpose. When Lee read the last of the statement, namely that the officers might retain their horses and side arms and that the paroled men were "Not to be disturbed by United States authority so long as they observe their parole and the laws in force where they may reside," he remarked with some feeling, General Grant thought, that this would have a very happy effect upon his army. He then explained that many of the Confederate cavalrymen and artillerymen owned their own horses, and he asked if they would be allowed to retain them. General Grant replied that the terms did not so provide. Realizing that this would probably be the last battle of the war and that "it was doubtful whether they would be able to put in a crop to carry themselves and their families through the next winter without the aid of the horses they were then riding," Grant said that he would instruct the officers administering the paroles to allow "every man of the Confederate Army who claimed to own a horse or mule to take the animal to his home." General Lee again remarked that this would have a very happy effect.

In his essay entitled "Gentlemen" Robert Louis Stevenson with rare appreciation of General Grant's consideration and delicacy in slipping in the permission for the officers to retain their side arms, has this to say: "On the day of the capitulation, Lee wore his presentation sword; it was the first thing Grant observed, and from that moment he had but one thought; how to avoid taking it. A man who should perhaps have had the nature of an angel, but assuredly not the special virtues of a gentleman, might have received the sword, and no more words about it:

he would have done well in a plain way. One who wished to be a gentleman, and knew not how, might have received and returned it: he would have done infamously ill, he would have proved himself a cad; taking the stage for himself, leaving to his adversary confusion of countenance and the ungraceful posture of a man condemned to offer thanks. Grant, without saying a word, added to the terms of this article: 'All officers to retain their side-arms;' and the problem was solved and Lee kept his sword, and Grant went down to posterity, not perhaps a fine gentleman, but a great one."

General Grant had had many informal conversations with President Lincoln and knew that the latter agreed with him as to his general attitude toward the now defeated Confederates and bringing the seceded states back into the Union. Nevertheless, that the terms he proposed at Appomattox were in no way dictated by the President is confirmed by Nicolay and Hay in their history of Lincoln: "He [Grant] ended with a phrase which he evidently had not thought of, and for which he had no authority, which practically pardoned and amnestied every man in Lee's army—a thing he had refused to consider the day before, and which had been forbidden him in President Lincoln's order of the 3rd of March." But this phrase was by military usage within the prerogatives of the successful commander. Today we know it was the phrase by which he was able to prevent vengeance when President Andrew Johnson (in pursuance of his threat. "Treason must be made odious" and "Traitors must be punished and impoverished") later wanted to prosecute General Lee and other Confederate commanders in the civil courts.

General Lee sat down and wrote a letter accepting the terms, and General Grant gave his pencil draft to Assistant Adjutant General T. S. Bowers, to make a fair copy of. But Bowers was so excited by the importance of the event and what he was to copy, that his hand shook and he had to hand the manuscript to the stolid military secretary, Colonel Ely S. Parker, for copying. While the copies were being made, General Grant presented the Union officers to General Lee, who shook hands with General Seth Williams (he had been General Lee's adjutant at West Point when the latter was superintendent) and with those who extended their hands. He acknowledged the introduction of the others with a formal bow. When he saw Colonel Parker's swarthy features he looked somewhat surprised, presumably wondering at the Union commander's having a full-blooded Seneca Indian on his personal staff.

General Lee then spoke of the fact that he had ordered rations and forage shipped from Lynchburg for his needy men and horses. He was not certain how many men had to be fed. General Grant proposed to issue them 25,000 rations (which General Lee said would be ample) but explained that his own cavalry had had to depend upon the country for forage. General Lee also said he had a thousand or more Union prisoners, whom he would be glad to turn over, as they had of necessity had to march along with his army and share its privations. The number of men surrendered was actually 27,516, in addition to the 46,495 captured between March 29 and April 9, making a total of at least 74,011 in the Confederate army when the final campaign started, not counting deserters who got away.

General Grant, conscious that his appearance—a soldier's blouse with the insignia of rank only, muddy boots, and no sword—might be considered intentional disrespect, then explained that he had been separated from his headquarters' baggage for several days and was not in the habit of wearing a sword when on the road. To which General Lee replied that he was in the habit of wearing his sword "most of the time when I am among my troops moving about through the army." Thus, when a sentimental and gushing lady in after years asked General Grant, "What were your thoughts, General, in that sublime moment when you knew that at last Lee would surrender, and the heavens of your glory were about to open?" he could truthfully reply, "My dirty boots and wearing no sword."

General Lee then complied with General Sheridan's request for the loan of two messages sent in such a hurry that he had not been able to enter record copies in his headquarter's file. After arranging for a Union and a Confederate officer to hasten through the Confederate lines to notify General Meade of the surrender and assure that firing would not break out by mistake, General Lee rose. He shook hands with General Grant, bowed to the other officers present, and left the house. He called for his horse, Traveler, held by his orderly in the yard, and mounted. Raising his hat, he returned the salute of General Grant, who had followed to the foot of the porch steps. Then General Lee rode sadly away to his army, who were now prisoners of war.

The news of the surrender reached Union lines, and the firing of salutes began at several points. But General Grant sent an order at once to have them stopped: "The war is over; the rebels are our countrymen again; and the best sign of rejoicing after the victory will be to abstain from all demonstrations in the field."

On May 30, 1892, Colonel Charles Marshall, the single staff officer General Lee took with him to the surrender and the only Confederate officer who was an eyewitness of the historical conference in the McLean house, said in a prepared speech:

The day after the meeting at the McLeans' house, at which the terms of surrender had been agreed upon, another interview took place between General Grant and General Lee upon the invitation of General Grant. . . . The conversation turned on the subject of a general peace, as to which General Grant had already declared the want of power to treat, but in speaking of the means by which a general pacification might be effected General Grant said to General Lee, with great emphasis and strong feeling; "General Lee I want this war to end without the shedding of another drop of American blood." Not "Northern" blood, not "Southern" blood, but "American" blood, for in his eyes all the men around him and all those who might be then confronting each other on other fields over the wide area of war were "Americans". . . .

On that eventful morning of April 9th, 1865, General Grant was called upon to decide the most momentous question that any American soldier or statesman has ever been required to decide.

The great question was: How shall the war end? What shall be the relations between the victors and the vanquished? Upon the decision of that question depended, as I believe, the future of American institutions.

If the extreme rights of military success had been insisted upon, and had the vanquished been required to pass under the yoke of defeat and bitter humiliation, the war would have ended as a successful war of conquest—the Southern States would have been conquered states, and the Southern people would have been a conquered people, in whose hearts would have been sown all the enmity and ill-will of the conquered to the conquerors, to be transmitted from sire to son.

With such an ending of the war there would have been United States without an united people. . . .

Southern military power was exhausted. He [General Grant] was in a position to exact the supreme rights of a conqueror and the unconditional submission of his adversary unless that adversary should elect to risk all on the event of a desperate battle, in which much "American" blood would certainly be shed.

I will say here that the question was gravely considered in Confederate

Councils, whether we should not accept the extreme risk and cut our way through the hosts of General Grant or perish in the attempt.

This plan had many advocates, but General Lee was not one of them, as will be seen by his farewell order to his army.

Under such circumstances General Lee and General Grant met to discuss the terms of the surrender of General Lee's army, and at the request of General Lee, General Grant wrote the terms of surrender he proposed to offer to the Confederate General. They were liberal and honorable alike to the victor and the vanquished, and General Lee at once accepted them. Any one who reads General Grant's proposal cannot fail to see how careful he was to avoid unnecessary humiliation to his adversary. As far as it was possible, General Grant took away the sting of defeat from the Confederate army. He triumphed, but he triumphed without exultation, and with a noble respect to his enemy.

Then Colonel Marshall concluded with the following complimentary paragraph, to which should be added great praise for General Lee's wisdom and courage in taking the responsibility for so promptly accepting the terms offered.

There was never a nobler knight than the Grant of Appomattox—no knight more magnanimous or more generous. No statesman ever decided a vital question more wisely, more in the interest of his country and of all mankind than General Grant decided the great question presented to him when he and General Lee met that morning of April 9, 1865, to consider the terms of surrender of the Army of Northern Virginia.

Surely such praise of the conqueror from one of his unsuccessful opponents is most unusual. But General Lee himself had great respect for his adversary, as this selection from James Grant Wilson's *General Grant,* indicates:

Within a few weeks of Grant's death a member of General Lee's staff said to a friend, who had mentioned Hancock's high opinion of his old chief; "That reminds me of Lee's opinion of your great Union general, uttered in my presence in reply to a disparaging remark on the part of a person who referred to Grant as a 'military accident, who had no distinguishing merit, but had achieved success through a combination of fortunate circumstances.' General Lee looked into the critic's eye steadily, and said: 'Sir, your opinion is a very poor compliment to me. We all thought Richmond, protected as it was by our splendid fortifications and defended by our army of veterans, could not be taken. Yet Grant turned his face to our capital, and never turned it away until we had surrendered. Now, I have carefully searched the military records of both ancient and modern history, and have never found Grant's superior as a general. I doubt if his superior can be found in all history.' "

After the interview with General Lee on April 10, General Grant returned to the McLean house, where many officers of both armies had gathered and were exchanging greetings and reminiscences. After an hour pleasantly passed in this way he set out on horseback with his staff and a small escort for Burksville Junction, to which point the railroad had been repaired. But the repairs had been made in great haste and the ground was soft. "The train got off the track frequently, and as a result, it was after midnight the second day [April 12] when I reached City Point," General Grant wrote. From there he hastened by boat to Washington, to stop the expenses of the war as soon as possible. He arrived in the capital on April 13.

When we remember the length of the Civil War, the will to win on both sides, the unusually heavy losses the troops on both sides suffered without giving up—over 82 per cent by the 1st Texas at Antietam and an equal percentage by the 1st Minnesota at Gettysburg—we cannot but be grateful for a peace that brought prosperity to a reunited country and leadership among free nations. Truly the men of that great generation not only knew how to fight a war, but also how to end a war.

Napoleon once remarked something to the effect that an army is very seldom beaten—it is usually the general who is beaten. General Grant was apparently never beaten personally. When the enemy was able to frustrate one plan, he tried another. He always had his troops arranged so they could support one another if something went wrong, or they could take advantage of any mistake of the enemy. Thus when General Lee changed his line of retreat to the direction of Lynchburg and started to cross the Appomattox River, Ord and Sheridan were in position to conform to the change and still get ahead of the enemy's column in time to stop it. Perhaps this explains why Grant is the only commander in modern history I know of to receive the surrender in the field of three enemy armies—at Fort Donelson, Vicksburg, and Appomattox.

Now free to send a very large contingent of his army to confront General Joseph E. Johnston, the Confederate commander in North Carolina, and co-operate with General Sherman, whose army was already superior to the force General Johnston had been able to gather together,

General Grant surmised that Johnston would most likely follow General Lee's example and surrender to General Sherman. Not wishing to appear to be claiming a share in Sherman's glory in securing the surrender of the opponent who had so skillfully maneuvered from Dalton to Atlanta, General Grant immediately sent Sherman by messenger a copy of the terms granted at Appomattox and authorizing him to accept Johnston's surrender on the same terms.

Sherman, however, recognized the need for definite terms to establish a peace and the return of the seceded states into the Union, and he remembered Mr. Lincoln's conciliatory attitude toward the South. Tentatively—and subject to approval by higher authority—Sherman concurred April 18 in a memorandum of agreement with General Johnston. It comprised many political conditions and provided "in general terms—the war to cease; a general amnesty, so far as the Executive of the United States could command, on condition of the disbandment of the Confederate armies," and so on. It was just the sort of agreement President Lincoln had intended to prohibit by his General Order No. 3 of March 3 but had given Sherman to understand he would now approve. But President Lincoln had been assassinated on April 14, and his successor, Andrew Johnson, and Secretary of War Stanton disapproved Sherman's action and denounced it publicly in bitter terms. A Cabinet meeting was called and General Grant invited to attend. Sherman's proposed agreement with Johnston was disapproved, and General Grant was ordered to proceed to North Carolina and take charge of the situation.

With characteristic consideration for his great subordinate, General Grant visited Sherman as secretly as possible in his headquarters and arranged for the latter to notify General Johnston that the tentative agreement had been disapproved and his surrender would be accepted on the same terms as General Lee's. General Johnston could not do otherwise than agree, and the whole matter was thus settled. But obviously Sherman could not forget or forgive the public insults he had received for preparing a formula for ending the war politically as well as militarily. In the persepective of 100 years we cannot but regret that politics prevented the settlement of peace without the mischances of Reconstruction.

Other Confederate commanders surrendered to nearby Union commanders. Finally, on May 4, General Richard Taylor, son of President Taylor of Mexican War fame, surrendered everything within his command east of the Mississippi; and General Kirby Smith surrendered the Confederate Trans-Mississippi Department on the twenty-sixth.

The armies of Meade and Sherman were brought to Washington, and on May 23, 1865, the Army of the Potomac with General Meade leading passed in review before President Johnson and General Grant, who occupied a reviewing stand built in front of the White House. The next day General Sherman led his four corps, numbering about 65,000 men, over the same route. However, because of the attack made on him by the new President and Secretary Stanton in connection with his tentative surrender agreement with Johnston, he did not shake hands with either of them. His veterans of the march across Georgia and up the Atlantic Coast were not so technically precise and military in review, but they had with them many souvenirs of their skill and organization as foragers on their long and historic march through the enemy's country, and dramatic bits of showmanship met with enthusiastic response from the populace.

As the great British (but half-American by parentage) statesman and war leader, Sir Winston Churchill, was to write 93 years later: "Thus ended the great American Civil War, which must upon the whole be considered the noblest and least avoidable of all the great mass-conflicts of which till then there was record. Three quarters of a million men had fallen on the battlefield. The North was plunged in debt; the South was ruined."

XII

Reconstruction

ON Tuesday evening, April 11, President Lincoln took advantage of a considerable and enthusiastic crowd gathered in front of the White House and addressed them. He spoke of his hope for "a just and speedy peace, the joyous expression of which cannot be restrained." He said a call for a national thanksgiving was being prepared. "By these recent successes the reinauguration of the national authority—reconstruction—which has had a large share of thought from the first, is pressed much more closely upon our attention. It is fraught with great difficulty. Unlike a case of war between independent nations, there is no organized organ for us to treat with—no one man has authority to give up the rebellion for any other man." After a further brief exposition of the problems, he referred to the settlement he had approved in Louisiana, and the two great principles on which it was based: (1) the mass of southern people should be restored to their rights of citizenship as soon as they desired it, and (2) if there had to be punishment it should be limited to those few who could be proved to have been influential in leading the southern states into rebellion. He added:

> It is also unsatisfactory to some that the elective franchise is not given to the colored man. I would myself prefer that it were now conferred on the very intelligent, and on those who serve our cause as soldiers. . . . These twelve thousand persons (who in Louisiana had concurred in the settlement) are thus fully committed to the Union and to perpetual freedom in the State—committed to the very things, and nearly all the things, the nation wants—and they ask the nation's recognition and its assistance to make good their committal.

He concluded with a reference to the evils of disapproving the Louisiana basis of settlement and pleading that the novelty of the problem precluded announcement then of any rigid and inflexible policy.

On reaching Washington April 13, General Grant busied himself with orders for stopping the war expenditures and with letters of information and direction to various separate department commanders. He had an interview with President Lincoln, and was invited to attend the Cabinet meeting the next morning, where he received the cordial welcome and congratulations of all those present. That evening was to be the occasion of the greatest American tragedy.

The President and Mrs. Lincoln invited the Grants to go to Ford's Theater and sit in the box with them that evening; but the general had to decline, as he and Mrs. Grant had made arrangements to go to Burlington, New Jersey, that afternoon to see their two sons at school there. The trip probably saved Grant from assassination.

Mrs. Grant's recollection of events on that fateful April 14, 1865, is quoted in full:

At about mid-day, a rap at my door was followed, in answer to my "Come in," by the entrance of a man, dressed in light colored corduroy coat and trousers and with rather a shabby hat of the same color. I remarked his dress; as he came in, I started up and said: "I thought it was the bell boy with cards. What do you want?" He reddened and bowing, said: "This is Mrs. Grant?" I bowed assent. "Mrs. Lincoln sends me, Madam, with her compliments to say she will call for you at exactly eight o'clock to go to the theatre." To this, I replied with some feeling (not liking either the looks of the messenger or the message, thinking the former savored of discourtesy and the latter seemed like a command), saying, "You may return with my compliments to Mrs. Lincoln, and say I regret that as Gen. Grant and I intend leaving the city this afternoon, we will not, therefore, be here to accompany the President and Mrs. Lincoln to the theatre." He hesitated a moment, then urged: "Madam, the papers announce that Gen. Grant will be with the President tonight at the theatre," I said to this: "You deliver my message to Mrs. Lincoln, as I have given it to you. You may go now." He smiled as he turned to leave. I have thought since, that this man was one of the band of conspirators in that night's sad tragedy, and that he was not sent by Mrs. Lincoln at all. I am perfectly sure that he, with three others, one of them Booth himself, sat opposite me and my party at luncheon that day.

As soon as I received the invitation to go with Mrs. Lincoln, I despatched a note to Gen. Grant, entreating him to go home that evening; that I did not want to go to the theatre; that he must take me home. I not only wrote to him but sent three of the Staff officers who called to pay their respects to me, to urge the General to go home that night.

I do not know what possessed me to take such a freak, but go home, I felt I must. The General sent me word to have my trunks ready and for Jesse and me to have our luncheon, and if he could be in time, we would take the late afternoon train for Philadelphia.

It was in obedience to this that I was at late luncheon with Mrs. Rawlins and her little girl and my Jesse, when these men came in and sat opposite to us. They all four came in together. I thought I recognized in one of them, the messenger of the morning, and one, a dark, pale man, played with his soup spoon, sometimes filling it and holding it half lifted to his mouth, but never tasting it. This occurred many times. He also seemed very intent on what we and the children were saying. I thought he was crazy. As we sat at table, I said to Mrs. Rawlins in a low tone: "Be careful, but observe the men opposite to us and tell me what you think." After a moment or so, she answered: "Since you call my attention, I believe there is something peculiar about them." I said: "I believe they are a part of Mosby's guerrillas and they have been listening to every word we have said. Do you know, I believe there will be an outbreak tonight or soon. I just feel it, and am glad I am going away tonight."

Afterwards, as Gen. Grant and I rode to the Depot, this same dark, pale man rode past us at a sweeping gallop on a dark horse, black I think. He rode twenty yards ahead of us, wheeled and returned and as he passed us both going and returning, he thrust his face quite near the General's and glared in a disagreeable manner. Mrs. General Rucker, in whose carriage we were, remarked: "General, every one wants to see you." "Yes," the General replied, "but I do not care for such glances. These are not friendly at least." I noticed the General draw back, as the man returned and came so close.

We arrived without incident at Philadelphia. We went through the city and stopped at a large restaurant, situated near where we had to take the ferry-boat, to reach the cars for Burlington, N. J. The General ordered some oysters, as he had had nothing to eat since nine o'clock in the morning. Before they were ready for him, a telegram was handed him, and almost before he could open this, another was handed him and then a third.

The General looked very pale. "Is there anything the matter?" I inquired. "You look startled." "Yes," he answered, "something *very* serious has happened. Do not exclaim. Be quiet and I will tell you. The President has been assassinated at the Theatre, and I must go back at once. I will take you to Burlington (an hour away), see the children, order a special train and return as soon as it is ready."

On the way to Burlington, the General was silent and in deep thought. When I questioned him as to who could have done it, and the object, etc., he replied: "Oh, I don't know. But this fills me *with the gloomiest apprehension. The President was inclined to be kind and magnanimous, and his death at this time, is an irreparable loss to the South, which now needs so much both his tenderness and magnanimity.*" I asked: "This will make Andy Johnson President, will it not?" "Yes," the General said, "and for some reason, I dread the change."

We none of us, retired for the night. Crowds of people came thronging into our cottage to learn if the terrible news were true. The General left for Washington while it was yet starlight. The first mail that sad morning, brought a letter to Gen. Grant. He having directed me to open all telegrams and letters, I read the following letter:

"General Grant, thank God, as I do, that you still live. It was your life that fell to my lot and I followed you on the cars. Your car door was locked and thus you escaped me, thank God!"

Years afterwards, after having met the rulers of almost every civilized country, General Grant said that Lincoln had impressed him as the greatest intellectual force with which he had ever come in contact. John Russell Young recalled how the general was grateful that so much of the President's last days had been spent with him, and spoke of him as "the greatest man I have ever known and the day of his death the darkest of my life." Years afterward he regretted that he had not been able to go to the theater with the President that fatal evening of April 14, 1865. He doubted that Booth could have entered the box undiscovered by him, and events "might have reached other conclusions."

The Vice President, Andrew Johnson, succeeded Mr. Lincoln without any difficulty, although Atzerodt, one of the conspirators, had been assigned the job of murdering him but lacked the courage to carry out his part. Johnson opened his Administration with two statements: "Treason must be made odious" and "Traitors must be punished and impoverished." This formula was repeated frequently. In a speech in Nashville on June 9, 1864, he defined what he meant by "impoverished," saying in the same connection that "great plantations must be seized and divided into small farms and sold to honest industrious men." Such statements were necessarily received with great applause and gratification by the radicals in Congress. Based on the suspicions and inadequate evidence in the Bureau of Military Justice under the Judge Advocate

General, Joseph Holt, the charge was also made that Jefferson Davis had been implicated in a conspiracy for the assassination of President Lincoln and had been influential in bringing about the suffering of Northern prisoners of war at Andersonville.

Of Andrew Johnson, the historian Rhodes wrote:

> A man of strict integrity, a fluent and ready speaker, he was at the same time extremely egotistical, the self-confidence of the self-made man obtruding itself in most of his utterances. He possessed physical courage; indeed no man could have taken part in the political life of Tennessee in his time unless he were ready to resent insult and defend himself against personal attack. As military governor his courage was put to the supreme test and apparently it never failed. But at some time during his occupancy of this office he began to drink to excess.

Of the last accusation, Colonel William H. Crook, bodyguard to President Lincoln and through four succeeding administrations on duty at the White House in various capacities, claims the President was not guilty:

> He had certainly acted in a manner to offend the men who were about him and to lower the Vice President before his subordinates. Since then the matter has been explained. We all know now that he was then recovering from a severe attack of typhoid fever. He was not in a condition to go through even the simple ceremonial which marked Mr. Lincoln's second inauguration. In order that he might be able to perform his part in the exercises of the day, he had taken a stimulant. The effect of alcohol on typhoid convalescents is well known, the smallest amount being intoxicating.

Evidently, he was selected for the nomination for strictly political reasons, the desirability of having a Democrat with strong Union principles on the ticket with Mr. Lincoln. I have been told, but have no evidence of the fact, that Mr. Lincoln never spoke to his Vice President after the inauguration.

In his description of Mr. Johnson, Rhodes, who seems to be a fair enough commentator on him, continues:

> Called to the high office by a calamity so appalling a modest man would have maintained a dignified reserve, taken counsel of others and considered soberly his position. But Johnson had an itch for speechmaking; and different delegations which came to Washington and called on him were eager to hear from the new President and incited him to utterance. Seeming to have a

certain jealousy of the memory of Lincoln he made a number of egotistical and commonplace harangues which had undoubtedly a certain vogue in the country at large but which were regretted by leading Republican senators and representatives as being unworthy of the place and the time. The manner in which he spoke persistently of the crime of the Southern leaders, the due punishment of which was death, tended to inflame Northern sentiment, already bitter enough in the lamenting of Lincoln's assassination.

It was evident that Mr. Johnson, who had little education (his wife taught him to read and write) but a certain gift of oratory, was strongly prejudiced against the well-to-do leaders in the South. He did not include Jefferson Davis in his first amnesty proclamation on May 29, 1865, and when General Longstreet in late November presented a letter to the President from General Grant recommending Longstreet's pardon, the latter described the interview:

> The President was nervous, ill at ease, and somewhat resentful . . . and at length closed the interview by saying, "There are three men this Union will never forgive—they have given it too much trouble. They are Jefferson Davis, Robert E. Lee, and James Longstreet." General Longstreet said, "Those who are forgiven much, love much, Mr. President." Johnson answered, "You have a high authority for that statement, General, but you cannot have amnesty."

However, the President about-faced in his message to Congress of December 5, 1865, which was written by George Bancroft and was "in striking contrast with the tiresome redundancy and offensive egotism of his speeches. It met in a conciliatory way the hostile or critical part of Congress; and to Republican members disposed to work with the President it was a cheering indication that they were separated by no chasm." However, approval of his policy by Congress was not possible. A joint Committee on Reconstruction had been set up in Congress and it would be outside the purpose of this biographical sketch of General Grant to attempt to describe in detail except when pertinent to our subject the quarrel of the President with Congress, which lasted about three years and ended with his impeachment.

Senator Chauncey M. Depew in his *My Memories of Eighty Years,* relates that General Grant, from his own experience with President Johnson, explained the latter's shift in attitude toward the southern states as follows:

Johnson, he said, had always been treated with such contempt and ignored socially by the members of the old families and slave aristocracy of the South that his resentment against them was vindictive, and so after the surrender at Appomattox he was constantly proclaiming "Treason is odious and must be punished." He also wanted and, in fact, insisted upon ignoring Grant's parole to the Confederate officers, in order that they might be tried for treason. On this question of maintaining his parole and his military honor General Grant was inflexible, and said he would appeal not only to Congress but to the country.

One day a delegation, consisting of the most eminent, politically, socially, and in family descent, of the Southern leaders, went to the White House. They said: "Mr. President, we have never recognized you, as you belong to an entirely different class from ourselves, but it is the rule of all countries and in all ages that supreme power vested in the individual raises him, no matter what his origin, to supreme leadership. You are now President of the United States, and by virtue of your office our leader, and we recognize you as such." Then followed attention from these people whom he admired and envied, as well as hated, of hospitality and deference, of which they were past masters. It captivated him and changed his whole attitude towards them.

He sent for General Grant and said to him: "The war is over and there should be forgiveness and reconciliation. I propose to call upon all of the States recently in rebellion to send to Washington their United States senators and members of the House, the same as they did before the war. If the present Congress will not admit them, a Congress can be formed of these Southern senators and members of the House and of such Northern senators and representatives as will believe that I am right and acting under the Constitution. As President of the United States, I will recognize that Congress and communicate with them as such. As general of the army I want your support." General Grant replied: "That will create civil war, because the North will undoubtedly recognize the Congress as it now exists, and that Congress will assert itself in every way possible." "In that case," said the president, "I want the army to support the constitutional Congress which I am recognizing." General Grant said: "On the contrary, so far as my authority goes, the army will support the Congress as it is now and disperse the other."

It was thus in an atmosphere replete with intrigue and passion—with an ignorant, stubborn, and loquacious President, a jealous and divided Cabinet, and a Congress still trying to work out its dominant policy—that "the honest-minded, trustful, straight-thinking Grant, after forty years of obscurity and four years of life in camp, received his first lesson in politics." In the President's proclamation of amnesty, he had omitted fourteen specific classes. Among these classes were 1) all men who held civil or military offices of any distinction in the Confederacy and 2) all those whose taxable property was valued at more than $20,000. Thus he eliminated from the possible leadership in the South those men who had intellectual attributes, possessed land, and otherwise had been popularly recognized as leaders.

The Reconstruction Act of March 2, 1867, stated that "no legal state governments or adequate protection for life or property" existed "in the Rebel states of Virginia, North Carolina, South Carolina, Georgia, Mississippi, Alabama, Louisiana, Florida, Texas and Arkansas"; therefore to enforce "peace and good order" those states were divided into five military districts and the President was to assign to the command of each an officer of the army, "not below the rank of brigadier general," who should be furnished "a sufficient military force . . . to enforce his authority." This general was to protect life and property, suppress disorder and violence, and punish all disturbers of the public peace; he could at his discretion "allow local civil tribunals" to try offenders or he could organize military commissions for that purpose. State officers were not to be allowed to interfere with the exercise of his military authority. Section four comprised some mitigating limitations on martial rule. Section five, except the last clause, provided for the elections in these ten states of conventions to frame new constitutions. All male citizens "of whatever race, color or previous condition" should have a right to vote for delegates "except such as may be disfranchised by participating in the Rebellion." The new state constitutions must provide for universal Negro suffrage, and must be ratified by a popular vote and approved by Congress. After the new constitution had been adopted and the legislature established, and after the latter had adopted the Fourteenth Amendment and this amendment had become a part of the constitution, then the senators and representatives of the state should be admitted to Congress if they had taken the oath that they had not been disfranchised, after which military rule in the state should cease.

President Johnson's troubles with Congress continued. He made strong efforts to pull General Grant into his quarrel with the lawmakers and on various occasions embarrassed the general by asking him to appear publicly with him. For instance, when he took his so-called "swing around the circle" he insisted that General Grant and Admiral Farragut accompany him and was undoubtedly angered by the fact that they got much more attention and many more cheers than he did. A meeting in Indianapolis was very turbulent, amounting almost to a riot, and General Grant rebuked the mob, telling them that he was ashamed of them and to go home and be ashamed of themselves. Hamlin Garland writes of this tour in his biography of Grant:

> In Cincinnati the demonstrations for him became so marked, and the defection from the President so great, that the general was obliged to utter himself upon the subject. He here said that he stood next to the President as the head of the army of the United States, but that he was not the leader of a political party; that he did not consider the army a place for a politician, and would not, therefore, be committed to the support of the present political party, or consent that the army should be made a party machine. He would not allow anything to be said which would seem to foreshadow his resignation from the army and his candidacy for political office. . . .

On another occasion the President rather insistently invited the general to attend a reception at the White House which he was giving for a group of his partisans. General Grant felt he could not refuse the President's invitation, but this sort of trickery, obnoxious to General Grant, lowered the President in his estimation; and doubtless it helped build up the enmity the President was feeling for him. As time went on the President devised a way of getting rid of Grant by sending him to Mexico as a representative adviser to the minister. Knowing General Grant's interest in Mexico and the Mexican people, and aware of the general's strong desire to see the French army recalled to France and Maximilian's government ousted, the President apparently expected the general to accept this appointment. However, he refused it. The President called him to a Cabinet meeting and there asked the attorney general whether General Grant should obey his order to go to Mexico; but the general told Johnson that he could answer the question without its being referred to the attorney general: that as an officer of the U.S. Army he had to obey and would obey any proper order of the President, but this was not a military matter. On the contrary it was a civilian position the President was trying to force upon him, and as an American citizen there was nothing to oblige him to accept such a position.

The President had ordered General Sherman to come to Washington to act in place of General Grant during the latter's expected absence in Mexico. When Sherman arrived, he was assured by the general that he would not accept the appointment to Mexico. Grant explained it was just a trick of the President to get him out of the way on the supposition that Sherman would be more ready to co-operate in putting over the President's policies. General Sherman informed the President that his old commander would certainly not accept the appointment and that he, Sherman, would not take the place of General Grant under the circumstances. To save face Johnson asked Sherman if he would go to Mexico, and on being told that Sherman would, Johnson accordingly sent him on the perfectly pointless errand.

The following statement of General Sherman about General Grant at this time seems very pertinent:

> I have been with General Grant in the midst of death and slaughter; when the howls of people reached him after Shiloh; when messengers were speeding to and fro from his army to Washington, bearing slanders to induce his removal before Vicksburg; in Chattanooga, when the soldiers were stealing the corn of the starving mules to satisfy their own hunger; at Nashville, when he was ordered to the "forlorn hope," to command the Army of the Potomac, so often defeated; and yet I never saw him more troubled than since he has been in Washington and been compelled to read himself a "sneak and deceiver."

As to the feeling in the South, the following extract from the Atlanta *Intelligencer* is evidence of the appreciation of General Grant's action in saving General Lee and other former Confederate officers from being indicted by the civil courts:

> While it is true that to General Grant the South owes her defeat in her attempt to establish an independent government, it is also true that at the surrender of General Lee, and ever since, up to the present time, his conduct toward the South has been most generous and in individual cases most magnanimous and just. The South owes much to General Grant, and its press has been too chary and tardy in its acknowledgment of the favors bestowed by this general upon the leaders of our armies. We should now make the amends. History does not make record of greater magnanimity than that displayed by General Grant to General Lee and the forces under his command. The faith plighted by him on the day of Lee's surrender has been kept inviolate.

General Grant turned his attention to the situation in Mexico. Nothing had come of efforts to get the President and Secretary of State Seward to take definite, positive action to require Napoleon III to evacuate Mexico and rid the country of Emperor Maximilian. The General felt compelled for patriotic reasons to take what action he could in a military way to stop this violation of the Monroe Doctrine and to help the Mexicans regain independence. Juárez, who had continued as President, was struggling to ease Maximilian out of the country. Realizing that what the Mexican patriots needed most was arms and ammunition, and knowing that there was a great quantity of arms and some ammunition in Texas (surrendered by Confederate forces), Grant suggested to General Sheridan that he store much of the supplies along the Rio Grande where the Mexican patriots could find them.

General Sheridan was assigned to command in Texas and Louisiana and immediately began to try to accomplish what he was sent there for, to wit:

Headquarters Armies of the United States.
Washington, D. C., May 17, 1865

General: Under the orders relieving you from the command of the Middle Military Division and assigning you to command west of the Mississippi, you will proceed without delay to the West to arrange all preliminaries for your new field of duties.

Your duty is to restore Texas, and that part of Louisiana held by the enemy, to the Union in the shortest practicable time, in a way most effectual for securing permanent peace.

To do this, you will be given all the troops that can be spared by Major-General Canby, probably twenty-five thousand men of all arms; the troops with Major-General J.J. Reynolds, in Arkansas, say twelve thousand, Reynolds to command; the Fourth Army Corps, now at Nashville, Tennessee, awaiting orders; and the Twenty-Fifth Army Corps, now at City Point, Virginia, ready to embark.

I do not wish to trammel you with instructions; I will state, however, that if Smith holds out, without even an ostensible government to receive orders from or to report to, he and his men are not entitled to the consideration due to an acknowledged belligerent. Theirs are the conditions of outlaws, making war against the only Government having an existence over the territory where war is now being waged.

You may notify the rebel commander west of the Mississippi—holding intercourse with him in person, or through such officers of the rank of major-general as you may select—that he will be allowed to surrender all his forces on the same terms as were accorded to Lee and Johnston. If he accedes, proceed to garrison the Red River as high up as Shreveport, the seaboard at Galveston, Malagorda Bay, Corpus Christi, and mouth of the Rio Grande.

Place a strong force on the Rio Grande, holding it at least to a point opposite Camargo, and above that if supplies can be procured.

In case of an active campaign (a hostile one) I think a heavy force should be put on the Rio Grande as a first preliminary. Troops for this might be started at once. The Twenty-Fifth Corps is now available, and to it should be added a force of white troops, say those now under Major-General Steele.

To be clear on this last point, I think the Rio Grande should be strongly held, whether the forces in Texas surrender or not, and that no time should be lost in getting troops there. If war is to be made, they will be in the right place; if Kirby Smith surrenders, they will be on the line which is to be strongly garrisoned.

Should any force be necessary other than those designated, they can be had by calling for them on Army Headquarters.

U. S. Grant,
Lieutenant-General

To Major-General P. H. Sheridan,
United States Army.

The situation with Mexico is well and briefly described by General Schofield in his *Forty-Six Years in the Army:*

If the American conflict had resulted in the triumph of secession, so also might Napoleon have succeeded in re-establishing monarchical government on the American continent. But from the moment when the Union of the States became reassured, European interference in the political affairs of the American republic became impossible. Upon this subject there appeared to be no division of sentiment among the people of the United States. Certainly there was none among the responsible American statesmen of that time. It was their unanimous voice that the French intervention in Mexico must be speedily terminated; but there was naturally some division of opinion respecting the means by which this should be effected. Some favored the most prompt and vigorous military action, while others, not unmindful of the long-existing friendship between the people of the United States and France, preferred more peaceful measures.

Upon reaching the mouth of the Red River, General Sheridan received word that Kirby Smith had surrendered under the terms accorded to Lee and Johnston; but the surrender was not carried out fully and some of the Texas troops marched off with their camp equipage, arms, ammunition, and even some artillery with the intention of going to Mexico. While they escaped in this way, General Sheridan thought it necessary to march two columns of cavalry through the state. About the time the two columns were ready to start, General Frank Herron occupied Galveston with one division of the XIII Corps, and General Steele had reached Brazos Santiago to hold Brownsville and the line of the Rio Grande in order to prevent the Confederates from escaping and joining Maximilian.

Convinced that the French invasion of Mexico was tied in with the rebellion, General Grant felt that the best way to prevent an outbreak of hostilities with the United States would be to establish a sizable body of troops (who would volunteer for this service) somewhere in Mexico in support of Juárez. As the troops in the army under Sheridan had volunteered or were conscripted for duty to re-establish the Union and fight the Confederacy, it would be improper to use them in intervening in Mexico in favor of the Liberal Party.

To investigate the matter and possibly organize such a force, General John M. Schofield was called to Washington in June 1865 for consultation on the subject. In the capital he had meetings with General Grant, Señor Romero (the Mexican minister), President Johnson, Secretary of State Seward, and Secretary of War Stanton. These high officials all concurred in having General Schofield assume control and direction of measures to be adopted for the purpose of compelling the French evacuation of Mexico. Accordingly, the War Department gave him a leave of absence for a year with permission to go beyond the limits of the United States and to take with him any staff officers necessary to perform this service. It was proposd to organize in Mexican territory an army corps under officers, commissioned by the Mexican Government, who would volunteer for this service from Union or Confederate forces. The Mexican authorities agreed to furnish the pay and expenses of military operations, for which purpose a loan by the United States was to be negotiated.

It was the view of Mr. Seward that Napoleon III would withdraw his army from Mexico as soon as he understood that the United States would never consent to the existence in Mexico of a government established and maintained by a foreign power. He therefore suggested that General Schofield be sent on a special mission to France, for the purpose of persuading the Emperor that such was the U.S. stand. As negotiations for the Mexican loan were making very slow progress and funds were not yet available for the purpose of General Schofield's "inspection tour," the general notified Mr. Seward on August 4, 1865, that he had decided to undertake the mission.

Accordingly, General Schofield went to Paris, arriving there December 2. General Schofield was able to accomplish his mission successfully without actually presenting any sort of ultimatum to the Emperor, revealing his mission to various high officials in the French Government who undoubtedly transmitted it to the Emperor.

The following intercepted cablegram from Napoleon III to General Castelnau in Mexico, dated December 13, 1866, shows that the Emperor had finally been driven to the conclusion that he had better pull out of the Mexican expedition:

> Received your dispatch of the third from Mexico. The evacuation will terminate in March. Unite or consolidate the Foreign Legion. Return all the French soldiers and Belgians, and some of the Austrians if they demand it. The transportation will leave here the last of December.

On August 5, 1867, President Johnson decided to remove Secretary Stanton from his position as secretary of war. Congress had adjourned by this time. Accordingly, he wrote to Mr. Stanton:

> Sir: Public considerations of the highest character constrain me to say that your resignation as Secretary of War will be accepted.

To this note Secretary Stanton replied:

> Public considerations of the highest character constrain me not to resign the office of Secretary of War before the next meeting of Congress.

The Reconstruction Acts, heretofore mentioned, had been passed and the President now proposed to test the validity of the Tenure of Office Act while ridding himself of Mr. Stanton's opposition in the Cabinet and again seeking to tie General Grant to his own chariot. So when Mr. Stanton refused to resign, the President suspended him and called on General Grant to act as secretary of war *ad interim*. The latter did not see how he could properly refuse the appointment pending action by the Senate.

In notifying Secretary Stanton of his assignment, General Grant concluded his note with the following:

> In notifying you of my acceptance, I cannot let the opportunity pass without expressing to you my appreciation of the zeal, patriotism, firmness, and ability with which you have ever discharged the duties of Secretary of War.

Mr. Stanton wrote to the President denying the legality of his suspension and concluding with the statement, "but inasmuch as the General commanding the armies of the United States has been appointed *ad interim,* and has notified me that he has accepted the appointment, I have no alternative but to submit, under protest, to superior force."

At nearly the same time the President ordered General Grant to remove Generals Sheridan and Sickles from their commands in the former Confederate states to which they were assigned. In notifying General Grant of this decision, the President indicated that he would be glad to have a comment on the matter. General Grant replied:

> I am pleased to avail myself of your invitation to urge—earnestly urge, urge in the name of patriotic people—that this order should not be insisted upon. It is the will of the country that General Sheridan should not be removed from his present command. This is a republic where the will of the people is the law of the land. I beg that their voice may be heard.

To this the president replied:

> I am not aware that the question of retaining General Sheridan in command of the Fifth Military District has ever been submitted to the people themselves for determination. . . . General Sheridan has rendered himself exceedingly obnoxious by the manner in which he has exercised the powers conferred by Congress and still more so by the resort to authority not granted by law. . . . His removal, therefore, cannot be regarded as an effort to defeat the laws of Congress.

On December 12, 1867, the President sent a message to Congress about Stanton's suspension, supporting his action with various documents and interesting revelations of Stanton's own opposition to the Tenure of Office bill when it was being considered. The Senate did not approve of Mr. Stanton's removal from office, and when he learned this fact General Grant vacated the office of secretary of war, turned in the keys to the adjutant general, and notified the President that he had done so. Stanton lost no time in returning to his old office, and with his usual churlishness sent a peremptory call to the Commanding General of the Armies of the United States to come to see him. General Grant had no reason whatever for wanting to keep Stanton in his high office; however, he was trying, in the difficult position of being between Congress and the President in their fight, to act strictly in accordance with the tenure law which had been passed by Congress over the President's veto.

President Johnson was furious and began a campaign of abuse against General Grant for allegedly failing to retain the position of secretary of war in order to force a decision by the Supreme Court on the constitutionality of the Tenure of Office Act. He did the one thing that General Grant could never overlook; namely, he accused him of breaking a promise and of making a false statement. General Grant denied the charge. The President summoned him to a Cabinet meeting on January 28, 1868, and made his accusations. Of this meeting General Grant wrote to Johnson on January 28, 1868:

At this meeting, after opening it as though I were a member of the Cabinet, when reminded of the notification already given him that I was no longer Secretary of War *ad interim,* the President gave a version of the conversations alluded to already. In this statement it was asserted that in both conversations I had agreed to hold on to the office of Secretary of War until displaced by the courts, or resign, so as to place the President where he would have been had I never accepted the office. After hearing the President through, I stated our conversations substantially as given in this letter . . . I in no wise admitted the correctness of the President's statement, though, to soften the evident contradiction my statement gave, I said (alluding to our first conversation on the subject) the President might have understood me the way he said, namely, that I had promised to resign if I did not resist the reinstatement. I made no such promise.

It is hardly necessary to reproduce here the entire correspondence, which included a verbal demand by the President that General Grant should not obey any orders given to him by the secretary of war, upon which the general asked for written instructions by the President to this effect. The general finally tried to conclude and summarize the situation in writing as follows (February 3, 1868):

I find it but a reiteration, only somewhat more in detail, of the "many and gross misrepresentations" . . . which my statement of the facts set forth in my letter of the 28th ultimo was intended to correct; and I here reassert the correctness of my statements in that letter; anything in yours in reply to it to the contrary notwithstanding. I confess my surprise that the Cabinet officers referred to should so greatly misapprehend the facts in the matter of admissions alleged to have been made by me. . . .

From our conversations, and my written protest of August 1, 1867, against the removal of Mr. Stanton, you must have known that my greatest objection to his removal or suspension was the fear that some one would be appointed in his stead, who would, by opposition to the laws relating to the restoration of the Southern States to their proper relations to the Government, embarrass the Army in the performance of duties especially imposed upon it by these laws; and it was to prevent such an appointment that I accepted the office of Secretary of War *ad interim,* and not for the purpose of enabling you to get rid of Mr. Stanton by my withholding it from him in opposition to law, or, not doing so myself, surrendering it to one who would, as the statement and assumptions in your communication plainly indicate was sought. . . . The course you would have it understood I had agreed to pursue was in violation of law, and without orders from you; while the course I did pursue and which I never doubted you fully understood, was in accordance with law, and not in disobedience to any orders of my superior.

And now, Mr. President, when my honor as a soldier and integrity as a man have been so violently assailed, pardon me for saying that I can but regard this whole matter, from the beginning to the end, as an attempt to involve me in the resistance of law, for which you hesitated to assume the responsibility in orders, and thus to destroy my character before the country. I am in a measure confirmed in this conclusion by your recent orders directing me to disobey orders from the Secretary of War,—my superior and your subordinate,—without having countermanded his authority to issue the orders I am to disobey.

He concluded with the assurance "that nothing less than a vindication of my personal honor and character" could have induced this correspondence on his part. He would have no further personal relations with the President who had so often tried to trick him into a false position and now had questioned his veracity.

The President continued in his determination to get rid of Stanton and would not recognize him as secretary of war. He tried to get Sherman to take Stanton's place, and Sherman refused. Johnson was bent on testing the constitutionality of the Tenure of Office Act in the courts. On February 21, he ordered Lorenzo Thomas, the adjutant general, to take possession and fill the office of secretary of war, giving him a letter (which Thomas handed to Stanton) removing Stanton from his position. Stanton kept Thomas out of the office. Then Thaddeus Stevens, representative from Pennsylvania, presented his report for the Republican members of the Reconstruction Committee, impeaching Andrew Johnson for high crimes and misdemeanors. Two days later the House adopted the resolution by a vote of 126 to 47. By only one vote did the President escape conviction by the Senate.

The final vote on the impeachment of the President was taken on May 26, 1868; but the Republican Convention had met in Chicago on May 20 and nominated General Grant for the presidency by acclamation on the first ballot. Schuyler Colfax, the speaker of the House, was nominated as Vice President.

Seven years after the impeachment proceedings, Andrew Johnson was again elected to the Senate and had to serve there with many persons who were or had been his enemies. It is interesting that he told Colonel Crook: "I have come back to the Senate with two purposes. One is to do what I can to punish the Southern brigadiers. They led the South into secession, and they have never had their deserts. The other is to make a speech against Grant. And I am going to make it this session." He made this speech within two weeks; presumably it was a relief to him to get the malice and anger out of his system.

XIII

President Grant

THE nomination as Republican candidate for President came to General Grant as a call of duty to render a service that was very unwelcome. However, the confusion in the minds of the American people resulting from President Johnson's quarrel with the Congress, and the procedure to impeach him, had created a situation which called for a popular leader and one of character to carry on the reconstruction of the country, so recently divided, and create conditions conducive to peace not only without arms but without violent emotional discord. It had become evident to General Grant that he was the most popular and most trusted citizen and consequently must assume the burden.

President Johnson's accusations had finally forced Grant to side with Congress, although he was anything but sympathetic with the policies of the extreme radicals. For a time these radicals doubted that he would be acceptable and they had one or two of their leaders investigate the matter and report. Senator Ben Wade at first reported that when he tried to talk politics to the general, he talked horses to him and Wade didn't know much about horses.

In this connection General Badeau, who was in his confidence at this time, said of the commanding general:

> When he was first approached on the subject [of politics] he resented the liberty and repelled all discussion of the theme. I have often seen men who hoped to draw him out receive very mortifying and unexpected rebuffs. They would make, perhaps, an elaborate little speech, devise a snare into which they thought he must certainly fall, invent a bait that must tempt him to talk; but Grant would simply look at them with no expression whatever on his

face, and say not a single word. If he had uttered anything at all they might have continued or renewed their wiles, but this absolute silence was the most embarrassing answer possible. It not only entirely baffled them, but was merciless in its way. They stammered and blushed, no matter how bold or adroit; then they attempted to change the subject, and invariably, before many minutes, took their leave. Sometimes, as the door closed, Grant would look up at me with a quizzical expression that showed he enjoyed their confusion. For a man unused to the stratagems of peace he was the most skillful and the most successful in these repulses I have ever seen. His interlocutors never returned to the charge.

To indicate how far things had gone between the President and Congress, Burr writes that President Johnson came to the general's office, presumably some time before the impeachment trial started. After talking for nearly an hour about commonplace subjects, he turned to General Grant before leaving and said: "General, I am very anxious to know, in case there should be an open rupture between myself and Congress, with which side you will be found." To this the general replied, "That will depend upon which is the revolutionary party."

To the general the laws passed by Congress over the President's veto in accordance with the provisions of the Constitution had become the laws he had sworn to maintain and enforce, no matter how the President personally felt about it. Lacking a Supreme Court decision to the contrary, he had no choice or doubt in his own mind. To complete the picture, as he saw it, reports had been made to him of the organization of an armed force in Maryland, and similarly, of the organization of 3,000 veteran soldiers in Washington under the command of a major general with many officers who had been conspicuous during the Civil War. However, no one had any information as to what General Grant would do in an emergency.

Badeau claims he was with the general when the secretary of war entered the room with the information of the convention vote. He exclaimed as he entered: "General! I have come to tell you that you have been nominated by the Republican Party for President of United States." General Grant received the intelligence seriously but without exaltation or emotion showing in his face. When public announcement had been made he responded extemporaneously: "Gentlemen, being entirely unaccustomed to public speaking, and without the desire to cultivate the power, it is impossible for me to find appropriate language to thank you for this demonstration. All that I can say is, that to whatever position I may be called by your will, I shall endeavor to discharge its duties with fidelity and honesty of purpose. Of my rectitude in the performance of public duties you will have to judge for yourselves by the record before you."

When formally notified of his nomination, General Grant accepted in the following letter:

> If elected to the office of President of the United States, it will be my endeavor to administer all the laws in good faith, with economy, and with the view of giving peace, quiet, and protection everywhere. In times like the present it is impossible, or at least eminently improper, to lay down a policy to be adhered to, right or wrong. Through an administration of four years, new political issues, not foreseen, are constantly arising, the views of the public on old ones are constantly changing, and a purely administrative officer should always be left free to execute the will of the people. I always have respected that will, and always shall. Peace and universal prosperity, its sequence, with economy of administration, will lighten the burden of taxation, while it constantly reduces the national debt. Let us have peace.

The statement was generally received with approval throughout the country, especially the final sentence, "Let us have peace"; because after the four years of civil war and, more recently, three years of war between the President and the Congress, the country was ready to welcome peace. Criticism of this letter principally focused on the fact that Grant had not committed himself on any one of the political questions then before the country, beyond taking a stand for the laws made in accordance with the Constitution. Very definitely, General Grant refused to commit himself on any of these questions or to make any promises in advance. Probably for the first time in U.S. history the president-elect made no campaign for his own election, not even from a back porch. In fact, he left General Rawlins in Washington to open his mail and reply to all military professional questions, and with Rawlins was Badeau, to reply to political questions.

Grant himself retired to his cottage in Galena and refused to take any part in the campaign. On election night he strolled down to the house of his old friend Representative Washburne, who had had a telegraph instrument installed there to receive the returns. When it was manifest that he had been elected, the general went home and, on entering, rather sadly took off his overcoat and said to his wife: "I'm afraid I am elected." He received the vote of 26 states having 214 electoral votes; the popular majority for him and Colfax was 308,584. Virginia, Mississippi, and Texas did not vote. Following his return to Washington, Grant was pursued, of course, by applicants for office. Feeling that a candidate's fitness was usually in inverse ratio to his eagerness for office, Grant turned these applications over to one of his aides. According to Church, they were never answered.

The city was more crowded than usual by those who had come to seek jobs and those who had come to participate in the inauguration. The day of the inauguration—March 4, 1869—was cold and overcast, but the streets were filled with the crowd and as the sun came out brilliantly before noon, the superstitious took this as an augury favorable to the coming administration. The new President had refused to drive to the Capitol in the same carriage with the outgoing President; he felt that Johnson had officially insulted him in a manner that could not be forgiven. Grant therefore drove to the Capitol with General Rawlins in a carriage of his own, a park phaeton. At the Capitol, after the usual ceremonies connected with swearing-in the new senators, he followed the Supreme Court out to a platform constructed on the east front. There Chief Justice Salmon P. Chase, who had been a candidate very eager for the presidency, administered the oath prescribed for the President of the United States. (Evidently Chief Justice Chase did not harbor any grudge against the successful candidate, as he very graciously sent to Mrs. Grant the Bible with which the oath had been administered.)

Many of the public present were disappointed to see the general in a plain dark, civilian suit. There was no dramatic ceremony to symbolize the laying down of his sword to take up the duties of the State—only the simple oath. After it, the President stepped forward to the lectern and read his inaugural address, the essential parts of which follow:

Your suffrages having elected me to the office of President of the United States, I have, in conformity with the Constitution of our country, taken the oath of office prescribed therein. I have taken this oath without mental reservation, and with a determination to do, to the best of my ability, all that it requires of me.

The responsibilities of the position I feel, but accept them without fear. The office has come to me unsought; I commence its duties untrammelled. I bring to it a conscious desire and determination to fill it, to the best of my ability, to the satisfaction of the people. On all leading questions agitating the public mind I will always express my views to Congress, and urge them according to my judgment, and when I think it advisable, will exercise the constitutional privilege of interposing a veto to defeat measures which I oppose. But all laws will be faithfully executed, whether they meet my approval or not.

I shall on all subjects have a policy to recommend, none to enforce against the will of the people. Laws are to govern all alike—those opposed to as well as those in favor of them. I know no method to secure the repeal of bad or obnoxious laws so effectual as their strict execution. . . .

A great debt has been contracted in securing to us and our posterity the Union. The payment of this, principal and interest, as well as the return to a specie basis as soon as it can be accomplished without material detriment to the debtor class or to the country at large, must be provided for. To protect the national honor, every dollar of the government indebtedness should be paid in gold, unless otherwise especially stipulated in the contract. Let it be understood that no repudiation of one farthing of our public debt will be trusted in public places, and it will go far towards strengthening a credit which ought to be the best in the world, and will ultimately enable us to replace the debt with bonds bearing less interest than we now pay.

The address was generally well received. Garland says that it "excited the most intense excitement. It was at once seized upon and twisted hard to wring some sinister meaning from it. Mainly it was approved. It was considered to be like him—firm, but gentle, sincere, and perfectly lucid. Only one paper in the North considered it 'empty and self-confident, and at the same time servile.' To others it read 'like the bulletin of a great general.' " The southern editors were favorably impressed by his failure to use the expressions of the radical party.

The Inaugural Ball was held in the newly finished wing of the Treasury Department Building. The Inaugural Committee had failed woefully to estimate the number who would attend and the space needed for them and for their wraps—indeed no such crowd had ever attempted to attend a ball, or to visit the Capital as for this inauguration. Mrs. E. F. Ellet described it thus:

The surging masses of humanity swelled and swayed, to the utter destruction of all comfort. A larger number was brought together than since the close of the war, and crowd jostled crowd; vast numbers unable to proceed finding their energies taxed to effect egress. The President, Vice-President and their ladies had a small reception room in another part of the building, and were supported by Generals Sherman, Terry, Kilpatrick, Pleasanton, Webb and Thomas, with General Grant's staff, and Admirals Farragut and Goldsborough—all in full uniform. Mrs. Grant was dressed in pearl-colored satin with long train, point lace fichu and pearl ornaments; a wreath of leaves and flowers on her hair; Mrs. Colfax in pink satin with an over-dress of white tulle caught up with pink flowers; etc. . . . The foreign ministers, as usual came in full court costume.

It was a cold night and overcoats and ladies' wraps got mixed. Many could not be found and their owners had to make their ways home without them.

No hint of who would be recommended for the Cabinet in the new Administration had slipped out, and when the recommendations were sent to the Senate the next day they were received with much surprise. Grant did not want any politicians in the Cabinet who had possibly committed themselves to policies upon which he had not yet had reason to make a decision. In other words, he wanted a Cabinet which was "untrammeled," as he had taken such care to be himself. However, this was such an unusual basis of choice that it did cause much discussion, and because most of the persons recommended had not been prominent in politics, their competence was in many cases questioned. As Colonel William Conant Church wrote, Grant "was a soldier, and not a politician. He was a statesman in his large views of public and national interests, but he lacked the experience that had once led Lincoln to make the extreme statement that 'honest statesmanship is the employment of individual meanness for the public good.' "

For secretary of state he had recommended Elihu B. Washburne of Illinois, with the understanding that this was a temporary appointment; Mr. Washburne preferred to have a high diplomatic post. Upon his resignation on March 17, 1869, he was appointed U.S. minister to France, in which position he distinguished himself greatly, remaining in Paris (at the President's suggestion) through the siege by the German army after the French Government had fled; Washburne was able to represent many of the neutral nations and give protection to the American citizens resident there.

Mr. Hamilton Fish, a former member of both the House of Representatives and the Senate and a governor of New York, was persuaded to accept the portfolio of secretary of state. Again, this Cabinet officer rendered outstanding service, including the difficult but successful negotiations with Great Britain for the Treaty of Washington and the peaceful settlement of the Virginius case.

With the perfectly common-sense notion that a successful businessman or financier would make an intelligent and efficient secretary of the treasury, he recommended for that position Mr. A. T. Stewart, the great dry-goods merchant of New York whom Grant knew to be not only an intelligent and outstanding executive, but also a man of high honor and thorough reliability. Moreover, Mr. Stewart was willing to transfer, during his term of office, his business to trustees who should give all the profits to charity. This nomination was promptly and unanimously confirmed with the others proposed, but almost immediately somebody dug up the Act of September 2, 1789, establishing the Treasury Department, which prohibited anyone directly or indirectly interested in trade or commerce from being appointed secretary of the treasury. In a special message of March 6, 1869, to the Senate, the new President quoted this law and asked for a joint resolution to exempt Mr. Stewart. The bill was introduced but never passed. The country was deprived, then, of Mr. Stewart's services, at a time when its Civil War debt was a heavy burden and overseas trade had to be re-established. The President, to fill the vacancy, appointed George S. Boutwell of Massachusetts, with Senate approval. He had been governor of his state, first commissioner of internal revenue under Mr. Lincoln, and a member of the House of Representatives.

For secretary of war, General John M. Schofield was persuaded to stay on for a short time. He was to be succeeded by General John A. Rawlins of Illinois, who had been chief of staff at headquarters of the Commanding General of all the Armies of the United States. Unhappily, he had an incipient case of tuberculosis and was not to live many months.

For secretary of the navy, Adolph E. Borie of Pennsylvania was recommended and appointed. He was a loyal Union man and a successful manufacturer and merchant in Philadelphia. The President knew he would be a thoroughly reliable and competent administrator. However, as he apparently had not had any political experience and actually did not want the position, the appointment caused surprise and considerable opposition among the strictly politically minded in the country.

For attorney general Grant chose E. Rockwood Hoar of Massachusetts, recognized as a lawyer of much ability and high principles. In view of Boutwell's appointment to the treasury, this made two members of the

Cabinet from Massachusetts, a violation of custom followed heretofore. Mr. Hoar had been a judge of distinction in Massachusetts from 1849 to 1869, ending in that year as judge of the State Supreme Court.

John A. J. Creswell of Maryland was named postmaster general. He was confirmed without opposition and performed an outstanding job. For secretary of the interior Grant nominated Jacob D. Cox, a meritorious veteran of the Civil War and former governor of Ohio, well known to be informed on biography, history, and the sciences, and a scrupulously honest and truthful man.

Of the Cabinet, Rhodes says: "Grant's independent essay at cabinet making had not been a complete success; nevertheless a cabinet which contained Fish, Cox and Hoar could not be accounted otherwise than strong." Mrs. Ellet, who probably reflected the view of Washington society and officialdom, wrote toward the end of the Administration that "General Grant's cabinet seemed to be selected with reference to the competence of the members to discharge their duties and second the President in the course of reform and retrenchment, and the press generally expressed approbation." Colonel Crook, White House majordomo through five administrations, concurred that there were three members of great ability, and that the Cabinet compared favorably with later ones he had known.

But the Cabinet appointments were a surprise. They had been selected by the new President without consultation with the political "pros," whose feelings were ruffled and who voiced objections. Certainly the Cabinet as proposed—Washburne's appointment being but temporary and he destined for the mission to France—contained no politician who would be trammeled by previous promises (something the President attached much importance to). And it contained no officer of the Regular Army; Rawlins was a volunteer from civil life. Certainly Mr. Fish, who replaced Washburne, became one of our outstanding secretaries of state and must be rated, in U.S. history, a very great one.

The White House staff had to be organized to handle the great flood of office seekers. There had never been so many. The two million ex-soldiers, sailors, and officers—many of whom had gone home only to find their former jobs occupied by others—all seemed to expect the Administration to have employment for them. One of Grant's first innovations was the setting up of a reception room, with Colonel Dent (the President's brother-in-law and onetime roommate at West Point) in charge and Colonel Crook as his assistant. No one was to be admitted to the President until the receptionist had ascertained his mission and considered it required the personal attention of the President. Two other aides, Colonels Horace Porter and Orville Babcock, received and handled the requests of non-routine applicants for appointments.

Every president has always brought to the White House with him some office assistants whom he knew and who knew his ways of doing business. Presidents who were former governors of states were likely to have a fully trained office staff enter the White House with them. It was natural that General Grant's personal office should, at least at first, be made up of army officers who had been close to him during the Civil War. But although they wore civilian clothes and there was no military formality in the way these friendly and co-operative officers handled the President's visitors, some narrow-minded politicians seemed to find it disagreeable to have to pursue their missions through them. Mr. Robert Douglas, the son of Stephen Douglas, was officially the secretary to the President, and Mr. Levi P. Luckey was the assistant secretary. For the former the situation was somewhat embarrassing for a time, but Luckey had been in Washburne's office and was a friend of Colonel Babcock.

The Johnson White House staff had been fearful of summary dismissal, as the public expected the new President to "make a clean sweep." For a time they were frequently reminded of this possibility by the "new brooms" sent to the White House with humorous intent, but they did not fully appreciate the joke. However, Johnson retainers soon found that they were to be continued in the service and were in no way connected with Mr. Johnson's ineptitudes. Only two clerks who had made themselves somewhat conspicuous by their personal abuse of General Grant were dismissed. They were probably removed by one of the aides without the general's knowledge; it was his practice to leave such details to his staff.

In his inaugural address, the President had said: "To protect the National honor, every dollar of Government indebtedness should be paid in gold, unless otherwise expressly stipulated in the contract. Let it be understood that no repudiator of one farthing of our public debt will be trusted in public place, and it will go far toward strengthening a credit which ought to be the best in the world, and will ultimately enable us to replace the debt with bonds bearing less interest than we now pay." The first legislation of his Administration was the act approved by him on March 18, 1869, which promised the carrying out of this pledge. Indeed, economy of administration of the affairs of the government and liquidation of the national debt (incurred mostly by the Civil War) were the primary objectives of the Administration. Secretary of the Treasury Boutwell reported on December 6 that the debt on December 1 had been reduced to $2,453,000,000—a decrease of $71,903,000 since March 1, 1869.

On February 7, 1870, Chief Justice Chase somewhat surprised the nation with a Supreme Court decision that the acts authorizing the issue of "greenbacks" during the war had been unconstitutional, and was justified only by the necessity for some means to carry on the war. The chief dissenter from this decision was Associate Justice Samuel F. Miller.

During the war the number of justices on the Supreme Court had been reduced from nine to seven. The Act of April 10, 1869, which was to become effective the first Monday in December, restored the number of Supreme Court justices to nine. Two vacancies were created by the death of Associate Justice Wayne and the resignation of Associate Justice Grier, enabling the President to nominate Lincoln's secretary of war, Edwin M. Stanton, as chief justice and E. R. Hoar as associate justice. Stanton's appointment was promptly confirmed by the Senate, but he died four days afterward. Judge Hoar's appointment was rejected by the Senate on February 3, 1870. The President on February 7 then nominated William Strong of Pennsylvania and Joseph P. Bradley of New Jersey for the two vacancies. These changes in the Supreme Court are pertinent because the enemies of the Administration accused the President of packing the court for some sort of approval of the view that the greenbacks were not unconstitutional. As neither of the new judges had apparently expressed any definite opinion on the subject, the allegation was merely one of the quite unjustified accusations made by the enemies of the President.

On July 14, 1870, a bill recommended by Secretary of the Treasury Boutwell for the refunding of the national debt became a law. On March 1, 1873, the public debt had been reduced by $368,000,000 and the interest on it by $25,000,000. In 1873, Mr. Boutwell was elected senator from Massachusetts and on March 17 resigned his position as secretary of the treasury, having made a record for economical and efficient administration and an outstanding achievement in the reduction of the national debt. On January 14, 1875, toward the end of his second Administration, President Grant had the pleasure of approving the Sherman Act for the resumption of specie payment on January 1, 1879; the economic problems arising from the Civil War had been successfully solved and the nation's credit re-established. At the same time the income tax had been reduced to 2½ per cent and was to expire December 31, 1871.

The President was pleased to announce by proclamation on May 19, 1870, that the eight-hour law for government employees would be "in force without reduction of wages for all workmen and mechanics employed by the United States."

In July 1868, Jay Gould and James Fisk, Jr., had acquired control of the Erie Railroad and with one other associate had become quite irresponsible owners of it. They operated without calling the executive committee together or consulting the other stockholders or considering their interests. Gould and Fisk now entered into a conspiracy to corner the gold market. Under Boutwell's administration of the U.S. Treasury, and with the approval of the President, the government every month had been releasing for sale on the open market $2,000,000 to $8,000,000 of gold, purchasing bonds with the proceeds. It was obviously imperative for the conspirators to stop this government sale of gold.

To achieve this end they approached A. R. Corbin, who had married a sister of the President and through whom they met the President and made a concentrated and clever effort to gain his confidence. They must have proven on further acquaintance anything but congenial company; however, the President did permit himself to be inveigled, June 15, 1869, into accepting their hospitality on the Fall River steamer to attend the Peace Jubilee in Boston. At the dinner that night the conspirators argued for the government leaving gold to reach its level naturally and suggested that he might well favor an upward movement in the cost of gold. The President's reply proved a wet blanket to the conspirators and Gould for the time gave up the hope of converting the President. However, on the President's return to New York, Fisk persuaded him to attend a performance of one of Offenbach's operettas, to show him off with Mrs. Grant and their daughter in a box occupied also by Fisk, Gould, and Corbin.

It is evident that speculation was active on the Gold Board of New York, and that fluctuations in its cost would have quite an impact on the business of importers of foreign goods and exporters of American crops. The following recollections of Mrs. Grant's are pertinent:

Our eight years in the Executive Mansion were delightful, but there were some dark clouds in the bright sky. There was that dreadful black Friday.— The papers seemed to say I knew something of it, but I did not,—only this. One day, while visiting a cousin at Washington, Pa. (a banker there), I sat in the library writing letters. Gen. Grant entered and asked: "Whom are you writing to?" I answered, "Your sister". He said: "Write this". Then he dictated as follows: "The General says, if you have any influence with your husband, tell him to have nothing whatever to do with ———. If he does, he will be ruined, for come what may, he (your brother) will do his duty to the country and the trusts in his keeping." I signed, "Sis."

He said: "Seal and send the letter by the first mail." And I did. That is all I knew about it then. After the letter was sent, the General told me he had received a letter from his brother-in-law, just before he came into the library, and supposing it had been brought up by one of my cousin's clerks (who always brought the General's mail), he then opened it and seeing it was from ——— glanced up at the man and said: "All right", meaning to dismiss the messenger and that there was no answer, who repeated: "All right?" The General nodded. Directly, Gen. Horace Porter, then on duty with my husband, entered and asked the General if the letter he had just received was important.

"No, it is from ———", Gen. Grant said. "Did you read it carefully?" Porter asked. "Do you know it was sent by special messenger from New York?"

"No", the General said, "was not that one of S—'s clerks?" "No", said General Porter, "what did you say to him?" "Nothing. I said, 'all right', meaning there was no answer and that he could retire." Porter said: "Yes! the messenger said he would at once telegraph your answer 'all right' ".

The General said to me: "I have read the letter carefully now and I find it is an earnest plea for a certain financial policy, which you know, he continually urges, saying if I will adopt it, it will make money plentiful and consequently make my administration popular. I always felt great respect for ——— and thought he took much pleasure in the supposition that he was rendering great assistance to the administration by his valuable advice. I blame myself now for not checking this (as I thought) innocent vanity. It is very sad. I fear he may be ruined and my poor sister!"

And sure enough, when we arrived in Washington, the papers announced a fearful financial panic in New York, and as I remember, the President did his duty, his whole duty, on that occasion.

The letter from Corbin, referred to above, was received by the President on September 19, 1869. In the meantime, Gould and Fisk had been buying gold and on September 20 its market price passed 137. By the twenty-third, Gould, who had purchased about $50,000,000—"merely enough to make believe I was a bull"—gave orders to his broker to sell. However, Fisk continued his purchases. On his return to Washington, D.C., from Pennsylvania, General Grant had a conference with Mr. Boutwell, and determined to intervene, should the excitement continue. The price of gold rose on September 23 to 144, and it became evident what was intended. On September 24, which came to be called Black Friday, because of the effects of Fisk's continued effort to corner the market, the secretary of the treasury ordered the sale of gold and the price fell rapidly from 162 to 135. The secretary's telegram ordering the sale of government gold had reached New York in the early afternoon and was made public. Gould's prompt reversal of policy saved him financially, but Fisk was obliged to repudiate his purchases. It would be interesting to know how they settled the matter between them.

In view of the erroneous impression some biographers have given that the General's acquaintance with Gould and Fisk in this case was an indication of a liking for their kind, it seems advisable to point out that they were introduced to him by Corbin and pushed their attentions and hospitality on him all for the purpose of persuading him to adopt a plan they claimed for the public good, and that as soon as he saw through the true objective of their scheme, he took appropriate action.

Reconstruction legislation passed by Congress during the Johnson administration effectively excluded from the vote and from any opportunity to exercise their leadership those who had been political or military leaders in the seceded states. This was a disappointment to General Grant, but his duty was to enforce the legislation, much of which had been passed over the President's veto. If Mr. Lincoln had lived he might have been able to control the action of Congress sufficiently to provide the conditions for readmission of the states. However, this was not to be, and Mr. Johnson's ineptitude and fight with Congress resulted in throwing both houses of Congress into the control of the radicals. This resulted in the XIV and XV Amendments and in the requirement by Congress that they should be adopted by each seceded state as a condition to its readmission into the Union.

President Grant had had nothing to do with the conditions for readmission of the states except in connection with the XV Amendment, which prohibited denial of the vote "by any State on account of race, color, or previous condition of servitude." This amendment had been declared ratified March 30, 1870. Although the President was inclined to favor some requirements as to education at least for eligibility to vote, he became convinced that the Negroes must have a vote in order to protect themselves against the violence of the Ku Klux Klan or similar groups formed by southern whites against the rule of the carpetbaggers and the too often ignorant and corruptible freedmen.

An act was approved January 26, 1870, providing for the readmission of the state of Virginia with certain conditions, and on that day the government of Virginia was turned over by the military to the civil authorities; her senators and representatives were quickly sworn in and Virginia was once again a member of the Union. Mississippi and Texas had duly ratified the XIV and XV Amendments and were readmitted as states February 23, 1870, and March 30, 1870, respectively. Because Georgia had excluded all Negroes from its legislature, there was some delay in getting this action modified and Georgia was readmitted to the Union on July 15, 1870. Thus all the seceded states were again participating members of the United States before the end of Grant's first Administration.

The Grant Administration necessarily inherited the problem of what has been generally called "the Alabama Claims." In violation of what the Lincoln Administration considered the neutrality of Great Britain, the *Alabama,* the *Florida,* and other cruisers had been built in England and had been permitted by English authorities to escape to the Azores, there to be equipped for the destruction of American commerce on the high seas. Appropriate protests had been made by the U.S. minister in London, Charles Francis Adams, with the backing of Secretary of State Seward. The British Cabinet declined to consider the protest, and nothing more could be done while the war lasted. However, the Andrew Johnson Administration in August 1868 sent Reverdy Johnson to replace Mr. Adams. The former with great enthusiasm went ahead and drafted with the English foreign secretary a treaty to be known as the Johnson-Clarendon Convention; it ignored most of the claims of the United States. When Johnson returned early in 1869 with details of the convention, it was generally attacked and overwhelmingly failed of ratification. On the occasion of its consideration by the Senate, Senator Sumner made a speech attacking Great Britain in undiplomatic terms, acknowledging the direct losses due to the operation of the destroyers at some $15,000,000, claiming national damages of $110,000,000 caused by the prolongation of the war and similar hypothetical injuries, and concluding with the statement: "To my mind our first duty is to make England see what she has done to us. How the case shall be settled, whether by money more or less, by territorial compensation, by apology or by an amendment of the law of nations, is still an open question; all may be combined."

Of this speech Charles Francis Adams, who was better informed than any American as to the probable reaction in England, wrote:

> The practical effect of this is to raise the scale of our own demands of reparation so very high that there is no chance of negotiation left, unless the English have lost all their spirit and character. . . . There were intimations made to me in conversation that the end of it all was to be the annexation of Canada by way of full indemnity. . . .

The London papers were excited and inflammatory and pointed out that their bonds on the Exchange had fallen 5 per cent and that the English people really expected war with us, counting on the aid of France. Evidently Sumner's was a very unwise speech, although the senator claimed that he had made no demands but merely stated his view of what the claims for damages might or should be. Coming from the chairman of the Senate Committee on Foreign Relations the speech, added to the debate in the Senate, was to make the reopening of negotiations on the subject a very real problem in tact and diplomacy for the new Administration.

The first step toward renewal of negotiations with England was taken through Caleb Cushing, who had become closely acquainted with John Rose, then acting as British commissioner in the joint tribunal on the claims of the Hudson Bay and Puget Sound Companies under the 1863 Treaty. Rose was described as a natural diplomat of a high order, and Cushing was able to arrange for an interview in Washington between Rose and Fish. At this time a complication arose from the fact that the American minister in London was the distinguished writer, John Lothrop Motley, and that it was discovered, largely from a memorandum he had given Mr. Fish on how the problem with England should be approached, that Motley was actually carrying out the instructions of

Sumner and ignoring those of his direct superior, Mr. Fish. Motley had to be recalled in December, 1870.

In the meantime the Franco-Prussian War had come into the picture; though not involved in the war, England had certainly become more inclined to settle its differences with the United States. These were to be settled by arbitration, conducted by a joint high commission composed of members named by each government. Sessions were held in Washington, and the British and American commissioners drafted a treaty which was laid before the Senate on May 10, 1871.

Ratification took place on May 24. The Treaty of Washington was a great, innovative step in the settling by arbitration of any international dispute that brought two countries to the brink of war. The next step toward a final settlement was the appointment of the arbitrators and representatives of the two nations involved. Great Britain appointed Chief Justice Alexander Cockburn; the United States, Charles Francis Adams. The King of Italy, the President of the Swiss Confederation and the Emperor of Brazil named three neutral arbitrators: Count Sclopis, Baron d'Itajuba, and Jacques Staempfli, respectively. Lord Tenterden was the British agent, and Sir Roundell Palmer the counsel. Assistant Secretary of State J. C. Bancroft Davis was agent for the United States, and the American counsel were William M. Evarts, Caleb Cushing, and Morrison R. Waite.

On December 15, 1871, the Board of Arbitration met in Geneva, Switzerland. Even here the threat of war, implicit in Senator Sumner's earlier demands, cropped up in the inclusion of the indirect claims in the American presentation. The firmness and diplomatic resourcefulness of Charles Francis Adams prevented the arbitration from failing, and on June 25, Bancroft Davis announced the plain and direct acquiescence of the President of the United States in the decision of the arbitrators and "two days later Tenterden announced the indirect, cautious and hesitating assent of Her Majesty's Government." Thus, the award of $15,000,000 to be paid in gold by Great Britain to the United States for the damages done by the *Florida, Alabama,* and *Shenandoah* was the settlement at the last meeting on September 14, 1872.

Another important international question that was settled by arbitration was the Northwest Boundary dispute under the Treaty of June 15, 1846. In this case the arbitrator was the Emperor of Germany, who on October 21, 1872, as reported to the Congress by the President, awarded as claimed by the United States "the important archipelago of the islands lying between the continent and Vancouver Island" (which had been contested for twenty-six years) and "leaves us for the first time in the history of the United States as a nation without a question of disputed boundary between this territory and the possessions of Great Britain on this continent."

Progress in the peaceful settlement of international disputes made during the Grant Administration and public interest in the same was evidenced by the formation in 1873 of two special non-governmental organizations to favor this progress by suitable public discussion and information: the American Society of International Law, and the French Institut de Droit International.

In 1868, Buenaventura Baez, again President of Santo Domingo, had sent a confidential agent to Washington, suggesting annexation of Santo Domingo to the United States. In his last annual message President Johnson on the advice of Secretary of State Seward recommended annexation of the entire island of Hispaniola, composed of Santo Domingo and the Republic of Haiti. Haiti formed the western part of the island—about one-third of Hispaniola's area with many times the population of its neighbor Santo Domingo. Haiti had apparently not been a party to the request for annexation. However, its troubled career in internal politics justified the belief that it would be easily acquired.

Baez again made overtures to the new Administration in 1869, but had little success except in the mind of President Grant, who doubtless saw the island's value to the United States (1) in furnishing an integrated source of tropical and semitropical products, and supposedly very great mineral resources; (2) in having a great harbor in Samaná Bay for a coaling station and naval base; (3) in offering a possible land for colonization by American Negroes, a special project of Mr. Lincoln; (4) in becoming a good foreign market for U.S. farm products; and (5) in giving an important point for the control of great commercial traffic to be expected through a canal across the Isthmus of Panama.

To investigate the situation, the President sent his private secretary, General Babcock, to Santo Domingo. Apparently General Babcock became very enthusiastic about the proposal of annexation, and he ventured to draft a protocol with the Santo Domingo authorities for annexation. When he returned with his draft of the treaty it was quite a shock to

Secretary of State Fish, and the Cabinet did not give it an enthusiastic reception. Action by the Cabinet was apparently stalled by Secretary Cox's question: "Is it really settled that we want to annex Santo Domingo?" Although the treaty had been drafted by an army officer without any diplomatic authority whatsoever, that could be adjusted. On November 29, 1869, the treaty was submitted to the Senate for ratification. It included a provision for the United States to pay $1,500,-000 to the Dominican Republic for the liquidation of its debt. Mr. Fish, who felt that his department had been compromised without his full knowledge, submitted his resignation; but in consideration of his great desire to conclude the negotiations with Great Britain on which he had been engaged, and at the serious urging of the President, he withdrew his resignation. On further consideration, he seemed to take a favorable view of the annexation of Santo Domingo.

The necessary two-thirds vote was not secured at the June 30, 1870, session of the Senate. Sincere in his belief that the annexation of Santo Domingo was greatly in the interests of the country, the President, in his annual message to Congress on December 5, 1870, again referred to the treaty for the annexation of the Republic of Santo Domingo, enlarging upon his previous recommendation and arguments in its favor. Wishing to avoid another defeat in the Senate of a program so earnestly urged by the President, Senator Morton introduced a compromise resolution to authorize appointment of a commission of investigation.

Senator Sumner, who had gone on record in his opposition to annexation, was now thoroughly enraged at the Administration and did not allow the Morton resolution to be passed; he even went so far as to assure Senator Morton that his life had been threatened at the White House by the President and Babcock. He could not be laughed out of this delusion. On December 21, 1870, he made a violent speech in a manner that seems to have been regretted by his best friends. Nevertheless, Morton's resolution was adopted by both the House and Senate. The commission was appointed by the President to be composed of Senator Benjamin F. Wade, a radical Republican, Andrew D. White, president of Cornell University, and Samuel G. Howe, an abolitionist, philanthropist, and friend of Sumner. Dr. White wrote:

On receiving notice of my appointment, I went to Washington, was at once admitted to an interview with the President, and rarely have I been more happily disappointed. Instead of the taciturn man who, as his enemies insisted, said nothing because he knew nothing, had never cared for anything save military matters, and was entirely absorbed in personal interests, I found a quiet, dignified public officer, who presented the history of the Santo Domingo question, and his view regarding it, in a manner large, thoughtful, and statesmanlike. There was no special pleading; no attempt at converting me; his whole effort seemed given to stating candidly the history of the case thus far.

There was much need of such statement. Mr. Charles Sumner, the eminent senator from Massachusetts, had completely broken with the President on this and other questions; had attacked the policy of the administration violently; had hinted at the supremacy of unworthy motives; and had imputed rascality to men with whom the President had close relations. He appeared, also, as he claimed, in the interest of the republic of Haiti, which regarded with disfavor any acquisition by the United States of territory on the island of which that quasi-republic formed a part and all his rhetoric and oratory were brought to bear against the President's ideas. I had long been an admirer of Mr. Sumner, with the feeling which a young man would naturally cherish toward an older man of such high character who had given him early recognition; and I now approached him with especial gratitude and respect. But I soon saw that his view of the President was prejudiced, and his estimate of himself abnormal. Though a senator of such high standing and so long in public affairs, he took himself almost too seriously; and there had come a break between him, as chairman of the Senate Committee on Foreign Affairs, and President Grant's Secretary of State, Mr. Fish, who had proved himself, as State senator, as Governor of New York, as United States senator, and now as Secretary of State, a man of the highest character and capacity. . . .

At various times I talked with the President on this and other subjects, and was more and more impressed, not only by his patriotism, but by his ability; and as I took leave of him, he gave me one charge for which I shall always revere his memory.

He said: "Your duties are, of course, imposed upon you by Congress; I have no right as *President* to give you instructions, but as a *man* I have a right in this matter. You have doubtless noticed hints in Congress, and charges in various newspapers, that I am financially interested in the acquisition of Santo Domingo. Now, as a man, as your fellow-citizen, I demand that on your arrival in the island, you examine thoroughly into all American interests there; that you study land titles and contracts with the utmost care; and that if you find anything whatever which connects me or any of my family with any of them, you expose me to the American people." The President uttered these words in a tone of deep earnestness. I left him, feeling that he was an honest man; and I may add that the closest examination of men and documents relating to titles and concessions in the island failed to reveal any personal interest of his whatsoever.

The commissioners and staff all embarked on the steam-frigate *Tennessee* on January 17, 1871, but nothing much came of the investigation and Santo Domingo, of course, was never annexed (although U.S. Marines had to occupy it from 1916 to 1934 and a United States customs receivership was in effect from 1905 to 1941).

One more event relating to the area south of the United States can best be mentioned here, although it occurred at the beginning of General Grant's second Administration. This event became known as the "Virginius Incident."

An American-built steamer rather frequently employed for landing military contraband destined for the revolutionists in Cuba was the *Virginius*. It was captured on October 31, 1873, by the Spanish gunboat *Tornado* while on its way from Jamaica to Cuba and while flying the American flag but carrying war material obviously intended for the insurgents. A hurriedly assembled court-martial condemned fifty-three of the crew and passengers to death; they were executed November 4–8; eight American citizens were among them. Secretary of State Fish promptly telegraphed General Sickles, American minister in Madrid, on November 7: "The capture on the high seas of a vessel bearing the American flag presents a grave question, which will need investigation . . . and if it prove that an American citizen had been wrongly executed this Government will require most ample reparation." Castelar, who was President of the then Spanish Republic, received word of the incident at seven o'clock on November 6 and immediately cabled the captain general in Havana that "the death penalty must not be imposed on any non-combatant without previous approval of the Cortes, nor upon any persons taken in arms against the Government without the sanction of the Executive." To General Sickles he deplored deeply the execution of four of the prisoners at Santiago on November 4 and exclaimed: "What a misfortune that my order was not received in time to prevent such an act! It was against the law and the only excuse offered is that a sentence of death had already been pronounced against these men. Such scandals must cease."

The Virginius affair caused great excitement in the United States

Popular sentiment was aroused and war looked imminent. The President authorized the Secretary of the Navy to put the navy on a war footing. However, the President and Secretary Fish did not lose their heads in this emergency. The entire matter was reported to Congress by the President in his message of January 5, 1874, and the following paragraphs summarize the view of the Administration:

No state of war existed conferring upon a maritime power the right to molest and detain upon the high seas a documented vessel, and it can not be pretended that the *Virginius* had placed herself without the pale of all law by acts of piracy against the human race.

If her papers were irregular or fraudulent, the offense was one against the laws of the United States, justiciable [sic] only in their tribunals.

When, therefore, it became known that the *Virginius* had been captured on the high seas by a Spanish man-of-war; that the American flag had been hauled down by the captors; that the vessel had been carried to a Spanish port, and that Spanish tribunals were taking jurisdiction over the persons of those found on her, and exercising that jurisdiction over American citizens, not only in violation of the rules of international law, but in contravention of the provisions of the treaty of 1795, I directed a demand to be made upon Spain for the restoration of the vessel and for the return of the survivors to the protection of the United States, for a salute to the flag, and for the punishment of the offending parties.

The principles upon which these demands rested could not be seriously questioned, but it was suggested by the Spanish Government that there were grave doubts whether the *Virginius* was entitled to the character given her by her papers, and that therefore it might be proper for the United States, after the surrender of the vessel and the survivors, to dispense with the salute to the flag, should such fact be established to their satisfaction.

This seemed to be reasonable and just. I therefore assented to it, on the assurance that Spain would then declare that no insult to the flag of the United States had been intended.

I also authorized an agreement to be made that should it be shown to the satisfaction of this Government that the *Virginius* was improperly bearing the flag proceedings should be instituted in our courts for the punishment of the offense committed against the United States. On her part Spain undertook to proceed against those who had offended the sovereignty of the United States, or who had violated their treaty rights.

The surrender of the vessel and the survivors to the jurisdiction of the tribunals of the United States was an admission of the principles upon which our demands had been founded. I therefore had no hesitation in agreeing to the arrangement finally made between the two Governments—an arrangement which was moderate and just, and calculated to cement the good relations which have so long existed between Spain and the United States.

The terms outlined above were carried out, the ship was surrendered to the American navy at Bahia Honda in Cuba, on December 18, but was wrecked in a bad storm on its way back to the United States. The surviving prisoners were released and two days later duly turned over to American authorities and reached New York safely. Investigation finally resulted in the conclusion that the *Virginius* was carrying the American flag without legal authority.

Many other diplomatic problems and negotiations were handled in the same manner and with equal success, but individually they were not important enough to summarize here. All the while, there were domestic affairs to attend to, and the never-ending requests for jobs.

To supplement his lack of knowledge of politicians and their friends and supporters throughout the country and to provide as far as he could for the appointment only of qualified persons, the President adopted a policy of requiring the recommendation of at least two reliable persons who did know applicants and their capabilities as a condition for appointing them. This did not work out as well as he had hoped. As General Porter at a later date stated, "If there were twenty applicants and only one could be appointed to the job, we found only too often that we had made nineteen enemies and one ingrate." In fact there was much criticism with the appointments made, and here was again a problem which the President wanted to solve in the best interests of the government. Accordingly, on December 19, 1871, the President sent a message to Congress on the subject of civil service reform, promising to adopt the suggestions of the report of a commission, of which George W. Curtis was chairman. In March 1871 the commission recommended a variety of rules, the object of which was to secure for the civil service of the government the services of persons qualified for each job by experience or education.

Grant also asked for "all the strength which Congress can give me to enable me to carry out the reforms in the civil service recommended and adopted to take effect, as before stated, on January 1, 1872." He further pointed out that no appropriation was available to maintain the commission and recommended "that a proper appropriation be made to continue the services of the present Board for another year." Congress

by the Federal Government and thereby exempt from local taxes.) Consequently, there was no general sewage-dispoal system, no general water supply (different neighborhoods were dependent upon local springs), and no adequate lighting or paving of the streets.

Visitors and temporary residents from abroad, like the diplomatic corps, were justifiably critical of the conditions under which they had to live and do business with the government. Cattle, hogs, and other domestic animals ran about the streets freely, on occasion knocking over pedestrians and otherwise being a nuisance entirely inappropriate to a national capital. The situation was further complicated by the fact that Georgetown, the county within the district but outside the planned city, and Alexandria were separate municipalities and had their autonomous governments. In 1846 the part of the original district on the Virginia side of the Potomac River was ceded back to Virginia on request of those who had settled there, thus taking the problems of Alexandria out of the congressional jurisdiction, and reducing the area of the district to some 69 square miles. The recession to Maryland of the parts of the district originally given by Maryland and not actually needed by the Federal Government was frequently discussed but not initiated. There has also been considerable division of legal opinion as to whether the Congress had a right to give back to Virginia its part of the district.

After the Civil War the citizens of the district were stirred up and most anxious to have a city that was not a disgrace to the country. Meetings were held and proposals made to Congress for changes in the district government that would permit this. A proposal to raise funds by a national exposition in Washington was turned down in Congress because it would be humiliating to have representatives of other countries visit the capital as it then was. Little could be done while the fight over the impeachment of President Johnson was going on and the enforcement of the Reconstruction legislation was being achieved.

However, it was evident to President Grant that something had to be done. He had already put an officer of the corps of engineers, General Orville E. Babcock, in charge of the public buildings and grounds, succeeding the commissioner who had been responsible for the maintenance and care of all Federal interests not taken care of by the individual departments or transferred to the city government. The law approved February 21, 1871, gave a territorial government to the entire district, subordinating Georgetown to it and merging the old county of

Washington with the new territory. Alexander H. Shepherd, who had authored the first draft of the bill and as a representative citizen was strongly in favor of it, explained that the bill gave the appointment of a council to the Federal Government, so that the government would do its part in paying for the cost of building up the capital. How much the Federal Government would or should contribute to the district budget was left to Congress to decide; but Congress avoided settling this matter in the bill that was passed, and there was therefore no provision for Federal aid except by implication.

The President appointed Henry D. Cooke as governor of the new territory and Alexander H. Shepherd to the Board of Public Works, of which he became chairman. The other four members of this board had been previously connected with his efforts to secure improvement of the city, except for A. B. Mullett, the supervising architect of the Treasury Department, who was an ex-officio member. Shepherd was undoubtedly the leading spirit and the chief administrator of the phenomenal job of constructing the city during the two years following. According to Bryan, as stated in *The Nation,* he was "a man 'who had never been known to cheat or steal' and this record remained unchanged. His large way of doing things was part of the nature of the man. . . . His imperious will recognized not merely no master, but no difficulty that stood in the way of what he wanted to do."

Within three weeks of the signing of the territorial bill, the President had appointed a council of eleven members (among them Frederick Douglas), the upper body of the legislature, and a Board of Health. An election was held for the House of Delegates and for one delegate to Congress, and the new District of Columbia Territorial Government was organized and the legislature convened in time to succeed the old municipal government on June 1, 1871. General Chipman was elected to represent the district in Congress; Edward L. Stanton, son of the great war secretary and a member of the bar, was appointed to succeed Chipman as secretary of the territory. A comprehensive plan for the improvement of the city was put before the legislature before it had been in session for a month. The improvements were estimated to cost $6,250,-000. This naturally shocked the conservative element in the community, which had haggled over the repaving of Pennsylvania Avenue after nearly twenty years of heavy use had made it unserviceable.

With the failure of Jay Cooke and Company on September 18, 1873,

Henry D. Cooke felt compelled to resign as governor of the D.C. Territory, and the President recommended Mr. Shepherd to fill the vacancy. He was confirmed. It is surprising how much work was accomplished under Mr. Shepherd's energetic guidance and sound planning. The plan for the territory had vision and appreciation of the true physical needs of the city; experience since has shown that it was generally sound. The cost of its execution was high because the old municipality had woefully failed in its duty to develop the city adequately, largely because it had been unable to enlist the help of Congress. Bryan writes, in his history of Washington:

> This plan provided for a sewerage system that would also care for the drainage and uniform street levels, both of which were so well devised for the needs of a large centre that they remain the foundation of the city today. In still another respect the plan proved enduring, for in reducing the broad thoroughfares to a practicable width for paving, the admirable device was adopted of a parking space between the building line and the sidewalk in residence streets. With a breadth of vision unknown in that day in city improvement work, tree planting was made an essential part of the plan, and unlike a great deal of street paving and sewer work, it was well done . . . Liberal bounds were given to what was described as the central section of the city, where every street was to be improved . . . In addition the main thoroughfares in all sections extending to the urban bounds were included in the area of improvements as well as connecting county roads . . . In all one hundred and eighteen miles of city streets were improved and thirty-nine miles of county roads.

The activities of the new government were not restricted to public works, but extended to the general clean-up of the city. "Murder Bay" received particular attention, as did the large number of gambling establishments. The issue of licenses for saloons was limited and some supervision over them exercised. Life and property enjoyed a protection previously lacking.

So much work by the authorities could not but be reflected in private activities. Real estate development, which had been stimulated by the increase of population and had made considerable progress in the last years of the Johnson Administration, now began to boom. The British Embassy on Connecticut Avenue and N Street, the Corcoran Art Gallery on Pennsylvania Avenue and 17th Street, and the houses built by Mr. Shepherd himself on K Street between 17th and Connecticut Avenue are among the most important buildings of the period. This increase in real estate activities was sufficiently pronounced to justify the hope that rising values in taxation would materially assist in paying within a reasonable time the indebtedness that had to be incurred for the public works.

It was the particular misfortune of the Administration that the wave of increasing values and local developments broke, when just about at its crest, on the rock of the panic of 1873. The financial distress that swept over the country from overdevelopment and speculation could not but be felt in the capital; it was most pronounced in the curtailment of loans for real estate developments and in the financial straits forced on developers who had already assumed obligations.

The government started out with an authorization from the legislature to raise a loan of $4,000,000 through the sale of bonds. Although this was acknowledged to be less than two-thirds the total amount that would be needed, it was an entirely unheard-of sum to be spent on public works in the city of Washington. The opposition to the government formed a citizens' organization, started a newspaper to voice its hostility, and applied for an injunction. But this opposition was still limited in extent, although organized and extremely bitter. Governor Cooke was able to arrange for the sale of the entire issue of the new bonds at 94, although the securities of the old municipal corporation were selling at only 80. However, the injunction did tie up the proceeds of the loan; but the new government was not of a character to be stopped by such devices. It obtained from the legislature a direct appropriation of half a million dollars in anticipation of the current revenues, in order to start work.

One of the claims made by the injunctionists was that the loan had not been submitted to the voters for confirmation and was, therefore, illegal. The government, without waiting for the decision of the courts, immediately secured the passage of another act authorizing a loan of the same amount but requiring confirmation by a vote of the people. The cost of such an election was an undesirable addition to the total cost of the work forced upon the government by the opposition itself. Another consequence was that in the meantime the work had to be started by hired labor, and the uncertainty of the amount of funds available made it impracticable to have recourse to contracts.

After some three months the courts rendered a decision favorable to the Board of Public Works, and at the same time the election endorsed the loan. These two victories for the Board of Public Works discouraged the opposition as to its chances of securing action through the courts or at the polls, and they had recourse to the not unusual device of congressional investigation. Although the suggestions made in both the House and Senate had given some hope for the assumption of part of the cost by Congress, the determined opposition to the government's work appears to have prevented the friends of the government from asking for any such legislation; then the appointment of an investigating committee made any such attempt impossible until receipt of the report of the investigation.

Although the investigating committee of 1872 found nothing to sustain any accusation of "corruption, misconduct or serious mis-government" on the part of the territorial government and found reason to praise its "zeal, energy and wisdom," the opposition was able to repeat the same tactics each year. They had investigations in 1873 and again in 1874, thus putting the territorial government on the defensive in Congress and temporarily doing away with any hope of assistance from the Federal treasury.

The government's counterstep was to secure legislation fixing the total authorized indebtedness at $10,000,000, hoping that this would be a low enough limit to dissipate any reasonable fears and at the same time sufficient to pay for the essential part of the work. In spite of all the alleged extravagance, the territorial government actually assumed obligations for only $8,883,940 of the authorized amount, although the subsequent commission government had to expend something over a million to finish some of the work. However, while this was true as to the funded debt incurred for the public works, bonds were authorized by the legislature for other purposes not included in the comprehensive plan, the $3,500,000 owed by the old municipal corporation were added, and the inability to collect about 47 per cent of the moneys assessed on private property forced the territorial government to have recourse to short-term loans and other less formal obligations which created a floating debt. The aggregate of all these items was alleged in the final investigation of 1874 to be over $22,000,000, an estimate that was probably the worst that could be claimed even by the government's enemies.

While sagacious and politic in his dealings with Congress and with other authorities, the exigencies of the work itself forced Mr. Shepherd to make many enemies. When the opposition to the public works program was found to be unyielding, somewhat arbitrary but effective means were found of performing the work regardless of the opposition, and doubtless these measures added yet more enemies.

The President's recommendation—that Congress contribute to the cost of the district as a taxpayer on the basis of the assessed value of the public buildings—did not pass. The territorial government was already embarrassed by its inability to pay some of the regular employees, and the blow of the 1873 panic destroyed any hope of the government's avoiding bankruptcy.

The congressional investigation of 1874, therefore, turned from a judiciary attitude to the problem of setting up temporarily some sort of government which would be relieved of the hostility felt for the territorial government, would stop the expenditure of funds, and apply itself in earnest to the work of liquidating the debt incurred. A temporary commission of three was instituted by Congress in order to have no one person with the authority that had enabled Mr. Shepherd to carry on his work so effectively in spite of the efforts made to stop it.

After three years of such temporary government and consideration of the problem, Congress finally passed an act, approved June 11, 1878, permanently establishing the present commission form of government, and doing away with the territorial form.

The liquidation of the debts resulted directly from the two factors which had been foreseen by the Territorial Government and on which it had confidently gone ahead with the work that it had to do: namely, the increased population and values directly resulting from and created by the completion of the needed municipal improvements, and secondly, a liberal contribution from the Federal Treasury in order to compensate for the difference between the cost of developing and maintaining a city worthy to be the National Capital, and the cost of a city appropriate merely to house an equal population.

The aggregate assessed value of real estate in 1869 was $58,639,000, while in the next five years it rose to $96,433,000, an increase of nearly 65 per cent which can be attributed to the improvements made by the Territorial Government and the consistent increase of the population and values. Manifestly the money spent on improvements made by the Shepherd government went a long way toward liquidating the debt incurred, which in any case would probably not have been too heavy a burden for the District to carry and liquidate, with reasonable Federal aid. In any case the President included in his annual message of December 1, 1873:

> Under the very efficient management of the governor and the board of public works of this District the city of Washington is rapidly assuming the appearance of a capital of which the nation may well be proud. From being a most unsightly place three years ago, disagreeable to pass through in summer in consequence of the dust arising from unpaved streets, and almost impassable in the winter from the mud, it is now one of the most sightly cities in the country, and can boast of being the best paved.
>
> The work has been done systematically, the plans, grades, location of sewers, water and gas mains being determined upon before the work was commenced, thus securing permanency when completed. I question whether so much has ever been accomplished before in any American city for the same expenditures. The Government having large reservations in the city, and the nation at large having an interest in their capital, I recommend a liberal policy toward the District of Columbia, and that the Government should bear its just share of the expense of these improvements. Every citizen visiting the capital feels a pride in its growing beauty, and that he too is part owner in the investments made here.

Theodore Noyes, for so many years the editor and publisher of the *Washington Evening Star,* in reviewing the relations of the various presidents with the District of Columbia, said that no President had shown the interest in the national capital and done so much for it as General Grant.

Even as a cadet at West Point, General Grant appreciated beautiful scenery and historical surroundings. It was only natural then that later he should have been intrigued and impressed with the stories of the natural wonders in Wyoming at the headwaters of the Yellowstone River in the area since known as Yellowstone Park. These natural wonders were known to the Indians by tradition and confirmed by John Colter, a member of the Lewis and Clark Expedition in 1807. As time went on other explorers confirmed or added to the information, and finally the report by Captain W. F. Raynolds, of the U.S. Topographical Engineers of an exploration of the region in 1859 gave official recognition to earlier accounts. Even so, the stories were so amazing that they were not generally believed. Finally in 1860 a private exploring party consisting of David E. Folsom, C. W. Cook, and William Peterson set out from the gold fields of Montana with the express purpose of verifying or refuting the rumor, and they returned full of enthusiasm. A semi-official expedition in 1870, led by Henry E. Washburn, surveyor general of Montana, and Lieutenant Gustavas C. Doane, 2nd U.S. Cavalry, spread the confirmation of "the Yellowstone wonderland." This was followed the next year by an expedition under Dr. Ferdinand V. Hayden. The President and some members of his family visited the area, probably with one of these last two expeditions. As a result he became convinced, along with many of our leading conservationists, that the area should be excluded from occupation under the various Homestead Acts. Thus an act of Congress, approved March 2, 1872, establishing the first National Park. This introduced a new policy to preserve by law the natural wonders of the country for the enjoyment and education of future generations.

In this first Administration many things were done and many things were begun. Some of the things—the reduction in Federal expenditures, the urban renewal (as it would now be called) of the Federal capital, and the attempts to establish civil service—caused considerable discussion and aroused many enemies to the Administration. For instance, of the initial attempt to do away with the spoils system, George William Curtis in 1869 wrote:

> Nor have we had from any President a single word of manly protest against this monstrous system, until now President Grant says in words which in spirit are worthy to stand with those of Washington, "There has been no hesitation in changing officials in order to secure an efficient execution of the laws; sometimes, too, when in mere party view undesirable political results were likely to follow. Nor has there been any hesitation in sustaining efficient officials against remonstrances wholly political." At last, thank God, we have got a President whom trading politicians did not elect and who is no more afraid of them than he was of the rebels, and these manly and simple words are as full of cheerful promise as the bulletins of his advance on Vicksburg.

However, when the President was unable to get his civil-service legislation adopted and appropriations made to carry it out, because of the unwillingness of the politicians to deprive themselves of the patronage that they had been accustomed to, the same George William Curtis became a political enemy. The Santo Domingo question made another group of enemies who imagined something sinister in the novel proposal of the United States becoming a colonial power. The National Parks program, which would take out of real estate development and mining much of the area and wealth that could be exploited selfishly for individual profit, doubtless stirred others to enmity.

Other reforms which did not seem practicable of accomplishment at the same time doubtless added to the hostility toward the Administration; hence a group, even in the Republican Party, grew up in opposition to the Administration and ready to accuse it of all sorts of mistakes and wrongdoing. The instance of the investigation of the Shepherd administration of Washington, an investigation which lasted three successive years and which found no evidence of corruption, is an example of what annoyance with the Administration's somewhat aggressive pushing of novel policies could do in the way of making enemies. One is inevitably led to belief that there was much valid experience in Bagehot's statement that "one of the greatest pains to human nature is the pain of a new idea."

The dissenters called themselves "Liberal Republicans" and issued a call to all Republicans opposing the Administration and favoring reform to meet in Cincinnati on the first Wednesday in May 1872. There was plenty of material at hand for such a gathering, although there was no common bond of sympathy except dissatisfaction with Grant and his Administration. In New York there was a factional quarrel. The two United States senators were in fighting mood. Reuben E. Fenton, crafty political manipulator, had been leader of the state while governor from 1865 to 1869, but Roscoe Conkling, from Utica, New York, had gained ascendancy with the Administration in Washington. Greeley, always afflicted with the itch for office, was Fenton's candidate for governor in 1870, but was beaten in the convention. In the New York convention of 1871 there was a titanic struggle for supremacy, and Conkling, taking command in person of his forces on the floor, had driven the friends of Greeley and Fenton out and assumed full control of the party organization.

Of the Cincinnati meeting, Grant's biographer Coolidge wrote:

> The Cincinnati gathering did not consist of delegates regularly chosen; but any person of Republican antecedents was permitted to participate. No such collection of curiously assorted men ever before or since has undertaken to organize a political party. The Liberal Republican movement, in so far as it embodied a real passion for reform, was peculiarly the product of writers for the Press.

The convention ended by nominating Greeley for President; he had kept the demand for tariff reform out of the platform and was a most irreconcilable protectionist who also expressed contempt for civil-service reform. For Vice President the gathering nominated Gratz Brown.

The Democrats, meeting in Baltimore on July 9, 1872, endorsed Greeley and his ticket. At Philadelphia on June 5–6, Grant had been renominated by acclamation and with great enthusiasm. The only suggestion of disagreement was in the selection of a candidate for Vice President, and Henry Wilson of Massachusetts was nominated.

There now began probably the most abusive, maliciously critical, and generally exaggerated campaign against the President personally. For instance, Senator Sumner in a more or less keynote speech accused the general of "Caesarism," a desire to have despotic control of the government. In reply to this accusation, Matthew H. Carpenter said:

> I was trying last night to recall a single instance if in conversation in regard to the late war I had heard General Grant allude to himself, and I could not. I have heard him speak in the most glowing terms of his comrades in arms. I have heard him speak of the exploits of Sherman. I have heard him allude to what was done by Logan, McPherson, and many other officers of the Union army. I never heard him say, speaking of a battle, "at such a juncture I thought I would do so and so," or, "I ordered a battalion this way or that," or, "I turned the scale by such a maneuver." I never heard him allude to himself in connection with the war. I believe you might go to the White House and live with him and converse about the war day after day, and you never would know from anything he said that he was in the war at all.

As a matter of fact if we except only Washington, probably no President took so little avantage of his office to satisfy personal interests and ambitions. Proposals were made to President Grant, as they had been to Washington, pointing out the possibility of taking in hand the government for the good of all when things were in the greatest confusion, but of course he didn't even listen to such suggestions.

Another instance of entirely mistaken and unjustified criticism was the introduction into the campaign, as an attack on the President, of the Credit Mobilier Scandal. This was a fiscal corporation established back in the Andrew Johnson Administration to assist financially the construction of the Union Pacific Railroad. The scandal was that a member of

Congress named Oakes Ames had distributed stock of the corporation to various members of both the House and the Senate to secure their interest in furthering construction of the railroad. In some cases the stock was sold to them allegedly at a cost much below par; in other cases it was a gift. Considerable financial return was paid by the corporation. While some of the most prominent members of the national legislature were accused, investigation showed that many had refused to have anything to do with it, others had returned the stock, and only a few were found deserving of criticism by the investigating committee of Congress which rendered its report February 18, 1873.

To Ames it seemed that what he had done was perfectly honest and aboveboard; "the same thing," he claimed, "as going into a business community and interesting the leading business men by giving them shares." However, he was one of those censured by the investigation. As the whole question of propriety involved members of Congress only, and no members of the Grant Administration, the accusations had no rightful bearing on the Administration; it was something which had occurred in the legislative branch of the government in a previous administration. Could the ill will of the opposition have reached further for an entirely unjustified criticism of the candidate for re-election?

A close friend of Grant, George W. Childs, was shocked by a report that things were not looking very bright for the election. He went to the general with this story, and the latter got out a map of the United States and named with confidence what states he would carry and what states might go to the opposition. The election proved him to have estimated the results very accurately. He received 286 electoral votes out of 349, and his popular vote was 3,597,132—an increase of 484,209 over the vote in 1868. It was an overwhelming popular demonstration of confidence, which was very gratifying to the candidate who had been so maliciously and unmercifully accused and abused.

As March 4 approached, the Congress on the third passed a bill increasing the salaries of the President, Vice President, members of the Cabinet, and members of the Senate and House. Coming at the very end of the session, there was not much time for discussion, and the raise was manifestly long overdue, considering the great increase in population of the country and consequent duties of all involved. Nowadays such an increase, or even a much greater one, is accepted by the country as normal and only fair, but such was the bitterness of some people against the Grant Administration that they set up a howl, calling this "the salary grab." But the law went into effect.

The following extracts from the general's second inaugural address show the purposes with which he had been impelled in his first Administration and his ideas of what still needed to be done:

It seemed to me wise that no new questions should be raised so long as that condition of affairs existed. Therefore the past four years, so far as I could control events, have been consumed in the effort to restore harmony, public credit, commerce, and all the arts of peace and progress. It is my firm conviction that the civilized world is tending toward republicanism, or government by the people through their chosen representatives, and that our own great Republic is destined to be the guiding star to all others. . . .

The effects of the late civil strife have been to free the slave and make him a citizen. Yet he is not possessed of the civil rights which citizenship should carry with it. This is wrong, and should be corrected. To this correction I stand committed, so far as Executive influence can avail.

Social equality is not a subject to be legislated upon, nor shall I ask that anything be done to advance the social status of the colored man, except to give him a fair chance to develop what there is good in him, give him access to the schools, and when he travels let him feel assured that his conduct will regulate the treatment and fare he will receive.

The States lately at war with the General Government are now happily rehabilitated, and no Executive control is exercised in any one of them that would not be exercised in any other State under like circumstances. . . .

In future, while I hold my present office, the subject of acquisition of territory must have the support of the people before I will recommend any proposition looking to such acquisition. I say here, however, that I do not share in the apprehension held by many as to the danger of governments becoming weakened and destroyed by reason of their extension of territory. Commerce, education, and rapid transit of thought and matter by telegraph and steam have changed all this. Rather do I believe that our Great Maker is preparing the world, in His own good time, to become one nation, speaking one language, and when armies and navies will be no longer required.

My efforts in the future will be directed to the restoration of good feeling between the different sections of our common country; to the restoration of our currency to a fixed value as compared with the world's standard of values —gold—and, if possible, to a par with it; to the construction of cheap routes of transit throughout the land, to the end that the products of all may find a market and leave a living remuneration to the producer; to the maintenance of friendly relations with all our neighbors and with distant nations;

to the reestablishment of our commerce and share in the carrying trade upon the ocean; to the encouragement of such manufacturing industries as can be economically pursued in this country, to the end that the exports of home products and industries may pay for our imports—the only sure method of returning to and permanently maintaining a specie basis; to the elevation of labor; and, by a humane course, to bring the aborigines of the country under the benign influences of education and civilization. It is either this or war of extermination. Wars of extermination, engaged in by people pursuing commerce and all industrial pursuits, are expensive even against the weakest people, and are demoralizing and wicked. Our superiority of strength and advantages of civilization should make us lenient toward the Indian. The wrong inflicted upon him should be taken into account and the balance placed to his credit. The moral view of the question should be considered and the question asked, Can not the Indian be made a useful and productive member of society by proper teaching and treatment? If the effort is made in good faith, we will stand better before the civilized nations of the earth and in our own consciences for having made it.

All these things are not to be accomplished by one individual, but they will receive my support and such recommendations to Congress as will in my judgment best serve to carry them into effect. I beg your support and encouragement.

It has been, and is, my earnest desire to correct abuses that have grown up in the civil service of the country. To secure this reformation rules regulating methods of appointment and promotions were established and have been tried. My efforts for such reformation shall be continued to the best of my judgment. The spirit of the rules adopted will be maintained.

I acknowledge before this assemblage, representing, as it does, every section of our country, the obligation I am under to my countrymen for the great honor they have conferred on me by returning me to the highest office within their gift, and the further obligation resting on me to render to them the best services within my power. This I promise, looking forward with the greatest anxiety to the day when I shall be released from responsibilities that at times are almost overwhelming, and from which I have scarcely had a respite since the eventful firing upon Fort Sumter, in April, 1861, to the present day. My services were then tendered and accepted under the first call for troops growing out of that event.

I did not ask for place or position, and was entirely without influence or the acquaintance of persons of influence, but was resolved to perform my part in a struggle threatening the very existence of the nation. I performed a conscientious duty, without asking promotion or command, and without a revengeful feeling toward any section or individual.

Notwithstanding this, throughout the war, and from my candidacy for my present office in 1868 to the close of the last Presidential campaign, I have been the subject of abuse and slander scarcely ever equaled in political history, which to-day I feel that I can afford to disregard in view of your verdict, which I gratefully accept as my vindication.

During Grant's first term the country had suffered two very serious fires which destroyed sufficient property and made sufficient number of people homeless to rank as national disasters: the Chicago fire, Sunday, October 8, 1871, which lasted for 24 hours, burned over an area of 2,100 acres, destroyed 17,500 buildings, and rendered 100,000 people homeless, with the destruction of property estimated at $200,000,000; and the Boston fire on November 9, 1872, which lasted about the same length of time, destroyed an area of about 65 acres with a money loss of $73,000,000. These two fires were the most serious that had occurred in the United States up to that time; they had a profound effect on business in the two cities. Many insurance companies were unable to meet their obligations, and the economic risk of inflammable wooden houses became a strong argument for fireproof construction which was subsequently developed.

The fiscal situation, as General Grant had pointed out in his first inaugural address, was obviously one of the most important problems of the country; a solution was needed immediately after the close of the war. He had, with great promptness, taken measures to stop the war expenditures, and then reduction of the national debt was necessary, to enable the country to return to specie payment. The solution of this problem was made more difficult by the number of so-called "greenbacks" in circulation at depreciated values, varying with the locality in which they were being used. It will be remembered that the greenbacks had been made legal tender by act of Congress for all payments except import duties and other Federal taxes; therefore, they were a lower class of currency, representing merely a paper promise of the government. They were not backed up with any metal or other property of real value. Then Chief Justice Chase rendered an opinion on February 7, 1870, that the Legal Tender Act itself had been unconstitutional, further lessening the value of the greenbacks in public estimation.

President Johnson's Secretary of the Treasury Hugh McCullough quite properly started taking in greenbacks and other more or less informal negotiable papers that formed part of the national debt and funding the debt by the sale of bonds. Evidently, such deflation brings with it a troublesome lack of currency in circulation, and such a move can progress only very slowly and with great caution. On occasion McCullough had to put back in circulation a certain number of the greenbacks which had been withdrawn, and the legality of this procedure even to meet a fiscal emergency of the government was questioned. McCullough had retired and canceled $44,000,000 out of $400,000,000 of greenbacks authorized by law. Mr. Boutwell continued the McCullough policy under General Grant. The country seemed to be doing famously financially: business was booming, construction work, especially on railroads and similar large undertakings, was going at full tilt, and for the moment things looked very promising. On Mr. Boutwell's resignation, March 17, 1873, in order to accept election to the Senate, Mr. William A. Richardson of Massachusetts was designated to succeed him in the treasury, and he continued the efforts to reduce the national debt.

In the meantime while the amount of currency available was gradually being reduced, the expenditures and use of materials were rising. It is generally conceded that the excessive railroad construction and its use of materials, especially iron and wood, had gotten to exceed the amount the business could pay for. In 1869, 4953 miles of railroad had been built; in 1870, 5690; in 1871, 7670; and in 1872, 6167. This totaled some 24,000 miles of new railroad in four years. In addition, Commodore Vanderbilt was starting to four-track the New York Central to Albany, constituting an additional demand for railroad tracks and cars to run on them. (Four-tracking would permit passenger trains to use one set of tracks while the slower-moving freight trains used the other set.)

Jay Cooke & Company had been most successful in selling at advantageous prices the new government bonds carrying a lower interest rate. Now it undertook to finance the building of the Northern Pacific. Fiske and Hatch were financing the Chesapeake and Ohio; Kenyon, Cox and Company, the Canada Southern. They advanced money for the work of construction, and when sufficient mileage had been built they would place an issue of bonds thereon and sell them to investors. Jay Cooke & Company failed on September 18, 1873, and many other bankers were also compelled to close, having exceeded the capital available to them because of their optimism and confidence in ample financial return. This set off the Panic of 1873. There had been a sharp financial panic on the Vienna Bourse in May 1873, which stopped to a great extent the purchase of American bonds in Europe and had forced the New York bankers to strain their credit to carry on. In November a number of railroads defaulted in the payment of the interest on their bonds. Many of the business concerns were dragged down in the general panic. Its effects were felt during the succeeding years and gave rise to many idle mills, furnaces, and factories, unemployment, reductions in wages, strikes, etc.

It was to be expected that the Congress meeting in December 1873 would be greatly concerned over the situation, and indeed a great number of bills aimed at remedying the financial situation were presented in the Senate. They were referred to the Committee on Finance headed by Senator John Sherman. For nearly four months the debate went on, culminating in a discussion of whether the greenback circulation should be increased by law. In the meantime, Secretary of the Treasury Richardson was inflating the currency by putting in circulation $3,000,000 or $4,000,000 of the greenback "reserve." He continued this policy until by January 10, 1874, $26,000,000 of greenbacks had been reissued. In the Senate, former Secretary of the Treasury Boutwell defended this action of his successor. The attorney general had considered the expedient legal. Finally, Senator Sherman proposed a compromise measure which would authorize a return to the former limit of $382,000,000, and would accordingly legalize and include the amount of greenbacks reissued by Richardson. This was amended to fix the limit at $400,000,000 and authorize the reissue of the whole reserve. The inflationists had a majority in Congress and scored a momentary victory. The $400,000,000 bill passed the Senate on April 6, 1874, and the House eight days later. This was the famous inflation bill presented to the President with, as far as he knew, the endorsement of the leaders of the Republican Party.

The President's action was described by John R. Young in *Men and Memories:*

"I hear a good deal in politics about expediency," said the General, one day. "The only time I ever deliberately resolved to do an expedient thing for party reasons against my own judgment, was on the occasion of the expansion or inflation bill. I never was so pressed in my life to do anything as to sign that bill, never. It was represented to me that the veto would destroy the

Republican party in the West; that the West and South would combine and take the country, and agree upon some even worse plan of finance; some plan that would mean repudiation. Morton, Logan, and other men, friends whom I respected, were eloquent in presenting this view. I thought at last I would try and save the party, and at the same time the credit of the nation, from the evils of the bill. I resolved to write a message, embodying my own reasoning and some of the arguments that had been given me, to show that the bill, as passed, did not mean expansion or inflation, and that it need not affect the country's credit. The message was intended to soothe the East, and satisfy the foreign holders of the bonds. I wrote the message with great care, and put in every argument I could call up to show that the bill was harmless and would not accomplish what its friends expected from it. Well, when I finished my wonderful message, which was to do so much good to the party and country, I read it over, and said to myself: 'What is the good of all this? You do not believe it. You know it is not true.' Throwing it aside I resolved to do what I believed to be right—veto the bill! I could not," said the General, smiling, "stand my own arguments. While I was in this mood—and it was an anxious time with me, so anxious that I could not sleep at night, with me a most unusual circumstance—the ten days were passing in which the President must sign or veto a bill. On the ninth day I resolved inflexibly to veto the bill and let the storm come. I gave orders that I would see no one, and went into the library to write my message. Senator Edmunds came to the White House and said he only wanted to say one word. He came in looking very grave and anxious. He said he wanted to speak of the inflation bill, to implore me not to sign it. I told him I was just writing a message vetoing it. He rose a happy man, and said that was all he wanted to say, and left. When the Cabinet met, my message was written. I did not intend asking the advice of the Cabinet, as I knew a majority would oppose the veto. I never allowed the Cabinet to interfere when my mind was made up, and on this question it was inflexibly made up. When the Cabinet met, I said that I had considered the inflation bill. I read my first message, the one in which I tried to make myself and everyone else believe what I knew was not true, the message which was to save the Republican party in the West, and save the national credit in the East and Europe. When I finished reading, I said that as this reasoning had not satisfied me, I had written another message. I read the message of veto, saying that I had made up my mind to send it in. This prevented a debate, which I did not want, as the question had passed beyond debate. There was only one word changed, on the suggestion of Mr. Robeson. I said, if I remember, that no 'patent-medicine' scheme of printed money would satisfy the honest sentiment of the country. Robeson thought the 'patent-medicine' allusion might be unnecessarily offensive to the friends of inflation. So I changed it, although I wish I had not. The country might have accepted the word as a true definition of the inflation scheme. The message went in, and, to my surprise, I received no warmer commendations than from the West. I remember one long dispatch from James F. Wilson, of Iowa, a glowing enthusiastic dispatch. Bristow also sent me a warm dispatch, and it was that dispatch, by the way, as much as anything else, that decided me to offer Bristow the Treasury. The results of that veto, which I awaited with apprehension, were of the most salutary character. It was the encouragement which it gave to the friends of honest money in the West that revived and strengthened them in the West. You see its fruits to-day in the action of the Republican Convention of Iowa."

"Nothing by the way," says the General, "shows the insincerity of politicians more than the course of the Democratic party on the financial question. During the war they insisted that the legal-tender act was unconstitutional, and that the law making paper legal tender should be repealed. Now they insist that there should be millions of irredeemable currency in circulation. When the country wanted paper they clamored for gold, now when we are rich enough to pay gold they want paper. I am surprised that our writers and speakers do not make more of this extraordinary contradiction. It only shows the insincerity of so much of our political action.

"Financial questions at home," continued the General, "are settling themselves in spite of the politicians. Wherever our friends have tampered with silver bills and inflation they have suffered. Political leaders who make these concessions will be in about the same position as those who went after Know-Nothingism at the time the country had that scare. With a people as honest and proud as the Americans, and with so much common sense, it is always a mistake to do a thing, not entirely right for the sake of expediency. When the silver bill was passed I wrote General Sherman, and advised him to suggest to the Secretary, his brother, the plan of paying Congress in silver. I made a calculation," said the General, laughing, "that it would have taken about twenty wagons to have carried silver enough to the capital to have paid the Congressmen and the employés for one month. They could not have carried their pay off except in wheelbarrows. As they passed the bill it was proper that they should enjoy its first-fruits. It would have made the whole thing ridiculous. If I had been President, and could have raised silver enough for the purpose, the Congressmen would have had silver at legal rates. The men who voted for the silver bill, like the old Know-Nothing leaders, will spend the remainder of their lives in explaining their course. Already in the West you see the reaction."

President Grant and Mrs. Grant arrived in St. Louis on October 5, 1874, to attend the St. Louis Fair. Their daughter and Secretary of the

Navy Borie and General Babcock accompanied them. They were welcomed at the station by ten old friends and Federal officials. Within the following year four of the ten were convicted of complicity in the "Whiskey Ring" and were in prison.

The President had bought his father-in-law's old farm on Gravois Road, and to it he sent frequently some of the presents of livestock he received, colts, calves, and pigs, but especially horses and colts. The manager of the farm was encouraged to enter some of the livestock for competition at the fair. So he entered two horses, Claymore and Young Hambletonian, in the President's name. Of the twelve or fifteen exhibits to be judged at this annual event in the Mississippi Valley, the two colts entered from the Grant farm were manifestly not in the same class as some of the other entries. The judges were tied as to the first-prize award, and it was suggested that General John McDonald be added to the two judges to secure a decision. The decision was quickly made, and the judges tied a blue ribbon on the President's colt. Embarrassed, the President threw his cigar to the ground, exclaiming, "That is an outrage!" He then turned and walked away.

This incident is worthy of mention only because of the part General McDonald was later found to have played in the Whiskey Ring. McDonald had been a "steamboat runner" on the St. Louis levee, a local name for one engaged in energetically securing passengers for the boat line. He was illiterate, but after his marriage his wife taught him to read and write. At the outbreak of the Civil War, McDonald's acquaintance with the river men and a certain quality of leadership made it possible for him to get recruits and to contribute greatly to raising the 8th Missouri. In recompense he became a major in the regiment and distinguished himself during the war under General Sherman, being breveted Brigadier General at the close of his service.

For some years he made considerable income from commissions paid him for pushing claims against the government. In 1868, Congress created supervisors of internal revenue to prevent frauds, and McDonald applied for appointment as supervisor. With his application he filed a surprisingly long list of recommendations, among them a recommendation from General Sherman and other well-known people connected with St. Louis. There was a protest against his appointment by a group which Senator Carl Schurz headed, but, owing to the very enthusiastic recommendations, he was appointed in November 1869 to the district comprising Arkansas, Indian Territory, and, three months later, Missouri, when St. Louis became his headquarters. He soon took an active part in politics and secretly organized the Whiskey Ring in September 1871. Members of the ring claimed its purpose was to raise a campaign fund to secure General Grant's re-election.

The ring's operation provided that certain corrupt government officials would exempt the distillers from paying taxes on part of their output, and require them to pay the ring half the amount that should have gone to the government as taxes. Of course the President was not informed of any of this, although an effort was made later to accuse him of complicity by proving that one of his personal aides, General Babcock, was a party to the ring.

Benjamin H. Bristow in June 1874 was appointed secretary of the treasury, succeeding Richardson, who had resigned. He discovered that there was a discrepancy between the taxes received and the amount of liquor manufactured in a number of cities in the West. The chief shortage was in the St. Louis district. In his effort to investigate the causes of the shortage, Secretary Bristow had the co-operation of the attorney general, Edwards Pierrepont, and his energetic solicitor of the treasury, Bluford Wilson.

Apparently the operation of the Whiskey Ring had gone smoothly enough before the 1872 election, and the ring was reorganized and resumed operations in 1873, without any pretense of providing funds for the Republican Party. According to Walter B. Stevens in *Grant in St. Louis,* the money was regularly distributed from St. Louis and "gaugers and storekeepers and other subordinates were carried on the ring payroll at from $50 to $100 a month. The greater part of the fund was divided into five parts, one of which was mysteriously set apart for 'the man in the country.' Each of the ringleaders netted $1,000 and upwards a week."

One measure proposed by Secretary Bristow, in an effort to secure definite evidence, was to transfer supervisors from one district to another. Evidently, this would have brought the malfeasance to light, but the order for shifting supervisors was revoked by direction of the President. For the moment the ring was saved and its leaders naturally thought McDonald's claim that "the old man knew" was true. President Grant later told why he revoked the order:

I resisted all efforts to have the order revoked until I became convinced that it should be revoked or suspended in the interest of detecting frauds that had already been committed. In my conversation with Supervisor Tutton, he said to me that if the object of that order was to detect frauds that had already been committed, he thought it would not be accomplished. He remarked that this order was to go into effect on the 15th of February. This conversation took place late in January. He alleged that it would give the distillers who had been defrauding the Treasury three weeks notice to get their houses in order, and be prepared to receive the new supervisor; that he, himself, would probably go into a district where frauds had been committed and he would find everything in good order, and he would be compelled to so report; that the order would probably result in stopping the frauds at least for a time, but would not lead to the detection of those that had already been committed. He said that if the order was revoked, it would be regarded as a triumph for those that had been defrauding the Treasury. It would throw them off their guard, and he could send special agents of the Treasury to the suspected distillers—send good men, such a one as he mentioned, Mr. Brooks. They could go out and would not be known to the distillers, and before they could be aware of it, the latters' frauds could be detected; the proofs would be complete, the distilleries could be seized, and their owners prosecuted. I felt so conscious that his argument was sound, and that it was in the interest of the detection and punishment of fraud that this order should be suspended, I then told him that I would suspend it immediately, and I did so without further consultation with anyone. My recollection is that I wrote the direction for the suspension of the order on a card, in pencil, before leaving my office that afternoon, and that the order was issued and sent to the Treasury by one of my secretaries.

But lightning struck and the ring was shattered when the President sent to the secretary of the treasury a letter dated July 19, 1875, from W. D. W. Barnard, telling the story of what was going on in the Bureau of Internal Revenue. Grant wrote in his own hand on the back of the letter the following endorsement:

I forward this for information and to the end that if it throws any light upon new parties to summon as witnesses they may be brought out. *Let no guilty man escape if it can be avoided.* Be specially vigilant—or instruct those engaged in the prosecution of fraud to be—against all who insinuate that they have high influence to protect—or to protect them. No personal consideration should stand in the way of performing a public duty.

Of course the evidence of corruption was picked up and made the most of by enemies of the Administration. Secretary Bristow received a tremendous amount of good publicity as a reformer who was trying to clean out the conspirators and distillers who had profited by the operation of the ring—so much publicity that it became evident that Mr. Bristow had the idea that his investigation might very well land him the presidency. One indication of such an ambition was the choice of a former senator, John B. Henderson from Missouri, to assist the district attorney in the prosecution of those accused. In one of the earlier trials, Henderson made a flamboyant speech with evident political inferences and with somewhat insulting and entirely improper references to the President himself. Henderson was necessarily removed from the investigation, and for a time at least the President thought that Bristow, his head turned by the popular attention he was getting, had transformed the investigation into an effort to try the Administration rather than the persons who had committed wrongs in the government.

However, it is noteworthy and rather unusual that here was a case of malfeasance in the government which had been discovered by the Administration itself and about which appropriate legal action had immediately been taken against those at fault. Many of the underlings, perhaps too many, were let off with light punishment on making pleas of guilty, and some were given immunity in order to secure their testimony involving the wrongful actions of others. McDonald was indicted and convicted, and served seventeen months in the Missouri penitentiary. Other ringleaders were also indicted and convicted; only one indicted man escaped punishment. This was General Babcock, who was indicted by a grand jury led by one of the endorsers of McDonald. In fact, General Babcock's conviction seems to have become the special object of the prosecution as a means of involving the President; but he was tried by a jury and acquitted.

General Babcock's acquittal was generally attributed to the deposition voluntarily made by the President, who did this in response to the plea of General Horace Porter. In his deposition the President could truthfully testify to no knowledge of Babcock's connection with the ring, and General Porter's intervention on Babcock's behalf seems to be very much in the latter's favor; they had been closely associated in the same office in the White House and General Porter had attended part of the hearings in St. Louis. It is pertinent that Justice David P. Dyer, U.S. District Court, who had been assistant to the attorney general in the prosecution of the whiskey ring, in later years stated for publication:

General Grant had no knowledge of the existence of the Whiskey Ring when the prosecutions began, and therefore was not in the remotest manner a party to or in any wise connected therewith. His great mistake was in trusting men who did know, and were parties thereto, and this after their connection with the ring was a matter of common information. Grant was an honest man and implicitly trusted those he believed to be his friends.

Likewise, Pierrepont testified before the House Committee:

I heard the President say five or six times in the progress of the case, "If Babcock is guilty there is no man who wants him so much proven guilty as I do, for it is the greatest piece of traitorism to me that a man could possibly practice."

Summarizing the story of the Whiskey Ring, it is manifest that there were dishonest distillers ready to profit by the corruption of some of the officers of internal revenue; that Secretary Bristow, representing the Administration, discovered what was going on and took immediate steps to investigate and to indict those who were guilty; that in the course of the investigation the Administration's enemies found so much delight in the facts brought out that Secretary Bristow and other prosecuting officers may have felt that they could climb to greater power and popular acclaim by trying to implicate General Babcock and through him the President himself; and finally, that those indicted were all punished, whether adequately or not is a matter of opinion, and that General Babcock was tried by due process of law and acquitted.

Another case which is often quoted with glee against the Grant Administration is that of General William W. Belknap, who as a volunteer officer had won the confidence and respect of Generals Grant and Sherman. On the death of General Rawlins, September 6, 1869, General Sherman, who was in command of the army, was charged with performing the duties of the secretary of war until a successor could be appointed. On the recommendations of General Sherman and others, and on his own record during the war, General Belknap was appointed secretary of war and entered on his duties October 25, 1869. He and General Sherman did have some misunderstandings because of Belknap's issuing orders to the army without consulting the commanding general. This had been a bone of contention between secretaries of war and commanding generals of the army for many years. Otherwise, General Belknap's administration of the War Department seems to have been free of criticism or difficulty; but there was one occasion before his resignation on which he had been overruled.

On the morning of March 2, 1876, the very popular General Belknap came to the White House and asked especially to see the President as soon as possible. On being admitted to the President's office he said, "I have come to offer my resignation, Mr. President," and he added a request that it be accepted without delay. According to the recollection of Colonel William Crook, who was in charge of the reception room and who was present at the interview, no one could have helped feeling sorry for General Belknap; "he looked heartbroken." The President apparently realized there was something that had caused his visitor great personal distress and simply shook hands with him and said, "I am sorry, Belknap." About half an hour afterward he accepted the resignation in writing, "with regret." It later developed that in the afternoon of that same day Hiester Clymer, chairman of the Committee on Expenditures of the War Department, reported to his committee that he had found uncontradicted evidence of malfeasance in office by General Belknap.

Belknap was accordingly impeached. The investigation that followed revealed that in 1870 Mrs. Belknap had suggested to Caleb P. Marsh of New York, at whose house she was visiting and who had been a business partner of Mrs. Belknap's sister's first husband, that he apply for a post-tradership on the frontier. Somehow it was hinted to him that she would accept a portion of the profits he would make. As the valuable sutlership at Fort Sill, in Indian Territory, was to become vacant, Mr. Marsh arranged with the incumbent, John S. Evans, who was seeking reappointment, to continue in the business and to pay Marsh $12,000 a year, one-half of which was to go to Mrs. Belknap. She died late that same year and the payments continued to be made to the secretary. This evidence seemed to implicate the secretary directly, but he claimed he had assumed the payments to be part of his second wife's income (he having married the first Mrs. Belknap's sister) and had passed them on to her. (She had, as a condition to accepting him, obtained his assurance that he would not try to exercise any control over her personal estate.)

My grandmother remembered in after years that the second Mrs. Belknap came to see her by appointment, "her pretty, rosy dimpled mouth now had its quivering lips drawn quite to one side." When asked,

"Why did you not tell General Belknap? He would have made it right," Mrs. Belknap drew back and exclaimed: "Tell Belknap! Why, he would have annihilated me. Oh! No, I could not." So there is this evidence that he really did not know—not being capable of suspecting his own womenfolk. At least in the Grant family he was believed to be ignorant of the bribe which had been paid for his reappointment of Evans. In fact, the members of our family always believed in General Belknap's innocence. The impeachment proceedings failed to have the votes necessary for conviction. General Belknap settled in Washington and practiced law there—evidently there were many, fully conversant with the facts, who still trusted him to handle their affairs and legal business.

At about the middle of his second term, General Grant's enemies raised an alarm that he was seeking a third; they ventured to predict that this was just another step toward his following Caesar's example of despotism. "Burleigh" of the *Boston Journal* wrote:

The cry of Caesarism has been sounded through the land. No King, No Emperor, No Third Term, in glaring capitals, meet the eye in sensational journals. A large and victorious party, that carried through the war, and has blessed the country with a marvelous peace and prosperity, are accused of a deep game to place in the chair of Washington, a permanent President. The quiet gentleman in the White House, who smokes his cigar, and most emphatically minds his own business; who spends his evenings with his family, and welcomes *all* comers with a genuine hospitality, is said to be deep in the plot. His aim is, it is said, to overturn the government that Washington gave us; to clothe himself with imperial power, and by changing the Constitution and the laws, by bayonets, or by ballots, or by some other force, to make himself Emperor. This attempt to alarm the country by the cry of Caesarism, may be a sensational joke; it may be a note of serious alarm; for the authors of this outcry "are all honorable men." But malevolent or serious, this outcry may have more in it than its authors intend. It has taught the people that they can elect General Grant for a third term, if they will. Neither the Constitution, the laws, nor the teaching of the Fathers, stand in the way of the third or the thirteenth term, if the people will. Furious and malignant attacks on General Grant have not so far borne the fruit expected. During the late canvass, the vilest things were said about him. His military abilities, and even his integrity were called in question. His home, his family, his children were not spared. The result showed that the people understood General Grant quite as well as his maligners. Had the canvass lasted six weeks longer, the General would have been elected by a unanimous vote. This new assault has commenced early, and if pressed with commendable vigor, will probably end in the renomination of Grant. What was intended as a political pleasantry may be taken up by the people in all seriousness.

I think that as a matter of fact the President had told his wife very definitely that he would not accept a third term unless forced to it as a matter of duty; and he announced to his Cabinet, early in 1875 when the Pennsylvania Republicans had indicated their readiness to nominate him for a third term, that he was replying in an open letter as follows:

> The idea that any man could elect himself President, or even renominate himself, is preposterous. Any man can destroy his chances for an office, but none can force an election or even a nomination. I am not nor have I ever been a candidate for renomination. I would not accept a nomination if it were tendered, unless it should come under such circumstances as to make it an imperative duty—circumstances not likely to arise.

Rhodes with the usual drop of poison in his sarcasm speaks of this letter "as a grudging declination to be a candidate for a third term," doubtless because of the obvious loophole it left for a change of attitude. In interpreting the letter, we must remember General Grant's fixed principle that it was his duty to render needed public service when it was officially and definitely offered to him by those having authority and responsibility to do so. Similarly, he felt that it was improper to refuse in advance any request to perform service before it had been properly and formally offered him. For example, Governor Yates asked in the early days of the mobilization at Springfield, Illinois, "What is the matter with this man Grant? He has not applied for any of the colonelcies or other appointments." Grant replied that he never would ask for an appointment and that the only way to handle the situation was to appoint him to some duty without consulting him. So Governor Yates made him colonel of a regiment which was probably on the verge of mutiny. Of this regiment he made an excellent organization which earned a fine record in the war.

In spite of the political attacks on the President, life in the White House was anything but melancholy. Colonel Crook left this sympathetic description of the Grant family life in the White House:

> I have never seen a more devoted family or a happier one. There never seemed to be the slightest jar. To begin with, I don't believe any man and

wife were ever more devoted than were President and Mrs. Grant. I am sure he thought she was absolutely perfect. . . . The President . . . wouldn't sit down to the table without her. In the morning he was always up first, and had time to read the morning papers—the Republican or the Post—before Mrs. Grant was dressed. But as soon as breakfast was announced at half past nine, he would knock at Mrs. Grant's door. Her voice would come from within: "I will be there in a few minutes, General."

The General would walk to the window of the library and wait, fidgeting, until she joined him. Then she took his arm, and they went down to breakfast together. The children were usually there, but whether they were or not, one of these inseparables never thought of eating a meal without the other. The breakfast, as a rule, was plain—broiled Spanish mackerel, steak, breakfast bacon and fried apples (a favorite dish), rolls, flannel cakes or buckwheat cakes, with a cup of strong coffee. When the President had signified that he had finished by pushing back his chair, Mrs. Grant would look up and say, "All right, Ulyss, I will be through in a few minutes." Then when she had had another half cup of coffee, she would take his arm again, and they would go upstairs to her room. There they always had a little talk to begin the day with, until he had to leave for his office in the Cabinet room.

At two, when lunch was announced, the President went to find Mrs. Grant in the library, where she sat crocheting or reading. Again they went arm in arm to and from the dining room. After lunch General Grant drove in his buggy, walked, or rested a short time. At dinner the family was all together. They went down together at seven. It was a jolly meal, with a great deal of fun and laughter. . . .

The public receptions, even, had an informality that pleased people. The military aids that are now so prominent a feature of state receptions were absent then; there were not so many uniforms to be seen among the guests. . . .

After relating an instance of Mrs. Grant's thoughtfulness, he goes on:

It was very largely the simple kindliness which Mrs. Grant showed in this instance—and which they all had—that made the Grant family so popular socially. It was the gayest, brightest of administrations. They had known what it was to be hampered by narrow means; they had been through the terrors and anxieties of war; they were warm-hearted, hospitable people—both General and Mrs. Grant thoroughly enjoyed the opportunity of making their official home the center of large hospitality.

It is hard to realize that this happy family life was lived during the most tempestuous period of expansion, construction, and speculation the country has known, while at the same time his administrations initiated the growth of the United States to greatness. But, except for the bitterness of political strife and the postwar psychology—always excited, confused, and propitious for the breaking down of moral standards—it was far from being a tragic era.

An important event was the opening in May, 1876 of the Centennial Exposition in Philadelphia to show to Americans and visiting foreigners the great progress made by the country in a hundred years. The exposition put special emphasis on the advances in steam power, farm implements, and similar initial steps marking the advent of the Industrial Age. The exposition was formally opened by President and Mrs. Grant and the Emperor of Brazil, who was visiting this country at the time. The Grants visited with the George W. Childs family in Philadelphia and were very cordially and sumptuously entertained. To one who knew General and Mrs. Grant there is nothing more absurd and manifestly untrue than the claims made by some biographers that he liked the company of vulgar men. Of course he always had a sentimental affection for the people he remembered in St. Louis and Galena, for the soldiers who had fought in the war and for other plain people who were found to be kind and loyal citizens; but his intimate friends were quite unpretentious but good people like Mr. and Mrs. George W. Childs, Mr. and Mrs. Anthony J. Drexel, the Bories, the A. T. Stewarts, *et al.,* whom this writer as a boy saw much of and heard more about while his grandfather and grandmother were still living in New York.

Aside from the Emperor of Brazil, other high-ranking foreign visitors during the Grant administrations who were suitably welcomed and entertained were the Grand Duke Alexis, third son of the Czar of Russia, the Prince of Wales, and King Kalakana of the Sandwich Islands. Thomas F. Pendel, doorkeeper at the White House from Lincoln to McKinley, noted that the King of the Sandwich Islands had three of his personal attendants stand immediately behind his chair during dinner and take dishes from the regular waiters and pass them to the King. All three of them wore special uniforms, a prominent feature of which was what Pendel called "ladies' Bertha capes; it certainly was a singular scene in the estimation of an American."

The President's father, old Jesse R. Grant, and Mrs. Grant's father, "Colonel" Frederick Dent, who had both attended the inauguration in 1869, were visitors at the White House for considerable periods, sometimes at the same time. Then they took advantage of the opportunity to tease one another about their ages and to argue politics, about which they never agreed. Mr. Dent was there for a considerable period and died in the White House in his eighty-fifth year.

The Republican Convention which had met on June 14, 1876, in Cincinnati nominated General Rutherford B. Hayes of Ohio for President and William A. Wheeler of New York for Vice President. The Democratic Convention, which met in St. Louis on June 28, nominated for President Samuel J. Tilden of New York and for Vice President Thomas A. Hendricks of Indiana. The election was exciting and hard-fought—so much so that when the polls closed on November 7 everyone had a sense of relief.

Now there arose a very serious problem, the peaceful solution of which was very much to the credit of the Administration and especially indicative of the public confidence in the President personally. On November 10 he had sent a message to Sherman, commanding the U.S. Army:

> Instruct General Augur in Louisiana and General Ruger in Florida to be vigilant with the first forces at their command to preserve peace and good order and to see that the proper and legal boards of canvassers are unmolested in the performance of their duties. Should there be any grounds of suspicion of a fraudulent count on either side it should be reported and denounced at once. No man worthy of the office of President should be willing to hold it if counted in or placed there by fraud. Either party can afford to be disappointed in the result. The country cannot afford to have the result tainted by the suspicion of illegal or false returns.

It was manifest from the beginning that South Carolina's electoral vote belonged to Hayes honestly, but that there was considerable doubt about Florida and Louisiana, there being differences of opinion among the canvassers.

Without attempting to narrate the details of the discussion, it is only necessary to point out that General Grant asked Senator Conkling to introduce a bill for the constitution of an electoral commission, one of the solutions that had been suggested. Senator Conkling promised to introduce such a bill and thought he could get it through Congress, which he did. On November 27, General Hayes wrote to Sherman:

> A fair election would have given us about forty electoral votes at the South—at least that many. But we are not to allow our friends to defeat one

outrage and fraud by another. There must be nothing crooked on our part. Let Mr. Tilden have the place by violence, intimidation and fraud, rather than undertake to prevent it by means that will not bear the severest scrutiny.

A joint rule adopted by the Congress in 1865 had provided that "no vote objected to shall be counted except by the concurrent votes of the two Houses." Therefore, with a Republican Senate and a large Democratic majority in the House it was evident that, when the President of the Senate opened the certificates and proceeded to count the votes, there would be disagreement on this election. The procedure prescribed by the Constitution as interpreted by the said joint rule would evidently not work and the resort to an electoral commission, extra-Constitutional as it was, seemed a practical solution that would be considered fair by a majority of the voters. The historian Coolidge wrote:

> There were reports of Southern rifle clubs to march on Washington to help seat Tilden; and Tilden minute men were said to be enrolling in the North—An Army of Democratic Veterans of the Civil War. Any mad story, no matter how impossible, was sure to have its dupes, and there was need of a firm hand in Washington. . . . Grant was self contained and imperturbable. He used all his influence to bring the embittered factions into line and so insure a peaceful settlement of the dispute.
>
> On January 29 Grant signed the bill [for the electoral commission] and at the same time sent a virile message announcing his approval. "It is the highest duty of the law making power," he said, "to provide in advance a constitutional, orderly, and just method of executing the Constitution in this most interesting and critical of its provisions. . . . It must be that one of the two candidates has been elected; and it would be deplorable to witness an irregular controversy as to which of the two should receive or which should continue to hold the office. . . . The country is agitated. It needs and it desires peace and quiet and harmony between all parties and all sections. Its industries are arrested, labor unemployed, capital idle and enterprise paralyzed by reason of the doubt and anxiety attending the uncertainty of a double claim to the chief magistracy of the nation. It wants to be assured that the result of the election will be accepted without resistance from the supporters of the disappointed candidate, and that its highest officer shall not hold his place with a questioned title of right.

The electoral commission was to be composed of five senators, five members of the House, and four justices of the Supreme Court who, equally divided in their political beliefs, would choose a fifth justice, making fifteen members in all. They chose Associate Justice Bradley. The commission declared General Hayes and Wheeler elected.

An unusual feature about this change in administration was that March 4, 1877, came on a Sunday, when it was thought improper to hold an inauguration ceremony. Therefore, General Hayes was quietly and privately sworn in as President on the evening of the third by Chief Justice Waite in order that there be no interregnum. General and Mrs. Grant had given a welcoming dinner that Saturday night at the White House for General and Mrs. Hayes with the Cabinet and other high officials. My grandmother remembered afterward that "Mrs. Hayes was dressed in a handsome white silk. Her hair was arranged in Madonna style. She was handsome, I saw, as she approached with Mr. Hayes. She trembled a little as we stepped forward to welcome them, but this slight agitation soon passed, as I said to her, 'Mrs. Hayes, these ladies are all eager to be presented to you.' We had a very pleasant evening."

My mother, whose first child was born in the White House, always had vivid recollection of that last evening, March 3, 1877, when the President remained at the Capitol to sign last-minute bills, with the members of the Cabinet involved in any legislation there to answer questions. During this period there was some waiting, as the different bills were brought to the President for signature. Not unnaturally the conversation turned to the subject of the unfair and malicious abuse that had been directed at the President, when actually the Administration was working along quite effectively and in accordance with the applicable legislation. General Grant said that he did not read all the things that were written, in fact he avoided reading the comments of his known virulent enemies.

Secretary of War James D. Cameron drew a newspaper from his pocket and said, "What do you think of this?" Then he proceeded to read a very abusive article about the President. General Grant acknowledged, "That is pretty bad." To which Secretary Cameron replied, "Yes, and that was written about George Washington in his day." So the Father of our Country had himself been similarly abused, as had Lincoln, but time has effaced any impression the public might have retained in their cases.

In regard to criticism of Grant, John Russell Young has this to say:

The politicians understood and feared Grant. *They could not use him,* and therefore strove to slay him. He had fought his long campaigns of war. It was hard to fight his long campaigns of calumny. He was assailed living, his memory traduced when dead. Calumny, one fears, is becoming history. . . .

This genesis of calumny will be traced some day, the historian, like Layard or a Brugsch Pasha, digging the truth from out the rock and sand. Calumny has fallen upon the memory of Grant with Pompeiian fury,—lies as of lava, and slag, and smoke, and fire. So that even to tell the truth about him, sounds like unreasoning adulation. One can readily see how the ingenuous reader coming freshly upon his studies will, if believing what he is taught, find little to admire in Grant, except the heroism with which he wrote a book while dying of cancer. Calumny is taken for granted and orators and writers deal with his memory as though he were a blending of Caesar with a ticket-of-leave man.

The cause of much of this calumny will be found in the remorselessness of politics. Grant was never loved by the politicians. Nor can it be said that any mere soldier ever held their regard. Washington may be cited by those who have forgotten the ferocity aroused by the Jay treaty, and Jackson by those who do not remember the war on the United States Bank. August as is the renown of Washington, stately and growing as is that of Jackson, appreciation came with death, when the shadows of envy could no longer dim the sunshine of fame. If Washington and Jackson in America, if Marlborough and Wellington in England, had never entered upon a political career, their renown would have attained its eternity without the intervening limbo of death and time.

William Conant Church, a journalist of some renown and a personal witness of what he talked about, had this to say:

The weakness of Grant was in his lack of experience in civil administration; in his inability fully to understand and to circumvent the intrigues of partisans and place-hunters; in his ignorance of the art of bending other men to his purposes, by consulting their wishes and their prejudices in lesser matters, that he might control them in the greater. In short, he was a soldier, and not a politician. He was a statesman in his large views of public and national interests, but he lacked the experience that had once led Lincoln to make the extreme statement that "honest statesmanship is the employment of individual meannesses for the public good."

Senator Morton asked the Senate:

"Has there been an Administration within the memory of any man on this floor that has more promptly punished crime when it has been brought to light, or has more promptly removed the offender from office?" Senator Edmunds declared that with respect to the fidelity of its agents the Administration of Grant would "compare favourably with any Administration that ever preceded it from the days of George Washington to this day, when you take into consideration the number of persons necessarily employed in the Government now, compared with its early days, and the large amount of the transactions that they are obliged to perform." There were thefts and embezzlements, but the percentage was phenomenally small as compared with previous Administrations.

The actual record of President Grant's tenure in office is its own best defense. However, the general air of national well-being that prevailed also bears witness to sound policies in the White House and effective government throughout the country; for it would be a mistake to suppose that these postwar years were a time of great political conflict and internal unrest. Except for the disorders of Reconstruction in the southern states, the period was one of great economic development and population growth. It was a time of industrial progress and intellectual advance. There was a flowering in the arts and in literature. Indeed, a great burst of creative energy seemed to fill the land.

XV

The Trip Around the World: Europe and Egypt

ALL his life General Grant had wanted to travel and see the world that he had read about. Having laid down the burdens of the presidency, he now at last was able to satisfy his longing to go to Europe. In May 1877, Secretary of State William M. Evarts notified U.S. representatives in foreign countries by letter that the former President and party had sailed from Philadelphia on the seventeenth for Liverpool. The secretary was confident that U.S. representatives would, as President Hayes wished, "find patriotic pleasure in anticipating the wishes of the Department by showing him that attention and consideration which is due from every officer of the Government to a citizen of the Republic so signally distinguished both in official service and personal renown." Once relieved of any political official position, the general had been the recipient, even while still in this country, of a surprising number of very flattering testimonials of respect and admiration from many of his fellow citizens. In Europe he was to be received with all the consideration and cordiality that could be shown a retired ruler of a great country.

For the trip he had chosen *The Indiana,* a vessel belonging to the only American line of steamships crossing the Atlantic at that time. The ship reached Liverpool on May 28, stopping at Queenstown (now Cobh, Ireland) on May 27. Captain Sargent of the *Indiana,* speaking of General Grant, commented on the fact that "there is no one who can make himself more entertaining or agreeable in his conversation, when nobody has an axe to grind." Indeed, the first morning at sea the general had expressed his sense of relief and said "that he felt better than he had for sixteen years from the fact that he had no letters to read and no telegraphic dispatches to attend to."

During the stop at Queenstown a delegation of local officials and representatives called on the general and pressed him to stay over as their guest, but he had to refuse regretfully because of engagements already made for his continued journey. With the Queenstown delegation had come Mr. John Russell Young, a native of Tyrone County, who had been brought to the United States in his infancy and was later to be U.S. minister to China (1882–85) and Librarian of Congress (1897–99). It is to Mr. Young that we owe the excellent historical record of General and Mrs. Grant's trip around the world and many equally interesting historical notes and descriptions of men and events.

At Liverpool the harbor was filled with ships decorated with their appropriate flags. The Grants were cordially welcomed at the dock by Mayor A. R. Walker. Such ceremonial factories recurred at nearly every stop, forcing the general to make a gracious and appreciative reply, a part he quickly grew to play with considerable skill. After visiting the docks and other sights of interest, the Grants' visit to Liverpool ended with a banquet given by the mayor.

On Wednesday morning, May 30, the party traveled by railroad to Manchester, where the general was officially received by Mayor Heywood. After a visit to celebrated manufactories, warehouses, and other local points of interest, he was enthusiastically received at the Royal Exchange by an assemblage of merchants, the two local members of Parliament, and the Dean of Manchester. In his address of welcome the mayor graciously recalled that fourteen years before he had gratefully welcomed the captain of the American relief ship, the *George Griswold,* which had brought a cargo of provisions to alleviate the hardships consequent to the cotton famine.

The general's response is worth quoting in full, as an example of his style and the general tenor of his replies in such cases:

> Mr. Mayor, Members of the Council of Manchester, Ladies and Gentlemen: It is scarcely possible for me to give utterance to the feelings called forth by the receptions which have been accorded me since my arrival in England. In Liverpool, where I spent a couple of days, I witnessed continuously the same interest that has been exhibited in the streets and in the public buildings of your city. It would be impossible for any person to have so much attention

paid to him without feeling it, and it is impossible for me to give expression to the sentiments which have been evoked by it. I had intended upon my arrival in Liverpool to have hastened through to London, and from that city to visit the various points of interests in your country, Manchester being one of the most important among them. I am, and have been for many years, fully aware of the great amount of manufactures of Manchester, many of which find a market in my own country. I was very well aware, during the war, of the sentiments of the great mass of the people of Manchester toward the country to which I have the honor to belong, and also of the sentiments with regard to the struggle in which it fell to my lot to take a humble part. It was a great trial for us. For your expressions of sympathy at that time there exists a feeling of friendship toward Manchester distinct and separate from that which my countrymen also feel, and I trust always will feel, toward every part of England. I therefore accept on the part of my country, the compliments which have been paid to me as its representative, and thank you for them heartily.

Of the speech he was to make on June 15, when presented in full ceremony with the freedom of the City of London, and having his health proposed by the Lord Mayor and drunk amid enthusiastic cheers, Mr. George W. Smalley, correspondent of the *New York Tribune,* wrote: "I never heard a more perfect speech of its kind than that. There is a charm, a felicity in the turn of one or two of its phrases that would do credit to the best artists in words—Mr. Kinglake or Mr. Matthew Arnold themselves."

On the morning after reaching the capital, General Grant went to the Oaks at Epsom, where he met the Prince of Wales (afterward to become Edward VII), and on June 2 he dined with the Duke of Wellington at Apsley House. On the evening of June 5, Edwards Pierrepont, the American minister, gave a reception in his house on Cavendish Square for the general. On the seventh he was presented at Court, and on the eighth he made a hurried visit to Bath to receive an address of welcome from the mayor, returning in time for dinner with the Duke of Devonshire, followed by a reception given by General Badeau (the American consul general), and so on. It was quite a heavy social program for the simple family from Galena, Illinois.

Later, on June 15, after the presentation by the lord mayor of London, the general was guest of honor at a quiet and almost private dinner in the Crystal Palace. In the evening, Russell relates in *Around the World with General Grant,* there was an exhibition of fireworks and the general's portrait was "drawn in lines of changing flame against the dark background of Beckenham Hills. The guest of honor showed no reaction whatsoever, not a movement of recognition for the cheers with which the great crowd below hailed the portrait. But when this had burned out, and the next piece—a sketch of a building which crowns the heights above the Potomac—was blazing, a slight smile caught at the general's lips as he remarked to Lady Ripon, who sat next to him: 'They have burnt me in effigy, and now they are burning the Capitol!' "

The general dined with the Prince of Wales at Marlborough House on June 19, where he renewed his acquaintance with Dom Pedro II, Emperor of Brazil. After the dinner he visited the office of *The Times* of London. J. C. Macdonald, manager of the paper, received him and showed him over all the departments.

One evening, after attending a reception given by Mrs. Hicks, an American lady living in London, he went with Mrs. Grant to hear the opera *Martha* at Covent Garden. When the curtain went up the full company were there on the stage to greet them, and American flags were grouped in back of them. "The Star-Spangled Banner" was played and sung with a full chorus, with the audience and the Grants standing. That same evening there was a banquet given by the Trinity Corporation in their hall on Tower Hill, at which the Prince of Wales presided.

Although the Court was in mourning for the recently deceased Queen of Holland, Queen Victoria invited General and Mrs. Grant to dine at Windsor Castle on Wednesday, June 27, and to remain until the next morning. Their son, Jesse, Mr. Pierrepont and his wife, and General Badeau were also invited.

Before the arrival of the general's party in England, Minister Pierrepont had attempted to make some advance arrangements for their royal reception. But the Earl of Derby told him plainly (as recorded by Jesse Grant in his book, *In the Days of My Father*) that General Grant was, under American laws, a private citizen and that England would therefore receive him unofficially, as a distinguished American. True, he would doubtless receive every honor that could be bestowed upon a "commoner," but the government could not recognize him, in his private capacity, as it would recognize an ex-ruler of royal blood. Mr. Pierrepont was much chagrined, but with the party now at Windsor, his hopes were more than satisfied. The explanation of this change in attitude seems to be that the overwhelming enthusiasm with which the general had been received everywhere and by all classes (especially by the laboring class) indicated to the very shrewd and perceptive prime minister, Benjamin Disraeli, that it would never do for the Tories to receive their distinguished visitor with the little formality Lord Derby had spoken of. Disraeli persuaded the Queen to invite the Grants to Windsor Castle for dinner and overnight.

During the dinner a dispatch was received from Governor Hartranft of Pennsylvania which read as follows: "Your comrades, in national encampment assembled, in Rhode Island, send heartiest greetings to their old commander, and desire, through England's Queen, to thank England for Grant's reception."

When the general had landed in Liverpool he had promised the mayor to return and accept a dinner from him and the corporation; so he returned to Liverpool on the twenty-eighth and was the guest of honor at a very splendid banquet, with the usual speeches of welcome and response.

On the twenty-ninth he dined with London newspapermen and journalists. It was of special interest to the general to meet and converse with the molders of English opinion and the reporters of daily events.

General and Mrs. Grant were launched in a veritable whirlwind of social activities, and even to list their engagements would require the repetition of the greater part of the 1262 pages of Mr. Young's two volumes of *Around the World with General Grant*. Therefore, we will restrict this account to a few highlights.

On his return from Liverpool the Grants found the season over in London and nearly everyone out of town, except for those who remained to attend the Pierreponts' party on July 4. (Mr. Smalley reported in the *New York Tribune* that "the Fourth of July was observed in London at the Legation, and so far as I know at the Legation only. . . . the Americans presented themselves in large numbers. It is the season when a good many of our countrymen are in London, on their way to the Continent, and not a few of such birds of passage thronged the rooms of the Legation yesterday afternoon. Of resident Americans there were also many—so many that I won't undertake to repeat their names. And there was a pretty large sidewalk committee outside, attracted by the American flag which floated over the doorway and by the carriages setting down company.") So it seemed a good opportunity for the Grants to make a hasty trip to the Continent, postponing their trip to Scotland and North England until later. On July 5, after dinner at the American minister's, the general, accompanied by Mrs. Grant, Jesse, and General Badeau, went to Ostend, where an officer of the King's household waited on him and tendered him the use of the royal car to Brussels. Other municipal and military authorities met the general on landing with an address of congratulation. The following account was given by Jesse Grant.

We were greeted at Ostend by what we had come to consider as "the usual crowd." There were personal friends to meet us and there was an address of welcome from the civil and military authorities. We planned to remain overnight at Ostend and we went to our hotel—father, mother and myself.

It was late in the evening when the badly flustered proprietor knocked at the door of our apartment to announce that King Leopold was calling. If we were as surprised as the boniface, I trust it was not so apparent.

King Leopold came up alone and announced that he came to pay his compliments and welcome father to his country because he wished to see and talk with him in freedom from the antiquated and foolish exactions of court etiquette.

The conversation that followed was a long one. The King remained several hours, asking questions and talking most interestingly of his Congo country.

When the tales of Congo atrocities spread over the civilized world they always brought back to me the memory of that strange evening in our hotel rooms in Ostend when King Leopold talked so earnestly and freely of his hopes and plans for developing the resources and bettering the condition of the natives of the Congo. The tales may have contained truth, many of them appeared to be well authenticated, but I could never credit them. Surely Leopold intended no evil to the Congo. For several years thereafter, King Leopold sent me each new map, as it appeared, of Belgium and the Congo.

We went to Brussels, and the King called formally upon father, and father as formally returned the call. Then the King gave a great banquet in father's honor, where every exaction of royal procedure was carefully observed. It was all most interesting, but, to me, in my knowledge of the unsuspected democratic intimacy at Ostend, it took on the character of a spectacular play. As long as King Leopold lived I thought of him, not as he appeared in the role of King in Brussels, but as my personal friend at Ostend.

While they were still in Brussels a German officer presented himself to the general with letters from General von Moltke and Prince Bismarck. Bismarck's letter was particularly friendly and cordial, and expressed his earnest desire to meet Grant. He said that the "old gentleman," meaning Emperor William I whose assassination had recently been attempted, was out of danger but would not be able to appear in public for some time; it might be well, then, to postpone the visit to Berlin until the Emperor had recovered. The letter from von Moltke introduced the bearer, a colonel in the German army, and assigned him as aide to General Grant. He also indicated his hope that he might welcome General Grant with full military honors. The general at once advised the colonel that he would not be able to reach Berlin for some months and that when he did so he would particularly request that there be "no military reception or display." This was hard for the German colonel to believe. Rallying from his surprise, he requested permission to accompany the party to the German border. This offer was accepted, and the colonel turned out to be an amazingly instructive and agreeable companion.

On Monday morning, July 9, the general's party left Brussels for Cologne, traveling in the Belgian King's railroad car. On his arrival he was greeted by the civil and military governors. The Grants and their party visited the cathedral, crossed the bridges, and made the tour down the Rhine as far as Coblenz.

On July 11 they visited Wiesbaden and on the twelfth Frankfurt. During the remainder of their German tour they stopped in Homburg-les-Bains, Heidelberg, Baden, and the Black Forest.

Going on into Switzerland, they stopped at Lucerne, Interlaken, and Berne, reaching there on July 24. On the twenty-sixth the party arrived in Geneva, where the general laid the cornerstone of the new American Episcopal Church. The church was built on the Rue des Voirons on the site given to the congregation by an American resident in Geneva. Speaking at the dedication, the General emphasized the pleasure he felt in being in the city where the *Alabama Claims* had been settled peacefully by arbitration, and expressed his hope that this method would be followed in other international disputes.

Of course a trip to Mont Blanc was arranged, and the party then crossed the Simplon Pass for a tour of northern Italy. After a few restful days in Ragaz, the group went into Alsace and Lorraine, which had been taken over by Germany as a result of the French defeat in 1870–71. There they visited Metz and Strassburg, including some of the major battlefields. They found the newly conquered provinces sad and desolate. Much of the population had returned to France; those remaining behind resented the Prussian occupation force.

From this digression to the continent the Grant party returned to

Scotland and were received by the Lord Provost, Sir James Fanshaw, on August 31 in Edinburgh, where they visited Holyrood Palace, the home of Mary, Queen of Scots, John Knox's little house at Hartelay, and the castle. That evening they attended the lord provost's banquet where they met General Stewart, army commanding officer in Scotland. They also saw Glasgow, of course, the Tay Bridge, and many other places of interest. Before leaving for England, the Grants visited Granttown, home of Clan Grant, but they did not visit the castle of the Earl of Seafield, head of the clan, because other engagements had already been accepted for the same date. They spent ten days, September 30–October 10 with their daughter Nellie, now Mrs. Sartoris, at Southampton, and then went to Birmingham. In a speech there the general touched on one of his favorite themes: the peaceful settlement of international disputes. He believed, he said, "that at some future time the nations of the earth would agree on some sort of Congress which shall take cognizance of international questions of difficulty, and whose decisions will be as binding as the decisions of our Supreme Court are binding on us. It is a dream of mine, that some such solution may be found."

The Grant party, with Mr. Young, left London for France on October 24, 1877. At Folkestone the mayor and many prominent citizens had gathered to cheer the party and wish them *bon voyage*. The trip was calm and pleasant, and at Boulogne the prefect of the department welcomed the general in the name of Marshal MacMahon, President of France. Just before their train reached the station in Paris, General Noyes (the American minister), General Torbert (the consul general), and an aide-de-camp of Marshal MacMahon entered the car to extend an official welcome. The Grant party saw all the sights of Paris they could, considering their heavy social schedule. The general was delighted to find men who had served with honor under him in the Civil War now representing the United States Government in official positions in France. Although the American colony in Paris revolved around the legation and the consulate, there were other centers—the newspaper houses on the Rue Scribe, the banking houses, and the leading hotels. Mr. Young comments, "*The* [New York] *Herald* office was one of the favorite haunts of General Grant in Paris. He would slip in of a morning and seek out a quiet corner, and brood over the newspapers for an hour or two."

Mrs. Grant, however, preferred to shop, and she had a splendid time.

Mr. Worth personally directed the fittings of her dresses, and Madame Virot took charge of her for any millinery she wished. These attentions were no small matter and privilege at the time. "The Paris I remember," as she later wrote, "is all sunshine, the people all happy. All places of note were visited of course, all famous art galleries, churches; and Versailles, so rich in history; and Sèvres, the famous porcelain and tapestry factories; and all places of historic interest in and around Paris. Many of these were visited with friends, but it would take a volume to tell this alone, but I must forbear."

Early in December the Grant party traveled south to Nice where they boarded the *Vandalia,* a man-of-war that had been cruising in the Mediterranean and which the American government placed at the general's disposal during his travels on that historic sea. They embarked on December 13, 1877, and reached Naples on the seventeenth. Expecting sunshine, they were much disappointed to find the weather on the Bay of Naples cold and raw. After visiting the Castle of San Martin, an old monastery which had been turned into a museum and barracks, they arranged to go to Mt. Vesuvius the next morning. The volcano was very quiet and failed to show any enthusiasm or give its distinguished visitors a warm welcome. The destitute beggars who followed the General's carriage aroused his sympathy and, in spite of his having been cautioned against encouraging pauperism, he would throw them all his change and have to borrow more pennies from other members of the party. Horsemen offered their services as guides and, as the carriage passed the huts of the peasants, women would stand in the doorways and offer wine, which was graciously accepted.

On December 19 they visited Pompeii. The guide was a soldier, who informed the party that he had waited on General Sheridan when the latter had visited the ancient city. As a special compliment to General Grant, the Italian authorities directed that during his visit a house in Pompeii should be excavated. It was evidently a disappointment to the Italian officials that, as Mr. Young states, "Nothing came of any startling import [from the excavation]. There were two or three bronze ornaments, a loaf of bread wrapped in cloth, the grain of the bread and the fiber of the cloth as clearly marked as when this probable remnant of a humble meal was put aside by the careful housewife's hands." The director proposed to open another ruin but one of the *Vandalia* friends, a gentleman of a practical turn of mind, remembered that it was cold and he was hungry, so he suggested that they should "excavate a beef-steak" at the restaurant near the gate instead of excavating another ruin.

On board the *Vandalia* the party sailed for Palermo, arriving at noon on December 23, 1877. The town was attractive enough, especially as it had been decorated for Christmas. The officers of the ship gave a dinner in the wardroom in honor of Mrs. Grant, who had proved such a good and agreeable traveling companion. She and the other guests were surprised at the transformation the younger officers had wrought in the narrow wardroom and at the excellent menu. Mrs. Grant recalled in later years:

> This dinner is a very pleasant memory to me. The menu could not have been better (8 courses), and the dinner was well served by their waiters, who wore white canvas jackets and black silk scarfs. The smilax was such a surprise and the pretty bon-bons! You were very good, dear gentlemen and brave sailors, and I will never forget this, nor any of your kind attentions to me and mine.

On Christmas Eve a delegation of captains of ships then in port, most of them plying between Palermo and New England, called and paid their respects to the General. Christmas morning the ships in the harbor were all a mass of color, with flags and bunting ornamenting them in honor of the general. The town was all abustle and alive with the ringing, pealing, and chiming of the many bells in celebration of the great Christian anniversary. The prefect came in state to pay his respects and was received with a salute of fifteen guns. The general declined with thanks the many invitations and visits to the sights offered, including the hospitality and courtesies of the town. After the authorities left the General and Captain Robeson took a walk through the town, which was something the General always liked to do when visiting a new place. His "bump of locality" stood him in good stead on these occasions and Mr. Young said that he was the only person who had taken a walk in Seville, gotten lost for a moment, but found his way back to the hotel without any help.

The shops in Naples had been attractive and full of carved tortoise shell, ivory, and coral. Mrs. Grant thought her husband somewhat unreasonable in objecting to her buying a lovely coral handle for her parasol, but his attitude was fully explained when on December 25 he gave her an exquisite one, saying, "Now you see why I did not want you to buy one. I wanted to give it to you as a Christmas present."

The party left Palermo with its Christmas bells still ringing merrily and steamed east then south, passing the volcanic island Stromboli, then coming to the rock Scylla and the whirlpool Charybdis, much less active and dangerous than they had expected. They went through the Strait of Messina and passed the city of the same name. After sailing in sight of the ancient city of Syracuse, they finally reached the island of Malta on the afternoon of December 28. Here the strains of "The *Star-Spangled Banner* mingled with the salutes fired. The very handsome Duke of Edinburgh called (his ship was anchored nearby), and in the evening the general made his official visit to the governor of Malta, General Van Straubeuzee.

On the thirty-first the party headed for Egypt on the *Vandalia*. Besides General and Mrs. Grant and their son Jesse, Mrs. Grant had a maid and the General had a courier. His name was Jacques Hartog. He was a native of Holland, educated in Paris, and a very efficient courier. He spoke the necessary languages and carried himself with quite an air, but he was a very poor sailor and subject to distressing seasickness. The wardroom officers had nicknamed him "the Marquis" in recognition of his stylish dress and accomplishments. Then a real storm overtook the ship and lasted for two days. The poor Marquis suffered excruciatingly and spent most of his time curled up in his overcoat in a corner of the deck.

Mrs. Grant, fully appreciating the courier's discomfort and the violence of the gale, ventured to make some suggestions to Captain Robeson. She called out to him as he was entering his cabin, "Captain, this is a stiff breeze?"

"Yes, Madam."

"Captain, don't you think it would be well to drop anchor here?"

"Cannot reach bottom, Madam."

"Then don't you think we had better go back to Malta?"

"It is just as far to Malta as to Alexandria, Madam."

The General overheard the conversation and called from his cabin, "I think, Julia, if I were you, I would not make any more suggestions to the Captain. I really did not suppose you would take charge of the ship."

The General fell into the ways of the ship and the life at sea with "the rapture of a boy going home for a holiday." He was reading Mark

Twain's *Innocents Abroad,* and a copy of the *Nasby Papers* which had been found in Naples.

The party arrived in Alexandria on January 5, 1878, where they remained three days. As the *Vandalia* lay at anchor, the governor of the district, the Admiral and the Generals, pashas and beys, the Consul General, the Vice-Consul, judges and missionaries all came on board. After each officer had been individually saluted according to his rank and the salutes returned, there was smoke enough in the air for a naval engagement. In the name of the Khedive, Ismail Pasha, the Governor welcomed General Grant to Egypt and offered him a special steamer to sail up the Nile and a palace in Cairo. In accordance with Oriental etiquette, the call was promptly returned by the general, his son, the *Vandalia*'s Commander Robeson, and two other navy officers. They were ushered into a spacious chamber and were seated on cushions or divans according to rank. A Pasha, who appeared to be a Greek, offered them cigarets. On a signal from him servants entered bearing little porcelain cups about the size of an egg held in filigree cases and containing coffee spiced with cinnamon. In about five minutes the party arose and proceeded slowly downstairs, the servants and guards saluting. That concluded the visit.

After another day of entertainment, including a meeting with Henry M. Stanley, just out of the African wilderness, the party left Alexandria by special train for Cairo. While Mrs. Grant pondered on the romance and poetry of the scene with its Biblical associations, the general noted the scenery and terrain and their resemblance to some portions of the western prairies in the United States.

Arriving in Cairo, the party was welcomed by a guard of honor, a carpet approach, and a group of officers and civilians. The general immediately recognized some old friends, like Confederate Major General William W. Loring, whom he had not seen for thirty years, and Union Brigadier General Charles P. Stone. (Ismail had increased the Egyptian army considerably and had induced a number of former American officers, both Union and Confederate, to accept commissions in it.) The party drove off with Generals Loring and Stone to the palace of Kassr-el-Noussa, placed at the general's disposal by the Khedive. The next day they called on the Khedive at eleven o'clock, state carriages having been sent for them a short time before that hour. The reception lasted about half an hour, giving the Khedive time to point out the murals commemorating the opening of the Suez Canal. The Grant party then returned to its palace and had been there only a few minutes when the Khedive and his secretary for foreign affairs were welcomed by the general in the grand salon. When that formal visit was concluded, official calls were made on the Khedive's two sons, which they returned at once. The party's official duties were ended.

At noon on Wednesday, January 16, farewells were said, the drawbridge opened, and the party embarked on the Nile. Emile Brugsch, one of the directors of the Egyptian Museum, was assigned to the party by the Khedive, presumably for their education, while an officer of the Khedive's household, Sami Bey, was assigned to act as executive officer of the expedition. He left the deciphering and translating of inscriptions and hieroglyphics and the explanation of the ruins to Mr. Brugsch. The general had had so agreeable a time with the officers on the *Vandalia* that he invited Commander Robeson to come and bring with him as many of his officers as could be spared; but after a night's rest Commander Robeson realized that he and most of the officers should stay with their ship so that only the Chief Surgeon (George H. Cooke), Lieutenant W. A. Hadden, and Ensign F. A. Wilner went upstream with the Grant party. Each of them had bought a Turkish fez and some even ventured on the luxury of an Indian hat. There was likewise a demand for dark spectacles and the Marquis with foresight based on past experience arrived on board with an astonishing umbrella. According to J. F. Packard's *Grant's Tour Around the World,* the trip was like this:

If there are ruins to be seen in the morning, he (the General) is generally first on the deck with his Indian helmet swathed in silk, and as he never waits, we are off on military time. If there are no sights to be seen, the morning hours drift away. We lounge on the deck. We go among the Arabs and see them cooking. We lean over the prow and watch the sailors poke the Nile with long poles and call out the message from its bed. Sometimes a murderous feeling steals over some of the younger people, and they begin to shoot at a stray crane or pelican. I am afraid these shots do not diminish the resources of the Nile, and the General suggests that the sportsmen go ashore and fire at one of the poor, patient, drudging camels, who pulls his heavy-laden hump along the bank. There are long pauses of silence, in which the General maintains his long conceded supremacy. Then come little ripples of real, useful conversation, when the General strikes some theme connected with the war or his administration. Then your serious correspondent wishes he were a Las Casas or a Boswell, that he might gather up and bind these sheaves of history. Or perhaps our friend Brugsch opens upon some theme connected with Egypt. And we sit in grateful silence while he tells of the giants who reigned in the old dynasties, of the gods they honored, of the tombs and temples, of their glory and their fall. I think that we will all say that the red letter hours of our Nile journey were when General Grant told us how he met Lee at Appomattox, or how Sherman fought at Shiloh, or when Brugsch, in a burst of fine enthusiasm, told us of the glories of the eighteenth dynasty, or what Karnak must have been in the days of its splendour and its pride. But you must not suppose that we have nothing but serious talk in those idle hours on the Nile. Hadden sometimes insists that Sami Bey shall become a Christian, and offers to have subscriptions raised for his conversion, and this generally superinduces a half-serious, half-laughing conversation, in which our Moslem friend shows how firmly he believes in the Prophet, and how it is that an accomplished and widely-traveled man of the world may see all the virtues of faith in the faith of Islam.

At Asyut (then Siout), the capital of Upper Egypt and a city of 25,000 inhabitants, the party saw many bazaars, narrow and covered with matting or loose boards to break the force of the sun. The avenues were not more than six feet wide, and the town, except for some fine houses and mosques, was otherwise a collection of mud hovels. The Grants and their entourage visited the tombs built in the sand and climbed the limestone rocks on donkeys. They came to accept the donkey as the normal means of transportation. They traveled to Aswan, the next important stop, by donkey. On the way back to Cairo they visited Philae, Memphis, and Thebes. After packing up again they bade good-by to their friends in Cairo and arrived at Port Said on February 9, 1878, boarding the *Vandalia* and feeling as though they had gotten home. They landed at Jaffa the next day. After the desert dryness of Egypt, Young reported that Palestine seemed "rich and fertile, sparkling with lilies and scarlet anemones, with groves of orange trees bending under their golden fruitage, the almond trees coming into bloom."

Visits to places of religious interest were tremendously appreciated, and the party enjoyed short stays in Damascus, which seemed vividly Oriental to them, and in Beirut. From there the travelers went on to Istanbul (then known as Constantinople), arriving March 5, just two days after the signing of the Treaty of San Stefano concluding the Russian-Turkish War. They stayed only five days, then sailed through the Dardanelles to the Piraeus, whence a short railroad trip took them to Athens. King George I and Queen Olga vied with the citizens of

Athens in doing Grant honor. Young writes, "More invitations, dinners and receptions were offered than the General could have accepted in many months."

The party deferred departure a day to visit the Parthenon at night, which was illuminated especially for the Grants' visit and made a very impressive and fine show. Many of the party left the Acropolis that night and walked down into the city under the spell of the Parthenon. In spite of his reputation for being imperturbable, none appreciated better than the general these relics of the past.

At the time of this visit, Greece was much in sympathy with Russia in the latter's war against Turkey. The Greeks had big hopes of an extension of territory as a result but the Treaty of San Stefano did not so provide. After leaving Greece for Rome, the general discussed the political situation in Turkey and Greece in a letter to his son, Colonel Frederick Grant:

> Since my last we have visited Constantinople for five days and Athens, Greece for five days. We saw Constantinople at a historically interesting time, but a very unfavorable time for seeing the Turks in their glory. They were very hospitable however notwithstanding their embarrassing situation. The Russian Army was but eight miles outside and the road entirely open from the city to the Russian camp. I was anxious to visit their camp but having received the hospitalities of the Turkish officials I doubted the propriety of such a visit, and therefore abstained.
>
> I differ from you in regard to the Greeks. They seem to me to be a very energetic and advancing people. Athens, which had not a single house forty-five years ago, is now one of the most beautiful, cleanest and best paved cities in Europe, containing a population of about 45000 people. The houses are substantial and present a fine architectural appearance, the people, high & low, are well and comfortably clad and every thing indicates prosperity. I am inclined to think that if they could regain their former territory, or a good part of it, with the addition of the Greek population this would give them, they would become a very respectible Nation. The Turco-Russian war may yet end in this. My visit through the Turkish Empire does not impress me favorably with their power to develop the resources of a country.

In Rome, Cardinal McCloskey, representative prelate of the Roman Catholics in the United States, and Monseigneur Chatard, rector of the American College, arranged for Grant's reception by the newly elected Pope, Leo XIII. Almost immediately upon his arrival, the general had also been called upon by an aide-de-camp of King Humbert, and every attention was given the party in its trips to the innumerable monuments and museums of the Eternal City.

On April 20 the Grants were in Florence where they perhaps appreciated the attractions of that city more because there were no special audiences or receptions. On April 23 the party reached Venice where they found special excitement traveling through the canals in gondolas, visiting the Piazza San Marco as well as many of the beautiful buildings and works of art. They reached Milan on April 27, the general's birthday. They were welcomed by the prefect, the syndic and other city notables. In addition to visits to the cathedral and the Church of Santa Maria della Grazie where they saw Leonardo's *Last Supper,* an amusing incident occurred. It was related by Captain Alfred M. Fuller, Second U.S. Cavalry, in *McClure's Magazine* of April 1897.

In the spring of 1878 I happened to be in the city of Milan. Returning to the hotel one afternoon, I saw an immense crowd gathered and a group of Italian officers mounted, their horses grandly caparisoned, themselves decorated with the most brilliant of uniforms. In front of the doorway, held by three uniformed grooms, was a beautiful blood-bay horse, equipped with a new English pigskin saddle. It kept the three busy to restrain his plunges; every moment it seemed as if he would leap on top of the holders and break away.

Going into the hotel, I asked what was the matter, and was told that General Grant was going to review the flower of Italy's army, the pride of all, the flying Bersaglieri. Taking my stand in the corridor in full view, I waited to see our famous general appear.

In a few minutes I saw the general coming down the stairs dressed in a plain black frock coat and trousers and high silk hat. He walked by unnoticed, unannounced, in his plain, unpretentious manner, towards the door. At this time one of the group of officers who had dismounted and were standing in the hallway to receive and escort him to the restless steed without, remarked loud enough for me to overhear, "Why does not General Grant come?" I said, "There he goes now," pointing proudly to the simply dressed figure. They looked at me with a doubting laugh, saying, "No, that cannot be he."

I replied, "I am a United States officer and know him well."

Meanwhile General Grant had come to a halt, having undoubtedly heard the remarks, as a good-natured smile lurked on his face. Finally, one of the officers, being sufficiently convinced, approached and asked if he was General Grant. Receiving an affirmative reply, a look of utter astonishment overspread their faces; they hastened to make amends for their apparent rudeness, accompanying him to the waiting horse, who was making frantic efforts to shake himself free from the three stalwart grooms.

A more restless, wicked-appearing horse I have seldom seen. I was in mortal fear that our general would be speedily thrown and crushed to death by the cruel hoofs. From the sly winks and nudges that passed between these dandyish young officers it looked to me very much as if they had assigned to the general of set purpose a young untamable horse that had never been ridden. My fears for him were somewhat removed when I saw General Grant's eyes lighten up with admiration as he gazed upon the horse. Whether it was that the general was not well or was merely assuming a sort of helplessness, I have never been able fully to determine; but in mounting he accepted the assistance of two officers (the horse fully occupied the attention of the three grooms), and from an apparent stiffness had some difficulty in getting his right leg over the saddle. So soon as he touched the seat, however, he grasped the reins, his form straightened, and the change in his appearance immediately so impressed those around with his thorough horsemanship that spontaneously a shout of applause went up from the crowd. The horse, after a few futile plunges, discovered that he had his master, and started off in a gentle trot. From that time on horse and rider were as one being. The bersaglieri are the brag foot-troops of Italy, and perform all their manoeuvres at a run. For two hours, most of the time with his horse at a gallop, General Grant kept both mounted and foot troops on the move. On his return to the hotel I could hear murmurs of wonder and admiration from his escort. They themselves looked much fatigued, but the general appeared as calm and unruffled as if he had been seated in a rocking-chair.

By May 7, they were again in Paris, where they attended the Paris Exhibition and planned a trip to Holland. They spent almost a fortnight visiting The Hague, Scheveningen, Rotterdam, and Amsterdam. In The Hague they lunched with Prince Frederick, the King's uncle, at the royal country seat, the Huis in t'Bosch. The next stop after Amsterdam was to be Berlin.

That Bayard Taylor, U.S. Minister in Berlin, had been one of the most abusive political opponents of General Grant apparently caused some anxiety in the American Legation. Young therefore preceded the party to Berlin in order to give assurance that there need be no apprehension, and Taylor went to meet the general at Stendahl sixty miles from Berlin. The general was in the best of spirits, still delighted from his visit to Holland and impressed with the prosperity and freedom of the Dutch people. Young relates that "Grant was polite in his calm way, and invited the minister into the car, where Mrs. Grant sat in a corner. 'This is Minister Taylor.' 'Yes,' and a pause. Bayard, also looking out toward the German plains, the prose and poems of the Greeley campaign and the arousing of the country against military despotism coming back to his troubled mind . . . 'Don't you remember,' said the General to his wife, 'the winter we were married, that among the books I read you of an evening was one about two young men traveling afoot over Europe?' 'Why, yes, and how charming!' 'This is Mr. Taylor who wrote the book.' 'How delighted I am to see you.' And what a flood of sunshine rolled in upon the heavy laden heart of Taylor. . . ."

The decisive and overwhelming military victory the Germans gained in the Franco-Prussian War had made it possible to unify all of Germany north of the Austro-Hungarian Empire, making it overwhelmingly influential in Europe. This newly formed empire, so much the work of Prince Bismarck politically and of von Moltke by military conquest, seems to have been of special interest to the general, who found Bismarck particularly interesting. (Von Moltke was not in Berlin at the time.) The prince and the general met several times and held long discussions. On the occasions of Grant's first visit to Bismarck's palace, the sentinels in the courtyard eyed him for an instant only and then instinctively presented arms. The visit had been expected, of course, but nonetheless he was recognized by the sentinels as a soldier despite his casual approach. (To the writer this is an interesting identification of a commanding general whose unimpressiveness our newspapermen have delighted in emphasizing.) Throwing away his half-smoked cigar, the general acknowledged the salute and quietly advanced to the door. Two liveried servants threw it open and he passed into the spacious marble hall to be greeted cordially by Prince Bismarck, certainly one of the greatest men of his day. He wore an officer's uniform and took the general's hand, saying, "Glad to welcome General Grant to Germany." (Bismarck spoke English with precision though somewhat slowly, and when he wanted a word had recourse to French.)

The general replied that there was nothing in his German tour more interesting to him than this opportunity of meeting the Prince. The Prince thereupon commented on the general's youthful appearance and attributed it to "the value of a military life, for here you have the frame of a young man, while I feel like an old one." In the meantime, the Prince had led the general into the library, a large, spacious room with gray marble walls and plain simple furniture. In one corner was a writing-desk, where the Chancellor worked, and on the waxed floors were a few Turkish rugs.

The general expressed the hope that the results of the Berlin Congress, which was holding its sessions in Bismarck's residence, would be peaceful. The Prince assured him that this was his hope and belief too, adding, "that is all our interest in the matter. We have no business with the Congress whatever, and are attending to the business of others by calling a congress. But Germany wants peace, and Europe wants peace, and all our labors are to that end. In the settlement of the questions arising out of the San Stefano Treaty, Germany has no interest of a selfish character. I suppose," said the Prince, "the whole situation may be summed up in this phrase, in making the treaty Russia ate more than she could digest, and the main business of the Congress is to relieve her. The war has been severe upon Russia, and of course she wants peace."

The Prince attributed his not being able to take the general around and show him Berlin as another cause of his regret that the Congress was in session, adding, "His Majesty has been expecting you and evinces the greatest interest in your achievements, in the distinguished part you have played in the history of your country and in your visit to Germany. He commands me to say that nothing but his doctor's orders that he shall see no one, prevents his seeing you." The general replied: "I am sorry that I cannot have that honor, but I am far more sorry for the cause, and hope the Emperor is recovering." William I had been severely injured in an assassination attempt some months before. General Grant felt most strongly about it. Young relates:

"In America," said General Grant, "some of our people are, as I see from the papers, anxious about it. There is only one way to deal with it, and that is by the severest methods. I don't see why a man who commits a crime like this, a crime that not only aims at an old man's life, a ruler's life, but shocks the world should not meet with the severest punishment. In fact," continued the General, "although at home there is a strong sentiment against the death penalty, and it is a sentiment which one naturally respects, I am not sure but it should be made more severe rather than less severe. Something is due to the offended as well as the offender, especially where the offended is slain."

"That," said the prince, "is entirely my view . . . if crimes like these are rampant they must be severely punished."

"All you can do with such people," said the General quietly, "is to kill them."

"Precisely so," answered the prince.

During this meeting with Bismarck, Grant revealed something about himself before going on to discuss the Civil War:

The General said that he had accepted the Crown Prince's invitation to a review for next morning, but with a smile continued: "The truth is I am more of a farmer than a soldier. I take little or no interest in military affairs, and, although I entered the army thirty-five years ago and have been in two wars, in Mexico as a young lieutenant, and later, I never went into the army without regret and never retired without pleasure."

"You are so happily placed," replied the prince, "in America that you need fear no wars. What always seemed so sad to me about your last great war was that you were fighting your own people. That is always so terrible in wars, so very hard."

"But it had to be done," said the General.

"Yes," said the prince, "you had to save the Union just as we had to save Germany."

"Not only save the Union, but destroy slavery," answered the General.

"I suppose, however, the Union was the real sentiment, the dominant sentiment," said the prince.

"In the beginning, yes," said the General; "but as soon as slavery fired upon the flag it was felt, we all felt, even those who did not object to slaves, that slavery must be destroyed. We felt that it was a stain to the Union that men should be bought and sold like cattle."

"I suppose if you had had a large army at the beginning of the war it would have ended in a much shorter time."

"We might have had no war at all," said the General; "but we cannot tell. Our war had many strange features—there were many things which seemed odd enough at the time, but which now seem Providential. If we had had a large regular army, as it was then constituted, it might have gone with the South. In fact, the Southern feeling in the army among high officers was so strong that when the war broke out the army dissolved. We had no army—then we had to organize one. A great commander like Sherman or Sheridan even then might have organized an army and put down the rebellion in six months or a year, or, at the farthest, two years. But that would have saved slavery, perhaps, and slavery meant the germs of a new rebellion. There had to be an end of slavery. Then we were fighting an enemy with whom we could not make a peace. We had to destroy him. No convention, no treaty was possible—only destruction."

"It was a long war," said the prince, "and a great work well done—and I suppose it means a long peace."

"I believe so," said the General.

The Crown Prince Frederick arranged a military review for General Grant on the Templehof, a large open field outside Berlin. When the general drove on the ground in a court carriage, he was met by the commander of the Berlin troops and a large staff. A wild rain swept in gusts across the open field, and even with the protection of a carriage the party was pretty thoroughly drenched. The maneuvers went on nevertheless. First were staged incidents of a battle complete to a charge at double quick with fixed bayonets, the soldiers shouting and cheering as they advanced.

The general complimented Major Igel, the attendant assigned him, on the movement of the troops but questioned whether in modern war a saber or bayonet were of much use. "What I mean," said the general, "is this: anything that adds to the burdens carried by the soldier is a weakness to the army. Every ounce he carries should tell in his efficiency. The bayonet is heavy, and if it were removed, or if its weight in food or ammunition were added in its place, the army would be stronger. As for the bayonet as a weapon, if soldiers come near enough to use it they can do as much good with the club-end of their muskets. The same is true as to sabers. I would take away the bayonet, and give the soldiers pistols in place of sabers. A saber is always an awkward thing to carry."

After the sham battle the troops marched by in review. This was followed by artillery practice, the guns firing and sweeping over the field at a whirling mad pace, then an artillery march-past, with cavalry following the artillery. During one phase of this display, the cavalry squadron broke into disorder and then rallied again. Major Igel explained that this was done to accustom the men with disorder on the field and to train every man to take care of himself. The movement was effective and showed, the general stated, "the highest state of discipline."

Prince Bismarck gave the party a twelve-course banquet on July 1. Afterward, the general and Prince Bismarck settled down on a small sofa near a window in an antechamber, with the Prince's large Danish dog, his constant companion, stretched out before them. There was a story going the rounds at the time that the dog had made an anti-Russian demonstration at the Berlin Congress against the legs of Prince Gortschakoff, which caused much amusement among the people at the conference. Young records:

> Mr. Taylor, the American Minister, was evidently impressed with the historical value of the meeting of Grant and Bismarck. He remembered a German custom that you can never cement a friendship without a glass of old-fashioned schnapps. There was a bottle of a famous schnapps cordial among other bottles. I am afraid to say how old it was. The Minister said, "General, no patriotic German will believe that there can ever be lasting friendship between Germany and the United States unless yourself and the prince pledge eternal amity between all Germans and Americans over a glass of this schnapps." The prince laughed and thanked the minister for the suggestion. The schnapps was poured out, the General and prince touched glasses, the vows were exchanged in hearty fashion, and the prince, rising, led Mrs. Grant through the hall.
>
> As the party passed into the room where the Congress meets the prince explained the position of the members and made some comments on the manner of doing business. "We do not get on rapidly for one reason," he said: "because nearly every member when he speaks does it in so low a voice that he has to say it all over again." At the head of the stairs the party separated, the prince kissing the hand of Mrs. Grant in knightly German fashion.

Of this dinner and the cordiality of their reception by Prince Bismarck and his family, as well as the perfection of the dinner itself, Mrs. Grant retained the most happy recollections. Referring to it in later years she said:

> I enjoyed every moment spent in his [Prince Bismarck's] company. His family, the Princess, and her son and daughter, were equally agreeable.
>
> I shall always remember this visit with the greatest pleasure. The dinner was early, as usual in this country. The Prince conducted me to the table and the Princess took Gen. Grant's arm, and she and the General sat opposite us at table, which brought us all quite near together and made conversation possible.
>
> I can remember even now, much that was said. After dinner, the Prince gave me his arm and asked if I would like to see where the Congress was sitting. I replied that I would.
>
> We entered the large room in which there was an immense table, long and wide. The Prince pointed out to me, the seat of each member of the Congress.

As he finished doing this, I looked up at him and inquired in a mystified manner, what the Congress was meeting for, and seeing his look of surprise, I said hurriedly, "Oh, I know. It is about Russia and Turkey. But what has Germany to do with that?" He laughed outright and said: "Well, to tell the truth, Russia has eaten too much Turkey and we are helping her to digest it."

We had the pleasure of meeting here several young gentlemen we had known in Washington at the German Legation.

When we made our adieux, the Prince and the Princess accompanied us to the entrance where our carriage stood. The Princess took my wrap from the attendant and wrapped it affectionately around my shoulders.

When I gave my hand to Prince Bismarck to say farewell, he bent low over my hand and kissed it. I said, laughing, "If that were known in America, Prince Bismarck, every German there would want to be kissing *my* hand." The Prince, still holding my hand in his great palm, looked down admiringly upon it and said: "I would not wonder at all at them."

I was, of course, enchanted with Prince Bismarck.

From Berlin the party went north to Hamburg. After a brief visit they decided upon a quick trip to Scandinavia, and by late July the general had been enthusiastically welcomed in Denmark, Norway, and Sweden. The towns through which they traveled were gaily decorated with flags. Their appetites were whetted by the cold fresh air and they especially enjoyed the singing of the peasants and the music, which seemed to be everywhere. In December of that year, the general wrote in a letter from Paris:

> I can say with great earnestness that no part of our journeyings gave us more pleasure than that through the Scandinavian countries, and no public have impressed me more favorably. If I were going to remain over another year I should go back to Norway at least and far enough north to see the midnight sun.

At the close of July the party sailed the 400 miles from Stockholm to St. Petersburg. The sea was not very cheerful, for it had no grand ocean swell and was quite turbid. The wind was brisk, not exactly a gale, but one felt the motion distinctly. As the ship skirted the shores of Finland, not quite halfway on the journey, the wind increased to a gale, but the vessel was an excellent one, the engines powerful, and in four hours the ship outsailed the squall. Occasionally, as the weather cleared, the coastline could be seen. In the far distance there was a bright spot shining by reflected sunlight: Kronstadt, the seaport of the

Russian capital of St. Petersburg. The ship sailed into the harbor past many vessels of war on July 30.

The reception at Kronstadt was brief, and after a short address of welcome the Grant party embarked on a steamboat and entered an arm of the sea into which the Neva pours her rapid stream. Soon St. Petersburg stood before them and the usual official welcome awaited.

The general made all the visits that etiquette required and was pleased with his interviews with the Czar Alexander and the Grand Duke Alexis. The Czar was much interested in American Indians. He was familiar with the recent wars with them but he wanted to know much more. General Grant had to go into great detail about plans of campaign and the peculiar methods of Indian warfare. At the close of the interview, the Czar accompanied the general to the door, saying, "Since the foundation of your government, relations between Russia and America have been of the friendliest character, and as long as I live nothing shall be spared to continue this friendship." To this the general replied, "Although the two governments are very opposite in their character, the great majority of the American people are in sympathy with Russia, which good feeling I hope will long continue."

The general's call on Prince Gortschakoff, who had suffered the indignity from Bismarck's dog, was an extremely sociable one, lasting for several hours. Prince Gortschakoff was then more than eighty years old and, though he was physically frail, no amount of mental work seemed to tire him. He and Grant discussed European matters, and the general attempted to give the Prince an insight into American politics.

The general was not always thus engaged. Mrs. Grant recorded her recollections of their visit to St. Petersburg:

The Winter Palace is indeed magnificent. Whilst we were there, some renovation was being made in parts of the palace. The different great halls we saw were magnificent in dimension and splendor of decoration. The floors were of inlaid wood of wonderful beauty. The walls of mirrors or else of tapestry or frescoing relating some historical event in the nation's life. Then great gilded columns supported the lofty ceilings all exquisitely frescoed. The corridors, and we passed through many of them, were I am sure not less than thirty feet wide, as down each side about twenty feet apart stood the most superb vases gathered from all parts of the world, mounted on stands from four to seven feet high, some made of onyx, some lapis lazuli, some of porphyry, some of malachite, some superb Sèvres, and everything else to correspond.

Here again in this great palace, I stopped to admire the apartments of Russia's fair Princess. The bath here called forth my special admiration. It was a bath for a goddess, and I could but wonder that she could consent to leave such surroundings.

We also visited a place where many wonderful jewels were shown us. Great ropes of pearls, rubies and diamonds, but these I did not care for. One sees so many, they cease to dazzle one. . . .

We found the magnificent churches with their columns of porphyry, malachite and lapis lazuli, and the balustrades of solid silver, crowded with devotees prostrating themselves until their foreheads touched the floor. We saw in the churches many caskets containing the remains of loved ones of the late war. These were entirely covered with faded flowers, but these again were covered with fresh flowers. Nearly every woman wore black.

We went out to see a great war ship and as we neared it, a salute of seventeen guns was fired. As the firing ceased, our Minister said (I thought with some surprise): "Madam, they are saluting your husband." I quickly replied, "Oh! no, that salute is for you, Mr. Minister. Gen. Grant's salute is twenty-one guns always." For a wonder, I had counted the guns.

The party was necessarily impressed with the large scale of everything in Russia; but while there was spaciousness, there seemed to be relatively few people. St. Petersburg was laid out according to a grand design probably more impressive than that of any other national capital. As a relatively modern city (Peter the Great had founded it in 1703), it lacked the congestion of most major European cities. Moreover, the needs of a great capital were magnificently provided for—impressive palaces, public buildings, and a great number of churches. An artistic people, the Russians also planned many monuments and beautiful grounds around their palaces.

The capital was joined to the largest city, Moscow, by a broad-gauge railroad constructed under the supervision of a commission of railroad engineers of which Colonel George W. Whistler (class of 1819 at West Point) was the head. He was the father of the American artist James McNeill Whistler and at one time commanded the 4th Infantry, with which Ulysses S. Grant served during the Mexican War. The party made the trip of about 400 miles in little more than twenty hours. They found the wide-gauged cars very comfortable and thought that there were many things that American railroad men might learn from the Europeans, especially in providing for the comfort of the traveler.

An old city, Moscow lacked the large spaces of St. Petersburg and was much more Russian in feeling. The party visited the Kremlin and viewed its treasures, not the least of which was a beautiful portrait of the Empress Catherine astride a superb charger. It is believed that this portrait was painted on the day she succeeded to the throne. Of this visit Mrs. Grant commented:

The great bell, the red gate, the treasury filled with beautiful things,—all these we viewed with pleasure. I must not forget to mention some curious Russian spoons I bought there, our polite military escort kindly indicating the best shops. These pretty coffee and tea spoons had in each bowl an etching of some one of the many churches or castles of Moscow, and with a twisted handle, curious if not quite pretty. I secured here also some very pretty trifles of malachite; also several very fine specimens of enameled wood, a portfolio, etc.

The governor, Prince Dolgoronki, and his niece entertained the Grant party at dinner. They had met the general's son, Frederick, when he visited Russia with General Sherman, and they were both inquired after. Mrs. Grant always remembered how intensely interested this lady, like the other Russians they met, was in the health and welfare—and, in fact, in everything—pertaining to the Russian soldier. They seemed very earnest and patriotic in their devotion to their country. Most of the men were tall and nobly formed, and the women also were handsome.

From Moscow the party went by special train to Warsaw, remembered afterward as full of sunshine. After a drive through the city and its beautiful suburbs, the party went on to Vienna, arriving August 18. The Grants never dreamed that their son Frederick would serve there in 1889 as American minister.

The general dined with Emperor Francis Joseph and with Count Andrassy. (The Empress was away, hunting in Ireland.) Although the social schedule was busy, it was late August and most persons of rank and society were out of the city, which was pleasantly quiet and easy to visit. The Emperor had a reception at the Schoenbrunn Palace, the American minister gave a dinner and ball, etc. One delightful day was spent on the Danube. The Grants went to Ischl and stayed at the Hotel Elizabeth, situated on the Russian water course, which the family found very pleasant and where they were joined by John Kasson, the American minister. They took many delightful rides and enjoyed the picturesque country.

Another diversion was a drive to Salzburg, which took all day. On arriving at about four o'clock, they met a dozen or more Americans and were impressed with what cosmopolitans Americans were becoming. That evening in Salzburg a message came from the Emperor William I of Germany saying that he was well enough then to receive the general, so he and Mr. Kasson left Salzburg by rail the next morning to meet the Emperor and returned the following day.

From Salzburg they went to Ragaz where Mrs. Grant insisted on staying for a fortnight. She, the general, and Jesse enjoyed hiking in the area. Mrs. Grant later described one expedition:

> I, too, became quite an expert in walking, once taking a walk of six miles from our hotel up the gorge to the baths of Pfeffers and back again, quite six miles.
>
> It happened in this way. One bright morning, the General and I started for a walk up the gorge. The road was clean and firm from a hard rain the previous night. We had been walking quite a while, I chatting away all the time, when the General remarked: "Why, you are walking finely, this morning. Do you think you can walk to the Half-way House?" (Just one and a half miles from our hotel.) I replied, "Yes, of course. I do not feel the least fatigued." He said: "If you feel tired when we get there, we will rest a while, have a glass of ale and I will get a carriage for you."
>
> We walked on and on, when the General said: "I think we ought to be getting near the Half-way House, do not you? Are you not tired?" "Not in the least," I said, walking on, when the General exclaimed, "I do believe we have passed the Half-way House. We have, for we are at the Baths." And how we enjoyed the surprise! A surprise to me, but not to the General, for when he asked me if I could walk as far as Half-way House, he knew we had already passed it. He was forever playing such practical jokes on poor me. He said it would be so fine for me to be able to say I had walked six miles once, and so it has been my one brag.

Eventually, the Grant party returned to Paris by way of Munich and historic Augsburg, arriving on September 25 and departing on October 10 for Bordeaux. They passed through interesting chateau country, industrial cities, and the wine-growing country, arriving finally at Biarritz, the beautiful French resort near the Spanish border that at one time was the residence of Napoleon III and his Spanish wife, the Empress Eugénie. Here Napoleon had met and been attracted by the young Bismarck, who was later destined to be the chief agent of his undoing and loss of his empire.

Orders had been issued that General Grant would be received with all the honors due a captain general of the Spanish Army—the question of how to receive an ex-President of the United States has long been a source of discussion in foreign capitals. Spain had solved it by giving the ex-President its highest military honors. Among the high Spanish officials and former officials gathered together on the border was the former President of Spain, Señor Castelar, and as soon as the general learned of his presence he sent word that he would like to meet him. Señor Castelar was presented, and there was a brief and rapid conversation in which General Grant thanked him for all he had done for the United States, for the many eloquent and noble words he had spoken for the North; he assured Castelar that he would have been greatly disappointed if he had visited Spain without meeting him. They met again on the platform of the railroad station where the American ex-President assured the Spanish ex-President: "When I reach Madrid, I want to see you."

"I will come at any time," said Castelar.

According to Mrs. Grant's recollection, they dined with Spain's King Alfonso in Vittoria by special invitation. The town was crowded with farmers bringing their products to market and with soldiers and natty young officers, their chests decorated with many medals bespeaking victories in Carlist and Cuban wars but all wearing mourning on their arms for the young queen, Mercedes.

General Grant was also received privately by the King. Alfonso spoke French as though it was his own tongue, German and Spanish fluently, and English with a good accent but a limited vocabulary. The general was offered a seat and after a little conversational fencing as to whether the conversation should be in Spanish or English, the general settled the matter by saying that he had known Spanish in Mexico but in the 35 years since he had forgotten much and would not venture to speak it. In English they discussed the general and his campaigns, the admiration each had for the other's country, and the tragic loss of the King's wife. The King said that he had been much touched to read of this sympathy in the American newspapers. He also said that his marriage had been one of love, not policy. No one knew what a help she had been to him in his trying position, for it was no pleasure or easy task to be an executive. The general told the King that his eight years as President of the United States had been the most difficult and burdensome of his life.

From Vittoria the party went directly to Madrid, arriving on October

28. The party was kept busy visiting the many great sights. The American visitors were interested and surprised at the uniformly observed "siesta hour" in the middle of the day when all the stores were closed and business suspended. Grant was called upon by many distinguished people and high-ranking officials. James Russell Lowell, the American minister to Spain, gave the party a dinner in Madrid and also took the general for a walk and sightseeing. Grant had never met Lowell before but found him very sympathetic and good company. Of course the previously agreed upon interview with ex-President Castelar was arranged.

But the most unusual event for the general was to witness from a window of the Hotel de Paris the attempt to assassinate the new King. Although the hotel was a considerable distance from the scene of the attack, it looked directly across the great central plaza and down the Calle Mayor. Young wrote: "The general, who was following with his eyes the progress of the Royal Cavalcade, which had just passed across the Puerta del Sol before him, said . . . that he clearly saw the flash of the assassin's pistol." The bullet did not reach the King.

From Madrid the party made a visit to the Escurial, then to Toledo, and finally to Lisbon, Portugal. From the river the city reminded them of Constantinople seen from the Bosporus, and the weather was like a Virginia spring. Of their stay in Lisbon, Mrs. Grant in later years remembered that:

> It was pleasant and full of interest. We were much pleased to meet and be entertained by their Majesties, King Louis and his beautiful Queen.
>
> The Queen, then only thirty-two years old, presented to me her two sons. Handsome youths, the eldest just sixteen and the other a year or two younger. The Queen looked more like the sister than the mother of the tall lads who leaned so lovingly over her chair. She was very lovely in her gown of rich mauve silk and her abundant beautiful hair, plaited in coils around her queenly head. This fair young creature was the daughter of Victor Emmanuel, King of Italy. I remember this reception by their Majesties of Gen. Grant, as a most brilliant one, the King and Queen being surrounded by a concourse of brilliant courtiers in rich uniforms and many fair women. As we were leaving the palace, after having been received by the King and his Queen, one of the gentlemen of the King's suite, came to the General and said: "General Grant, this is the birthday of the ex-King Ferdinand, King Louis' father, who would be gratified and pleased if you would call."
>
> The General said he was not only willing, but would be much pleased to

call. We were at once escorted to the ex-King's palace.

As we entered the drawing-room, we were met by a handsome, stately woman, who at once approached and taking the General's hand, said in the most charming manner, "General Grant, I am a countrywoman of yours, and I am so happy to welcome you to my house."

Just then, the ex-King entered and after welcoming us, said: "General Grant, let me present to you and Mrs. Grant, my wife, your countrywoman." [She was a Bostonian who had married Ferdinand after the death of his wife, the queen of Portugal. She was given the title of Contess d'Edla.]

We had a delightful call. The palace was full of beautiful things. The choicest and loveliest I saw while I was away. I remember particularly a kneeling figure by Thorwaldsen. It was so pure and chaste. I could not help admiring the lover king who abdicated his throne [he served as regent until his son, the heir to the throne, came of age] to enjoy the society of this truly beautiful woman. He showed me some finely decorated plates he was painting for her.

He was, I should think, about sixty-two or sixty-three years of age, and the lady was about ten years his junior. They were both handsome and happy with the prospect of many long years before them.

He had presented his wife with a beautiful palace, Cintra, about ten or fifteen miles out of the city, where we all made a lovely visit. This is one of the most beautiful palaces I remember, and like their residence in Lisbon, is overflowing with all that heart could desire.

We had the honor and pleasure of dining with King Louis and his Queen at the palace, when we met many of the court. King Louis conducted me to the table and I suppose General Grant escorted the Queen. They sat exactly opposite the King and myself. I enjoyed the dinner and especially the conversation of my interesting young host. I remember he was much interested and seemed to take great pride in the work he was then engaged upon, translating Shakespeare into his own language (Portuguese), a copy of which he presented to General Grant.

The ex-King Ferdinand was present at this dinner and when I inquired how the countess was, the dear kind old lover smiled and beamed like a boy of seventeen and exclaimed rapturously, "Is she not a darling?" Of course I assented, and she really was charming. From this dinner, we attended the Opera, where we again met King Louis and his Queen. She was of course dressed as she was at dinner, in a robe of rich white silk and such wonderful pearls adorned her slender throat.

We found Lisbon delightful and full of interest. I sent home a plane tree from Lisbon.

After visiting a few more days in Portugal, the Grant party went to Cordova, in Spain, and on to the quaint and beautiful city of Seville, where they arrived on the morning of December 4. The day after they arrived the Duke of Montpensier called on them and the following day entertained them in the hospitable halls and gardens of St. Telmo, his residence. The duke expressed his regrets that, because of the recent death of his daughter, Queen Mercedes, he could not give the general a more elaborate welcome.

The party's next stop was in Cádiz, a port on the coast, where they saw the remains of the Moorish occupation. The visitors were much impressed with the ringing of the many bells in the churches. The party left Cádiz on November 17 and proceeded to Gibraltar. As they approached Gibraltar they met the *Vandalia,* and the general had their steamer sail around her when they recognized Captain Robeson and many of their old friends. The party went ashore in a barge, and were met by the American consul and two officers of Lord Napier's staff. A guard of honor presented arms. General and Mrs. Grant drove directly to the house of the consul, Mr. Sprague, who had lived in Gibraltar for many years and was said to have been the oldest consular officer from the United States. General Grant was the third ex-President to be a guest in his house.

The commander of Gibraltar, Lord Napier, had telegraphed to Cádiz asking the general and his party to dinner on their first evening in Gibraltar. After a very fine banquet there was a review of the garrison and a sham battle, at which the general accompanied Lord Napier on horseback, while Lady Napier took Mrs. Grant in her carriage. The English bands, as a compliment to their distinguished visitor, played American tunes. Lord Napier was greatly pleased with the appearance and proficiency of his command, and he acknowledged to General Grant that he had never seen them do so well. The general examined them very closely and added: "I have seen most of the troops of Europe; they all seemed good. I liked the Germans very much, and the Spaniards only wanted good officers, so far as I could see, to bring them up to the highest standard; but these have something about them—I suppose it is their Saxon blood—which none of the rest possess; they have the swing of conquest."

According to Mrs. Grant's recollection, Lord Napier had sent them in an English revenue cutter to Málaga, as there was no commercial ship between the two ports. After spending one night in Málaga they started early for Granada and on arriving went to the Hotel Washington Irving. They visited the Alhambra, churches, and other places of interest, and she especially remembered their visit to the crypt which contains the remains of Ferdinand and Isabella. As she told the story:

The General and I had entered the church together. The others of our party passed on as I lingered to look at something. They entered the Crypt before us. So, entering last (and the General in advance of me), we were the last to leave,—as we could only move single file around the caskets lying side by side. I had reached the head of the caskets, the last visitor had passed out, the General was half way to the door, when I called to him, "Ulys, here are Ferdinand and Isabella." "Yes, I know," he said, "come on." "Oh no! let us linger a while, do! It was this woman who enabled Columbus to fit out his ships" [for the discovery of America]. The General here called: "Come! Come!" "Only think," I said, "they have been lying here side by side for nearly four hundred years. Let us stop and reflect." The General said: "Come on, or I will leave you and will shut the door after me." Of course, I went then, and he said to me, "I knew that threat would bring you."

But soon revenge was mine. Soon we entered a large room in which there were closets filled with church embroideries. The priest took a great deal of pleasure and pains in showing these to me. After seeing two or three, the General said more than once, "Come, they are all alike. Let us go on," and, "Now, have you not seen enough of them?" But no, to tease him, I exclaimed, "Oh no! they are all different and very beautiful."

I told the kind old priest how interested I had been in touching and seeing the casket containing the sacred remains of Ferdinand and Isabella; that every child in America knew the story of the jewel box of Isabella and of all she had done to aid the great navigator Columbus.

The priest was so pleased to hear this, that he asked: "Would you not like to see that little jewel box?" Of course I would, and the whole party moved into an inner room, this kind, good man leading the way. We all stood around until the casket was taken out of a doubly locked closet with iron doors.

It was silver, about eighteen inches long, eight or ten inches wide, and deep, with a rounding top or lid, and ornamented in repoussé. It was perfectly white and looked as though it had just come from Tiffany's.

The box was opened and I put my hand into its depths again and again, telling the party to do the same. The General was skeptical about a great deal he saw abroad and said to me in a whisper: "It looks very new."

Then the good priest asked if I would not like to see Queen Isabella's crown? Indeed! I would. He unlocked another dark chamber and brought forth the crown.

It was silver, but it looked like iron and perhaps it was. (Isabella was a stern and austere woman.) But there were no jewels in this crown and I was disappointed. He held it up a moment for me to see and smiling, said: "May I place this crown upon *your* head?" "Oh, yes," I said, bending low to receive the crown, which he placed on my head. And placing the sceptre in my hand, he said: "It is fitting that Queen Isabella's crown should rest upon the brow of America's first lady, if it is only for a brief moment."

I held the sceptre up and with an air of command, waved it towards the gentlemen, when Mr. Young, shading his mouth with his hand, said to me in a loud whisper, "I am going to telegraph to the New York Herald, that Mrs. Grant is here in Europe trying on crowns."

I at once asked the kind old priest to remove the crown, saying, "It is too heavy for my American head, too heavy."

After brief stops at Valencia and Barcelona, they then proceeded to Paris via Pau, where they learned (just before leaving) that Mrs. Abraham Lincoln was stopping there. They regretted very much they had not learned this sooner so that they could have made a call on her, but they had their tickets and a train scheduled, and a party going with them, and could not change their plans. The 36–38-hour trip to Paris was cold and uncomfortable.

Originally the Grants had not expected to go all the way around the world and include India, China, and Japan in their trip. This was partly because they did not believe they had funds enough to meet the expenses of such a long voyage. I have a vague recollection of a family understanding that the general had left something like $100,000 with his second son, Ulysses S. Grant, Jr., who was in business in New York, to take care of and if possible enhance. The young Ulysses, commonly known as "Buck," had become acquainted with a speculator in Wall Street named Ferdinand Ward, and with his counsel Buck had been able to double the $100,000, as related in family tradition. So when the Navy Department assigned the U.S.S. *Richmond,* ordered to the China station, to pick up the general and party in England and take them to visit India and China and Japan, it seemed evidently practicable that they continue their journey and return to the United States by San Francisco. This was naturally good news for the Grant party, but made the few days in Paris and London, waiting for the *Richmond,* very busy.

However, the general felt that he must make a visit to Ireland, even if it had to be much shorter than at first desired, and Mrs. Grant wanted to visit their daughter, Mrs. Nellie Sartoris, who had not been able to join them in Paris but was awaiting her mother's visit in her house in Southampton, with her infant son, Algernon Edward.

The general's trip to Ireland was very agreeable, if rushed a little, and he was received everywhere with great cordiality and popular applause. He found many veterans who had fought in the Civil War, some on one side and some on the other, but mostly on the Union side. The government of Cork indicated to the American representative there that they were not desirous of having Grant visit their city because of something he had said in some public statement which they thought prejudicial to the Catholic Church.

In Dublin he was welcomed and entertained by the lord mayor, who also saw the party off when it left on a Monday morning, January 6, 1879, for Dundalk. In spite of a storm, a very large and enthusiastic crowd had assembled to welcome the general there, and similarly large crowds cheered him on his way at Omagh, Strabane, Londonderry and other stations. He enjoyed a particularly warm reception in Belfast and then returned to Dublin, where he took a steamer to London and then proceeded to Paris. In Paris he picked up Mr. Borie, secretary of the navy in his first cabinet, Mrs. Grant, Colonel Frederick D. Grant, Dr. Keating, and Mr. Young. (Jesse had left the party to return to California and Hartog, the courier, was not to go to India.) The party went via Marseilles to board the *Labourdonnais,* an old-fashioned ship, not in the best of order but comfortable enough, which was to carry them safely as far as Alexandria.

Mr. Young records that the general seemed much pleased and somewhat relieved on finding that he was escaping a salute and reception, having no hands to shake and no speech to make and being able to sit in an ordinary railway car, en route to Suez, in conversation with General Stone, Mr. Borie, and the consul general. Generals Grant and Stone talked about the days at West Point, about friends, and about the new days, doubtless including the misfortunes that had fallen on their friend, the Khedive. Mr. Borie, who had not been with the party on its former trip through Egypt, looked longingly from the car to catch a glimpse of the Pyramids and questioned some of the party about the excursions they had made. They were late for India, and he realized they could not stop for him to get a better view of Egypt.

They stayed overnight in Suez, but the next morning the steamer which was to carry them to India had not arrived, having been blocked in the canal; but they were not forced to delay another night, as the steamer *Venetia* appeared about five in the afternoon. Everything was hurried on to the tender and as the sun went down they went on board, General Stone staying until the last moment to say good-by. The date was January 31, 1879.

The general's party, the only Americans on the *Venetia,* pre-empted an unoccupied space, about six feet square, behind the wheel in the stern, and they formed a group of their own. Here they could lounge and look out at the water, and even at night some members of the expedition could be found there. Mr. Young described the scene:

> Mrs. Grant sits back in a sea chair, wearing a wide-brimmed Indian hat, swathed in a blue silk veil. There is the sun to fight, and our ladies make themselves veiled prophetesses, and shrink from his presence. The General has fallen into Indian ways enough to wear a helmet, which shields the face. The helmet is girded with a white silk scarf, which falls over the neck. We all have helmets which we bought in Suez, but only wear them as fancy seizes us. Mr. Borie has one which cost him eight shillings, an imposing affair, but no persuasion has as yet induced him to put it on. Dr. Keating wears his so constantly that an impression is abroad that he sleeps in it. This, I fear, arises from envy of the Doctor, who takes care of himself, and comes out of his cabin every morning neat enough to stroll down Chestnut Street, and not, like the rest of us, abandoned to flannel shirts and old clothes and frayed cuffs and cracked, shiny shoes. The ship goes on in a lazy, lounging motion. Mrs. Grant looks out of her cloud of blue silk. She has brought up the interesting, never-failing question of mails. That is the theme which never dies, for you see there are boys at home, and if only boys knew the interest felt in their writings what an addition it would be to our postal revenues. Colonel Grant, curled up in a corner, is deep in *Vanity Fair.* The Colonel is assuming a fine bronzed mahogany tint, and it is suggested that he will soon be as brown as Sitting Bull. You see it is the all-conquering sun who is having his will upon us. I am afraid the General's complexion failed him years ago, in the war days, and I do not see that the sun can touch him further. But the rest of us begin to look like meerschaum in various degrees of hue. What shall we be when we reach India?

XVI

The Trip Around the World: India and the Far East

THE British Government had a rule that every vessel passing through the Red Sea with more than a limited number of first-class passengers must stop at Aden to insure the ship's having a clean bill of health. (More probably the rule was made to enable the government to scrutinize everyone entering Indian waters and to give the local government an income.) In any case, after a very hot voyage through the Red Sea, the *Venetia* reached Aden on February 6, but stayed only long enough to leave mail and take on supplies.

About 3 A.M., Colonel Grant and Mr. Young were aware of the fact that the engines had stopped and that coal was being taken on; the iron pipe for conveying the coal ran through their cabin and the noise made sleep impossible. Young went on deck and found Borie already there, prepared to go on shore as soon as the sun rose. This proved impossible because the ship was to sail at eight o'clock. As the dawn came over the sea and the darkness turned to gray, more passengers came on deck; the general appeared about sunrise. About eight the engines started, and the *Venetia* set her course for Bombay. During the voyage, the general's party had an opportunity to become better acquainted with the English passengers and to size up the sort of person England sent to govern her colonies. The Americans found them less reserved than Englishmen generally and with more of the shrewdness and energy of Americans.

Although the departure from Europe had been hurried and no notice had been sent by the party to Bombay, as soon as the *Venetia* entered the harbor there were evidences that the general had been expected. The ships in the harbor were dressed with flags, and there was a large crowd of soldiers, natives, and Europeans gathered on the wharf. As the new arrivals passed the English flagship a boat came alongside the *Venetia* with an officer representing Admiral Corbett to welcome the general. Soon another boat brought Captain Frith, military aide to Sir Richard Temple who was the governor of the Presidency of Bombay. He brought a letter from the governor welcoming the general to Bombay and offering him the use of the Government House at Malabar Point. Captain Frith further expressed Sir Richard's regrets that he could not be in Bombay to welcome the distinguished visitor in person because he was detained in Sinde by duties connected with the Afghan war. The American consul, Mr. Farnham, likewise came with a committee of American residents.

By nine o'clock the last farewells were spoken and the Americans took leave of the *Venetia.* They boarded the government yacht and landed at the Apollo Bunder, the very spot where the Prince of Wales had landed. As the yacht approached the shore they saw an immense crowd again lining the wharf and a company of Bombay volunteers in line. The general was met by Brigadier General Aitcheson, commanding the forces; Sir Francis Souter, commissioner of police; Mr. Grant, the municipal commissioner; and Colonel Sexton, commanding the Bombay volunteers. The latter presented arms, the band played the U.S. national anthem, and amid loud cheers from the Europeans present the general walked slowly with uncovered head to the state carriage. Escorted by Captain Frith and attended by an escort of native cavalry, the general and his party started for Government House at Malabar Point, which was to be their home while in Bombay.

Malabar Point is an edge of the Bombay island jutting out into the Indian Ocean, with a bluff overlooking the waters at a height of 100 feet. There was a battery of five large guns overlooking the sea and keeping guard over this part of the British Empire. Nearby were the ruins of a pagan temple which had been destroyed by the Portuguese years before. Government House was actually a group of buildings. The party went through gates and what seemed like porters' lodges of an English mansion, proceeded on an avenue bordered with mango trees and beds of flowers giving off a delicate fragrance, coming finally to a one-story house surrounded with spacious verandas. The state entrance was covered with red cloth, and an Indian guard at the foot was dressed in the usual English scarlet uniform. Servants lined both sides of the stairs. These were Mohammedans in long scarlet gowns, white turbans, and a belt with the imperial crown. The servants touched their foreheads and bent their heads low in token of welcome. Entering a hall and passing between two rooms—large, high, and decorated in blue and white—the party looked out upon the gardens below, with the sea beyond and the towers of Bombay in the distance. One of the rooms they passed was the state dining room, of a size to entertain fifty people; another room was the state drawing room. This house was used only for ceremonies and entertainment.

Passing on for a hundred paces under a covered way over a cement and stone path, through flower beds and palm trees, they came to another house where the principal bedrooms and private chambers were located. This house was also one story high and built so near the sea that from a balcony a biscuit could be thrown into the white surf. Here apartments were assigned to General Grant and his wife. There were drawing rooms, anterooms and chambers with high walls, and rugs and cool matting covering the floors. As the party passed in, the servants, who had been sitting crouched around on the floor, rose up and bowed. A little group of shoes was noticeable at the door; the custom of the country required those in service to take off their slippers before entering their master's house.

Another house about a hundred paces farther on, somewhat larger, contained guest chambers in which a part of the party would reside. Mr. Young was assigned quarters in a house still farther on, where he could write his story in sight and sound of the white surf breaking over the rocks.

What impressed Mr. Young and other members of the party was the tremendous number of servants on hand and how they would help at any possible opportunity. For instance, if one of the party walked from one house to another a servant would appear with an umbrella to hold over him and protect him from the sun. On one occasion Mr. Borie had to be rescued from the attentions of a native servant who was, with the best intentions in the world, trying to put buttons in his shirt in preparation for dinner. Mr. Borie was unable to make the native understand that this was something he would like to do for himself, until they found Captain Frith and persuaded him to explain to the servant.

Mr. Borie's bungalow was nicknamed "Tiger Hall," and the one in which Mr. Young was quartered had been given the name of "Cobra Castle," although he could not find any adequate cause for this gruesome name and he was inclined to attribute it to the colonel's imagination. Certainly Mrs. Grant had been duly warned about cobras, and when taking a bath she was horrified and badly frightened to see one coiled up in the corner of the room. She called for help in great fear and was much relieved when the servant who responded to her call discovered that what she had taken for a cobra was one of her stockings coiled up. Of course she had always been nearsighted, and this condition had become more pronounced with the years.

There were many signs of prosperity in Bombay and some of this was attributable to the American Civil War. An Englishman remarked, "It is odd that Bombay and General Grant should be face to face, for the general ruined Bombay." Then came the story of the cotton mania which raged during the Civil War. During the war India had exported $100,000,000 in cotton because the cotton of the Confederate South could not be shipped abroad in sufficient quantities. This great addition to the city's wealth engendered every form of speculation. Since the gambler never reasons, when the South again began shipping cotton the panic that followed the cutting off of the market ruined many of the commercial enterprises which had been established in the days of prosperity. Probably no city in the world was so prosperous as Bombay in 1865, but with the news of Lee's surrender the prosperity of Bombay collapsed. Thus the year 1865 meant a year of panic and bankruptcy for Bombay.

As some gentlemen who would like to have called on the ex-President belonged to castes whose religion imposed dietary habits differing from Europeans', a time was fixed after a state dinner for the general to receive callers, and great numbers took advantage of the invitation. This after-dinner reception closed the visit to Malabar Point. Young wrote of that visit:

> The attentions paid to the General and his party by the people of Bombay have been so marked and continuous that most of our time has been taken up in receiving and acknowledging them. What most interests us, coming fresh from Europe, is the entire novelty of the scene, the way of living, the strange manners and customs.

It was decided that the party would have to have some servants. Mr. Borie fell into the hands of an imposing man named Peter Marian, who was of a Christian Portuguese family and looked somewhat like General Burnside. Colonel Grant's servant was a boy with all the brightness and activity of youth but without much sense. He was known as Genghis Khan. Mr. Young's servant, whom he called Kassim (not his name but the nearest his master could get to it), was a serious middle-aged Hindu who spoke some English. He had a mania for packing and unpacking Mr. Young's portmanteau and apparently an aversion to papers and any form of manuscript, so that Mr. Young was constantly apprehensive that his notes and reports to the papers at home would be destroyed. The servants were paid a rupee a day, or about 40 cents in American money.

On leaving Bombay two sleeping cars were put at the disposal of the party, which arrived the next evening about nine o'clock at Icbulpur. Early the next morning they went by carriage on a picnic and to visit the famous white rocks. After a ten-mile drive they left the carriages and continued the journey on elephants over a bad road. The first elephant was covered with scarlet cloth and carried a platform which accommodated four people: General and Mrs. Grant, and two others. The rest of the party rode another elephant. Their progress took them near the Neirhedda, a sacred river believed to wash away the sins of the Hindu. They then took a small rowboat up the river, which cut through a marble hill. The steep sides of pure white marble, some sixty feet high in places, had an almost polished surface that alternated with ragged and cracked spaces. As they were leaving they were caught by a rainstorm which cooled things off and turned the dust into slippery mud. However, the trip back to the train was much more comfortable.

The next stop was at Allahabad, where they were greeted by colonial officials and the ruling prince of that part of the country. At first Mrs. Grant had mistaken the prince for a young lady, presumably because of his dress, he being radiant "in rose-colored trousers with a tunic and turban of fleecy gauze, bound and looped with bands of pearls." Later in the day he called on her dressed in a suit of black velvet knickerbockers with large diamond buttons. Later she learned that he was soon to be married and naturally asked if his intended bride was beautiful, to which he replied: "I hope so, but cannot tell as I've never seen her."

From Allahabad the party proceeded to Agra; they felt they must not leave the country without seeing the Taj Mahal, reputedly the most beautiful building in the world.

Mr. Borie, standing looking at the exquisite towers and marble walls, said: "It was worth coming to India to see the Taj." From a practical business man this was great praise.

When the party had been at Allahabad, an official impressed the general by his description of Jaipur and his high opinion of the Maharajah of Jaipur. So the schedule was modified to permit a brief digression to Jaipur, where they met the maharajah, whose official title was, His Highness Dhiraj Sewae, Sir Ram Singh Bahadur, Knight Grand Commander of the Most Exalted Order of the Star of India. He enjoyed a personal salute of twenty-one guns—the highest of any Indian prince—given only to those who have been submissive and loyal to England or who have rendered the Crown a distinguished service. He was commonly called Maharajah Ram Singh.

They returned to Agra by way of Bhurtpore, where they found a vast concourse of people assembled to meet the general, the Maharajah of Bhurtpore at their head. The prince was accompanied by the British officers attached to his court, and he advanced, shook hands with the general, and welcomed him to his capital. The maharajah looked older than his years, but this was often the case with Indian princes. He wore a blazing uniform covered with jewels, and had a firm stern face with strong features and a good frame, unlike his brother of Jaipur who gave his days to prayers and his evenings to billiards. The Maharajah of Bhurtpore was a soldier and a sportsman and was called a firm and energetic ruler, but he was very serious and unsmiling.

The general's party drove from the station to the palace, passing through bazaars and under a high archway into a courtyard. There was little to the palace except that it was very large and very uncomfortable, with odd decorations. The prince did not live there, and it gave the impression of being a sort of storeroom, in which the keepers had stored everything that came along. The maharajah lived in a palace more suited to Oriental tastes, where he had received the Prince of Wales in 1876. A meal had been prepared, and the prince left them to enjoy it in the company of their English friends. The rules of caste were very marked, and the partaking of food by an Indian ruler with persons of another caste or of another race was considered a defilement; but at the end of the American party's meal the prince returned in state and there were exchanges of good feeling between the maharajah and the general.

After the farewell ceremony the party drove to the station and after a ride of a few miles stopped to change to carriages, each drawn by two camels, that would take them to the ruins at Futtehpoor Sikra. This was the party's first experience with camels, about which they were not at all enthusiastic. They traveled for miles over the sandy plains and then came to a road parallel to a red stone wall which they followed until it was growing dark. Finally they turned into an enclosure and there were the ruins. The general was fortunate in making his way to the ruins without incident, but the carriage in which Mr. Young and others were riding was not so fortunate. Their animals seemed to have scruples of conscience about climbing the hill and stopped obstinately. "No inducement could move them," as Mr. Young reported.

The driver pronged them with his goad, called them names, adjured them by all the gods in the Hindoo mythology to make their way to Futtehpoor Sikra. There they stood. Perhaps under a severe pressure of the goad they would move a few paces and stop again. The camel is an imperturbable beast. He makes no display, shows no violent critical temper, does not jump or prance or resent the goading or the bad language. He moves his head to one side or the other, gives you an affectionate, imploring look, as though appealing to your sympathies, but does not move. He has gone beyond reason. He throws himself upon your generosity, but will not move. Here we were in India, on a lonely highway, the sun going down. Here the sun falls like a drop curtain at the play. There is no twilight. In an instant the sable clouds sweep over the earth and you are in darkness. To be belated on any road, hungry and dinner waiting, is disagreeable; but in India, with servants around you who do not know English, away from any town or village, on your way to a ruin, knowing that when night comes the lords of the jungle will come forth, was certainly not what we came to India to see. We tried all experiments to encourage the camels even to the extent of putting our shoulders to the wheels and urging them on. This had little effect, and we might have had a night bivouac on the highway if, after a long delay, the camels had not changed their minds, and, breaking into a speedy pace, carried us into the ruined city. The night had fallen, and the General, when we arrived, was strolling alone about the courtyard smoking his cigar.

The party the next morning walked around to see some tombs that were marvelously carved and covered with exquisite embroidered covers. They saw men jump from a wall 80 feet high, performing this stunt for a tip of one rupee. They were supposedly guides, but they had little or nothing to tell the visitors.

The ride back to Agra was very agreeable, and there the party made farewells to the pleasant people they had met on the previous visit. In the cool of the morning they left with the sound of booming cannon in their ears to go to Delhi. After a hot and uncomfortable ride, General and Mrs. Grant were conducted to Castle Ludlow, the home of Gordon Young, the chief officer, and others in the group were quartered in a hotel near the railway station.

There are probably few cities in the world that have had a more varied and changeable career than Delhi, going from years of splendor to those of destruction and back again. For the people of India it is what Rome was to the Christian world. Its splendor was greatest with the Mogul Empire, and in driving about one could observe, both from what they built and from what they destroyed, the severity of their creed. Passing out of the English section, the visitors were saddened by the sight of miles of ruins, the ruins of many wars and dynasties, a record of what was destroyed by the Turks in the twelfth century to what was destroyed by the English in the nineteenth. Even with the best disposition to restore the monuments and historic sights on the part of the rulers of India, this could hardly have been undertaken, even by a rich and generous government, because of the cost. It seemed at the time of the Grants' visit that the English authorities were quite properly more interested in spending available funds for irrigation and for relief of famines and poverty, than for the restoration of the ancient monuments and buildings.

W. C. Capper had been a fellow passenger on the *Venetia* and had pressed his invitation that the Grants visit him in Lucknow. He was chief judicial officer of the district and lived in a large, pleasant house in the English quarter. Lucknow had been the capital of the old kingdom of Oudh. It was annexed in 1856 by the East India Company under Lord Dalhousie, whose policy was "to persevere in the one clear and direct course of abandoning no just or honorable accession of territory or revenue, while all existing claims of rights are scrupulously respected." Lucknow is especially famous for its heroic defense by the handful of English residents against overwhelming forces of Sepoys in 1857. Capper had been one of the garrison during the siege, and he showed General Grant every point of military interest.

After arriving at Lucknow, and having a bath and a cup of tea, Mrs. Grant had fallen back on her bed utterly exhausted. Her maid called the general, who at once sent for a doctor. The latter after his examination assured them both that the patient was only suffering from extreme fatigue. She needed a rest and could not attend the banquet and ball that night.

After the general and doctor left her, as she recalled in later years, she said to the maid: "I am very, very ill and they do not know it, and I wish to tell you this before it is out of my power to do it, and if the worst happens say to General Grant that I told you to tell him that if I died here, under no consideration was he to take me home. It was my wish to be buried right here at Lucknow." The maid protested that she did not think her mistress so ill but she promised to do as asked. Mrs. Grant was wont to explain that she did not want to mar the pleasure of the little party and she thought of what a nightmare the taking of her remains home would be to them, and so made her wish imperative. But of course the next morning she appeared at breakfast as usual.

When the Grants and their entourage left the city, a hundred elephants in gorgeous trappings were lined up along the road, and at the command of the head mahout they all raised their trunks high in the air in salute as the party passed.

The Grants now went to the holy city of Benares. The city is as sacred to both Buddhists and Hindus as Mecca to the Moslems and Jerusalem to Christians and Jews. British rule had given the Indians an opportunity to rebuild monuments the Mohammedan invaders had destroyed, and now the city fairly teemed with pilgrims. The streets were so narrow that only in the widest could an elephant make his way.

The party ascended the steps of a very beautiful temple, much gilded. (All the temples, wells, shrines, and streams—indeed, the city itself—were governed by priests.) The court, the temple, and the steps were crowded with people. The visitors entered and passed by the shrine near which stood a very handsome young man, who seemed to be exhorting the people to some greater enthusiasm. This young priest was a Brahman and as the party approached he held up a wreath of marigolds, strung on a thread, and offered it to Mrs. Grant's Indian escort, who with some show of scorn refused it. The young priest's handsome countenance changed its expression to that of a demon; but Mrs. Grant smiled and leaned forward and motioned that she would like to have one. His face lighted up and he placed two of the pretty wreaths about her neck. The wreaths became objects of interest to the sacred cows, who came up and nibbled at them, causing many kind smiles to fall on her as it was considered a good omen. She had been a little startled at the near approach of these cows, but the other women around showed by their expression that there was no reason to fear and, throwing their white scarves around the necks of the creatures, drew them away quietly and caressingly.

They also visited some of the temples built on the Ganges and watched the pilgrims bathe in the sacred waters, "prince and pauper side by side." They returned home when they began to feel the heat and found the piazza filled with people offering meats, fruits, vegetables, sugar, coffee, tea, spices and confections of the country. As always, the gifts were received with much ceremony and after the donors departed the foodstuffs were turned over to the servants of the house in which the Grants were guests.

The general had received an invitation from the viceroy to visit him in Calcutta, and the Grant party arrived there from Benares on the morning of March 10, 1879. The American consul general, General Litchfield, the aide-de-camp of the viceroy, and a guard of honor of Bengal troops escorted them to Government House. The streets had been watered and there was just a suspicion of a cool breeze from the Hoogly River. Policemen lined the two-mile route from the railway station to the door of Government House, a large, ornate building standing in an open park. Its cornerstone was laid about the time that Washington laid the cornerstone of the U.S. capitol. The mansion was designed to resemble the country house of Lord Scarsdale in Derbyshire.

The viceroy of India was Lord Lytton, better known to Americans as the poet Owen Meredith. He received General Grant with great cordiality and said in greeting him that he was honored to receive a gentleman whose career he had followed with respect and interest, and that it was especially agreeable to receive one who had been chief magistrate of the country in which he had spent some of his happiest years. (Lord Lytton was referring to his years in Washington as a member of the British Legation when his uncle, then Sir Henry Bulwer, was British minister. He had himself later been British minister.)

Each day brought its banquet, picnic, tour, and different guests. The

Indian princes, as Mrs. Grant remembered, looked magnificent in their flowing robes of soft, silken texture and their beautiful jewels. Lady Lytton was very charming, and "spirituelle in her beauty." At a state dinner General and Mrs. Grant met members of leading Indian native families. After dinner Lord Lytton escorted Mrs. Grant to the reception room. The hall was already filled with a brilliant and picturesque assembly of leading natives, princes, and merchants, who gave the affair the look of a fancy-dress ball. The son of the King of Oudh was there. (The King lived in Calcutta on a British allowance of $600,000 a year as compensation for the 1856 annexation of Oudh. He did not go near Government House, partly because he was so fat that he could not move around.) A young prince and princess from Burma were also present, their king having taken to evil ways, including, it was said, the murder of his relations. According to report he also threatened to kill the British resident in Mandalay, and the British sent a force of troops to protect the resident. In his book Young ventures to question whether this report was not just the usual introductory accusation which so often preceded the taking over of an area desired by the British. The Princess made friends with Mrs. Grant and they spent a part of the evening together.

The party had found Calcutta more European than any city they had yet seen in the East, perhaps because of its use by the English as the capital. The party had to leave rather hurriedly. They received word that the *Richmond,* which they had expected to meet at Ceylon, had not yet passed through the Suez Canal. The general was disappointed by this news, because he had hoped to visit Ceylon and Madras, having a pressing invitation from the Duke of Buckingham, who was governor of Madras, as well as from the governor of Ceylon. But to have waited for the steamer would have prolonged the party's stay for many days, and the general did not want to trespass further on his hosts, who had been so hospitable and courteous to him. Therefore, hearing that the steamer *Simla* was to sail for Burma within a few hours, it was decided that the party would take it and visit Rangoon.

In a letter dated Rangoon, March 20, to his brother-in-law, the Rev. Michael J. Cramer, General Grant summarized his impressions of India in the following words:

> I have been very much pleased with English rule and English hospitality in India. With that rule two hundred and fifty millions of uncivilized people

are living at peace with each other, and are not only drawing their subsistence from the soil but are exporting a large excess over imports from it. It would be a sad day for the people of India and for the commerce of the world if the English should withdraw.

The *Simla* proved very comfortable, and Mrs. Grant enjoyed the luxury of a bathroom connected with her stateroom, and the easy chairs under the heavy awnings on deck. The steamer trip provided an opportunity for relaxation and the exchange of views and opinions among members of the party. Mr. Young kept a careful record of General Grant's statements about persons and public affairs. Some of these were published, with the General's permission, in various American newspapers and in Mr. Young's book, *Around the World with General Grant*. "There are few men," Mr. Young wrote, "more willing to converse on subjects on which he is acquainted than General Grant. The charm of his talk is that it is never about anything that he does not know, and what he does know he knows well. He is never vindictive, and never gossips, and when referring to men and things in his eventful career seems passionless and just."

The party arrived in Rangoon on March 19 and found all the shipping in the harbor dressed in English and American flags and bunting, as was the little *Simla*. The British commissioner and the American vice consul came aboard to welcome them. They drove to Government House, a handsome and commodious residence in a forest of trees and flowers. Here the Grants were given a banquet and reception. They were also entertained with a banquet and ball at the American consulate.

In Rangoon the Hindu civilization and customs were behind them; they now encountered the Chinese. Chinese signs were on the houses, Chinese workmen were in the streets, and there were shops where one could smoke opium. While politically Burma was part of the British Empire, it was commercially an outpost of China. The influence of that country was to follow the Grants until they reached Japan.

Streets were wide, rectangular, and shaded with trees. From a distance a pagoda, one of the most famous in Asia, was visible on a hill, which signaled to the party that they had left India, the land of Brahma, and had come to the land of Buddha.

The prosperity of Burma at the time of the general's visit impressed him. There was an enormous rice crop; tobacco, betel nut, and banana were also successful crops. Considering the good sanitary regulations and the low cost of labor, Burma seemed to be a fine example of the wisdom and excellence of British administration. In addition there was trade in rubies, sapphires, gold, and silver. But the general was disturbed by the fact that the United States had practically no commerce here and no place in the markets they were visiting. He thought this was well worth considering by U.S. trade authorities. He believed that the strengthening of the American Consular Service would help stimulate trade between the Far East and the United States.

On leaving Rangoon the Grants crossed to the little town of Moulmein, stayed briefly, and then sailed on to Penang in what is now Malaysia. The general with some of the party and an escort of honor went up a mountain to a reception and dinner given by the government. Mrs. Grant had refused to go with them, but they had hardly left when the wife of the chief justice came on board the ship and insisted that she should go and stay all night with her. The next morning the visitors rode over the island among nutmeg orchards and coconut trees growing in forests.

The Chinese community also gave General Grant a reception. In the speech of welcome he was asked why America refused the same home and liberty to Chinese immigrants that she offered to the rest of the world. The general diplomatically replied: "It is true, the United States have made laws discouraging immigration from China, the Chinese immigrants are sent by contract and become, as it were, slaves for the time being. You must remember the great struggle the United States has just passed through in which so much precious blood and treasure were lost, to wipe out slavery. You must not, therefore, expect the United States to tolerate even temporary slavery on her shores." This speech pleased his wife immensely and was remembered by her as the best speech she ever heard him make.

From Penang their next stop was Malacca, where the general was met by the naval commander and driven to see some ruins, but Mrs. Grant did not accompany him. Finally, they arrived at Singapore. The party's stay there was full of engagements for dinners, receptions, and garden parties, and included a delightful trip to Johore where they were entertained by the maharajah at his residence in a charming manner. He also gave them a dinner at his city residence in Singapore.

There was some mistake as to the time the *Richmond* would arrive for them, and they were delayed at Singapore longer than expected.

Having received an invitation to visit the King of Siam, it was decided that this could be accepted and they could still be back in time for the *Richmond,* so the general engaged a ship to take them to Siam on the morning of April 14. On coming ashore in Bangkok, the Grant party was received with great ceremony by the minister of foreign affairs and a brilliant retinue, then driven to the Suranrom Palace, the home of His Royal Highness the Celestial Prince (and the King's brother).

At that time Siam had two sovereigns: a first King who did everything and whose power was absolute; and a second King who appeared to do nothing except draw a large income. Interestingly enough the second King was named George Washington by his father, who admired the Americans. His Majesty (the first King) had taken the deepest interest in the general's visit and wished to do special honor to him.

As the party had driven past the artillery barracks the artillery was drawn up in battery and fired a 21-gun salute. As they reached the palace another guard was drawn up, and a band played the American national anthem. (Earlier they had been serenaded by "Hail Columbia.") At the gate of the palace the foreign minister again met the general and escorted him to the door. At the head of the marble steps stood the Celestial Prince, in full dress regalia, with members of the household. He advanced and shook hands with the general and offered his arm to Mrs. Grant, leading the party to the great audience chamber. Here the rest of the party met the prince, a young man of about twenty with a clear, expressive face, who spoke English well enough but during the interview spoke Siamese which was translated by a royal interpreter. The prince regretted the weather, which was untimely and severe, but it would be a blessing to the country and the people—a blessing of rain which General Grant had brought with him to Siam. He added that this palace was the general's home, and he had been ordered by the King, his brother, to say that anything in the kingdom that would contribute to the happiness, comfort, or the honor of General Grant was at his disposal. The general responded in appreciation and delight with the cordiality of his welcome, and said he would have been greatly distressed not to have seen Siam. The prince then offered his arm to Mrs. Grant and escorted her and the general to their apartments while the members of his suite assigned the remainder of the party to the quarters they were to occupy. That evening the general and party dined quietly with the prince. The program for the entertainment of the party was discussed, and as there were only five days for Bangkok, one or two dinners were eliminated and the visits to temples and to see the white elephants were concentrated into one day.

The next morning the ex-Regent of Siam called, a venerable nobleman and foremost in influence and authority in the realm. He was a friend and counselor of the late King and governed the kingdom during the minority of the then present sovereign. Due to his influence, His Majesty's accession was secured without question or mutiny, and he had become chief of the Council of State and governor of several provinces. When the call of the ex-Regent was returned, he placed the general on his right and had the other members of the party sit about him on chairs. He was a grave person who showed honor by speaking slowly, saying little, and making pauses between his statements. Rapid and flippant speech was not indulged in and a gay, easy talker would give offense. This was in accord with the general's habits and left him in an advantageous position.

It was said that in Siam there were four persons to mark: the first King, the second King, the ex-Regent and the British consul general. Colonel Grant and Mr. Young made a formal call on the second King, a gentleman of much intelligence, and an informal call after the exchange of visits of ceremony. The second King said that he concentrated his attention and time on study and science, having time enough for the most abstruse calculations. He nevertheless seemed somewhat tired and perhaps bored, and when the visitors took their leave he asked them to come again to see him, wished them a happy journey home, and requested them to accept a couple of ivory boxes and a cup and saucer he made as souvenirs of their visit.

The real King was in his twenty-fifth year and had ascended the throne eleven years before on the death of his father. The latter had been a distinguished and able man, and first opened Siam to the outside world by treaties with other countries. He had learned the English language and wrote it fluently; he had taught his sons English, had opened embassies in France and England, and sent young Siamese noblemen to be educated in England. Evidently it was a result of this policy that the noblemen who attended General Grant spoke English. The King himself and the princes always spoke Siamese at the official audiences, but in private conversation the King spoke English as fluently as his interpreter.

The Grant party had their official audience with the King on April 14 at three o'clock. The band in the courtyard played the national air, and as the general came to the head of the stairs the waiting King, wearing a magnificent jeweled decoration, advanced and shook the general's hand in the warmest manner. Then shaking hands with Mrs. Grant, he offered her his arm and walked into the audience hall. As they entered the hall, the King paused before a marble bust and, pointing to it, said to Mrs. Grant: "Do you recognize it?" "Of course I do," she answered, "it is General Grant. Where did you get it?" To which the King rejoined, "I had it made in Paris and I had the model destroyed so that no one could have one just like it." When they passed on into the second salon, the King led her to a sweet-looking little lady and said, "My consort." The two ladies shook hands and the King's wife led Mrs. Grant to a sofa where they settled themselves. Then an attendant entered bearing a salver on which were several Siamese curios and specimens of fine Siamese work. There was a toilet set in pure gold for a lady. This Her Majesty presented to Mrs. Grant, who thought the set extraordinarily beautiful. The King handed to the general a gold cigar case and to Colonel Grant a bowl of cigars.

The King returned the general's visit on April 15 by going in state to the palace Grant was living in. They were told that this was a most unusual honor and was intended as the highest compliment His Majesty could bestow. Long before the hour the space in front of the Suranrom palace was filled with curious Siamese and Chinese, heedless of the rain and waiting to gaze upon the King's celestial countenance. As the hour of the visit approached there was a bustle of preparation. First a guard formed from the palace gate to the porch; then a band appeared at the rear of the inner guard; then attendants carrying staves in their hands to clear the street and give warning that the King was coming and that the street must be vacated by all. Then came a squadron of royal bodyguard in scarlet uniforms under command of a royal prince. The King sat in a carriage alone, on the back seat, with two princes sitting on the front seats.

The prince who was the general's host and the members of his household were dressed in state garments, the Prince wearing a coat of purple silk. To balance all this gorgeousness as far as they could, the general and his party wore evening dress. When the trumpets announced the arrival of the King, the general, accompanied by the prince, the members of his household, and the Americans, came to the foot of the stairs. Colonel Grant, wearing his uniform of lieutenant colonel, went to the gate to receive the King in his father's name. Dressed simply, the King wore the decoration of Siam. At the meeting the King and the general talked for about an hour. Among other subjects, the question of opium and the emigration of Chinese to America were discussed. The King regretted that the opium habit was spreading among his people and the general urged him, among other things, to send young men to study in American schools. His Majesty announced that he thought of sending a special embassy to America. At the end of the conversation the King rose and walked hand in hand with the general to the foot of the stairs, the band played the national air, cavalry formed in line, the princes and high officers walked to the carriage door and the King drove off to his palace.

The next evening there was a state dinner at the King's palace. The prince escorted Mrs. Grant, and she found him handsome as well as fun. He turned to her and said: "Madam, I wish you to know how much we appreciate this visit from General Grant, and how honored we are to hear him speak." The King conducted General Grant to the table and he and Mrs. Grant sat next to him. From the distance came Thai music, which Mrs. Grant found delightful. After three hours at the table they assembled in the audience hall again and Mrs. Grant was taken to an inner room where once more she met the young Queen. Mrs. Grant fastened on the Queen's wrist a little gold and enamel bracelet, in the form of a serpent, which she told the Queen was a fine specimen of American workmanship. She also asked her to accept a little crystal and gold watch, one of those in which the works are visible and which Mrs. Grant had been wearing and thought rather unusual. The Queen was much pleased and Mrs. Grant hung it on her sash.

The party returned to Singapore on April 22. The general, disappointed at the nonarrival of the *Richmond,* decided to take passage on the French ship the *Irrawaddy,* for Saigon and Hong Kong.

While steaming up the Saigon River the general, and some others were sitting in a group near Mrs. Grant when she heard a snap and felt an unusual shiver of the ship. She started up and exclaimed: "Did you hear that, and feel the motion?" No one had heard it and the suggestion was made to her that she should not get excited; she insisted that they should tell the captain something was broken; but, no, it was not their business . . . the captain would find it out if anything was wrong. Presently about thirty men came running up on deck with axes and began cutting and splitting the vessel's deck, and the mammoth ship began to stagger and plunge like a drunken animal. For a while there was some confusion, and Mrs. Grant got much satisfaction out of pointing out to the gentlemen that she had been right in knowing that something had broken. The ship's rudder chain had snapped asunder; but it was soon remedied and they proceeded on their way.

The next morning they drove through Saigon, returned to the ship to rest, and left for a large dinner and reception, after which they went back to the *Irrawaddy*. The following morning they were off again into the China Sea. As they turned toward Hong Kong the weather grew cooler. At the Crown Colony Governor and Mrs. Pope Hennessy met the party and took them to their house, where they did everything to make their visit agreeable. Dinners, receptions, and garden parties were given for them, and there were many very pleasant drives.

On May 5 they went aboard the U.S. ship *Ashuelot* to go to Canton, where they spent four very social days before sailing on May 9 to Macao, where they passed one day before returning to Hong Kong. Governor Hennessy gave the General a banquet that night and at the close of it made a speech in which he pointed with pride to the fact that during our Civil War two men so diverse in person and disposition and party connections as John Bright and Benjamin Disraeli were sagacious enough to know that their own country and the welfare of the world were bound up in the cause for which General Grant was then contending.

After leaving Hong Kong, the Grant party cruised along the coast of China, in very pleasant circumstances, so far as winds and waves were concerned. While there was a monsoon blowing, it was only just enough to help them along. Their next stop was Swatow where the Chinese governor called in state and said he had orders to pay all possible attention to General Grant. As it was the custom of the country to bring an offering in making these calls, and as nothing could be more useful than food, he had brought a live sheep, 6 chickens, 6 ducks, and 4 hams. While the governor was in conference with the general the animals remained outside, but there was nothing for the general to do but accept the offering and present it to the servants.

Amoy was another treaty port open to foreign trade, and the Grants were entertained there before steaming on to Shanghai, which they approached on May 17. When their ship came in sight of the Woosung forts, 21 guns were fired in welcome. Chinese gunboats joined the chorus and the vessel returned the salutes. The party had arrived a little ahead of time, and the American man-of-war *Monocacy,* dressed from stem to stern, steamed toward them and when a cable's length away dropped anchor. A boat was dispatched carrying the American consul to China, Mr. D. W. Bailey, who presented the members of a committee, consisting of Messrs. Little, Forbes, Helland, Purden, and Hübbe, and Mrs. Little and Mrs. Holcombe who had come to meet Mrs. Grant. The committee lunched with the general, and about half past one the general's ship slowly steamed up to the city of Shanghai, greeted by fired salutes, a throng of some 100,000, and a formal welcoming party.

The next day, a Sunday, General Grant attended services in the cathedral. Monday was passed visiting a dairy farm, roaming the city, and making a few calls. In the evening the party dined with Mr. and Mrs. Little and afterward went to a reception and witnessed the beautiful illumination and torchlight procession from windows and balconies. Almost every house was illuminated, and words of welcome were seen on most of them and thousands of lanterns lighted up the darkness. "China," as Mrs. Grant remembered, "the land of pyrotechnics, entirely overwhelmed us with its great display that night. I can not do justice to this ovation. It was simply grand!"

On the advice of a physician, Mr. Borie sailed for home May 21, as it was getting hot. The rest of the party remained for a few days more at Shanghai and on May 24 left for Peking, the capital. At Tientsin the party was met by the famous viceroy, Li Hung-chang, probably the most eminent man in China, whom his admirers generally called "the Bismarck of Asia." He seemed to have conceived a very special admiration for General Grant, which gradually developed almost into affection. With some pride he told the general that the two of them had conquered and put down the two most violent and dangerous revolutions in history, Li Hung-chang having suppressed the Taiping Rebellion, which had been almost contemporaneous with the U.S. Civil War. As a result he was a nobleman with the rank of earl, grand secretary of state, guardian of the heir-apparent, head of the War Office and of the Chinese Armies, and director of the coast defenses. Finally, he was in command of the province which guarded the road to Peking, the most honorable viceroyalty in the empire. Li was an imposing personality, over six feet tall with keen eyes, a large head, and a wide forehead.

Young wrote of Li and Grant:

> Between the General and the Viceroy friendly relations grew up, and while we were in Tientsin they saw a great deal of each other. The Viceroy said at the first meeting that he did not care merely to look at General Grant and make his formal acquaintance, but to know him well and talk with him. As the Viceroy is known to be among the advanced school of Chinese statesmen, not afraid of railways and telegraphs, and anxious to strengthen and develop China by all the agencies of outside civilization, the General found a ground upon which they could meet and talk. . . . During his stay in China, wherever the General has met Chinese statesmen he has impressed upon them the necessity of developing their country, and of doing it themselves. No man has ever visited China who has had the opportunities of seeing Chinese statesmen accorded to the General, and he has used these opportunities to urge China to throw open her barriers, and be one in commerce and trade with the outer world.

The journey upstream to Peking, about 150 miles from Tientsin, had to be made in small flatboats and it took considerable preparations to hire and equip such a flotilla. The general's boat had two cabins and a dining room; their cooking was done in another vessel. The journey was primitive and simple but Mrs. Grant rather enjoyed it, although she discovered reflected in the mirror, when she was doing her hair, three smiling eager faces that seemed almost at her shoulder. They disappeared as soon as she turned but soon reappeared again, apparently eager to see how an American lady did her hair. Mrs. Grant frightened them away with a flourish of her hairbrush, and learned later that they lived in the lower deck of the boat.

On their arrival at the head of the Pei Ho River they left the boats and began the overland journey. The general rode a fine horse, and Mrs. Grant had a palanquin. It was very light and cool, and when she took her seat the maid brought her two bottles of claret. When they had gone about halfway, a halt was made. The men were gray with dust and red from the heat. They came to Mrs. Grant and were astonished to find her quite comfortable and free of dust. And they were more than happy when she produced her two bottles of claret and stipulated only a single draught for herself.

After a long weary ride they reached the gates of Peking, which was surrounded by very high and very wide walls. The party soon noticed that the people in Peking were larger and taller than those in Canton and Shanghai; that the streets were wide, unpaved, and very dusty; and that the American flag was floating over the legation, where they would be staying.

Inevitably there was a discussion as to whether the Emperor in person could grant an audience to the distinguished visitor. Because of the Emperor's youth (he was seven) audiences had for some time been postponed, but there seems to have been some feeling on the part of a foreign representative that a point should be made of obtaining an audience for the general. However, he was not one to ask favors of this kind and the matter was settled by the general's having an audience with Prince Kung, Prince Regent of the Empire. Grant and his party were received by Prince Kung, who chatted and then invited his guests to lunch. The luncheon comprised dishes of soups, sweetmeats, sharks' fins, roast ducks, bamboo sprouts, bird's-nest soup, and a hot, insipid tipple made of rice, "tasting like a remembrance of sherry," which was poured into small silver cups. Neither the general nor the prince was hungry, and the former soon lighted a cigar, while the prince toyed with the dishes as they came and went and then smoked a pipe.

The prince was of middle stature with a sharp, narrow face and high forehead. He had been head of the Chinese Government since the English invasion and the burning of the summer palace, and as the only prince who had remained at his post at that time it devolved upon him to negotiate the peace, which gave him a certain European celebrity and experience that was an advantage. The European powers had gladly kept him in power, and he had shown courage and ability.

Prince Kung was punctual in returning General Grant's call, and the general invited several officers of the *Richmond,* who happened to be in Peking on a holiday, as well as those of the *Ashuelot,* to assist in receiving the prince. As soon as they had all been presented the party moved into the dining room and sat around the table garnished with tea, sweetmeats and champagne. Prince Kung then stated that China had never been more fairly treated than by America during the Administration of General Grant, and General Grant responded: "We believe that fair play, consideration for the rights of others, and respect for international law will always command the respect of nations and lead to peace. I know of no other consideration that enters into our foreign relations. There is no temptation to the United States to adventures outside of our own country."

Prince Kung then said China had one question pending with Japan. If he could secure the general's good offices or advice in the matter, a solution of benefit to all nations of the East might result. The question concerned sovereignty of the Loochoo (or Ryukyu) Islands. These islands had for many years been a kingdom paying tribute to China and recognized as a part of the Chinese Empire; but they had been seized by Japan with the evident intention of absorbing them into the Japanese Empire. Kung would not have mentioned it except for the fact that the viceroy of Tientsin had written to him about the kind and sympathetic manner in which the general had listened to his statement on the subject, that he was now going to Japan as a guest of the people and the Emperor and would have opportunities to present the views of China to the Japanese Cabinet. The prince averred that Loochoo had recognized the sovereignty of China as far back as the Ming Dynasty, but the King of the islands had been taken to Japan and his sovereignty extinguished. The Japanese would not discuss the question, either with their minister in Peking or with the Chinese minister in Tokyo. Would General Grant help?

The general pointed out that he was only a traveler seeing sights and looking at new manners and customs, but he would upon going to Japan take pleasure in informing himself on the subject and conversing with the Japanese authorities. He did not know what their argument would be, and of course they had an argument. He did not suppose that the rulers were inspired by a desire to wantonly injure China, but he would inform himself fully on the Chinese side and also learn what he could of the Japanese side. The general referred to the arbitration between Great Britain and America on the "Alabama Claims" as an example for China and Japan to follow. "That arbitration between nations may not satisfy either party at the time," he said, "but it satisfies the conscience of the world, and must commend itself, as we grow in civilization more and more as the means of adjusting international disputes."

When the prince and general had finished their discussion, Prince Kung, speaking to the translator Mr. Holcombe, said he wished again to express to the general the honor felt by the Chinese Government at having received this visit. He made special inquiries as to when the general would leave, the hour of departure, the ways and periods of his journey, and asked if there was anything wanting to complete the happiness of the general or show the honor in which he was held by China. The general rose and returned the prince's good wishes and thanked him. The prince entered his chair and was snatched up and carried away by his bearers, the guard of honor hurriedly mounting and riding after him.

On one of their tours the party climbed the wall that surrounded the city and looked upon the yellow roofs and domes of the buildings of the Imperial Palace from a distance. The Imperial Palace was a sacred enclosure forbidden to all except those in immediate attendance on the Emperor. It covered a large area of ground and as seen from the wall appeared a green, inviting place and, from the number of yellow-roofed buildings, the home of a large retinue. The travelers also visited the Temple of Heaven, one of the most important monuments in China and one that is usually closed to the outside world. However, it seemed that most of those whom the party met in Peking had made their way into the sacred enclosure by climbing over the wall and acquiring the friendship of the guard by a judicious use of money. But in this case the government sent a mandarin and escort to open the sacred portals for the general's party, the first time that such a compliment had been paid to any foreigner.

General Grant and his party left Peking for Tientsin and reached that city at daybreak on June 12. Breakfast had not been finished before a message was received from the viceroy stating that he was on his way to meet the general. When the viceroy stepped out of his chair, the general advanced to meet him and welcomed him. Together they passed into an inner room, and Li Hung-chang repeated his and Prince Kung's arguments for the general's intervention in the matter of the Loochoo Islands. The general assured the viceroy that he would, if possible, confer with the Japanese authorities on reaching Japan. If the matter reached a point where it appeared that he could advise or aid in a peaceful solution, he would be happy to do what he could, as he had assured Prince Kung.

The night before they left Tientsin, Lady Li Hung-chang, the viceroy's wife, gave a dinner for Mrs. Grant which was a great and unusual honor. Mrs. Grant remembered that there were six American women invited—Mrs. and Miss Denny, Mrs. and Miss Dillon, a missionary lady who interpreted for them, and herself. The ladies assembled at the consulate where the viceroy's chairs were sent to convey them to his palace. Mrs. Grant's chair was the first to arrive at the viceroy's. The bearers ascended a few steps and, amidst a great flourish of trumpets, her chair was placed on the stone floor of the grand vestibule. As she stepped out of it the door near her rolled back and a Chinese lady and her attendant stood before Mrs. Grant, the usher simply saying "Lady Li" and "Madame Grant."

Lady Li took her hand and welcomed her in a dignified but cordial manner. She then took her guest's arm and, with her attendant walking on the other side, walked through a long corridor to the library where a teapot, cups, and saucers of dainty blue china were laid out on a simple table of natural wood. The library was also in plain wood, the shelves and upright pieces all being of the same wood as the table, without either lacquer or varnish. The books were in rolls like manuscript, tied with dark silk cords. The polished floor was covered by a rug of soft white matting. The appointments were exquisitely elegant and simple. When Mrs. Grant had finished her cup of tea, Lady Li took her by the hand and led her into the drawing room where the other ladies of the party had assembled. They met a daughter and daughter-in-law of Lady Li. The Chinese ladies were dressed in the costumes of their country: long jackets, very beautifully embroidered, and skirts of rich material. Their hair was elaborately dressed.

In the dining room the table setting was similar to those Mrs. Grant was accustomed to in her own country. In addition it was handsomely decorated with many flowers, and at each place there was a variety of glasses and porcelain plates filled with nuts, which the Chinese ladies were constantly nibbling between courses, a custom which had the cordial approval of the Americans. A course of European food and cooking alternated with a course of Chinese food. As a compliment to her hostess, Mrs. Grant partook only of the Chinese courses. The bird's-nest soup was served in a small bowl, and was so delicious that she ate the whole of hers and was entirely satisfied. Madame Li was astonished when she proposed to drink the health of her visitor in a glass of sparkling champagne and found that her visitor merely tasted it. She turned to the missionary lady and said she had wished to drink her guest's health, to which Mrs. Grant said: "Yes, I knew that and fully understood her and acknowledged her compliment by tasting her delicious wine." Lady Li said: "I have been told that it is the custom to take a full glass when one's health is drunk." To which Mrs. Grant replied, laughing: "Oh, no, that is not the case. What I did is our custom. If we finished the glass I am afraid we should stay all night."

After dinner Miss Dillon and Miss Denny played on the piano and sang a few ballads and even waltzed. While this was going on, a handsome young son of the viceroy entered the drawing room. He wore a long, pale blue silk gown, which was very becoming, and his hair hung down his back in a long single plait.

Mrs. Grant thought it time for them to say their adieus. Farewells were cordially exchanged and wishes expressed that they might meet again. On arriving home they found, as a souvenir of their visit to Lady Li, a roll of pretty china silk for each lady.

The Grant party left their friends that night at the consulate and went aboard their ship, which early in the morning weighed anchor and steamed down the Pei Ho to the blue waters of the China Sea. They followed the coast as far as the end of the Great Chinese Wall, which they reached about noon. All went ashore.

The Chinese wall has long been a curiosity, known for its great length and for its purpose: to protect China from the Mongolian people to the north. It was built in the third century B.C., and it took over fifteen years for all the labor power of the empire, mostly convict, to complete it. When the Grant party visited it, parts had begun to crumble.

By five o'clock the same afternoon the party was under way again on a dead calm ocean. By early morning they had reached Chefoo, a port and summer watering-place for European residents of Shanghai and Tientsin. After the usual tumultuous reception and warm hospitality, their brief visit ended and they bade China farewell and sailed toward Japan.

By way of comment on the Chinese tour, General Grant said:

> My own visit has . . . been under the most favorable circumstances for seeing the people and studying their institutions. My impression is a very favorable one. The Chinese are enduring, patient to the last degree, industrious, and have brought living down to a minimum. By their shrewdness and economy they have monopolized nearly all the carrying trade, coastwise, of the East, and are driving out all the other merchants. Through India, Malacca, Siam, and the islands from the shores of Africa to Japan, they are the mechanics, market gardeners, stevedores, small traders, servants, and in all callings that contribute to material progress. The Chinese are not a mili-

tary power, and could not defend themselves against even a small European power. But they have the elements of a strong, great, and independent empire, and may, before many years roll around, assert their power. The leading men thoroughly appreciate their weakness, but understand the history of Turkey, Egypt, and other powers that have made rapid strides toward the new civilization on borrowed capital and under foreign management and control. They know what the result of all that interference has been so far as national independence is concerned. The idea of those leading men of China with whom I have conversed—and I have seen most of those in the government of the empire—is to gradually educate a sufficient number of their own people to fill all places in the development of railroads, manufactories, telegraphs, and all those elements of civilization so new to them but common and even old with us. Then the Chinese, with their own people to do the work, and with their own capital, will commence a serious advance. I should not be surprised to hear within the next twenty years, if I should live so long, more complaints of Chinese absorption of the trade and commerce of the world than we hear now of their backward position. But before this change there must be a marked political change in China. It may even affect the dynasty, although that will depend upon the dynasty. The present form gives no State powers whatever. It may take off the heads of weak offenders or of a few obnoxious persons, but it is as weak against outside persons as America would be if States rights, as interpreted by Southern Democrats, prevailed. There are too many powers within the government to prevent the whole from exercising its full strength against a common enemy.

On June 21 their ship was threading its way through beautiful islands and rocks covered with green, looming up out of the sea and standing like sentinels along the coast. On the coast were trees, hills terraced to their summits with gardens, and high, commanding cliffs. Through green, smooth, tranquil waters the *Richmond* steamed into the bay of Nagasaki and the party had their first glimpse of Japan. They could see with their field glasses the picturesque city and hills beyond and the multitude of flags which indicated the population knew of their coming. When the *Richmond* ran up the Japanese standard and fired twenty-one guns in honor of Japan, the forts on the land and the Japanese gunboats responded in honor to General Grant. American Consul W. P. Mangum and his wife came on board, and in a short time a Japanese barge approached with Prince Dati, Mr. Yoshida, and the governor of Nagasaki, each in the full splendor of his court uniform. They were received with due honors and escorted to the cabin. Prince

Dati said the Emperor had directed him to meet General Grant on his landing and to welcome him in His Majesty's name and to attend upon him as the Emperor's personal representative so long as the general remained in Japan. Prince Dati was one of the highest noblemen in Japan, one of the old feudal barons who had had the power of life and death in his own dominion before the revolution. But he had accepted the change in governmental organization with enthusiasm, believing it best for the country, and had become one of the most influential nobles in the empire. His appointment as special escort to the general was manifestly a special compliment.

The Japanese man-of-war *Kango,* commanded by Captain Ito, had been sent to Nagasaki to welcome the general. The landing was made in the Japanese barge, and as soon as the general stepped into the latter the Japanese vessels and batteries on shore thundered out their welcome, the yards of the vessels were manned, and as the barge moved slowly along, the crews of the ships in the harbor cheered. As it was the intention of the Mikado that the general should be the guest of the Japanese Government while in his country, the *Richmond* was taken to a landing place arranged in the strictly Japanese part of the city and not in a foreign section. Lines of troops were formed, the steps were covered with red cloth, and every space was covered with people.

The general's boat touched the shore and with Mrs. Grant on his arm—followed by the colonel, Japanese officials, and members of his own party—he slowly walked up the platform, bowing to the multitude who were bowing to him. The principal citizens of the city came forward and were presented. After a short pause the party stepped into jinrickshas.

Mrs. Grant remembered these beautiful little vehicles as not much larger than a baby's perambulator. Although generally drawn by one man only, those bearing the Grant party had come from Tokyo and were drawn by two men. The party traveled through streets adorned with flags, flowers, and lanterns for about a half mile, to the attractively furnished house that had been prepared for them. The American minister, John A. Bingham, had also come, on June 22, from Tokyo to meet them. He brought sad news of the cholera ravaging the empire which would necessarily limit their journey. He also brought news of home affairs.

The governor gave a state dinner on the twenty-third for the general and the men of the party. On this occasion Mr. Bingham made a speech, as did the governor of Nagasaki, Utsumi Togatsu, proposing General Grant's health. A part of the general's response seems worth quoting as a matter of historic interest:

> The spirit which has actuated the mission of Judge Bingham—the spirit of sympathy, support, and conciliation—not only expressed my own sentiments, but those of America. America has much to gain in the East—no nation has greater interests; but America has nothing to gain except what comes from the cheerful acquiescence of the Eastern people and insures them as much benefit as it does us. I should be ashamed of my country if its relations with other nations, and especially with these ancient and most interesting empires in the East, were based upon any other idea. We have rejoiced over your progress. We have watched you step by step. We have followed the unfolding of your old civilization and its absorbing the new. You have had our profound sympathy in that work, our sympathy in the troubles which came with it, and our friendship. I hope it may continue, that it may long continue. As I have said, America has great interests in the East. She is your next neighbor. She is more affected by the eastern populations than any other power. She can never be insensible to what is being done here. Whatever her influence may be, I am proud to think that it has always been exerted in behalf of justice and kindness. No nation needs from the outside powers justice and kindness more than Japan, because the work that has made such marvelous progress in the past few years is a work in which we are deeply concerned, in the success of which we see a new era in civilization and which we should encourage.

On the twenty-fourth there was a real Japanese dinner, given by the merchants of Nagasaki and lasting several hours. The menu was wonderful, both in novelty and variety. The entertainment included a short scene comprising a forest, a lake, and a fisherman who caught fish that were served alive at the table. When Mrs. Grant mentioned this to a Japanese gentleman, he said smilingly: "I am sure you serve live oysters as a favorite course at your tables in the United States, do you not?"

The party and their Japanese hosts with Consuls Mangum and Denny and their families did not exceed twenty or thereabouts. Each guest was served at a table of his own. The merchants themselves waited on the party, assisted by a swarm of attendants wearing old Japanese costumes. The bill of fare embraced over 50 courses and was almost a volume by itself, and the wine was served in unglazed porcelain cups on white wooden stands. The feast began with dried fish, edible seaweeds, and isinglass, in something of the Scandinavian style. The first serious course was composed of crane, seaweed, moss, rice bread, and potatoes. The soup, when it first came—it was to come again and again—was remembered as an honest soup of fish, like a delicate fish chowder. Then followed in bewildering confusion other dishes composed of such things as truffles, dried bonito, aromatic shrubs, snipe, lassfish, orange flowers, powdered fish flavored with plum juice and walnuts, sliced raw carp, and rice.

With the first pause in the dinner a merchant came forward and read an address to General Grant. After this the guests all rose from their tables and sauntered about on a gravel walk, viewing the bay and enfolding hills.

Then the servants brought in candles, setting one candle in a pedestal in front of each table, and the merchants entered bearing meats. In the middle of the room they knelt and pressed their foreheads to the floor. With this demure courtesy the second period of the dinner started, the attendants placing on each table lacquer bowls and dishes and tempting the guests with side dishes of watermelon seeds and almond kernels. To the Western guests there was a dearth of bread and wine, the only drink being saki, a hot preparation from rice, with a sherry flavor, which was poured from a teapot into shallow, lacquer saucers for sipping.

The feast continued, and then came music and dances by ladies whom Mrs. Grant was assured were not professionals but the daughters of merchants and leading citizens of Nagasaki. The first three entered, one with an instrument like a guitar, another with one somewhat like a banjo, and the third with a drum. They wore blue silk gowns with white collars and heavily brocaded pearl-colored sashes. Others then entered, presenting a very attractive picture. They sang an original composition to the glory of America and the honor of General Grant. This completed, twelve dancing maidens entered. They performed the beautiful butterfly dance, playing their own accompaniment. They were followed by a group of performers with masks and later a group of children. Thus the evening ended. General Grant and his party stayed in Nagasaki six days and nights, and every night the city was illuminated with fireworks and bonfires on the hills.

The governor asked the general and Mrs. Grant if each would plant a tree in Nagasaki to commemorate their visit and requested the general to write an inscription. This he did, expressing the hope that both trees in Nagasaki Park should prosper, grow large and live long, and in their vigorous growth and long life be emblematic of the future of Japan.

On leaving Nagasaki, the party re-embarked on the *Richmond*. Prince Dati remained on his own ship, but Mr. Yoshida and the other gentlemen in attendance accompanied General Grant to the *Richmond*. The *Ashuelot* remained with the flotilla, and from their entry into Japanese waters they were accompanied by one of the Japanese gunboats under the command of Captain Ito. During their first days on the Sea of Japan they were denied permission to land because of the cholera epidemic in many parts of Japan. But although no foreign ships had been permitted to anchor in Sumida Bay, the *Richmond* with its party aboard were guests of the Emperor and not subject to this prohibition. So the party left the ship and traveled by jinrickshas to Shiguoka, which they reached about noon.

Since visitors hardly ever came there, the people were eager to see the party from across the ocean. Bazaars were full of fine Japanese lacquer work, and after luncheon wonderful daytime fireworks were set off. One of the pieces was a sort of bomb making a cloud effect in the sky and shooting out fans and ribbons. Another rocket burst and a young woman appeared and deliberately raised her umbrella, then walked across the sky with a stately and measured step. Mrs. Grant was told that this one represented the "girl of the period." After a pleasant day, the group returned to the ship and resumed the voyage to Yokohama.

About ten o'clock on July 3 they came in view of the seaport and a salute of twenty-one guns was fired by Admiral Patterson's flagship, the *Monongahela*. As the *Richmond* and *Ashuelot* entered the harbor slowly, the *Richmond* saluted the Japanese flag; this salute was responded to and the guns of various other countries thundered out their welcome so that the cannonade lasted for nearly an hour. On the deck of the *Richmond* the general received calls from various officials, making a brilliant scene in their full-dress uniforms. When the imperial barge came alongside, the general with Prince Dati, Mr. Yoshida, Colonel Grant, and several of the naval officers passed over the side and went aboard the royal yacht.

The party proceeded to Tokyo by special train, and General and Mrs. Grant entered the Emperor's private carriage, which had been waiting, and were escorted by a troop of cavalry to the Emperor's summer palace, the beautiful Enriokwan, where they were to be lodged.

The Emperor Mutsuhito had thought it would be especially appropriate to receive the general officially on July 4, and arrangements were accordingly perfected for a reception at the Emperor's Palace at two o'clock on the afternoon of America's Independence Day. The general had invited Mr. Bingham, our minister, Admiral Patterson and a number of his officers, and his own entourage to accompany him. It was a long drive, and when they arrived they were somewhat surprised at not finding a palace full of beautiful cloisonne, lacquer work, embroideries, and so on. Instead, the palace contained only the simplest furniture and ornaments. It turned out that this palace was a temporary replacement of the old one which had recently burned down.

The Emperor and Empress were awaiting them at the end of the audience hall. The Emperor was dressed in uniform and the Empress in a court robe of ruby velvet over a white silk skirt. Her hair was dressed in beautiful wide plaits arranged in a large bow on the back of her head. On her forehead she wore a small jeweled coronet resembling the end of a peacock feather. Young, fair, and delicate-looking, she said a few words of welcome to Mrs. Grant through an interpreter, to which her guest made suitable reply. On this occasion Mrs. Grant wore a lovely mauve silk gown, demitrained, trimmed with exquisite Brussels lace and made by Worth. As she looked in a mirror she was reminded of the statement, "A pretty gown gives the greatest peace of mind to a woman."

The Emperor stood quite motionless, apparently unconscious of any homage paid to him. He was a young man with a slender figure, taller than the average Japanese. He had a striking face, with a mouth and lips that could have reminded one of the Hapsburg family. His forehead was narrow and his hair, mustache, and beard intensely black. His face was expressionless, save for the dark, glowing eyes directed at the general.

While the reception up to this point seemed somewhat cold and formal, it was quite revolutionary when he advanced and shook hands with General Grant. Such an action on the part of the Imperial Majesty had never been known in Japanese history. Mr. Bingham advanced and bowed, but received just the faintest nod of recognition. The other members of the party were each presented individually, standing about a dozen feet from the Emperor and bowing. Then General and Mrs. Grant were presented to the princesses, each bowing to the other in silence. The Emperor then gave a signal to one of his attendants, who advanced to the general and said he was commanded by his Majesty to make the following statement:

> Your name has been known to us for a long time, and we are highly gratified to see you. While holding the high office of President of the United States you extended toward our countrymen especial kindness and courtesy. When our ambassador, Iwakura, visited the United States, he received the greatest kindness from you. The kindness thus shown by you has always been remembered by us. In your travels around the world you have reached this country, and our people of all classes feel gratified and happy to receive you. We trust that during your sojourn in our country you may find much to enjoy. It gives me sincere pleasure to receive you, and we are especially gratified that we have been able to do so on the anniversary of American independence. We congratulate you, also, on the occasion.

At the close of the address, read in English, General Grant said:

> Your Majesty: I am very grateful for the welcome you accord me here to-day, and for the great kindness with which I have been received, ever since I came to Japan, by your government and your people. I recognize in this a feeling of friendship toward my country. I can assure you that this feeling is reciprocated by the United States; that our people, without regard to party, take the deepest interest in all that concerns Japan, and have the warmest wishes for her welfare. I am happy to be able to express that sentiment. America is your next neighbor, and will always give Japan sympathy and support in her efforts to advance. I again thank your Majesty for your hospitality, and wish you a long and happy reign, and for your people prosperity and independence.

The rest of the afternoon was spent in receiving what seemed to be all the distinguished people in Japan who had come to meet the visitor. Since this was the Fourth of July, the American colony of course had to have a party for the general and his group; so they gave a dinner followed by a ball, which gave the Americans in Tokyo an opportunity to celebrate the American holiday and become better acquainted.

July 7 was indicated by the Emperor for a review of the troops in honor of General Grant. This was conducted with much panoply, after which the Emperor gave a breakfast for the general at Shila Palace. And thus the days in Tokyo passed, filled with official visits, social calls, stops in the bazaars.

On July 17, the Grant party accompanied by Prince Dati, Mr. Yoshida, and Mr. Tateno, left Tokyo to visit the shrine and temple at Nikko. They had expected to visit many other famous places, but the prevalence of cholera prevented these plans from being carried out. The little villages they passed en route to Nikko became more and more picturesque; everywhere the population was assembled, and the aspect of the people changed as the Americans in the party felt they were coming closer and closer to the ancient customs and manners of the people. For example, the Grants became accustomed to the very little clothing that the lower-class Japanese wore.

The capability of the jinricksha men to go up to 40 to 50 miles a day was to be wondered at. The first day the party made 28 miles and spent the night at a village in the house of the governor. The next day they stopped at noon at a small teahouse where they rested for two or three hours because the heat was so great.

At four o'clock the following day, they reached Nikko, where all the town seemed to be out to welcome them. Here they lived for ten days, enjoying the scenery, visiting the waterfalls, and strolling about the temple, tombs, and monuments.

Upon his arrival in Tokyo the general had indicated to the Japanese hosts that he had a communication from the Chinese Government relative to the Loochoo Island question which he would like to present to the Japanese Cabinet, if he could do so without appearing to interfere. When the Grants were in Nikko, the Emperor sent Minister of the Interior Ito and Minister of War Saigo to receive the statement. This was a somewhat formal meeting in which the general presented the problem as it appeared to him and the ministers gave formal replies and of course expressed the views on behalf of Japan. However, the Emperor had also indicated that he would like to have a personal interview with the general after his return from Nikko; as this would be the opportunity to discuss the Loochoo Islands question with the Emperor in person, the general postponed further discussion of the matter.

The Grant party left Nikko on July 28, visiting the falls of Hong-Toki and silk factories at Kanagana before returning, on July 31, to their pleasant quarters at Enriokwan.

The informal conference with the Emperor soon took place, on a very hot day at half-past two in the afternoon, in his summer house on the banks of a lake. Very simple preparations had been made. In the center of the room a table had been placed with chairs arranged around it, and behind a screen was another table near the window which looked out on the lake. As the general entered, the prime minister and the minister of the imperial household advanced and welcomed him. Then, after a pause, the three men passed behind the screen and found themselves in the presence of the Emperor, who was standing before a table in an undress uniform adorned only with the ribbon of a Japanese order. The general advanced and the Emperor shook hands with him, merely bowing to the rest of the party.

The Emperor said: "I have heard of many of the things you have said to my ministers in reference to Japan. You have seen the country and the people. I am anxious to speak with you on these subjects, and am sorry I have not had an opportunity earlier." The general assured him that he was entirely at His Majesty's service, and that he was glad indeed to have the opportunity to thank him for all the kindness shown to him in Japan. He might say that no one outside of Japan could have a greater interest in the country, or a more sincere friendship for its people.

There arose the subject then very urgent in political discussions in Japan—namely, the granting of an assembly and legislative functions to the people. The general said this seemed to be the only question about which there was much feeling in Japan, as far as he had observed. It was a question deserving a very careful consideration, and no one could doubt but that governments became stronger and nations more prosperous as they became more representative of the people. No one could doubt but that a legislative system dependent upon a popular parliament would be an advantage to Japan; but the question of when and how to grant it required careful consideration, a consideration which needed a clearer and more thorough knowledge of the country than he had had time to acquire. It was necessary to remember that rights of this kind—rights of suffrage and representation—once given could not be withdrawn. They should be given gradually. It would probably be an advantage to have an elective assembly meet in Tokyo and discuss all the problems connected with the change. Such an assembly should not have legislative power in the beginning. This seemed to General Grant the first step; the rest would follow as a result of the admirable system of education they seemed to have in Japan.

Nothing had been of more interest to the general than the study of the growth of foreign influence in Asia. He thought the British rule in

India was advantageous to the Indian people and he could see no alternative at that time except anarchy. There were some things to regret but a great deal to admire in the way India was governed; but since he had left India he had seen things which made his blood boil; namely, the way some European powers were attempting to degrade Asiatic nations and extinguish their independence. On this subject he had spoken strongly, and in writing to friends in America he had been emphatic. It seemed inconceivable that rights we considered essential in America were being denied to China and Japan, such as the control of their commerce. Japan especially seemed to him to be in a position where the control of her commerce by her own statesmen might relieve the people of a great burden, namely, their land tax. He had no doubt that if the land tax could be diminished the people of Japan would be enriched and so be able to buy more and the country would benefit. He thought he knew the American people well enough to say that they had, without distinction of party, the warmest wishes for the independence of Japan. The General also said there was nothing Japan should avoid more strenuously than borrowing and incurring debts to European nations. He pointed to the experience of Egypt in this regard.

Having spoken to the Emperor with great earnestness on these subjects, he went on to say that he had been asked by the Prince Regent of China and the viceroy of Tientsin to use his good offices with the Japanese Government in an effort to settle the question of the Loochoo Islands. This was a matter about which he would rather not have troubled himself, as it belonged to diplomacy and government, and he was not a diplomat and not in government. At the same time he could not ignore a request made in the interest of international peace. While he had read with great interest and listened to all the arguments from both the Chinese and Japanese sides, he felt it would hardly be becoming in him to express an opinion. He recognized the difficulties that surrounded Japan, but China evidently felt hurt that she had not received the consideration due her. It seemed to him that His Majesty could advantageously strive to remove that feeling even if it were necessary to make some sacrifices.

He was thoroughly satisfied that China and Japan should make what sacrifices were necessary to settle all questions between them and become friends and allies, without consultation with foreign powers. He had urged this on the Chinese Government and was glad of the opportunity of saying the same thing to the Emperor. China and Japan were then the only two countries left in the East capable of becoming great and independent of European dictation and laws.

The prime minister then said that Japan felt most friendly toward China and valued the friendship of that nation very highly. She would certainly do what she could, without yielding her dignity, to preserve the best relations. General Grant said he could not speak too earnestly to the Emperor on this subject, because he felt earnestly. Nothing would give him greater pleasure than to leave Japan, as he soon would be doing, confident that there was a cordial feeling between China and Japan. Other counsels would certainly be given His Majesty, because there were powerful influences in the East fanning trouble between China and Japan, and he was convinced that giving way to them would bring unspeakable calamity to both China and Japan.

In relating these events, Young called attention to the difference between the treatment of Seward when he came to Japan in October 1870 and that accorded General Grant on this occasion. The same Emperor was on the throne, several ministers in the Cabinet had remained, and Mr. Ishibashi, who had escorted Mr. Seward to his interview with the Emperor, was the same man who escorted General Grant and interpreted for him. According to a detailed description of the formalities and ceremony with which Seward was received, it was evident that this later reception had become more friendly; indeed there was an actual exchange of ideas between the general and the Emperor, whereas in the case of Mr. Seward the Emperor had not spoken at all. He had merely from the throne touched the message of welcome with his scepter, which was then read. The Grant party felt not only that they had been received with greater consideration and graciousness, but that the change showed a great advance in the Japanese progress toward the adoption of Western ideas.

A public festival at Uyeno Park in Tokyo on August 25 excited much public attention and proved rather a culminating incident in the general's visit. There was the noticeable increase and consideration in the cordiality of the Japanese. While the Emperor had never failed in courtesy to the princes of other royal families who had visited him, he had treated General Grant as a friend and had also shown him the honor given the reigning head of a nation. In addition it was noticeable that the people had taken a novel and unusual interest in General Grant. While the courtesy of princes and gentlemen was noteworthy and had been unusual, the part taken by the people in his reception was unique.

As the August 25 fete was in the general's honor, it was thought that the presence of naval officers would be a compliment to the citizens and add to the interest of the day; so the general invited Admiral Patterson, Captain Benham, and the leading officers of the American ships to join him at the palace, have luncheon with him, and go to the park with him. The party rode in the Emperor's state carriages, preceded and surrounded by cavalry going at a slow pace, so that the crowd could see the general. The distance from Enriokwan to Uyeno was three miles, and every step of the way was through a dense crowd. Every house was decorated with flags and lanterns, and the people rushed to their windows and looked out as the general's carriage passed; but there was perfect order and courtesy. When the party came to the park a line of infantry had been formed, and as the general's carriage slowly turned into the park, the soldiers presented arms and a Japanese band played "Hail Columbia."

A committee requested General and Mrs. Grant each to plant a tree, which they were happy to do. A tablet recording the event, engraved both in English and Japanese, had been prepared beforehand.

This ceremony over, they re-entered their carriages and drove to a pavilion prepared for the general. Soon the Emperor arrived, and after formal ceremonies the assemblage witnessed sports, amusements, and fireworks.

The Grants' formal farewell interview with the Emperor was at an audience on Saturday, August 29. After exchanging formalities, General Grant took out of his pocket a manuscript on which he had written a prepared speech, breaking his usual custom of not preparing anything in writing and of speaking extempore. Here is what he read:

Your Majesty: I come to take my leave, and to thank you, the officers of your government, and the people of Japan, for the great hospitality and kindness I have received at the hands of all during my most pleasant visit to this country. I have now been two months in Tokio and the surrounding neighborhood, and two previous weeks in the more southerly part of the country. It affords me great satisfaction to say that during all this stay and all my visiting I have not witnessed one discourtesy toward myself, nor a single unpleasant sight. Everywhere there seems to be the greatest contentment among the people; and while no signs of great individual wealth exist, no absolute poverty is visible. This is in striking and pleasant contrast with almost every other country I have visited. I leave Japan greatly impressed with the possibilities of her future. She has a fertile soil, one half of it not yet cultivated to man's use, great undeveloped mineral resources, numerous and fine harbors, an extensive sea-coast abounding in fish of an almost endless variety, and, above all, an industrious, ingenious, contented, and frugal population. With all these nothing is wanted to insure great progress except wise direction by the government, peace at home and abroad, and non-interference in the internal and domestic affairs of the country by the outside nations. It is the sincere desire of your guests to see Japan realize all possible strength and greatness, to see her as independent of foreign rule or dictation as any Western nation now is, and to see affairs so directed by her as to command the respect of the civilized world. In saying this I believe I reflect the sentiments of the great majority of my countrymen. I now take my leave without expectation of ever again having the opportunity of visiting Japan, but with the assurance that pleasant recollections of my present visit will not vanish while my life lasts. That your Majesty may long reign over a prosperous and contented people and enjoy every blessing is my sincere prayer.

The Emperor read in a clear and pleasant voice a response which Mr. Ishibashi then translated. The Empress spoke to Mrs. Grant and expressed her great pleasure that the general and party had been in Japan and her fear that the unusual heat and pestilence had perhaps prevented them from enjoying their visit. In reply, Mrs. Grant said that her visit to Japan had exceeded all possible expectations and she had enjoyed it thoroughly, and hoped some day to have an opportunity of acknowledging and somehow returning the hospitality she had received in Japan.

This audience with the Emperor was necessarily the end of all festivities connected with the Grants' visit, but Sunday was crowded with friends coming and going all day to say good-by, and Monday was spent in making ready for the steamer which was to depart from Yokohama on Wednesday.

On Tuesday the general gave a dinner for Admiral Patterson, Captain Benham, Commander Boyd, and Commander Johnson (who were commanding the American men-of-war), and several members of the Japanese Cabinet and their wives. It was to be the Grants' last dinner in Japan, and it became a reception and a crowded one.

The next day the weather was fine and the departure from Tokyo was attended with almost the same formalities as their reception. Troops were posted, the station was crowded and the committee of citizens who had originally received the general were there to bid him a formal farewell. As the train moved out and troops presented arms and friends waved good-by, the general stood on the platform and waved his hat in a farewell salute. There were also crowds at the stations they passed through, but the train did not stop at any of them. On their arrival in Yokohama the governor was there, with troops and a band playing U.S. national airs. The governor escorted the party to the admiralty wharf, where they found Admiral Patterson, Captain Benham, and Commanders Boyd and Johnson waiting for them and where they remained for luncheon.

The general then went aboard the admiralty barge, while Admiral Kawamura escorted Mrs. Grant. They moved on to the *City of Tokyo* amid the roar of cannon, music, the flashing of fireworks, and cheers. They were received by Commodore Maury. It was hard to say all they wished to say in appreciation of how they had been treated in Japan, and many of their Japanese friends escorted them out to sea some distance on board a Japanese man-of-war. The weather was like the American Indian summer, and the accommodations on the *City of Tokyo* were luxurious. It was on September 3 that they began the long voyage to San Francisco. They had been in Japan more than two months, and out of the country almost two and a half years.

XVII

Intermezzo

THE arrival in San Francisco, on September 20, 1879, brought them into the midst of a reception such as they had not expected—salutes and naval display and committees from smaller boats to welcome them. The American crowd was much less quiet than the Oriental crowds had been, and they showed enormous enthusiasm for the returning travelers. One incident is illustrative perhaps of the extent of this enthusiasm. A little boy, whom I afterward knew as Sol Bloom—a member of Congress and co-director for the George Washington Bicentennial Celebration—had invested his small capital in purchasing some flowers, hoping to find buyers in the crowd. But he became so stirred up by the enthusiasm of the crowd in the streets that as the general's carriage passed on its way to the Palace Hotel the little boy quite lost his head and threw the flowers into the general's lap.

Traveling eastward the party stopped in Stockton, Lake Tahoe, and Yosemite Valley en route to Virginia City. There they descended some 1700 feet into a mine. Mrs. Grant boldly accompanied the party, having dressed appropriately for the expedition and having heard confidentially from Mr. Mackay that the general had bet she would not go down. After the descent into the mine they stopped at Carson City, Cheyenne, and Omaha, and finally reached Galena, where they were really at home again. The town was decorated as on the occasion of the general's return from the war, and everything was done to welcome back their citizen, General Grant.

There was a wonderful and very cordial reception for them in Chicago, with a banquet and fine speeches. Then in Philadelphia, which had always been so loyal to the general, he rested for a week or two before visiting the southern states, Cuba, and Mexico. General and Mrs. Sheridan, Colonel Grant and his wife, and Miss Felt of Galena joined the Grants, and they started south on December 27, 1879, stopping for a few days in Washington as the guests of their old friends, the Beales.

Again the citizens of the cities of the South—in Jacksonville, St. Augustine, Savannah, and many other places—were most cordial and greeted them with every possible hospitality. In Key West there was an impressive reception for them, but the ladies did not leave the ship and after a run of some hours they arrived in Cuba. An officer of the Spanish captain general's staff arrived in an especially fine gig to welcome the general and to conduct him to the Governor's Palace. This was a pleasant surprise, as they had expected to go to one of the hotels. It was like visits to European capitals all over again.

They remained in Cuba until after carnival time, and then they took a steamer to Vera Cruz, Mexico, going from there by train to the City of Mexico. They were received and made at home in the palace of President Diaz, and were most comfortably taken care of. Visits to the places of interest naturally took the general to the suburbs where he remembered the military operations, and he was able to reminisce about where he found his brother-in-law, Lieutenant Frederick Dent, wounded and lying by the roadside. The party enjoyed the fine paintings, the cathedral, many historic sights, and the lovely villages in the suburbs. The ladies of the party took pleasure in collecting some old silver, beautiful fans, and, in the curio shops, opals and other products of the country.

The return trip to Galena was via Galveston, Texas, where General and Mrs. Sheridan left the party; he was anxious to hurry back to his headquarters in Chicago. General and Mrs. Grant and Miss Felt went by steamer to New Orleans, where they received an ovation equaling those elsewhere. There was a dinner in New Orleans at which the guests presented the general with a souvenir album in which they had signed their names. They traveled on through Mississippi and the intervening states to Illinois, stopping at Little Rock for two days. Finally they arrived in Galena, where they remained, except for an occasional visit to Colonel Fred, who was stationed in Chicago on General Sheridan's staff.

At this time—in the spring of 1880—the politicians were looking forward to the Republican Convention scheduled for Chicago on June 2.

The general's loyal friends and admirers were urging him to be a candidate. The ovations with which he had been received in the United States must have made some impression on the general. He felt, too, that if he was really wanted as President again, he was better fitted and informed for it after his travels in Europe and Asia and his frank exchanges of ideas with the rulers of various countries. On the subject of Grant's candidacy, here is what Young wrote:

> Thus with comparative youth, Grant would have brought to the Presidency the education of eight years in the White House and the unrivaled experience which came from his journeys around the world. He would have governed with a broad mind. Although I never heard from him any expression of a wish for a third term, deprecating rather than otherwise any reference to the subject, it must not be forgotten,—and he was undoubtedly conscious of the fact,—that he returned home in 1879 the most accomplished and best informed statesman of his time. The book of the world had been opened to him. He saw the relative proportion of things, the true place of America in the economy of nations, and, under wise, intrepid statesmanship, the magnificence of her opportunities. "How I wish I had known this ten years ago," he was wont to say, as the truth of some new experience burst upon him, and he realized what he might have done when he had the power to do it.
>
> He knew the inner meaning of those subtle influences which form civilization—the meaning of Austria and Russia, of Germany and France and Spain. He saw the good in each of them, and believed they could, in time, be fused into harmony and peace; that the federation of man was more than a poet's dream. He rejoiced in the unification of Germany under whatever system it might be governed,—dynastic or democratic, and yet was profoundly interested in the Republic of France. His heart went out to the smaller nationalities,—Holland, Denmark, and Sweden. He conceived an affection for Greece, not alone as he saw it in the person of her sovereign, but in the genius of her people.
>
> Above all else, Grant was impressed with the East. He divined China and Japan; how necessary was their commerce to our Pacific commonwealth, and that the time was coming when we could no longer be indifferent to the autonomy of these ancient empires. Had Grant lived, or had his counsel been duly followed, there would have been no war between China and Japan.

As the time for the convention approached it became evident that there would be a really sharp and determined fight made against the renomination of General Grant. John Russell Young made a trip to

Galena and, in opposition to the wishes of the family and friends, induced General Grant to write a letter to Cameron, once in his Cabinet and now chairman of the Republican National Committee, requesting his supporters to withdraw his name at any time they thought it desirable. But no copy of the letter seems to have been preserved and it was never used, so that the exact statement is not known.

In the convention Garfield was manifestly to be the leader of those opposed to the nomination of General Grant and the fight was going to be between the "stalwarts" and the opponents of the former President. Garfield had been expected to nominate James G. Blaine, but that was forgotten in the course of the succession of votes taken. The friends of General Grant had foreseen two steps necessary for the assured election of their candidate: (1) the adoption for all the states of the unit rule—that is, that the majority of each delegation should determine the candidate for whom all the votes of that delegation would be cast and counted; (2) a plank in the platform endorsing the establishment of civil service based on competence and efficiency. Such a plank was adopted. One objection was made by Mr. Flannigan of Texas, who sprang up to say, "To the victors belong the spoils. What are we up here for? I mean that members of the Republican Party are entitled to office, and if we are victorious, we will have office." This caused general and hearty laughter, but in spite of it and other objections the civil service reform plank was adopted.

Conkling's speech nominating the general was unusual. He declared that with Grant the Republican Party could "grandly win." As James Ford Rhodes describes it:

> Pointing out in well-chosen words Grant's title to greatness, he was never effusive, tawdry or grandiloquent. He seized the salient points that suggested to all grateful recollections. Certainly he was a strong candidate who was victor in war, magnanimous at Lee's surrender, a lover of peace as shown by the Geneva arbitration, a believer in sound money as exemplified by the veto of the inflation bill. The only objection to Grant, Conkling said, was the "third term" and to this objection he applied his scathing ridicule. He was heard all over the hall and the long applause that followed was not entirely that of a claque; part of it was in genuine approval of an eloquent speech. Benjamin Harrison, a delegate from Indiana, a cold critic of oratory, who later developed into an excellent public speaker, unconsciously applauded as vigorously as Grant's most sympathetic friends, although he himself was opposed to the General's nomination. Conkling's was an effective speech in

holding together his solid phalanx, but it failed in conciliation. As the necessary votes to nominate Grant must come largely from the supporters of Blaine and Sherman, it was not a happy stroke to cast a slur on each of those candidates. After Grant's nomination had been seconded in a five-minute speech, Garfield rose to present the name of Senator John Sherman. To follow Conkling's oration was a difficult role and his subject was far less inspiring, yet he made a great speech, presenting strong reasons for the nomination of Sherman and receiving an enthusiastic acclaim from the audience in the Convention hall. Afterwards it was often sneeringly suggested that Garfield spoke for himself rather than for Sherman, but this sneer was prompted by the outcome of the Convention.

When the convention recessed on Saturday, no ballot was taken and the main business went over until Monday. There had been 34 ballots without a decision, for which 378 votes were necessary. On the first ballot General Grant had received 304 votes. During the recess they did not fall below 302, and even on the thirty-fifth ballot, after the tide had begun to set for Garfield, there were still 313 votes for General Grant. On the last ballot (the thirty-sixth), when the stampede was on, the line of the "Old Guard" still gave him 306 votes—a devotion and loyalty unmatched at any convention, and the 306 who, to the end, had voted for the general, had won their place in history. As a gesture of courtesy to the Grant followers, Chester A. Arthur, whom the general had appointed collector of the Port of New York only to be removed by Hayes, was nominated for Vice President.

There is no question but that Mr. Conkling's handling of the case (with offensive references to the opposition in the convention) was tactless and doubtless alienated some delegates who might have been won over. On the other hand, Garfield's courteous and pleasant manner to everyone had the opposite effect.

The general undoubtedly felt that his friends, who might have withdrawn his name at a suitable moment, had unnecessarily exposed him to the humiliation of being voted out of the candidacy. He had followed in Galena the accounts of what was going on at the convention and one evening, leaving the group who were listening to the returns, he went home saying that he was afraid he would be nominated. When it seemed imminent that Garfield would be nominated, he said he was a good man, and indeed he did do what he could to assure Garfield's election.

In the meantime, General and Mrs. Grant were vouchsafed a short period of relative prosperity, during which they decided to settle in New York and bought a house there at 3 East 66th Street, a double four-story, brownstone-front house.

It will be remembered that the Grants' second son, Ulysses S. Grant, Jr., had associated himself in some financial activities in Wall Street with young Ferdinand Ward, who was then winning the esteem of many by his successful operations in high finance; he soon became known as the Napoleon of Wall Street. The funds necessary for the general to complete his tour around the world had been gained in this way, and in the autumn of 1880, Ward had proposed a private banking firm to be called Grant & Ward. He was to be financial agent, while Ulysses, Jr., was to be an active partner and the general and James F. Fish, Ward's father-in-law and president of the Marine Bank of Brooklyn, were to be silent partners. With a paid-in capital of $400,000, mostly contributed by Senator Chaffee (Ulysses, Jr.'s, father-in-law) and other members and connections of the Grant family, in three years the bank acquired a rating of $15,000,000 and had a deposit of nearly a $1,000,-000 in Fish's bank.

The general had implicit confidence in Ward, who talked about rail-road contracts and huge rates of interest for emergency loans to sub-contractors. But in violation of his definite understanding of the general's stipulation that the firm should *never* undertake anything in con-nection with government contracts, Ward surreptitiously talked to other customers about the influence General Grant's membership in the firm had in getting contracts with the government.

The income, supposedly being earned by the firm, continued to come in in generous amounts and now for the first time General Grant—who as a lieutenant had hung on to his commission and assured salary while serving under most disagreeable circumstances in California, and who had written his wife that only the terrible fear of not being able to earn enough to support his family prevented his resigning immediately from the army and attempting to go it alone—felt confident that he would not have to face such dire circumstances. At last he could enjoy his comfortable home, filled with the trophies acquired during a successful career in the army, the presidency, and during the trip around the world. Also he could now meet on a basis of social equality with the wealthy and socially prominent people who were proud to claim his acquaintance.

Then, on Sunday evening, May 4, 1884, Ward came to see Grant and told him of the trouble the Marine Bank was in and that the bank's reserve had been imperiled by funds drawn late the afternoon before by the City Chamberlain. He added that unless $400,000 could be raised at once, the bank would be compelled to close its doors Monday morning and tie up the firm's deposit of $660,000 and possibly bring ruin to it. Ward said that he had raised $250,000 for it himself but could do no more; the general must look for the other $150,000. The general could think of nobody but Commodore Vanderbilt to ask for such a loan. Vanderbilt said he would lend it to him as a personal loan, but not for the sake of the Marine Bank or the firm of Grant & Ward. The next day the firm's check repaid the loan, so the general supposed; but when Tuesday morning the general limped to the firm's office (he had injured one leg on Christmas Eve in getting out of the carriage and slipping on the ice), he was stunned by Ulysses, Jr.'s, greeting that "Grant and Ward have failed and Ward has fled!" He turned without a word, ascended slowly to his own private room, and late that afternoon was found there by the cashier with his head bowed. Before night it was known that every dollar he possessed had been swept away, the firm had no deposit in the bank, and the securities Ward had talked about were worthless.

In talking it over with Mrs. Grant they were both appalled to realize they really had nothing left, as the general insisted upon considering the Vanderbilt loan as a personal debt for which he was personally responsible. The house in New York and the cottage at Long Branch were in Mrs. Grant's name but certainly should be retained at least for the present so that they might have a roof over their heads. However, the general immediately transferred his farm, his wife's real estate in Philadelphia and Chicago, and all his personal property, including the trophies of the war, his medals, swords and uniforms, and the keepsakes acquired during the trip around the world, to Mr. Vanderbilt. Vanderbilt tried to transfer the property to Mrs. Grant but she refused the offer except for the trophies, which she accepted in trust to be placed at the disposal of the government.

In fact the whole family, brothers and cousins and their in-laws, were now stripped of their funds and denied the income they had been receiving from the firm of Grant & Ward, which had no assets within reach. Special efforts were made by the general's sons to ease the position of other members who had nothing at all to fall back on. The question of how they could continue to afford to live in New York of course required an immediate answer, as bills from the tradesmen came pouring in. However, the situation was somewhat alleviated by the prompt and generous action of a stranger (Charles Wood of Lansingburg, New York) who sent a check for $1,000 which he insisted on the general's accepting as a loan "on account of my share for services ending April 1865." This unexpected cash certainly helped to meet the living expenses of the household for a short time. Even this generous and loyal action could not restore the general's faith in human nature, and in the midst of his troubles he said, "I have made it the rule of my life to trust a man long after other people gave him up; but I don't see how I can ever trust any human being again."

Before the failure of Grant & Ward the Century Company had started to publish a series of articles by persons who had taken part in the Civil War, telling of their experiences in it and their actions as they saw them. The Century Company had approached General Grant through Badeau as to the possibility of his writing some articles; but he had encouraged Badeau to write what was expected to be the general's military history (published in three volumes from 1881 to 1882), and he doubted that anybody would be particularly interested in his retelling the same story in different words. However, now that he was in such need of funds, it seemed as though the offer of the Century Company was something to be considered, although he did not have much confidence in his ability to write anything that would have a popular appeal.

Nevertheless, when Robert Underwood Johnson, assistant editor of the *Century* magazine, called on him in early June 1884 and again offered to print some articles by the general if he would write them, the general, still fearful that he might not be able to do as good a job as he would like (and also, I feel, with some lingering fear of competing with the book he had encouraged Badeau to write and which had failed to sell very well), again refused to undertake the writing of such articles. Apparently Mr. Johnson left with a refusal at the time but with the promise he would consider trying to write two articles. The sum of $500 offered for each was certainly an inducement he could not refuse, in view of the need for cash.

It should be added that Mark Twain and many other friends of the general had felt that he should write his memoirs. This would put in the public records all the facts that he alone knew of his military and political life.

In some campaigns, when his initial plan was often frustrated or stopped in a particular part, General Grant had shown unusual ingenuity and powers of recovery in pushing for success in some different part of the battlefield and thereby, to the surprise of the enemy and often of his own army, earned a decisive success. So now he saw in this offer of a considerable payment for his writings a possible unexpected way of earning his living and perhaps even writing a book which might bring in enough cash to put his family in reasonably comfortable circumstances. He thereupon agreed to try his hand at this new adventure of authorship and to write two articles. If they were successful, he might write four.

Instead of finding the work tiresome or boring, he found the recollections of victories won pleasant and interesting. It is true that the first draft of the article on Shiloh was completed in four pages and that was all the general intended to say about it, feeling that he had told the essential facts and that the public must know the rest of the story. However, with the family's and Badeau's urging, he realized that there might be interest in some of the incidents and how he felt toward them—for instance, that his sword had been hit by a bullet and a horse killed under him. There were other incidents which he was persuaded to write about, and in the writing of them he became interested and was led to add comments and tell of other people's actions. Having cast off the requirements of formal detachment that he imposed upon himself in all his official writings, he now found some interest in describing the picture more completely. And so he produced an article of reasonable size which, with the one that followed on Vicksburg, was interesting enough to the public. In fact, he was surprised at his ability to produce something with so much human interest.

Articles on Chattanooga and the Wilderness followed. The *Century* managers were delighted with the increase in the magazine's circulation by fifty thousand and doubled the payment for each article. A means of keeping the wolf from the door had been found, temporarily at least.

During a call on the general, Mark Twain with William Dean Howells had gotten him to talk about various things he remembered. And so Mark Twain records that he had tried very hard to get the general to write his personal memoirs for publication, but the general would not agree. His inborn diffidence made him shrink from voluntarily coming forward before the public and exposing himself to criticism as an author. He had no confidence in his ability to write well, whereas everybody else in the world, excepting himself, was aware that he possessed an admirable literary gift and style. He was also sure that the book would have no sale, and of course that would be a humiliation, too. He noted that General Badeau's *Military History of Ulysses S. Grant* had had but a trifling sale, and that John Russell Young's account of General Grant's trip around the world had hardly any sale at all. But Samuel Clemens (*i.e.,* Twain) said that these were not instances in point; that what another man might tell about General Grant was nothing, while what General Grant should tell about himself, with his own pen, was a totally different thing. Mark Twain assured him that the book would have an enormous sale; that it should be in two volumes, sold at $3.50 apiece, and that the sale would certainly reach half a million sets; that, from his personal experience, he (Twain) could save the general from making unwise contracts with publishers, and could also suggest the best plan of publication—the subscription plan—and find for him the best men in that line of business.

A word seems necessary about the meeting of the general and Mark Twain, which grew into a close friendship. In his autobiography Mark Twain noted that he first met the general in the fall or winter of 1866 at a reception in Washington. There he merely saw him and shook hands with him but had no opportunity for conversation. The description of their next meeting had best be told in Mark Twain's own words:

I next saw General Grant during his first term as President. Senator Bill Stewart, of Nevada, proposed to take me in and see the President. We found him in his working costume, with an old, short, linen duster on, and it was well spattered with ink. I had acquired some trifle of notoriety through some letters which I had written, in the New York *Tribune,* during my trip round about the world in the *Quaker City* expedition. I shook hands, and then there was a pause and silence. I couldn't think of anything to say. So I merely looked into the general's grim, immovable countenance a moment or two, in silence, and then I said: "Mr. President, I am embarrassed. Are you?" He smiled a smile which would have done no discredit to a cast-iron image, and I got away under the smoke of my volley.

I did not see him again for some ten years. In the meantime I had become very thoroughly notorious.

Then, in 1879, the general had just returned from his journey through the European and Asiatic world, and his progress from San Francisco eastward had been one continuous ovation; and now he was to be feasted in Chicago by the veterans of the Army of the Tennessee—the first army over which he had had command. . . .

There was to be a prodigious procession. General Grant was to review it from a rostrum which had been built out for the purpose from the second-story window of the Palmer House. The rostrum was carpeted and otherwise glorified with flags and so on.

The best place of all to see the procession was, of course, from this rostrum, so I sauntered upon that rostrum while as yet it was empty, in the hope that I might be permitted to sit there. It was rather a conspicuous place, since upon it the public gaze was fixed and there was a countless multitude below. Presently two gentlemen came upon that platform from the window of the hotel and stepped forward to the front. A prodigious shout went up from the multitude below, and I recognized in one of these two gentlemen General Grant; the other was Carter Harrison, the Mayor of Chicago, with whom I was acquainted. He saw me, stepped over to me, and said wouldn't I like to be introduced to the general? I said I should. So he walked over with me and said, "General, let me introduce Mr. Clemens." We shook hands. There was the usual momentary pause, and then the general said: "I am not embarrassed. Are you?"

It was probably late in the autumn of 1884 that General Grant visited the stock farm of Alden Goldsmith at Goshen, New York. He had often been a welcome guest there and enjoyed very much looking at the horses and hearing about the characteristics of each. C. B. Meade, who had been raised at Goshen, tells that as he rode by the Goldsmith place he saw General Grant looking over some fine colts in the stableyard and at once turned in.

A man took the horse he had been driving. Meade walked over to where the general and Mr. Goldsmith were standing and renewed his boyhood acquaintance with the latter, for whom he had worked as a printer's devil on the *Goshen Democrat*. He was introduced as a relative of General George G. Meade and the representative of a New York paper. He noted that the general looked worn and somewhat haggard but was the same "unassuming Grant that the world knew so well." As the conversation drifted on he reached in his pocket and drew out a handful of chestnuts and handed them to the general. The latter took them with thanks and then remarked in his quiet way: "Ah! These remind me of my early days at West Point and the more recent and stirring times down in Virginia. I have always been fond of chestnuts and have gathered many of them, but I am afraid my affliction will prohibit my swallowing these." (In the summer of 1884, General Grant had first consulted a physician about a persistently sore throat.)

"I'll fix them all right, General. I will have them boiled, and then they are as soft as cooked potatoes," said Mr. Goldsmith.

To this the general replied with a smile: "All right, Goldsmith, you may be the doctor."

Shortly after this exchange the general took out his cigar case and said: "Gentlemen, this is the last cigar I shall ever smoke." He continued, "The doctors tell me that I will never live to finish the work on which my whole energy is centered these days [meaning the *Memoirs* he was then engaged in writing] if I do not cease indulging in these fragrant weeds. It is hard to give up a cherished friend, that has been your comforter and solace through many weary nights and days. But my unfinished work must be completed, for the sake of those that are near and dear to me." Then the general lighted the cigar and for a few moments gazed over the browning fields and the autumn foliage and at the sky filled with myriads of migrating blackbirds, and golden sunshine filled the world about them.

XVIII

Grant's Last Victory

THE general had been conscious of a sore throat ever since early summer. He found great pain in swallowing tomatoes and peaches, which warned him that something was very wrong. He finally went to see Dr. Di Acosta, a prominent throat specialist, because his own doctor, Fordyce Barker, was in Europe and would be absent until the middle of October. Without giving him any diagnosis, Dr. Di Acosta advised him to see his own doctor, and when Dr. Barker returned he advised his illustrious patient to see Dr. John Hancock Douglas, the leading throat specialist of New York City. Grant saw Douglas on October 22, 1884.

Douglas, an old friend, had taken care of General Rawlins during his fatal illness, had been associate secretary of the U. S. Sanitary Commission throughout the Civil War, and was an admirer of General Grant. He had been impressed by the general's quiet, unobtrusive manner, as well as the quickness of observation and alertness which distinguished him when they had met at the battle for Fort Donelson—qualities which the two men shared.

Dr. Douglas, unlike the other doctors who had examined him and had not dared give their diagnoses, now told the general that his throat had a definite cancerous condition which might not be curable, but he and the other doctors would certainly do their best to relieve him of this danger and the pain that would accompany it. The general knew that this was practically a death sentence; but as had happened on many occasions before, this blow of fate proved a challenge and only stirred him to an almost superhuman struggle to finish his book before he had to answer the last roll call. Considering that the sale of the book might bring in a considerable sum of money for his widow and children and also that the memoirs would say for the record many things he wanted to say, he became possessed of a desire to survive long enough to complete the memoirs with such skill and enthusiasm as he could muster.

Dr. Douglas kept a diary of the general's case which has obviously been very useful in establishing specific dates in the progress of the illness. Except as noted, the patient's progress had been relatively uneventful until April 2, 1885, when, after completing the description of the Battle of Chattanooga, a crisis occurred in his condition and the doctors thought that a dangerous situation had arisen.

During January and February the disease had made somewhat routine progress but the pain suffered by the patient had persuaded the attending doctors of the advisability of calling other specialists in consultation on occasion, for by this time the country's sympathy and interest had been aroused. Indeed, the newspapers were issuing daily reports (the first on February 20, 1885) of the general's condition, and even established a press room of sorts in a house across the street from 3 East 66th Street so that any goings and comings could be watched and the cause of any special activity inquired into promptly. An enormous mail flooded the house, in volume quite beyond the ability of Colonel Fred, with the occasional help of his brothers, to handle. The mail and the interruptions of callers and inquiries added to the family's distress and anxiety. They worried not only about the fatal illness of the beloved head of the family but also about the interference with his writing. The situation imposed an almost unbearable burden upon the family.

Of course, this was not spoken of to us children (I had been born in 1881 and was living at 3 East 66th at this time) and our lives were kept as normal as possible, but we could not help being aware of the strain under which our parents were living, though it was never mentioned to us. We were just required to refrain from being noisy, and from intruding on Grandfather and Grandmother (who had always been so friendly in the past), and from talking (probably indiscreetly and certainly in ignorance) to the newspaper reporters who would often catch us on the street or on our daily walk to Central Park and ask us questions to which we did not know the answers.

The doctors consulted for their opinions were Dr. T. W. Markoe and Dr. H. B. Sands, while arrangements were made with Dr. George F. Shrady to replace Dr. Douglas when necessary.

Dr. Douglas noted in his diary:

January 28, 1885: The General had, at this time, more neuralgia in the head; interfering with his work upon his *Memoirs,* which up to this date had occupied him quite assiduously. He had to intermit his labors more frequently, and this added to his trouble, for he was very anxious to complete his work, upon which he was constantly engaged.

February 2: Suffered much last night. Great pain in right ear. Did not sleep until six in the morning, then at intervals until noon.

February 18, 1885: Made a local application of cocaine to the throat to diminish as much as possible the pain of digital examination. When this was done we all met in the General's room, the one occupied by him in writing,—into which a flood of sunlight was pouring—and a close and searching examination was made, both by direct light, and by the concentrated light from a frontal mirror, and finally by the finger. Returning to the parlour, each gentleman gave his separate individual opinion confirming the diagnosis. Both Doctor Markoe and Doctor Sands agreed that surgical interference was impracticable.

One event which had a definitely favorable effect on the general was the passage by the Senate of a bill to restore him to his previous rank of General of the Army on the retired list with the retired pay. He seemed to consider this a restoration by official act to the position he had fairly won and an indication of his return to his former high place in popular esteem. However, it was indicated by President Arthur that he would veto this bill because he felt it was an intrusion on the Chief Executive's prerogatives for the legislature to indicate by name such action in favor of any particular person. So on the last day of Congress, March 4, 1885, the bill, amended as the President had wished, was rushed through the House and Senate by unanimous consent amid cheers, and Arthur sent in Grant's name for confirmation just in time. It fell to Cleveland, Arthur's Democratic successor and the first Democratic President since the election of Mr. Lincoln in 1860, to sign the commission—the second act of his Administration. The general's telegram of acceptance to the adjutant general was written in his own hand and the receipt of his first month's pay was "touching in the evidence of his struggle to repair his shattered fortunes." Mark Twain wrote to his wife on March 4, 1885: "We were at General Grant's at noon and a telegram arrived that the last act of the expiring Congress late this morning retired him with full general's rank and accompanying emoluments. The effect upon him was like raising the dead. We were present when the telegram was put in his hand."

In the meanwhile Mark Twain's conviction and eloquence had been effective in convincing the general that the writing of his *Memoirs* was a challenge he should meet. On February 27, 1885, spurred on also by the fact that the *Century* people feared he might not be able to finish his four articles, the general had decided to sign the contract with Mark Twain's firm, Charles L. Webster and Company, which was done with appropriate witnesses. The contract had been drawn by the great law firm of Alexander & Green on Mark Twain's part and by Clarence Seward, son of Lincoln's secretary of state, for the general.

In the conversations preliminary to this the question had been raised as to the general's right, in accordance with the usual custom, to incorporate in his *Memoirs* the articles he was writing for the Century Company; in this connection there arose also the question as to the right of the Century Company to republish the magazine articles in a composite book of Civil War articles they were planning. Both of these matters were satisfactorily agreed to and in the course of the discussion relative thereto to, Roswell Smith, head of the Century Company, said to Mr. Clemens: "I'm glad you've got the general's book, Mr. Clemens, and glad there was somebody with courage enough to take it, under the circumstances. What do you think the general wanted to require of me?"

"What?"

"He wanted me to insure a sale of twenty-five thousand sets of his book! I wouldn't risk such a guarantee on any book that ever was published."

As of September 10, 1885, 250,000 sets of the *Memoirs*—500,000 single volumes—had been sold and only half the ground covered; it is obvious, then, that Mark Twain's estimate was not unduly exaggerated and that the Century Company had no remotely correct idea of how the book would sell.

On his return from his trip west, Mark Twain had been very much pleased by reports in New York papers that the general (according to his physicians) was a great deal better and was getting along comfortably. When he called on the general February 21, he expressed his pleasure at this good news, but the general only smiled and said, "If it were only true." Mark Twain, surprised and discomforted, inquired of Dr. Douglas if the general were not progressing as well as he had supposed; but Dr. Douglas intimated that the reports were rose-colored and the affliction was no doubt cancer.

Thereupon Mark Twain said that he and the other excessive smokers like him must take warning from this case; but Dr. Douglas spoke up and said that the result was not to be attributed *entirely to smoking,* it had probably had its *origin* in excessive smoking; but that was not the certain reason for its manifesting itself at this time, it was more than likely that the general's distress of mind and long worry over the effects of the failure of Grant & Ward had caused the very serious nature of his affliction.

This started the general talking on the subject of the Grant & Ward failure, a subject most important to him and to the whole Grant connection, as they had all been hurt by Ward's robberies. Mark Twain noted that while the general was evidently outraged by the way he had been treated, he never uttered a phrase concerning Ward which was abusive or other than what an outraged adult might have uttered concerning an offending child; he spoke as a man speaks who has been deeply wronged and humiliated and betrayed, but never used a venomous expression or one of a vengeful nature.

While Mark Twain was boiling inwardly and for flaying Ward alive, breaking him on the wheel, pounding him to a jelly, and cursing him with all the profanity of the one language with which he was acquainted, the general told his story with deep feeling in his voice, but no betrayal on his countenance of what was going on in his heart.

Before his trip west Mark Twain had become interested in a young sculptor, Karl Gerhardt, who came to his residence one evening to show him a small bust he had been making in clay from a photograph of General Grant. Mark Twain was somewhat irritated, he remembered, as he had never seen a portrait of any kind of General Grant that was at all satisfactory to him; therefore he did not expect a person who had never even seen the general to produce anything close to a likeness of him. But when Gerhardt uncovered the bust, Mark Twain's prejudices vanished immediately. Overlooking incorrectness of detail, it seemed to him the closest approach to a likeness of the general that he had ever seen. Gerhardt explained that he had brought it in the hope that Mark Twain would show it to some member of the general's family who would point out its defects. Glancing at the bust, Twain assured the artist that he would go to New York the next morning and ask the family to look at it; Gerhardt must come along.

Although conscious that the family must have been pestered with such matters by many artists, the next day Twain went to the family and explained that he had a young artist downstairs who had been making a bust of the general from a photograph; would they look at it? Jesse Grant's wife spoke up and asked: "Is it the artist who made the bust of you that is in *Huckleberry Finn?*" Mark Twain said, "Yes," whereupon Mrs. Jesse Grant said with great animation: "How good it was of you, Mr. Clemens, to think of that!" She added: "How strange it is; only two nights ago I dreamed that I was looking at your bust in *Huckleberry Finn* and thinking how nearly perfect it was, and then I thought that I conceived the idea of going to you and asking you if you could not hunt up that artist and get him to make a bust of Father!"

The other persons present were Colonel Fred Grant and Dr. Douglas. Somewhat jubilant at the success so far of his mission, Mark Twain ran down to get Gerhardt, who brought up the bust and uncovered it. They began to discuss the details of the bust and then suddenly begged Gerhardt's pardon for appearing to criticize; but of course he assured them that their criticisms were exactly what he wanted and asked them to go on. In the meantime Mrs. Grant had come in, taken some part in the discussion, and finally had hesitatingly suggested: "The general is in the next room. Would Mr. Gerhardt mind going in there and making the correction himself?"

While the discussion was going on concerning the nose and the forehead, Mrs. Fred Grant joined the group, and then the ladies went off for a few minutes and each came back with a handful of photographs and hand-painted miniatures of the general. These pictures had been made in every corner of the world, and one of them had been painted in Japan. But good as many of these pictures were, they were worthless as evidence because they contradicted one another in nearly every detail. No two noses and no two foreheads were alike.

They stepped into the general's room and found him stretched out in a "reclining chair with his feet supported upon an ordinary chair. He was muffled up in dressing gown and afghans, with his black woolen skull cap on his head." The ladies took the skull cap off and began to discuss the nose and forehead and asked him to turn this way and that way, which he did patiently and without complaint.

Twain said: "Mrs. Fred Grant, who is very beautiful and of the most gentle and loving character, was very active in this service and very deft, with her graceful hands, in arranging and rearranging the General's head for inspection, and repeatedly called attention to the handsome shape of his head."

Here Mark Twain was reminded that Gerhardt "had picked up an old plug hat of the General's downstairs, and had remarked upon the perfect, oval shape of it, this oval being so uniform that the wearer of the hat would never be able to know by the feel of it, whether he had it right end in front or wrong end in front, whereas the average man's head is broad at one end and narrow at the other."

Without further description of the details of the discussion, Mark Twain remarks, "in passing, that the General's hands were very thin, and they showed, far more than did his face, how his long siege of confinement and illness and insufficient food had wasted him. He was at this time suffering great and increasing pain from the cancer at the root of his tongue, but there was nothing ever discoverable in the expression of his face to betray this fact, as long as he was awake. When asleep, his face would take advantage of him and make revelations." At the general's suggestion Gerhardt brought his clay model to the sickroom. The general watched Gerhardt's "swift and noiseless fingers" for some time with manifest interest, until he slowly fell asleep, when everybody left except Gerhardt and Mr. Clemens himself, the latter moving out of sight as far as possible.

Harrison, the general's old Negro servant, came in presently and remained a while watching Gerhardt, and then broke out with great zeal and decision: "That's the general! Yes, sir, that's the general! Mind! I tell you that's the general!"

This was the first sleep the general had had for several weeks uninduced by narcotics, and Mark Twain adds in his description of the incident that, "To my mind this bust, completed at this sitting, has in it more of General Grant than can be found in any other likeness of him that has ever been made since he was a famous man. I think it may rightly be called the best portrait of General Grant that is in existence. It has also a feature which must always be a remembrancer to this nation of what the General was passing through during the long weeks of that spring. For into the clay image went the pain which he was enduring, but which did not appear in his face when he was awake.

Consequently, the bust has about it a suggestion of patient and brave and manly suffering which is infinitely touching."

According to Garland, about March 10 a piece of diseased tissue had been placed before Dr. G. R. Elliott, an expert microscopist, who also submitted it to Dr. Shrady. The latter agreed, without knowing from whom the piece of tissue came, that it was from the throat and base of the tongue and was affected with cancer. Dr. Elliott then said that it came from the throat of General Grant and Dr. Shrady replied, slowly, "Then General Grant is doomed." This diagnosis was publicized and there was corresponding response and expressions of sympathy.

On March 12 the general was reported to have done some work on his book in the morning and in the afternoon was cheerful and talkative when Dr. Shrady and Dr. Douglas visited him. But the report on March 17 was: "Bad night. A report that the General had died during the night. In the morning both Dr. Barker and myself were visited by reporters to ascertain the correctness of report. Neither knew anything concerning it." Here are other entries from Dr. Douglas' diary:

> March 28: Not as well. Consider that the restlessness and appearance of failure is due to the fatigue after the examination in the Fish trial. [This refers to the ordeal of the General's making a deposition in connection with the trial of Mr. Fish for his part in the Grant & Ward failure.]
>
> March 29: When I returned from my night visit, I had not noticed anything particularly alarming, but I had hardly reached my room, when I was aroused by a message from Colonel Grant, stating that his father wished me to come to him at once. We found the General much agitated from an accumulation of mucus in the throat. . . . The throat was immediately relieved of the accumulation of mucus, and soon after (the apprehension of dreaded suffocation having subsided) the General fell into a quiet slumber, which lasted several hours.
>
> April 1, midnight: After partaking of nourishment (following a severe coughing spell and pain due to accumulated secretions) the General appeared to be sleeping, but the almost imperceptible movement of the respiration, and the feebleness of the heart's action . . . made me so solicitous that . . . about 4 A.M. I aroused Doctor Shrady who was sleeping in the adjoining room.

The crisis which had been feared and for which some preparations had been made had evidently arrived. The family were summoned and for the first time Mrs. Grant, who previously had refused to believe that any immediate danger was imminent, now faced the facts. Dr. Douglas pointed to the syringe filled with brandy which was behind Dr. Shrady and said: "Use it, doctor, if it is just as convenient to you." The injection of brandy at first brought on no noticeable effect, but a second injection caused the heart at once to regain action. Throughout this time the general was conscious, spoke clearly when addressed, and was the least perturbed of those present.

With the family's consent, the Rev. Dr. Newman (of the Metropolitan Methodist Church, Washington) was now permitted to enter the sickroom for the purpose of baptizing the supposedly dying patient. Following the solemn words of the baptism and a brief prayer by Dr. Newman, the general slowly raised his eyes and looking about him said: "Thank you. I had intended to have attended to this myself."

Dr. Douglas feared the worst day would be when the general had finished his book, evidently fearful of the general's succumbing to his illness when he had accomplished the mission he had set himself. However, that time had not come yet and slowly he made a partial recovery. He was fearful of choking to death. Light hemorrhages of the throat relieved the congestion but weakened the patient. Drops of digitalis strengthened the heart, and solutions of cocaine applied to the throat were helpful, and when necessary hypodermic injections were given.

On April 14 he was able to walk from the library to his bedroom several times and enjoyed the company of several members of the family. On April 20 he drove out in the park with Dr. Douglas, and on April 23 he drove with the ladies of his family. His weight had dropped from 200 pounds to 146 pounds.

This writer remembers distinctly two occasions on which the general was able to stand at his window and review from there some military organization; once it was the 7th Regiment New York National Guard, and the other time it was part of the Grand Army of the Republic, probably the U. S. Grant Post and others from nearby. I was allowed to stand by my grandfather and was duly impressed with the military ceremony. I remember that one of these reviews was on his sixty-third birthday, April 27, 1885. He also received several friends on his birthday, and he appeared to have come back to a semblance of improved strength with his mind and his purpose clear and fixed throughout the crisis just concluded.

He was always on the lookout for any happening that might add to Mrs. Grant's worry or appear to the physicians as criticism or otherwise hurt their feelings. The doctor was conscious one afternoon of his being somewhat disturbed, and soon after General Grant handed the doctor a weekly paper in which the medical treatment he was receiving was criticized. He then gave Dr. Douglas some slips with his comments thereon to the following effect:

> This paper [naming it] is a reformer in medicines. It is an advertising medium for quack medicines prepared by ignorant people. If I were left to their treatment, I would die within a few days, suffering the extremest agony in the meantime. I would not have entire faith in the four doctors attending me, unsupported by the judgment of anybody else. But they are all distinguished in their profession. They reject no treatment because it is not given at their own suggestion.
>
> It is not true that they are experimenting on me with a single medicine about which they know little or nothing. It is not true that they are persisting in a single treatment. The medicine alluded to as the one being "experimented with" is, I presume, Cocaine. That has never been given as a medicine. It has only been administered as an application to stop pain. It is well known that it accomplishes that result without leaving injurious effects behind. It is only applied when much needed.
>
> As to the treatment of Garfield [President Garfield, who had been shot] I knew nothing about that.

On May 10, Dr. Barker had been so overworked that he considered it necessary to leave for Europe, and the general said good-by to him with every evidence of suppressed emotion. He expressed his appreciation of the doctor's long-continued professional friendship and care and added, "I suppose you never expect to see me again." The doctor replied, "I hope I may." To this the general answered sadly, "You do not say 'expect,' but 'hope.' "

Dr. Douglas at this time favored moving the patient to a high dry climate if possible, with the observation that the warm, moist weather always weakened him. Thereupon the family agreed to accept Joseph W. Drexel's offer of his cottage at Mt. McGregor, not far from Saratoga Springs, New York. The voice and general condition of the patient became so feeble that Dr. Douglas was able to add to his collection a little penciled memoranda of the general's: "June 23, 4:30 P.M.—I said I had been adding to my book and to my coffin. I presume every strain of the mind or body is one more nail in the coffin." That was the date on which they had intended to move to Mt. McGregor but the move was advanced to June 16.

Under date of June 27, 1885, *Harper's Weekly* noted: "At station after station on the route knots of people were found gathered to wave greeting and godsend. At West Point he beckoned to Dr. Douglas and with a smile motioned toward the Military Academy (where the Corps of Cadets stood at present arms as the train passed on the opposite side of the Hudson) . . . as though the sight were dear to him." His gaze was fixed on West Point until it was out of sight.

The journey to Mt. McGregor of course was tiring for the general, and on his arrival he went to bed and slept well and long for the first time in many weeks. On the afternoon of the seventeenth he had himself helped to a chair on the verandah of the cottage, where he sat a long time looking at the scene before him. Suddenly he decided to test his strength and try walking. With Harrison to help in case of need, he walked down the steps from the porch and up the inclined path toward the Hotel Balmoral, where he rested again on a rustic bench, thoughtfully gazing at the Schuylerville Monument on the Saratoga Battlefield.

In the evening he handed Dr. Douglas a folded yellow paper on which he had written: "Dr., since coming to this beautiful climate, and getting a complete rest for about ten hours, I have watched my pains, and compared them with those of the past few weeks. I can feel plainly that my system is preparing for dissolution in three ways; one by hemorrhage; one by strangulation, and the third by exhaustion. The first and second are liable to come at any moment to relieve me of my earthly sufferings. The time of the arrival of the third can be computed with almost mathematical certainty. With an increase of daily food, I have fallen off in weight and strength very rapidly for the last two weeks. There cannot be hope of going far beyond this period. All my physicians, or any number of them can do for me now, is to make my burden of pain as light as possible. I do not want any physician but yourself, but I tell you, so that if you are unwilling to have me go without consultation with other professional men, you can send for them. I dread them, however, knowing that it means another desperate effort to save me, and more suffering."

He had calls from many friends: from his old West Point friend Confederate General Buckner, Mark Twain, and Robert Underwood Johnson. Mr. Johnson wrote about a week before the end:

At Colonel Grant's request I visited Mt. McGregor to confer with him concerning our articles . . . but the Colonel arranged for me to see him

[General Grant]. The General, fully dressed, sat on the piazza in the sun, wearing something over his head, like a skull cap, and wrapped in a plaid shawl, looking thinner than before, and with a patient, resigned expression, but not with a stricken look. As he could communicate only in writing I did the talking . . . merely conveying the sympathy of my associates and the assurance that we should gladly do anything we could for the success of the book in Mr. Clemens' hands, adjusting our [magazine] plans to his. He smiled faintly and bowed his acknowledgment, and as I rose gave me his hand. I could hardly keep back the tears as I made my farewell. . . . The story may well be taught in all our schools as a lesson of fortitude, patriotism, and magnanimity. . . .

General Buckner had a special object in view in paying this visit. He wanted to assure Grant that every Confederate soldier held him in kindly memory, not only for his magnanimity at the close of the war, but also for his just and friendly act afterward in preventing Federal authorities from violating the terms of the military convention that Grant had offered and the South had accepted.

Certainly nothing could have pleased the dying Union general more than to hear this from his old friend and so he replied, by a pencil note on his pad:

I have witnessed since my sickness just what I have wished to see ever since the war—harmony and good feeling between the sections. I have always contended that if there had been nobody left but the soldiers, we would have had peace in a year. Jubal Early and [Daniel H.] Hillare are the only two that I know of who do not seem to be satisfied on the Southern side. We have some on ours who failed to accomplish as much as they wished, or who did not get warmed up to the fight until it was all over, who have not had quite full satisfaction. The great majority, too, of them who did not get into the war have long since grown tired of the long controversy. We may now look forward to a perpetual peace at home and a natural strength that will secure us against foreign complications. I believe myself that the war was worth all it cost us, fearful as it was. Since it was over, I have visited every state in Europe and a number in the East. I know, as I did not before, the value of our inheritance.

General Grant touched on the same theme in a note to his son Frederick:

You ought to feel happy under any circumstances. My expected death called forth expressions of the sincerest kindness from all the people of all the sections of the country. The Confederate soldier vied with the Union soldier in sounding my praise. The Protestant, the Catholic, and the Jew appointed days for universal prayer in my behalf. All societies———passed resolutions of sympathy for me and petitions that I might recover. It looks as if my sickness had had something to do to bring about the harmony between the sections. The attention of the public has been called to your children and they have been found to pass muster. Apparently I have accomplished more while apparently dying than it falls to the lot of most men to be able to do.

The rest of the story is quite fully told in General Grant's notes to the doctors and to his son Frederick, which had perhaps best be presented in the general's own words, and in the order in which they were preserved by Mr. Horace Green.

June 27: I feel worse this A.M. on the whole than I have for some time. My mouth hurts me and cocaine ceases to give the relief it did. If its use can be curtailed however I hope it will soon have its effect again. I shall endeavor to rest again if I feel it possible.

June 28: I feel much relieved this morning. I had begun to feel that the work of getting my book together was making but slow progress. I find it about completed, and the work now to be done is mostly after it gets back in gallies [spelling is the general's]. It can be sent to the printer faster than he is ready for it. There [are] from one hundred and fifty to two hundred pages more of it than I had intended. Will not cut out anything of interest. It is possible we may find a little repetition. The whole of that, however, is not likely to amount to many pages. Then, too, there is more likelihood of omission.

June 30, P.M. It will probably take several days to see the effect of discontinuing the use of cocaine. It might then be used once a day, might it not? Say when I am retiring for the night. It is no trouble, however, to quit outright for the present.

June 30, P.M. I see the *Times* man keeps up the character of his dispatches to the paper. They are quite as untrue as they would be if he described me as getting better from day to day. I think he might spare my family at least from reading such stuff.

July 1, 8 A.M. I feel weak from my exertions last night in throwing up. Then since that I cannot help repeating two advertisements of the B. & O. Railroad when I am half awake. The houses in this part of Deer Park are advertised as a sure cure for Malaria, or the place is, signed by Robert Barrett, Pres. The other is that the water—I think—is a sure cure for catarrh, signed same. There may be no such advertisements, but I keep dreaming them all the same. It strikes me as a very sharp dodge for a gentleman to advertise his own wares in such a way. When you consider Barrett owns the water and buildings at the park; is Pres. of the road over which invalids must pass to get to the place and is a very large owner in the stock of the road, it strikes me as another instance of what a man will do for money.

July 6, 5 P.M. The injection worked very well, and I hope at not too great a cost. The pain left me entirely so that it was an enjoyment to lay awake. I did get sleep, however, from the mere absence of pain, and woke up a short time before four. I then took my food, washed out my mouth and put in a little cocaine which went to the right spot the first time. I have felt no pain until within the last few minutes.

Undated: I know that what you are doing will be as likely to cure me as anything else. Nature is given a good opportunity to act and if a cure is possible it will develop itself. All the medical skill in America, including Dr. Brown, could not find a cure.

July 7, 11 A.M. I have had a pleasant morning. When my throat commences to hurt it begins with a cough. I then clean it out, either coughing up the phlegm, gargling out or the use of the syringe. It is then the cocaine would come in. I feel the want of it very much. But by keeping quiet the pain diminishes and finally disappears entirely so long as the hypodermic remains.

July 8, 7 P.M. [after writing on Mexican expedition] I must avoid such afternoons as this. We had company since four and I was writing all the time.

July 11, 1 A.M. Not sleeping does not disturb me because I have had so much sleep. And then, too, I have been comparatively free from pain. I know a sick person cannot feel just as he would like to all the time; but I think it a duty to let the physician know from time to time just my feelings. It may benefit some other fellow-sufferer hereafter. Wake the Doctor [probably Doctor Shrady] up and advise with him whether anything should be done . . .

July 12, 4 A.M. I notice that your little girls and Julie get along very happily together. With their swing, their lawn tennis and nice shade they seem very happy.

July 16, P.M. I feel sorry at the prospect of living through the summer and fall in the condition I am in. I do not think I can, but I may. Except that I do not gather strength, I feel quite as well from day to day as I have done heretofore. But I am satisfied that I am losing strength. I feel it more in the inability to move about than in any other way, or rather in the lack of desire to try to move.

Then there are some entries without dates in which he tries to be cheerful:

If Henry [the night nurse] can get me in bed . . . he has me just where he wants me. . . . You must have been dreaming. I heard no rain fall and I was here all the time.

If that is the case do you not think it advisable for me to get up and rest as the tailor does when he is standing up? . . . I was going to say you always catch me at it when you go out and come in again. I have been asleep three times since you went out, and once made enough noise to propel a Hudson river boat.

Here is the note which perhaps prompted Dr. Douglas to keep the entire lot confidential:

I will have to be careful about my writing. I see every person I give a piece of paper to puts it in his pocket. Some day they will be [coming?] up against my English.

July 20, 2 A.M. In making the summary of progress for the 19th of July, I stated that all the sores of the mouth were still there; this is hardly correct. The palate is about well, and along the tongue considerably improved.

The following letter, dated July 2, had been written and evidently mailed to Dr. Douglas:

Dr.: I ask you not to show this to any one, unless physicians you consult with, until the end. Particularly I want it kept from my family. If known to any one, the papers will get it. It would only distress them almost beyond endurance to know it, and by reflex, would distress me.

I have not changed my mind materially since I wrote you before in the same strain. Now, however, I know that I gain in strength some days, but when I do go back it is beyond where I started to improve. I think the chances are very decidedly in favor of your being able to keep me alive until the change of weather towards the winter. Of course, there are contingencies that might arise at any time that would carry me off very suddenly. The most probable of these is choking. Under these circumstances life is not worth living. I am very thankful I have been spared this long because it has enabled me to practically complete the work in which I take so much interest. I cannot stir up strength enough to review it and make additions and subtractions that would suggest themselves to me, and I am not likely to, to any one else.

Under the above circumstances, I will be the happiest the more pain I can avoid. If there is to be any extraordinary cure, such as some people believe there is to be, it will develop itself. I would say therefore, to you and your colleagues, to make me as comfortable as you can. If it is within God's providence that I should go now, I am ready to obey His call without a murmur. I should prefer going now to enduring my present suffering for a single day without hope of recovery. As I have stated, I am thankful for the providential extension of my time to enable me to continue my work. I am further thankful, and in a much greater degree thankful, because it has enabled me to see for myself the happy harmony which has so suddenly sprung up between those engaged but a few short years in deadly conflict. It has been an inestimable blessing to me to hear the kind expression towards me in person from all parts of our country; from people of all nationalities, of all religions, and of no religion; of Confederate and National troops alike; of soldiers' organizations; of mechanical, scientific, religious and all other societies, embracing almost every citizen in the land. They have brought joy to my heart if they have not effected a cure. To you and your colleagues I acknowledge my indebtedness for having brought me through the valley of the shadow of death to enable me to witness these things.

On July 10, Ulysses, Jr., had brought, in print, the last pages of the first volume. This gave everybody in the family something of interest to examine and check for errors. The general commented in one of his penciled notes: "In two weeks if they work hard they can have the second vol. copied ready to go to the printer. I will then feel that my work is done!"

The foregoing note by the general oddly enough predicted correctly within one day the end of the *Memoirs* and the general's death.

On May 23 General Grant had dedicated the *Memoirs* "to the American soldier and sailor." In July, however, it was suggested that he dedicate the volumes to the Union forces alone. The general said in a note to Frederick:

It is a great deal better that it should be dedicated as it is. I made what reputation I have as a soldier. The troops engaged on both sides are yet living. As it is, the dedication is to those we fought against as well as those we fought with. It may serve a purpose in restoring harmony. If it does it is of more importance than to simply gratify a little vanity. You will die. It is hoped the book will live. After you and the soldiers who fought are all gone the dedication will have more value than now.

The race with death had been won and his last contest had ended in victory—indeed a greater victory than he could have foreseen since the *Memoirs* have been recognized as a historical record of much greater value for future generations than he could have expected, and the fortune that derived from their sale—"the general's legacy," as he always called his manuscript—was much greater than even Mark Twain had prophesied.

On the twentieth he had attempted to go to the South Outlook in his bath chair, as he called it; he enjoyed sitting there and looking at the view, but on coming back over a different path the chair got stuck in some way and the general got up and walked several paces before the chair could be brought to where he was standing. On getting back to the cottage he looked very pale and somewhat weary.

On July 21, after a hot and sultry afternoon during which he was restless in search of comfort and relief from the heat, he gratefully accepted Mrs. Grant's assistance back to his chair, letting his cane fall to the floor. Later when the chair pillows and cushion had to be re-adjusted, the general rose and walked over to the cot nearby, practically falling over on it, weak and weary. He seemed to revive with the cool of night coming on, but was unable to take any food.

On the twenty-second the doctors realized that the general was sinking and that the signs of weakness and dissolution were noticeable. The patient's respiration had quickened, the pulse became weak (frequently so weak it could hardly be counted), and the limbs became cold.

For many weeks he had slept in an upholstered chair with his feet on another chair, but on the evening of July 22 he indicated he would like to be laid on his bed, a change for the worse that the doctors knew how to interpret. At seven o'clock, while Dr. Douglas was at the hotel eating dinner, the general's servant, Harrison, came for him because the general had become much weaker. Dr. Douglas immediately administered a hypodermic of brandy and waited; a slight revival occurred and in ten minutes he administered another hypodermic. Soon thereafter both Dr. Sands and Dr. Shrady came down from the hotel and remained up, prepared for the end to come at any moment.

During the night there were evidences of his appreciation of what those about him were doing for him. When he was asked if he were in pain, he distinctly answered, "No." One time during the night the colonel asked if he would have some water, to which he whispered, "Yes." Mrs. Grant sat near the head of the bed, at times cooling his forehead with a damp cloth and holding his hand. His three sons, their wives, and his daughter, Nellie Sartoris, were present most of the time.

On the last page of Dr. Douglas' diary he entered his last entry: "The intellect remained unclouded and he had been enabled to accomplish his great desire, the completion of his *Memoirs*."

Toward morning, July 23, a heavy fog crept up from the valley and surrounded the cottage. As the first rays of sunrise began to sweep away the mists, Dr. Douglas stepped out to the brow of the hill—to that view which had so often been enjoyed by the general. On coming back to take his place among the watchers, he found the heart rhythm so irregular that the pulse could not be counted, and gradually the respiration became shorter and even more shallow. There was no expiring sigh. Just before eight o'clock there seemed to be a stoppage in the breathing. They waited for a full minute, but the breathing was not resumed. Colonel Fred arose and stopped the clock at the time that the general's breathing had stopped. The general's children withdrew from the room and closed the door, leaving their mother alone with her "Victor" as she had so often liked to call him, while "over the soldier's granite features, inscrutable as always, now slowly settled a blanket of unending calm."

Fastened to his clothing was found a paper with the following note for Mrs. Grant in pencil:

> Look after our dear children and direct them in the paths of rectitude. It would distress me far more to hear that one of them could depart from an honorable, upright and virtuous life than it would to know that they were prostrated on a bed of sickness from which they were never to arise alive. They have never given us any cause for alarm on this account, and I trust they never will. With these few injunctions and the knowledge I have of your love and affection and the dutiful affection of all our children, I bid you a final farewell, until we meet in another and, I trust, better world. You will find this on my person after my demise.

Mrs. Grant knelt there for a long time by the side of her general, who had fought his last campaign.

Organizing the funeral and preparing for it took quite an effort, but the problems encountered were all successfully and harmoniously solved by New York City authorities and Federal Government officials, and especially the U. S. Army. General Winfield Scott Hancock was selected to be grand marshal of the funeral procession.

A brief funeral service was held in the Drexel cottage on Tuesday, August 4, 1885, at which the Rev. John P. Newman presided, preached a eulogy, and turned the body over to General Hancock. The latter with the guard of honor led the procession through the city of Albany to the new state capitol, where the body lay in state until the following day, Wednesday, August 5.

The morning of August 5 the general's remains were carried to the Albany station and placed in a special funeral car that had been draped in black. The family and such other persons as were to participate in the funeral ceremonies also boarded the train and proceeded to New York. As the train passed through the intervening towns their populations for the most part gathered at the stations to pay their respects, and at West Point the corps of cadets had been turned out and stood at present arms.

In New York City the general's body lay in state three nights and two days until on August 8 the final funeral services were held and the body carried to and placed in the temporary tomb on Riverside Drive.

Harper's Weekly of August 15, 1885, carried a full description of the funeral, as did many of the papers throughout the country:

> The funeral, however, was the greatest feature of this half week of national sorrow. It was under the control of the city of New York, and incidently of the National Government. The remarkable spectacle of three Presidents of the United States [Hayes, Arthur, Cleveland] come to the grave of a fourth may never be seen again by the living generation, if indeed in another century. No similar scene has been witnessed since Jefferson, Madison and Monroe walked together in the grounds of the University of Virginia. The President [Grover Cleveland] brought his whole cabinet; the United States Army and Navy may be said to have collected in all their enterprise and leading biography here. The pall-bearers selected by the President were typical of the highest respect and career in the land. SHERMAN and SHERIDAN, Grant's old lieutenants, JOHNSTON and BUCKNER, his old opponents, gave a picture of American fraternity astonishing almost to ourselves who remember the terrible conflicts within the present generation, and how it seemed that the American flag was doomed to be seen only in museums and old paintings.

In addition to the four generals mentioned above, President Cleveland appointed the following pallbearers: General John A. Logan, Illinois; Admiral David Porter, USN; Rear-Admiral John L. Worden, USN; Mr. George S. Boutwell, Massachusetts; Mr. A. J. Drexel, Pennsylvania; Mr. George Jones, New York; and Mr. Oliver Hoyt, New York.

The number of people who witnessed the procession was estimated at 1,000,000. The high and heavily draped hearse was drawn by twenty-four jet black horses with a black groom at each horse's head.

Mrs. Grant had requested only that, if any prominent Union generals were appointed pallbearers by the President, a corresponding number of Confederate generals be appointed.

Epilogue

BY April 27, 1897, seventy-five years to the day after the birth of Ulysses S. Grant in the little cabin at Mount Pleasant, Ohio—his monumental tomb on Riverside Drive in New York City was completed with funds donated by his compatriots, from the pennies of schoolchildren to the thousand-dollar subscriptions of the well-to-do. This was the day designated for its formal dedication and presentation to the City of New York. The President of the United States, William McKinley, a former major of Ohio Volunteers who had served in the army commanded by the famous occupant of the tomb, made the principal dedication address; General Horace Porter, the devoted aide of the general, who had been leader of the volunteer committee which raised the funds and built the tomb, made the presentation; and Mayor Strong accepted it for the city of which he was head.

The proposed ceremonies had been widely publicized throughout the country, and the city was crowded with more than half a million visitors who came by railroad, street cars, ferries, passenger boats, and over the bridges—all to witness the ceremonies with which the American metropolis would receive the remains of its hero President in the shrine so appropriately built by the donations of the people. The President and Mrs. McKinley came by special train, and with his usual consideration and thoughtfulness the President had invited the general's widow to come to New York on the same train. The Grant family gathered together with the widow in a parlor of the Fifth Avenue Hotel. The diplomatic corps and the high officials of the United States were also gathered there before starting in procession to the tomb.

A large fleet composed mostly of ships from the American navy and merchant marine was anchored in the Hudson River just west of the tomb; the American craft had been joined by many vessels of foreign nations. When the President stepped on the deck of the presidential yacht, the *Mayflower,* the first gun of the 21-gun salute went off. The scene and the noise reminded observers of the many salutes the general had received during his triumphant world tour.

At about a quarter to 11 o'clock the high officials and guests took their seats in the grandstand, which had been built in front of the huge tomb. A large crowd was gathered in the street facing the grandstand. The President and Vice President drove up together in a carriage and took seats in the front row, closely followed by General Porter. Mrs. Grant and her family had seats in an adjacent section, with her in the first row. The newspapers agreed that the approach of this first part of the party was a pretty sight, and that upon its arrival the crowd burst into cheers which were kept up for several hours. The President and Vice President were escorted by Squadron A, New York National Guard, while the Grant family was escorted by the Society of the Army of the Tennessee, the New York Commandery of the G. A. R., the Military Order of the Loyal Legion, and members of the G. A. R. Meade Post No. 1 in carriages, under the command of Gen. Daniel Butterfield. Squadron A and General Butterfield's guard of honor took their places in the column of march behind the line of mounted police when the distinguished guests they had been escorting were seated. The presidential party included Secretary of State Sherman, Secretary of War and Mrs. Alger, Attorney General and Mrs. McKenna, Secretary of Agriculture and Mrs. Wilson, and Gen. Miles. Former President Cleveland went up to his successor with a cordial, "How de do, glad to see you." After a warm handshake the two sat down together and conversed with an air of good fellowship. The arrival of the general's oldest son, Colonel Fred Grant, brought many hearty greetings. Mrs. McKinley entered on the arm of her physician and escorted by Abner McKinley. It was a scene not to be forgotten.

The official party and invited guests were served a light hot lunch in the back of the grandstand, and resumed their seats after finishing it, to listen to the speeches and then view the procession. President McKinley delivered an eloquent eulogy of his former commanding general, in which he said:

A great life, dedicated to the welfare of the nation, here finds its earthly coronation. Even if this day lacked the impressiveness of ceremony and was devoid of pageantry, it would still be memorable, because it is the anniversary of the birth of one of the most famous and beloved American soldiers.

Architecture has paid high tribute to the leaders of mankind, but never was a memorial more worthily bestowed or more gratefully accepted by a free people than the beautiful structure before which we are gathered.

In marking the successful completion of this work we have as witness and participants representatives of all branches of our government, the resident officials of foreign nations, the governors of states and the sovereign people of every section of our country, who join in this tribute to the soldier, patriot and citizen. . . .

Faithful and fearless as a volunteer soldier, intrepid and invincible as commander-in-chief of the Armies of the Union and confident as President of a reunited and strengthened nation, which his genius had been instrumental in achieving, he has our homage and that of the world; but brilliant as was his public character, we love him all the more for his homelife and homely virtues. . . .

Victorious in the work which under Divine Providence he was called upon to do, clothed with almost limitless power, he was yet one of the people—patient, patriotic and just, success did not disturb the even balance of his mind, while fame was powerless to swerve him from the path of duty. Great as he was in war he loved peace, and told the world that honorable arbitration was the best hope of civilization. . . .

General Porter's speech thrilled with strong emotion and the admiration in which he held his former commander through the last year of the Civil War, the years of Reconstruction, and as Secretary in the White House. He spoke of the propriety of this ceremony being presided over by the President—a former officer who had fought in the army under General Grant and who was performing the duties of President with so much grace and ability. He went on to say:

There is a source of extreme gratification and a pronounced significance in the fact that there are in attendance here today not only the soldiers who fought under the renowned defender of the Union, but also the leaders of armies who fought against him, all uniting in testifying the esteem and respect which he commanded of friend and foe alike.

This grateful day which we discharge is not unmixed with sadness, for the occasion brings vividly to mind the fatal day on which his generous heart ceased to beat and recalls the grief which fell upon the American people. And yet it is not an occasion for tears, not a time to chant requiems or display the sable draperies of mourning. He who lies within the portals is not a dead memory.

He pointed out that this was not a funeral, but the transfer with appropriate ceremony, after twelve years, of the President's remains to a suitable tomb erected in his honor by a grateful people.

John Russell Young wrote in the *Herald* of the day's festivities:

The world came not to his Funeral but to his Festival. The metropolis yesterday gave welcome to all the world. It was the day of the Apotheosis of Grant.

To the mere man whose dust was so reverently committed to the dust the funeral rites had been paid (twelve years before). Then we mourned the man. Yesterday we honored the hero. Then we paid tribute to sorrow. Now we pay tribute to fame.

It was a wondrous Babylon. It was therefore fitting that the metropolis should throw open its gates and bid mankind to his festival. Nor was the metropolis ever in a more gracious, hospitable mood. The city seemed a moving mass of light, order of chivalry, beauty, also fashion and pride. So much to show to those kind friends who came to spend the day with us. The beauties of river and bay, and highlands, the noble avenues, the pleasure grounds, hills crowned with homes of wisdom, piety and benevolence, stupendous forces of business and energy which buttress the fair city as if with fortifications. . . .

All this time the bands played and the procession—and New York had certainly never before had such a procession—went marching on until after dark, and no one was left to review its end but the kind Vice President, the President having had to leave to fulfil an engagement at the Union League Club; the Grant family because of old age or the children's youth; and a small part of the spectators for similar reasons; but a large host remained until the last devoted marcher had passed.

Bibliography

Abbott, John S. C. *The Life of General Ulysses S. Grant.* Boston: Russell, 1868.

Adams, George Washington. *Doctors in Blue: The Medical History of the Union Army in the Civil War.* New York: Collier Books, 1961.

Badeau, Adam. *Grant in Peace from Appomattox to Mount McGregor: A Personal Memoir.* Hartford, Conn.: S. S. Scranton & Co., 1887.

———. *Military History of Ulysses S. Grant, from April, 1861, to April, 1865* (3 vols.). New York: Appleton, 1881–82.

Bancroft, Frederic. *Slave Trading in the Old South.* Baltimore: J. H. Furst Co., 1931.

Barton, William E. *The Life of Abraham Lincoln* (2 vols.). Indianapolis: Bobbs-Merrill, 1925.

Battles and Leaders of the Civil War (4 vols.). New York: Century, 1887–88.

Bearss, Edwin C. *Decision in Mississippi.* Jackson, Miss.: Mississippi Commission of the War Between the States, 1962.

Brinton, John H. *Personal Memoirs.* New York: Neale, 1914.

Brown, D. Alexander. *The Bold Cavaliers: Morgan's 2nd Kentucky Cavalry Raiders.* Philadelphia: Lippincott, 1959.

Brown, D. Alexander. *The Galvanized Yankees.* Urbana: University of Illinois Press, 1963.

Browne, Francis F., ed. *Bugle-Echoes: A Collection of the Poetry of the Civil War.* New York: White, Stokes, & Allen, 1886.

Bryan, Wilhemus Bogart. *A History of the National Capital* (2 vols.). New York: Macmillan, 1914–16.

"Burleigh" of the *Boston Journal.* "Caesarism: General Grant for a Third Term." New York: Hurd & Houghton, 1873.

Burr, Frank A. *An Original and Authentic Record of the Life and Deeds of General Ulysses S. Grant.* Philadelphia: National, 1885.

Butler, Benjamin F. *Butler's Book.* Boston: A. M. Thayer & Co., 1892.

Carruth, Gorton, and Associates, eds. *The Encyclopedia of American Facts and Dates.* New York: Thomas Y. Crowell, 1956.

Catton, Bruce. *Grant Moves South.* Boston: Little, Brown, 1960.

———. *U. S. Grant and the American Military Tradition,* ed. by Oscar Handlin. Boston: Little, Brown, 1954.

Chaplin, Jeremiah, ed. *Words of Our Hero Ulysses S. Grant.* Boston: D. Lothrop and Co., 1880.

Church, William Conant. *Ulysses S. Grant and the Period of National Preservation and Reconstruction.* Garden City, N.Y.: Garden City Publishing Company, 1926.

Churchill, Winston S. *A History of the English-Speaking Peoples* (4 vols.). New York: Dodd, Mead, 1956–58.

Civil War Times, Illustrated (magazine). Gettysburg, Pa.: Historical Times, Inc.

Clemens, Samuel. *Mark Twain's Autobiography,* with an introduction by Albert Bigelow Paine (2 vols.). New York: Harper, 1924.

Conger, A. L. *The Rise of U. S. Grant.* New York: Century, 1931.

Coolidge, Louis A. *Ulysses S. Grant.* Boston: Houghton Mifflin, 1917.

Coppee, Henry. *Life and Services of Gen. U. S. Grant.* New York: Richardson, 1868.

Cramer, Jesse Grant, ed. *Letters of Ulysses S. Grant to His Father and His Youngest Sister 1857–78.* New York: Putnam's, 1912.

Cramer, M. J. *Ulysses S. Grant: Conversations and Unpublished Letters.* New York: Eaton & Mains, 1897.

Crook, William H., compiled and edited by Margarita Spalding Gerry. *Through Five Administrations: Reminiscences of Col. William H. Crook, Body-guard to President Lincoln.* New York: Harper, 1910.

Cross, Nelson. *The Life of General Grant, His Political Record, etc.* New York: J. S. Redfield. (no date)

Dana, Charles A. *Recollections of the Civil War.* New York: Appleton, 1902.

Dana, Charles A., and Wilson, J. H. *The Life of Ulysses S. Grant, General of the Armies of the United States.* Springfield, Mass.: Gurdon Bill, 1868.

Depew, Chauncey M. *My Memories of Eighty Years.* New York: Scribner's, 1922.

Dodge, Major General Grenville M. *Personal Recollections of President Abraham Lincoln, General Ulysses S. Grant and General William Sherman.* Council Bluffs, Iowa: Monarch Printing, 1914.

Donald, David. *Lincoln Reconsidered: Essays on the Civil War Era.* New York: Knopf, 1956.

———. *Lincoln's Herndon.* New York: Knopf, 1948.

DuFour, Charles L. *Gentle Tiger: The Gallant Life of Roberdeau Wheat.* Baton Rouge: Louisiana State University Press, 1957.

———. *Nine Men in Gray.* Garden City, N. Y.: Doubleday, 1963.

DuPont, H. A. *The Campaign of 1864 in the Valley of Virginia and the Expedition to Lynchburg.* New York: National Americana Society, 1925.

Dupuy, Colonel R. Ernest, and Dupuy, Colonel Trevor N. *The Compact History of the Civil War.* New York: Hawthorn Books, 1960.

Eaton, John. *Grant, Lincoln and the Freedmen: Reminiscences of the Civil War.* New York: Longmans, Green, 1907.

Edmonds, Franklin Spencer. *Ulysses S. Grant.* Philadelphia: George W. Jacobs & Co., 1915.

Ellet, Mrs. E. F. *The Court Circles of the Republic or the Beauties and Celebrities of the Nation.* Hartford, Conn.: Hartford Publishing Co., 1870.

Foster, John W. *A Century of American Diplomacy.* Boston: Houghton Mifflin, 1900.

Freeman, Douglas Southall. *R. E. Lee, a Biography.* New York: Scribner's, 1934–35.

Fuller, Colonel J. F. C. *The Generalship of Ulysses S. Grant.* London: John Murray, 1929.

———. *Grant and Lee: A Study in Personality and Generalship.* New York: Scribner's, 1933.

Galwey, Thomas Francis, ed. by Colonel W. S. Nye. *The Valiant Hours.* Harrisburg, Pa.: Stackpole, 1961.

Garland, Hamlin. *Ulysses S. Grant, His Life and Character.* New York: Macmillan, 1898.

Gerrish, Reverend Theodore. *Army Life: A Private's Reminiscences of the Civil War.* Portland, Me.: Hoyt, Fogg & Donham, 1882.

Goodrich, Arthur. *Mr. Grant.* New York: Robert McBride & Co., 1932–34.

Graham, C. R., ed. *Under Both Flags* (Tales of the Civil War as Told by the Veterans). Baltimore: R. H. Woodward Co., 1896.

Grant, Arthur Hastings. *The Grant Family: A Genealogical History of the Descendants of Matthew Grant of Windsor, Conn. 1601–1898.* Poughkeepsie, N. Y.: Press of A. V. Haight, 1898.

Grant, Jesse R. *In the Days of My Father, General Grant.* New York: Harper, 1925.

Grant, Ulysses S. *Personal Memoirs of U. S. Grant* (2 vols.). 2nd ed. New York: Century, 1903.

Green, Horace. *General Grant's Last Stand, a Biography.* New York: Scribner's, 1936.

Hanly, J. Frank. *Vicksburg.* Cincinnati: Jennings and Graham, 1912.

Hart, B. H. Liddell. *Sherman: Soldier, Realist, American.* New York: Dodd, Mead, 1929.

Healy, George P. A. *Reminiscences of a Portrait Painter.* Chicago: A. C. McClurg & Company, 1894.

Henderson, Colonel G. F. R. *Stonewall Jackson and the American Civil War* (2 vols.). London-New York: Longmans, Green, 1913.

Henry, Robert Selph. *The Story of the Confederacy.* Indianapolis: Bobbs-Merrill, 1936.

Hesseltine, William Best. *Civil War Prisons: A Study in War Psychology.* Columbus: Ohio State University Press, 1930.

———. *Ulysses S. Grant, Politician.* New York: Dodd, Mead, 1935.

Holcombe and Adams. *An Account of the Battle of Wilson's Creek.* Springfield, Mo.: Springfield Public Library and the Green County Historical Society, 1961.

Howland, Edward. *Grant as a Soldier and Statesman, being a Succinct History of His Military and Civil Career.* Hartford, Conn.: J. B. Burr & Co., 1868.

Illustrated Life, Campaigns and Public Services of Lieutenant General Grant. Philadelphia: T. B. Peterson & Brothers, 1865.

Jones, George R. *Biography of J. Russell Jones.* Chicago: privately printed, 1964.

Jones, Virgil Carrington. *The Civil War at Sea, I the Blockaders, II The River War.* New York: Holt, Rinehart & Winston, 1960–61.

King, General Charles. *The True Ulysses S. Grant.* Philadelphia: Lippincott, 1914.

Larke, J. K., and Patton, J. Harris. *General U. S. Grant: His Early Life and Military Career.* New York: Thomas Kelly, 1885.

LeConte, Joseph. *'Ware Sherman.* Berkeley: University of California Press, 1937.

Lee, Captain Robert E. *Recollections and Letters of General Robert E. Lee.* Garden City, N. Y.: Doubleday, Page, 1924.

Lewis, Lloyd. *Captain Sam Grant.* Boston: Little, Brown, 1950.

———. Sherman, *Fighting Prophet.* New York: Harcourt, Brace, 1932.

Livermore, Thomas L. *Numbers and Losses in the Civil War in America 1861–65.* Boston: Houghton Mifflin, 1900.

———. *Numbers and Losses in the Civil War in America 1861–65.* Bloomington: Indiana University Press, 1957.

Longstreet, James. *From Manassas to Appomattox, Memoirs of the Civil War in America.* Philadelphia: Lippincott, 1896.

Lossing, Benson J. *A History of the Civil War, 1861–1865* (with reproductions of the Brady war photographs). New York: War Memorial Association, 1895.

McClellan, Carswell. *The Personal Memoirs and Military History of U. S. Grant versus the Record of the Army of the Potomac.* Boston: Houghton Mifflin, 1887.

McClure, A. K. *Abraham Lincoln and Men of War-Times.* Philadelphia: Times Publishing Company, 1892.

McCormick, Robert R. *Ulysses S. Grant, the Great Soldier of America.* New York: Appleton, 1934.

———. *The War Without Grant.* New York: Bond Wheelwright, 1950.

Macartney, Clarence Edward. *Grant and His Generals.* New York: McBride, 1953.

Mahan, D. H. *A Treatise on Field Fortification.* Richmond, Va.: West & Johnston, 1862.

Marshall, Edward C. *The Ancestry of General Grant and the Contemporaries.* New York: Sheldon & Co., 1869.

Masters, Edgar Lee. *Lincoln the Man.* New York: Dodd, Mead, 1931.

Maurice, Major General Sir Frederick. *Robert E. Lee, the Soldier.* Boston: Houghton Mifflin, 1925.

Mearns, David Chambers. *Largely Lincoln.* New York: St. Martin's Press, 1961.

Mende, Elsie Porter, in collaboration with Henry Greenleaf Pearson. *An American Soldier and Diplomat: Horace Porter.* New York: Stokes, 1927.

Meredith, Roy, ed. *Mr. Lincoln's General U. S. Grant: An Illustrated Autobiography.* New York: Dutton, 1959.

Miles, Nelson A. *Personal Recollections and Observations of General Nelson A. Miles.* Chicago: Werner, 1896.

Mosby, John S. *Stuart's Cavalry in the Gettysburg Campaign.* New York: Moffat, Yard & Co., 1908.

Munden, Kenneth W., and Beers, Henry Putney. *Guide to Federal Archives Relating to the Civil War.* Washington: National Archives and Records Service, General Services Administration, 1962.

Newman, Ralph G., ed. *Lincoln for the Ages.* New York: Pyramid Books, 1964.

Nicolay, Helen. *The Boy's Life of Ulysses S. Grant.* New York: Century, 1909.

Nicolay, John G., and Hay, John. *Abraham Lincoln: A History* (10 vols.).

Nicolay, John G. *A Short Life of Abraham Lincoln.* New York: Century, 1904.

New York: Century, 1904.

Oberholtzer, Ellis Paxson. *A History of the United States Since the Civil War* (5 vols.). New York: Macmillan, 1917–26.

O'Connor, Richard. *Sheridan the Inevitable.* Indianapolis: Bobbs-Merrill, 1953.

Pendel, Thomas F. *Thirty-Six Years in the White House.* Washington: Neale, 1902.

Penniman, Major. *The Tanner-Boy and How He Became Lieutenant-General.* Boston: Roberts Brothers, 1864.

Perkins, J. R. *Trails, Rails and War: The Life of General G. M. Dodge.* Indianapolis: Bobbs-Merrill, 1929.

Personal Reminiscences and Experiences, by Members of the One Hundred and Third Ohio Volunteer Infantry. Oberlin, Ohio: News Printing Company. (no date)

Phisterer, Frederick. *Statistical Record of the Armies of the United States.* New York: Scribner's, 1883.

Porter, General Horace. *Campaigning With Grant.* Bloomington: Indiana University Press, 1961.

Post, James L., compiler. *Reminiscences by Personal Friends of Gen. U. S. Grant and the History of Grant's Log Cabin.* St. Louis: 1904.

Provisional and Permanent Constitutions of the Confederate States. Richmond, Va.: Tyler, Wise, Allegre and Smith, 1861.

Randall, Ruth Painter. *Lincoln's Sons.* Boston: Little, Brown, 1955.

Rhodes, James Ford. *History of the United States from the Compromise of 1850 to the Final Restoration of Home Rule at the South in 1877* (8 vols.). New York: Macmillan, 1906–19.

Richardson, Albert D. *A Personal History of Ulysses S. Grant,* revised and completed by R. H. Fletcher. Hartford, Conn.: Winter & Hatch, 1885.

Richardson, James D. *A Compilation of the Messages and Papers of the Presidents, 1789–1908.* Bureau of National Literature, vol. VII, 1909.

Ross, Ishbel. *The General's Wife: The Life of Mrs. Ulysses S. Grant.* New York: Dodd, Mead, 1959.

Russell, William Howard. *My Diary North and South.* New York: Harper, 1954.

Sanborn, John B. *The Crisis at Champion's Hill, the Decisive Battle of the Civil War.* St. Paul, Minn., pamphlet, 1903.

Schenck, Martin. *Up Came Hill.* Harrisburg, Pa.: Stackpole, 1958.

Schildt, John W. *September Echoes* (The Maryland Campaign of 1862). Middletown, Md.: The Valley Register, 1960.

Schofield, Lieutenant General John M. *Forty-Six Years in the Army.* New York: Century, 1897.

Seifert, Shirley. *Captain Grant: A Novel.* Philadelphia: Lippincott, 1946.

Sheridan, Philip H. *Personal Memoirs of P. H. Sheridan* (2 vols.). New York: Webster, 1888.

Sherman, William T. *Memoirs of General William T. Sherman* (2 vols.). New York: Appleton, 1886.

Shrady, George F. *General Grant's Last Days.* New York: privately printed, 1908.

Simmons, Ralph. *The Union Spy, the Autobiography of Private L. W. Simmons, Co. 1 11th Illinois Cavalry, U.S. Army.* 1961.

Small, Harold Adams, ed. *The Road to Richmond.* Berkeley: University of California Press, 1939.

Smith, Colonel Nicholas. *Grant, the Man of Mystery.* Milwaukee: Young Churchman Co., 1909.

Smith, William Farrar. *From Chattanooga to Petersburg Under Generals Grant and Butler.* Boston: Houghton Mifflin, 1893.

Stackpole, Edward J. *Chancellorsville—Lee's Greatest Battle.* Harrisburg, Pa.: Stackpole, 1958.

———. *Drama on the Rappahannock—The Fredericksburg Campaign.* Harrisburg, Pa.: Military Service Publishing Co., 1957.

———. *From Cedar Mountain to Antietam, August-September, 1862.* Harrisburg, Pa.: Stackpole, 1959.

———. *They Met at Gettysburg.* Harrisburg, Pa.: Eagle Books, 1956.

Steele, Matthew Forney. *American Campaigns* (2 vols.). Washington: Byron S. Adams, 1909.

Steere, Edward. *The Wilderness Campaign.* Harrisburg, Pa.: Stackpole, 1960.

Stern, Philip Van Doren, ed. *The Civil War Christmas Album.* New York: Hawthorn Books, 1961.

Stevens, Walter B. *Grant in St. Louis.* St. Louis, Mo.: The Franklin Club, 1916.

Stewart, Lucy Shelton. *The Reward of Patriotism.* New York: Neale, 1930.

Strode, Hudson. *Jefferson Davis: American Patriot.* New York: Harcourt, Brace & World, 1955.

———. *Jefferson Davis: Confederate President.* New York: Harcourt, Brace & World, 1959.

———. *Jefferson Davis: Tragic Hero.* New York: Harcourt, Brace & World, 1064.

Taylor, Richard, ed. by Richard B. Harwell. *Destruction and Reconstruction.* New York: Longmans, Green, 1955.

Tenney, W. J. *The Military and Naval History of the Rebellion in the U.S.* New York: Appleton, 1866.

Terrell, W. H. H. *Indiana in the War of the Rebellion.* Indiana Historical Bureau, 1960.

Throne, Mildred, ed. *The Civil War Diary of Cyrus F. Boyd, Fifteenth Iowa Infantry, 1861–1863.* Iowa City, Iowa: State Historical Society of Iowa, 1953.

Todd, Helen. *A Man Named Grant.* Boston: Houghton Mifflin, 1940.

Turner, George Edgar. *Victory Rode the Rails.* Indianapolis: Bobbs-Merrill, 1953.

Twain, Mark. *See* Clemens, Samuel.

Virginia Civil War Commission, Clifford Dowdy, ed. *The Wartime Papers of R. E. Lee.* Boston: Little, Brown, 1961.

Welles, Gideon. *Diary of Gideon Welles* (3 vols.). Boston: Houghton Mifflin, 1911.

White, Andrew D. *Autobiography of Andrew Dickson White* (2 vols.). New York: Century, 1905.

Wiley, Bell Irvin, and Milhollen, Hirst D. *They Who Fought Here.* New York: Macmillan, 1959.

Williams, Kenneth P. *Lincoln Finds a General: A Military Study of the Civil War* (5 vols.). New York: Macmillan, 1949–59.

Wilson, James Grant. *General Grant.* New York: Appleton, 1897.

———. *The Life and Public Services of Ulysses Simpson Grant.* New York: DeWitt, 1885.

Wilson, James Harrison. *The Life of John A. Rawlins.* New York: Neale, 1916.

Winters, John D. *The Civil War in Louisiana.* Baton Rouge: Louisiana State University Press, 1963.

Wister, Owen. *Ulysses S. Grant.* Boston: Small, Maynard & Co., 1907.

Wittenmyer, Mrs. Annie. *Under the Guns: A Woman's Reminiscences of the Civil War.* Boston: E. B. Stillings & Company, 1895.

Woodford, Frank B. *Father Abraham's Children.* Detroit, Mich.: Wayne State University Press, 1961.

Woodward, C. Vann. *Reunion and Reaction.* Garden City, N. Y.: Doubleday Anchor Books, 1956.

Woodward, W. E. *Meet General Grant.* New York: Horace Liverwright, 1928.

Young, Agatha. *The Women and the Crisis.* New York: McDowell, Obolensky, 1959.

Young, John Russell. *Around the World with General Grant* (2 vols.). New York: Subscription Book Department, The American News Company, 1879.

———. *Men and Memories: Personal Reminiscences,* ed. by his wife, May D. Russell Young. New York and London: F. Tennyson Neely, 1901.

INDEX

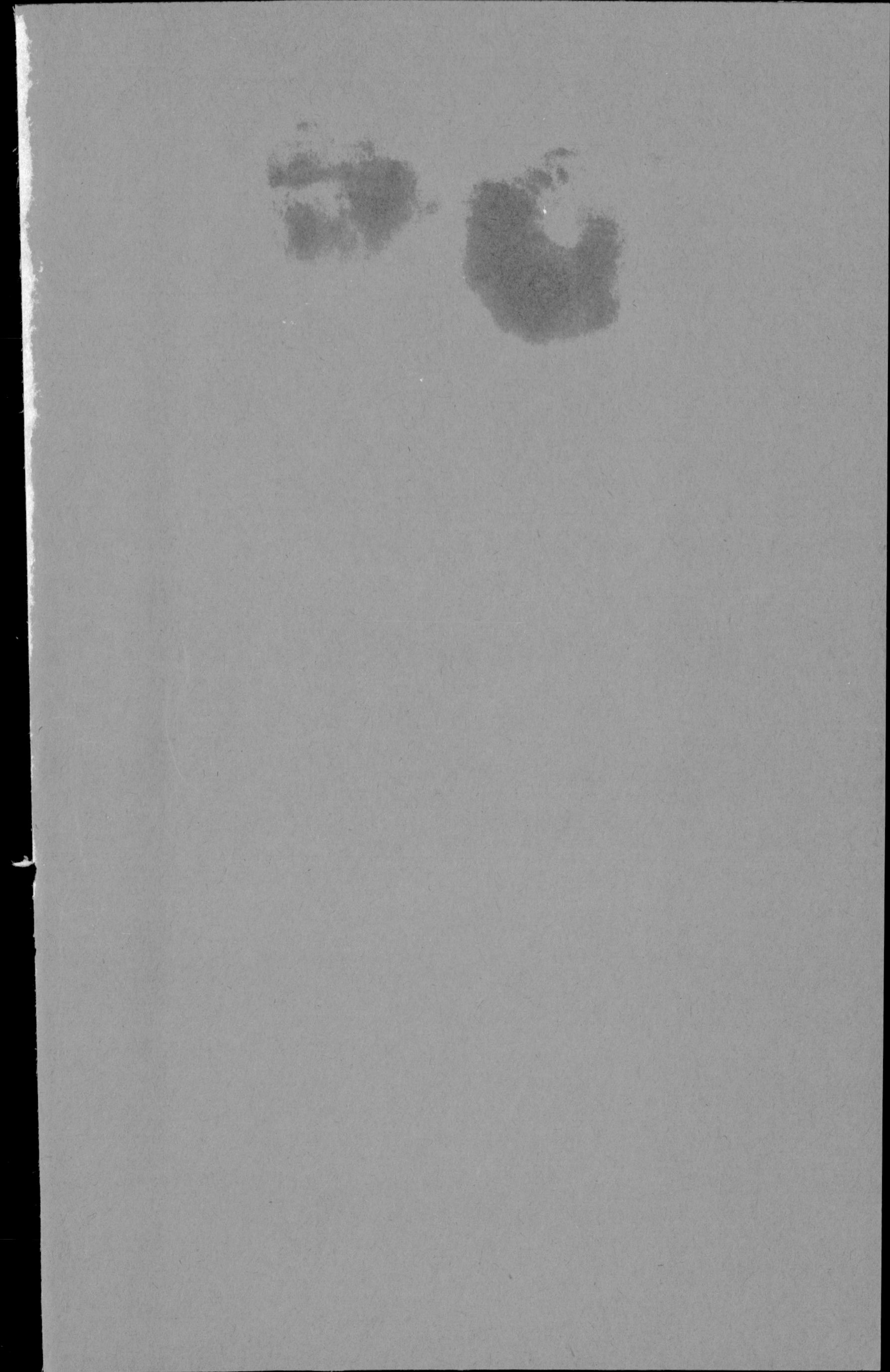